Manipulating the Ether

MANIPULATING THE ETHER

The Power of Broadcast Radio in Thirties America

by

ROBERT J. BROWN

McFarland & Company, Inc., Publishers
Jefferson, North Carolina and London

All photos courtesy of the National Archives, Washington, D.C.

British Library Cataloguing-in-Publication data are available

Library of Congress Cataloguing-in-Publication Data

Brown, Robert J. (Robert John), 1969–
    Manipulating the ether : the power of broadcast radio in thirties
America / by Robert J. Brown
        p.   cm.
    Includes bibliographical references and index.
    ISBN 0-7864-0397-7 (library binding : 50# alkaline paper) ∞
    1. Radio broadcasting—United States—History.   2. Radio
broadcasting—United States—Social aspects.   3. Radio in politics.
4. Radio journalism.   5. War of the worlds (Radio program)
6. Roosevelt, Franklin D. (Franklin Delano), 1882–1945.   I. Title.
PN1991.2.B76   1998
302.23'44'0973—dc21   97-43336
                                                                          CIP

Manufactured in the United States of America

McFarland & Company, Inc., Publishers
    Box 611, Jefferson, North Carolina 28640

For my parents,
Robert and Susan Brown

Table of Contents

Preface

For the average American listener in the latter part of the twentieth century, it is difficult to imagine radio as anything other than late-night talk shows and Top 40 music. While most listening today is done either in the car or shower, sixty years ago this activity took center stage in a living room tradition that served as an important aspect of family life during the Great Depression. During the 1930s, radio rose to a level of influence over the lives of everyday Americans that has never been rivaled by any other medium, before or since.

This book is an investigation into the origins of modern broadcasting. Whereas the 1930s have traditionally been dismissed by historians as merely a continuation of the groundbreaking developments of the previous decade, *Manipulating the Ether* attempts to focus attention on the formative aspects of this period in radio by examining the efforts of some of its most resourceful personalities: FDR, Orson Welles, and the network newscasters. There has been relatively little written about Roosevelt and the media, and what does exist in print tends to concentrate primarily on the president's use of the press and the newsreels, with insubstantial references to his exploitation of radio. This book attempts to fill that gap in media historiography. Despite the enormous debt today's newscasters owe to the trailblazing correspondents and radio reporters of the thirties, *Manipulating the Ether* is one of the first detailed treatments of the rise of network news broadcasting. As far as Orson Welles and the *War of the Worlds* broadcast are concerned, this work constitutes one of the most in-depth analyses yet. Welles biographers and radio historians have curiously refrained from presenting anything but the most impressionistic of studies of that 1938 broadcast, despite its reputation as the single most famous program of all time. In exploring the reasons for the program's believability and analyzing its impact, I have tried to integrate the findings of Hadley Cantril's distinguished 1940 study and other contemporary evidence with more recent research. Few other works have dissected the script in an attempt to reconstruct the mental state of the panic-stricken listener.

Each of these phenomena—the triumph of FDR via the airwaves, the rise of the network newscasters, and the panic of the American public in the face of Welles's famous broadcast—is fascinating in its own right. Yet *Manipulating the Ether* seeks to make a further contribution by demonstrating the links among the three stories as part of a much larger trend in American culture.

In many respects, I feel this work is long overdue. The infatuation that most broadcast historians have maintained for the entertaining aspects of radio's golden age have routinely led them to neglect the significant political, informational and psychological revolution that was occurring in broadcasting during this period. It seems that in analyzing specific programs and genres, broadcast historians have tended to lose sight of the big picture.

A useful feature of the work in hand is the light it sheds on the nature of contemporary broadcasting. Rush Limbaugh did not emerge in a vacuum. By examining the techniques of his many predecessors, *Manipulating the Ether* offers insight into how a man with virtually no previous experience as a professional broadcaster could exploit the airwaves to capture a mass audience and convince it of the rectitude of his own peculiar political philosophy. Recent years have witnessed an enormous proliferation of such "radio demagoguery" as a means to exploit racial tension and as a device by former politicians (such as Mario Cuomo and Oliver North) to acquire the influence they were denied at the polls.

Another contemporary parallel lies in the work's treatment of early World War II news coverage. Just as televised images of lifeless children and shell-ravaged towns have recently elicited heartfelt international sympathy for the peoples of the former Yugoslavia (sentiment which has translated into overt United States material assistance and even the dispatch of American troops to the war zone), so did 1940s sounds of air raid sirens and bomb explosions in London turn American public opinion away from its traditional isolationism and towards a more active anti-fascist foreign policy, thus laying the foundation for United States participation in the most monumental conflict of all time. Given the frequency and vividness of these aural impressions from the world's battle zones, *Manipulating the Ether* advances the argument that World War II, and not Vietnam, constituted the first "living room war" in American history.

Manipulating the Ether is the product of several years of intensive research. Most of the material contained within its pages is the result of countless hours spent in the sound-rooms and archives of such institutions as the Franklin D. Roosevelt Library in Hyde Park, N.Y., the Library of Congress, and the Museum of Broadcasting. To their staffs, I extend my warm appreciation for their valuable assistance.

To Syracuse University's Bird Library and Belfer Sound Archive, I am equally grateful for their accommodating my mammoth request for some fifty volumes of *Broadcasting*. I would also like to thank CBS and the crew of the National Archives' Motion Picture, Sound and Video Research Room for allowing me generous access to the Milo Ryan collection of World War II recordings.

Additional audio material was supplied through the graces of the University of Memphis Learning Media Center, the Radio Historical Association of Colorado, SPERDVAC, the Metropolitan Washington Old-Time Radio club, the Old-Time Radio Club of Buffalo, and a host of other nonprofit organizations faithfully dedicated to preserving our broadcasting heritage. Of these, I feel a particular need to single out one for praise: the North American Radio Archives, which not only graciously complied with all of my requests for materials on tape (cassettes and reels), but whose publication editor, James L. Snyder, gave unstintingly of his time and advice.

On the personal level, I would like to acknowledge my gratitude to Dr. Richard Kendall, Edward Tallon, Kenneth Kresse, and Debbie Neuls at the State University of New York at Albany; Dr. Robert Frost at the University of Michigan; and Dr. J. Fred MacDonald of Northeastern Illinois University; Norman Rudman, and Mitch Douglas.

For her generosity in allowing me to reproduce extracts from her late husband's masterful radio play, "Invasion from Mars," I am deeply indebted to Anne Koch. Likewise, Robert Rosenman and James R. Rowen proved equally kind in granting permission for use of Samuel Rosenman's *Working with Roosevelt*.

Most of all, I would like to thank Kathleen & Francine Cournoyer, and Robert and Susan Brown for their continual encouragement and extraordinary patience, without which this work would never have been possible.

Rochester, New York
October 1997

Introduction

In the late 1930s radio broadcasting exerted a powerful influence over the lives of the American people. By the beginning of the decade, many of the elements that would characterize the American system of broadcasting were already in place. Much of the basic technology had been developed and was becoming available to a wider public. It was clear that the medium was to be "dominated by large corporations and advertisers, and that it would be loosely governed by federal regulatory agencies."[1] While many of the precedents that would determine how broadcast media would develop in the United States had been established in the twenties, the process had in no manner reached a conclusion. One historian has argued that "what scholars have identified as the functions of the mass medium in the late twentieth century were being formulated and refined during the first 23 years of radio's history [1899-1922]"[2]; yet the purposes of the medium as something more than popular entertainment were not defined until a decade later. Only in the 1930s did radio reach a thorough understanding of its own capabilities. As late as 1937, acute observers could still remark, "Although the ether is a comparatively new means of communication and lends itself nationally in many useful ways, we find ourselves continually amazed at the things which have been accomplished and the development of future potentialities."[3] In the hands of skillful manipulators, much of the potential would be fully realized. Franklin D. Roosevelt would discover radio's unsurpassed usefulness as a political instrument with which to win elections, silence opponents, and sell domestic and foreign policy measures. The network news bureaus would exploit the medium's quickness and directness to make radio the most effective means of disseminating information yet devised. At the same time, Orson Welles would demonstrate radio's intense psychological hold on listeners and its dangerous power to deceive. In all three cases, radio would manifest its ability not only to mirror popular sensibilities, but also to influence individual habits and mold public opinion.

Radio and Thirties America

Systematic radio broadcasting began in the United States in 1920 when stations KDKA in Pittsburgh and WWJ in Detroit went on the air. Following

1

the almost instant success of these two stations, the next five years witnessed a rapid increase in the number of broadcasting establishments. In 1926 enough stations existed to link many of them into a permanent regional hook-up. Thus was born the first radio network in broadcasting history, the National Broadcasting Company (NBC).

Despite this expansion, radio remained a small-scale phenomenon during most of the 1920s. Not only was the overall listening audience relatively tiny, the quality of programming was of a distinctly primitive nature, consisting mainly of phonograph recordings of popular music, short vaudeville sketches and makeshift variety programs.

It was not until the mid–1930s that radio became a pervasive influence in American life. Whereas there were only three million sets in 1924, this number increased tenfold by 1936. Four years later, there were over fifty million receivers in America.[4] By 1938 it was estimated that 91 percent of all urban households and 70 percent of all rural homes in America contained at least one radio.[5] At this time the United States could boast over half of the world's radios, and more homes possessed sets than telephones, vacuum cleaners, and electric irons. Between 1930 and 1940, the number of radios in America grew by more than 100 percent. In 1939 alone, more than nine million new sets were sold, and in 1940 over eleven million.[6] Contributing to this great explosion were the 2.5 million automobiles in the country that became equipped with new Motorola receivers, and the countless "portable" battery-operated units that were made available to rural listeners. In 1938, the average price for a set had been reduced to ten dollars, enabling poorer families to purchase one while encouraging those with higher incomes to own many.[7] An Indiana University survey revealed that most homes that did not possess their own sets had regular access to a neighbor's.[8]

To cater to this expanding listening audience, over 275 new radio stations took to the air between 1935 and 1941, bringing the total to 882 nationwide.[9] The geographic proliferation of broadcasting facilities enabled many communities to tune in for the first time. By 1936, 43 percent of all cities with a population of 100,000 could claim their own station. With the development of regional and "highly powered clear-channel transmitters," many smaller municipalities of 10–50,000 citizens and some rural areas were assured of service.[10] Whereas access to the radio had been confined to a few densely inhabited areas in the 1920s, the 1930s witnessed the development of broadcasting into an institution of truly national proportions.

For many Americans, the radio set became a highly valued and permanent piece of living room furniture, and an integral part of family life. Unlike the shapeless television boxes of today, radio sets were often finely crafted with the best wood and intricately decorated. They came in a variety of shapes and sizes, from slender floor models of fluted pine to art deco shelf units of colorful Bakelite. Families across the country looked forward to gathering around the Philco, Zenith or Stromberg-Carlson every evening to listen to favorite programs. According to one observer, "the greater association of family members in this common activity" provided a measure of cohesion for many households plagued by economic insecurity.[11] During the Depression, when countless citizens found themselves with hours of involuntary leisure time and a need for escape, radio fulfilled a vital role in American cultural and social life.

Even in the midst of fiscal privation, many people still managed to scrape together the resources to obtain a cheap "midget" set. After the small initial investment, radio provided unlimited hours of free entertainment. Social workers frequently observed that destitute families would give up iceboxes or beds before they would relinquish their radios.[12]

A 1939 *Fortune* poll revealed that listening to the radio was overwhelmingly preferred as an inexpensive leisure-time activity over such pursuits as reading and moviegoing. (The reliance on radio became all the more keen as financial difficulties compelled one-third of all cinemas to close between 1930 and 1940.) In an NBC survey two years later, radio was voted the "Most Popular Family Servant," by a margin of 2 to 1 over such items as automobiles, electricity, and gas heat.[13]

The increasing importance of radio in American life during the thirties can be deduced from a well-known sociological study of Middletown, U.S.A. (Muncie, Indiana). In 1929 researchers Robert and Helen Lynd discovered that reading, automobile riding, and gramophone music dominated the leisure-time habits of the midwestern urban community, while radio was barely mentioned at all.[14] When they returned to Middletown in 1936, they found that listening constituted "the area of leisure where change in time spent has been greatest."*

In the decade of the Depression, radio reached an unprecedented apex as a medium of mass entertainment. With the comedic excellence of Jack Benny, Fred Allen, Bob Hope, Ed Wynn and the enormously popular Amos 'n' Andy, radio programming allowed the public a humorous reprieve from its many troubles. It "vastly enriched the lives of shut-ins and residents of remote places."[15] It stimulated a deep appreciation for classical music and "did more than any other medium to popularize and disseminate previously isolated kinds of folk music such as country and blues."[16] For sports fans, radio provided the most extensive coverage in history; the 1938 Joe Louis–Max Schmeling fight, for example, was carried to every corner of the world except east Asia, and was translated into five different languages by ringside announcers.

The 1930s also saw the origin of one of America's cultural mainstays: the daytime serial or "soap opera." (The name derived from the fact that each show

*In 1924 only one in every eight Middletown homes possessed radios. By the early 1930s this figure was one in two.

was invariably sponsored by one of Procter and Gamble's wide array of soap products—Ivory, Boraxo, Tide, Lux, Oxydol, etc.) One historian of broadcasting has called this development the "most important program phenomenon of the decade."* Appealing principally to mothers and wives, these daily fifteen-minute programs "commonly revolved around strong female characters who provided advice and strength to indecisive friends." Contemporary critic Herta Herzog explained how the "stories [became] an integral part of the lives of many listeners" by providing both "an emotional release and a model of reality by which one [was] taught to think and act."[17] So attached were some housewives to certain characters that they wrote weekly letters offering them advice.

In the evening hours, the finest talent in Hollywood could be heard on such programs as the *Lux Radio Theater*, the *Silver Theater* and the *Gulf Screen Guild*. The late night hours were usually dominated by the high adventure, horror, and whodunit thrills of *Suspense*, *Escape*, *Inner Sanctum*, and *Lights Out*. Many of these programs fully exploited radio's power as a dramatic medium, utilizing "sophisticated music patterns and unique sound effects to sharpen their impact."[18]

Beginning in the late 1930s, the networks began to offer unique presentations that were both amusing and intellectually stimulating. CBS began a prestigious Shakespeare series in the summer of 1937, and NBC aired a regular program of concerts by Arturo Toscanini and the NBC Symphony Orchestra. To further lend credibility to their efforts, the networks carried various programs of serious drama that were unsponsored. With the *Columbia Workshop* and the *Mercury Theater*, radio reached an aesthetic peak that has never since been rivaled.

As an "instrument for the general diffusion of knowledge," radio was "surpassed by neither school nor press."[19] With mind-enrichers like *Music Appreciation Hour*, *Torch of Progress*, *Science on the March*, *Pilgrimage of Poets*, and *Great Plays*, broadcasting was hailed as "the most versatile educator of all time."[20] In 1938, the Federal Communications Commission underscored its commitment to educational programming by declaring that at least one quarter of the broadcast spectrum must be reserved for public, non-commercial use.[21]

Radio played a strong role in drawing the country closer together and making it more homogenous. In a decade of "coast-to-coast airplane flights, streamlined trains, and multi-lane turnpikes," broadcasting proved to be the most efficient means of "erasing the old barriers of time and space"[22] and forging a sense of national unity.[23] As a "means of communication that reached millions of listeners simultaneously," broadcasting represented "as powerful an assault upon sectional and parochial mentalities as any other single force in American history."[24] By enabling people to listen "to the same things at the

---

*In December 1941, listeners had over 54 different soap operas to choose between the hours of 9 A.M. and 5 P.M. (Willey, p. 339).

same time," radio "helped to abolish distinctions between rural and urban communities, men and women, age and youth, social classes, and various creeds." Radio became a major force of democratization. As if "by magic, the boundaries of social stratification disappear and in their place comes a consciousness of equality and a community of interest." Commenting on the leveling quality of the medium, psychologist Hadley Cantril stated:

> When millions of people hear the same subject matter, same arguments and appeals, music and humor, when their attention is held in the same way and at the same time to the same stimuli, it is psychologically inevitable that they should acquire in some degree common interests, tastes, and attitudes. In short, it seems to be the nature of radio to encourage people to think and feel alike.[25]

Indeed, the networks acknowledged their important role in this process. One observer remarked that the "daily experience of hearing the announcer say, 'This program is coming to you over a coast-to-coast network,' inevitably increases a listener's sense of membership in a national family."[26] In a letter to National Association of Broadcasters (NAB) president Neville Miller, FDR stated: "As millions of American families gather each day about their receivers, we have become neighbors in a new and true sense."[27] In a widely circulated advertisement, CBS displayed a picture of a farmer and a city dweller with the caption, "They've never met, but they're all one family ... to CBS."[28]

Unfortunately, there are significant drawbacks involved in the process of fostering cultural homogeneity. Despite its "variety and stimulating diversion, radio could not avoid becoming an agency for standardization." Cantril notes that since not "every opinion could be aired, nor every variety of cultural interest represented," listening often meant adapting one's own "personal taste to the program that most nearly approximated it." In the era before cable and satellite television, when the number of program options was severely limited, "sacrificing individuality" to "fit one of the common molds that broadcasting offered" was not at all uncommon.[29] By creating a mass audience with a more or less unified disposition and cultural mindset, radio made it much easier to inform the public of important issues, but it also facilitated the efforts of ambitious politicians, propagandists and experimenting dramatists who sought to manipulate the ether.

Part I
The "Radio President"

1. Roosevelt and Radio

Franklin D. Roosevelt was one of the most successful politicians in American history. Not only was he elected to the presidency for an unprecedented four terms, but his skillful leadership helped the nation weather two of its greatest crises, the Great Depression and the Second World War. While many scholarly works describe the president's success as the result of various political, economic, and social factors, very few detail the relationship between Roosevelt's ability to achieve his goals and the technology that made it possible. While Roosevelt was not the first chief executive to utilize the medium of radio, he was undoubtedly the first to recognize its full potential as a political instrument. As a true "radio president," FDR realized the enormous role that the medium played in national life, and its power to mold public opinion.[1] During his long tenure in the White House from March 1933 to April 1945, Roosevelt communicated directly to the people in over 300 radio addresses and "fireside chats."[2] With his remarkable gift for oratory, Roosevelt was able, through his radio speeches, to persuade a majority of the American people to accept his domestic and foreign policy agenda, and to support his personal political ambitions. By the time of his death in April 1945, FDR had exploited the advantages of broadcasting so successfully that he was able to radically reshape the political, social, and economic structure of the nation through the New Deal; to adequately prepare his nation for war; and to become the longest serving chief executive in American history.

Roosevelt's Views on Radio

Among his American political contemporaries, Roosevelt alone possessed an uncanny appreciation of radio's power. On numerous occasions he voiced his admiration for the educational and cultural contributions the medium had made to American life, and his awe at what he considered its future promise. To Merlin Aylesworth, president of NBC, he asserted his belief that "nothing since the creation of the newspaper has had so profound an effect on our civilization as radio."[3] Its capacity for "promoting national unity, banishing geographic provincialism and sectionalism and preventing the disunity of our vast population into classes" had clearly demonstrated its considerable social

The "radio president": Franklin Roosevelt delivering a fireside chat.

worth. In politics, the medium significantly furthered the cause of democratic government in the United States. The president felt that "amid many developments of civilization which lead away from direct government by the people, radio is one which tends on the other hand to restore contacts between the masses and their chosen leaders."[4] For one such elected official, the medium was "the greatest force for molding public opinion" yet devised, and could be of inestimable value in "promoting policies and campaigning."[5]

While Roosevelt believed that radio had accomplished much, he did not think it had fully realized "the opportunities that it [had] in store."[6] Only through the systematic and creative use of radio's many political applications could "the staggering potentialities of this medium be exploited to their fullest measure."[7]

FDR's intense interest in radio derived from the fact that it presented him with options denied him by other media. In the 1930s, radio's main rival for the public's attention was the newspaper. Unfortunately for the president, many of the nation's largest publishing houses, like Robert McCormick's *Chicago Tribune* and the extensive Hearst chain, were owned and operated by individuals who were hostile to him and his policies. Radio, on the other hand, being a new medium, was not yet controlled by any one faction. In 1939 *Broadcasting* noted: "Because the bulk of the dailies are predominently anti–New Deal, it has long been an open secret in Washington that radio more and more was being relied upon to disseminate Administration views." Broadcasting offered

FDR an effective vehicle for countering the "loudly proclaimed untruths and greatly exaggerated half-truths" of the press.[8] By embracing radio, Roosevelt became the first chief executive to free himself from the restraints imposed by the print medium. Through broadcasting, the president retained a far greater degree of control over his message. A speech could reach the public directly "without the intercession of reporters, editors, or publishers, and their journalistic filtering."[9]

Strict control of message content was paramount. The executive secretary of the Democratic National Committee, Richard Roper, observed in 1934:

> The average American's mind works simply and it is not hard to keep him behind the President if we can properly inform him as to what is going on in Washington, what the President is trying to do, and the specific objectives he is seeking. Only by providing information from a source of confidence like radio, would it be possible to make absolutely sure that the public gets all the facts we wish to present.[10]

To ensure that editorial opposition found no outlet on the airwaves, Roosevelt and FCC chairman Frank McNinch spearheaded a crusade to "divorce newspapers from station ownership."[11] Not surprisingly, one of the first targets of the official ax was William Randolph Hearst, who had been steadily building a nationwide radio empire from the proceeds of his publishing activities.

Not only could radio be used to transmit the president's message "without adulteration" and color, it could "carry it farther, more immediately, and more persuasively than newspapers." Through the airwaves, FDR could enjoy "direct access to the people on a scale that the public speaker addressing a crowd could never match."[12] By means of a nationwide network hookup, the president could simultaneously reach millions of Americans, many of whom were unable to read or lived in areas not served by newspapers. Since broadcast material was usually presented in a more straightforward and comprehensible manner than the printed page, the complexities of modern government could be explained so that the average listener gained a clearer "understanding of the purposes, methods, and policies of the federal system."[13] Through frequent radio talks, the president could win the trust of the people and enlist their support, as the "legitimate vox populi, in any legal battle with an intractable Congress." According to radio commentator Drew Pearson, "FDR knew that his only hold on Congress was to be stronger with the country than they were." While the president communicated with his national constituents dozens of times each year, Congress was allowed the air only on special occasions such as the opening and closing of a term or during emergency sessions, and thus was "never given the opportunity to bond with the public in any politically useful way."[14] By frequently invoking his radio prerogatives, Roosevelt gave "a plain hint to Congress of a recourse which [he] could employ if it proved necessary to rally support for the legislation which he asked and which

the lawmakers were reluctant to give him."[15] In this way, FDR consistently utilized broadcasting as a means of maintaining and enhancing presidential
authority, often at the legislature's expense.

In August 1921, Roosevelt contracted poliomyelitis while vacationing in
Campobello, New Brunswick. The illness left him severely paralyzed from the
waist down. As a purely auditory medium, radio allowed FDR another advantage that the press did not: the ability to conceal his physical handicap from
the general public. In this act of deception, the president would no longer be
exclusively dependent on the "gentlemen's agreement" among cameramen that
he would not be photographed with his leg braces or wheelchair.* The image
that most Americans received of their president was a strong and decisive one,
as projected through the "authority of his voice." By communicating his messages orally, FDR generated a "strong sense of intimacy" that was completely
absent in a "cold text."[16]

Roosevelt was not unique among heads of state in recognizing radio's
political usefulness. Instead, he belonged to a much wider trend in which many
world leaders became "constantly more aware of the ether as an essential element of power over men's minds" during the 1930s.[17] Europe, in particular,
witnessed the accession of leaders who appreciated the striking political power
that could be wielded through radio. In the hands of the dictators Adolf Hitler
and Benito Mussolini, and their clever propaganda ministers, radio became a
"wonderful and intricate instrument for influencing the masses." All three
used the medium to maintain themselves in authority, and as a "means of
accomplishing wide-ranging national aims that ultimately plunged the whole
of Europe into devastating conflict."[18] With martial pomp, strong emotional
appeal, and the effective use of nationalistic and jingoistic themes, the total-
itarian governments used broadcasting to "form a vital link between leader and
people, and as an unsurpassed vehicle of propaganda."[19]

No discussion about Hitler's spectacular rise to power is complete without mentioning the critical role of radio. According to one observer: "The
organizers of the German revolution of 1933 knew how to put broadcasting
completely at the service of their aims." During the January elections, the
National Socialist party used radio as a principal means for disseminating
their campaign propaganda. The Nazis placed loudspeakers in virtually every
town square so that all Germans were sure to hear the speeches of Hitler,
Göring, Goebbels and others. Many of the addresses were recorded and replayed
to ensure maximum coverage. Every time the polls indicated an increase in the

---

*Many historians have argued that if FDR had lived during the age of television, he would
never have been elected. It is interesting to note, however, that Roosevelt was the first president actually to use the emerging medium. On April 30, 1939, he "inaugurated the first regular high definition television service" as he delivered the opening address at the New York
World's Fair to local viewers (Broadcasting, April 15, 1939, p. 15). Before his death, FDR
would use television on several more occasions.

number of votes for the Nazis, the pace of political broadcasting was quickened. When President Hindenburg announced the formation of the Hitler government on January 30, the celebratory torchlight activities were broadcast throughout Germany and Austria.

Once established, Hitler introduced two inexpensive midget sets, the "Volksempfaenger" (People's Receiving Set) and the "Kleinempfanger" (Small Receiver), which were so under-powered they could receive only domestic broadcasts from the Propaganda Ministry.[20] At 75RM ($24) and 36RM ($12) respectively, these units were deliberately priced so as to allow virtually every German to own one.[21]

The Führer frequently "commandeered" time for special broadcasts, and members of the party hierarchy spoke almost daily. "Never before," *Broadcasting* observed, "since the inception of radio, has the whole German nation been able to follow the activities of the Government to that extent."[22] On February 4, Hitler used the airwaves to proclaim his auspicious decree "For the Protection of the German People," and on March 21 he broadcast the ceremonies officially "re-opening" the Reichstag. German radio abounded with "plays and musical concerts devoted entirely to national events and Prussian history." The playing of jazz music was strictly forbidden. An American observer witnessing these events in Germany remarked:

> The National Socialists have done away with the idea that broadcasting should be an unpolitical institution of entertainment and education. They have done away with the idea that German broadcasting should be used as an open forum for all points of view, political or otherwise.... Goebbels uses German broadcasting for one purpose—to awaken the German people from their political lethargy and win them over to the ideals of National Socialism, to incorporate them into the ranks of Herr Hitler's enthusiastic followers...."[23]

From 1932 to 1939, the number of receivers in Germany rose steeply, from 3 million to 12.5 million. Propaganda minister Joseph Goebbels had a special circuit placed in his office that enabled him to preempt broadcasts anywhere in the nation for important official announcements. According to Ward Rutherford, the Nazi hierarchy "felt confident that it could reach the entire population at any given moment." To stimulate regular listening, the party organized community wireless groups and appointed "radio wardens" to publicize special programs.[24]

Radio was also a prominent tool of the European democracies. During the 1930s both the prime minister of Great Britain and the premier of France frequently addressed their people through the airwaves, with varying degrees of success. In Britain, while Stanley Baldwin and Neville Chamberlain continually fumbled before the microphone, Winston Churchill proved himself a superlative radio communicator whose defiant voice in the face of national adversity became as familiar to Americans as it was to Britons during the initial stages of the Second World War. In France, the beleaguered Third Republic produced its share of uninspiring speakers such as Leon Blum and Edouard Daladier, but it also spawned men of considerable vocal talent like Charles de Gaulle, whose broadcasts from London to his occupied homeland after 1940 restored the faith and determination of Free France during its darkest hour. For both Churchill and de Gaulle, effective communication became a major prerequisite of wartime leadership.

While Roosevelt shared many affinities with other "radio leaders," his method of wielding power through the medium was quite different.

Roosevelt's Special Relationship with Radio

Whereas in Europe radio was usually owned or administered by the state, in the United States the government had virtually no hand in the operation of broadcasting facilities. In the absence of direct federal control or regulation, Roosevelt had to secure the cooperation of the radio industry by other means. He offered assurance that the government would not commandeer the airwaves during the emergency situation posed by the Depression and the war; he gave benevolent consideration to FCC appointees who were favorably disposed toward the industry; and he made concessions such as allowing radio correspondents into press conferences. The networks generously reciprocated. In March 1933, Alfred McCosker, NAB president, pledged the administration "radio's full and unqualified cooperation in the tasks before it."[25] As a gift for his first inaugural, Herbert Glover, NBC's news director, presented the president with a specially designed microphone stand, complete with handlebars and fittings for his leg braces. NBC, CBS and the Mutual Broadcasting Company all willingly gave FDR airtime for his speeches and for pro–New Deal congressional talks "on any wavelength and upon instant demand." In another gesture of gratitude, the networks adopted a "right of way" policy in which their hundreds of affiliate stations were obligated to interrupt local schedules in order to air the president's speeches.[26] In the autumn of 1933, CBS and NBC offered, at considerable expense to themselves, to install land lines to independent stations so that they too would be able to transmit presidential broadcasts.[27] Roosevelt's "fireside chats" were the only occasion in broadcasting in which all national and regional networks would drop prior commitments and link together into "one huge chain," giving the president access to the largest audience ever assembled for a single speech.[28] In 1936, CBS graciously offered Roosevelt access to its studios any time he wished. Through annual renewals, FDR was to enjoy this concession throughout his entire stay in office.[29] During election time, the networks stood solidly behind Roosevelt, leading to frequent GOP charges of partisanship and the denial of equal access to airtime. One writer for *Broadcasting* went so far as to say that "the perpetuation of the Roosevelt Administration and its continuance in office" was due largely to the "friendliness of radio."[30]

On a more personal note, Roosevelt maintained cordial relations with many prominent members of the broadcasting world. FDR carried on a lively written correspondence with NBC chairman David Sarnoff, whom he addressed as "Dave," and CBS executive William Paley was a frequent lunch guest at the White House.[31] Together, Paley and the president worked out a plan to expand the scope of CBS's shortwave activities to include much of South America, "ostensibly to counteract fascist propaganda but actually to allow the U.S. government to blanket the area with pro–American programs in Spanish from more than 64 stateside transmitters"[32] (and, coincidentally, to provide additional market opportunities for Columbia's advertisers). Roosevelt won the affection of those further down the broadcast hierarchy as well. Engineers and announcers were delighted by the cooperation the president extended to them in the "technical task of getting his voice on the air." He was one of the few political speakers who "paid attention to microphone angles and responded to his cues."[33]

As the 1930s saw the rise to prominence of the radio news commentator, Roosevelt recognized the strategic necessity of forging an alliance. During press conferences, FDR often joked with reporters and created an atmosphere of "mutual respect and cordiality." Through a working relationship by which Roosevelt gave the newsmen scoops and inside information, he secured the loyalty of such influential broadcasters as Dorothy Thompson, Walter Winchell, and Gabriel Heatter.[34] In their nightly newscasts, these radio commentators were expected to present a pro-administration interpretation of the events they were reporting. Because of the enormous audiences these individuals commanded and their ability to sway opinion, Roosevelt created another useful way of bypassing the hostile press.[35] FDR's esteem for these newscasters was such that near the end of his life he once remarked, "I know what I'll do when I retire. I'll be one of these high-powered commentators."[36]

Radio commentators who were not well disposed toward the Roosevelt administration enjoyed short careers. FDR used his Washington connections with the broadcasting and advertising industries to have outspoken critics such as Boake Carter quickly removed from the air.[37] Any station that continued to support Carter's activities, or refused to carry the president's speeches, unexpectedly found itself devoid of a broadcasting license the next time it came up for renewal by the FCC.[38]

The Roosevelt Method

While Roosevelt sought the support of other broadcasters (commentators, presidential spokesmen, announcers, Democratic congressmen, etc.) to sell himself and his policies, his appeal was most effective when the president personally took to the air. FDR was a "pre-eminent political persuader whose gift for oratory was well suited to the medium that delivered it." *Broadcasting* declared: "FDR is the greatest public speaker in the nation. No doubt about it, he's top in speech on or off the air."[39] Often referred to as the first "rhetorical president," Roosevelt was enormously successful in conveying his thoughts to audiences through the "sheer artistry of his words" and the "artifice of his skills in speech delivery."[40]

Recognizing that his speeches were instrumental to the success of his presidency, FDR spent countless hours preparing his texts, developing the proper delivery techniques, and refining his voice and sense of timing. He also assembled a formidable staff of writers to help compose the speeches that he would deliver over the air. Such notable literary figures and intellectuals as Judge Samuel Rosenman, Harry Hopkins, Robert Sherwood, Thomas G. Corcoran, Raymond Moley, Rexford Tugwell, Archibald MacLeish, Hugh Johnson, Louis Howe, Ben Cohen, and Felix Frankfurter took a hand in producing the initial drafts.[41] Whenever the topic to be discussed required expert input, FDR did not hesitate to consult relevant non-governmental sources. On matters of economic or foreign policy, he routinely sent sketches to the Treasury and State departments, and thoughtfully considered their criticisms, corrections and suggestions.[42] He carefully read each draft that was presented to him and inserted his own lines and comments in the margins. When he encountered passages he did not like, he and his writers would toil for hours to perfect the phrasing.

Sometimes FDR would scrap speeches prepared for him and begin anew in his own words. At the 1932 Chicago convention, when Louis Howe handed him a speech the moment he got off the plane, the president-elect stayed in his automobile for an hour revising it. He informed his eager Brain Trust writer: "You know I can't deliver a speech that I've never done any work on myself."[43]

Speechwriting was a laborious and time-consuming process. It was not unusual for an address to undergo between four and ten drafts before reaching its finalized form. The president would then read the text aloud, again and again, in order to obtain a sense of how it would sound to the listening audience. Words or phrases that were aurally ineffective, or were constructed in an overly complex way that might confuse the average listener, were stricken. For FDR, every word was to be judged by how it would play on the airwaves.

In 1936, FDR engaged the Radio and Film Methods Corporation to regularly make phonograph recordings of his speeches and deliver them to the White House, where he would "listen to himself and improve his delivery for the next address."[44] Being a keen observer of the prevailing mood of the nation, he also paid close attention to the reactions of the radio audience through listener telegrams, public opinion polls and industry ratings for each of his broadcasts.

After constant practice, Roosevelt thoroughly memorized his speeches by the time he approached the microphone. "Time after time, Roosevelt delivered his addresses flawlessly, from a typewritten page and without the aid of modern devices like teleprompters."[45] According to his speechwriter Samuel Rosenman:

> The speeches as finally delivered were his—and his alone—no matter who the collaborators were…. No matter how frequently the speech assistants were changed through the years, the speeches were always Roosevelt's. They expressed the personality, the convictions, the spirit, the mood of Roosevelt. No matter who worked with him in the preparation, the finished product was always the same—it was Roosevelt himself.[46]

In the days prior to the delivery of a radio address, the president and his staff employed a variety of tactics designed to expand the capacity of the projected listening audience. One such device was to issue a release date for a speech without going into any detail as to its content. By this method "an air of uncertainty" was created, and interest would build as the public began to speculate on the nature of the forthcoming address.[47] Other times, the president would increase the expectations of his listeners by "hinting at what he would discuss and allow[ing] the press to report and comment on it." In either case, the "pre-speech publicity would assure FDR of a large audience at airtime."[48]

Through the skillful orchestration of White House press-radio secretary Steve Early, the speeches were scheduled so the maximum number of people could tune in. The best time slot was undoubtedly Sunday night at 10:00 P.M. At this time, the public was "relaxed and in a benevolent mood." According to one observer: "The hour was not so late that eastern listeners had gone to bed, and on the west coast, many families had just finished dinner and were ready to gather around the radio in the living room."[49] In all, over 50 percent of the president's major speeches were delivered on Sunday, Monday and Tuesday, all days in which news coverage would be the most intensive.[50] By contrast, none were given on a Friday or Saturday. Roosevelt employed his broadcasts tactfully, "avoiding overuse and airing them sparingly so that they became nationwide events." Because many listeners "may not have been enthusiastically predisposed to the type of material to be broadcast," Roosevelt's speeches were most effective, and listener interest was sustained longest, when they were concise. Realizing the value of Princeton psychologist Hadley Cantril's finding that the optimum length of a political or educational program should be limited to 10–20 minutes, the president rarely exceeded this recommended time limitation.[51] Roosevelt's ability to terminate his broadcast speeches precisely "on the nose" made him a favorite of clock-conscious networks anxious to maintain their regular programming schedules.[52]

Ultimately, FDR's mastery of timing "paid handsome political dividends." By frequently synchronizing his speeches with the days his proposals went before Congress, he was able to win public support for his initiatives. His ability to persuade listeners of the need to pressure their representatives "translated into a plethora of executive legislation becoming law."[53]

Roosevelt also took pains to develop his "uniquely successful style of speech presentation." Despite his physical disability, critics admired his vigor and dynamism before the microphone. FDR refreshed himself before every broadcast with a brief nap.[54]

Even when delivering a speech to Congress or some other group, Roosevelt addressed himself not to his immediate audience, but to his larger national body of listeners.[55] Unlike the majority of his political contemporaries, FDR "never forgot that radio listening was done by individuals and small family groups, and not by masses who filled an auditorium." As a result, he never had to roar into the microphone, and could adopt a much more informal manner of speech. He routinely referred to himself in the first person and always addressed the American public as "you."[56] Thus, his words came across more as an "intimate conversation between friends and less as a formal political address."[57]

The utter naturalism of his approach was revealed during a July 24, 1933, fireside chat. While speaking over a nationwide hookup from the Oval Office in the ninety-degree summer heat, FDR suddenly inquired, "Where's that glass of water?" After a brief pause, during which he poured and drank the water, he told his audience: "My friends, its very hot here in Washington tonight." [58]

In this manner, "talking to and not at the American public, FDR could speak into the microphone as if talking to one single American listener, and personally project the full range of his feelings in a manner that was both direct and sincere." [59] This casual approach was the essence of the renowned "fireside chats." This phrase was coined by the CBS manager of the Washington Bureau in 1933 to describe the president's unique speaking style. As explained to Steve Early, "The President likes to think of the audience as being a few people around his fireside, and the public imagines [him] sitting comfortably at his desk, conversing easily in their living rooms." [60] In reality, the small diplomatic reception room where FDR delivered many of his broadcasts was anything but informal and cozy.

> Standing on either side of the President's desk were Carleton Smith, NBC announcer, and Bob Trout of CBS, each having a microphone on a platform in front of them. Aimed at FDR were four huge motion picture cameras heavily blanketed to suppress the noise…. Also pointed in the President's direction were about five cameras for still pictures. The room was cluttered with all sorts of portable electrical apparatuses and the floor was strewn with electric cables leading to the President's desk. Lining the room facing the President, and watching his every move, were about twenty to twenty-five radio engineers, and sound and still photographers.[61]

To those closest to him, there is no doubt that he enjoyed the "illusion of close interaction with his people." Secretary of labor Frances Perkins described how the president would "picture in his mind the audience he was addressing and then, his face would smile and light up as if he were actually sitting on the front porch or in the parlor with them." [62] This impression was maintained by a majority of the public as well, as is evident by the large number of letters written by listeners inviting FDR "into my home through the medium of radio."[63] Many were enchanted by the thought that the president was "speaking directly to them and not to the fifty million others listening in." [64]

Broadcasting noted that through his cultivation of the fireside chat technique, FDR had effected a "one man revolution of modern oratory." Because of the marked success of the "Rooseveltian radio way," the "older generation of modern political speakers" largely abandoned "bombast rhetoric and the grand eloquent platform manner for the informal, conversational, person-to-person technique demanded by the microphone." While William Jennings Bryan and Daniel Webster were the "speech-making heroes of the nineteenth century," the journal remarked, "FDR is the oratorical model of the twentieth."[65]

A good part of the success of the fireside chat was due to Roosevelt's ability to "project himself to any listener's economic or social level, and thus appeal to all Americans regardless of class."[66] The president realized that in order to make his messages more fathomable to a heterogeneous audience, he would have to address them to a perceived "common denominator." To avoid alienating significant a number of Americans, he "could not afford to be either too high brow or too base," and he had to "avoid subtlety and sophistry."[67] One way that he could make his speeches consistent with the average American's intelligence level was to employ simple terminology. A contemporary study found that between 70 and 80 percent of the vocabulary in his fireside chats consisted of the "1,000 most common words in the English language."[68]

FDR also toned down the rate at which he delivered these words. While most radio orators were accustomed to speaking at 175 and 200 words per minute, the president consistently addressed the American people at a much slower 120 words. Only rarely did he exceed 130, and during crucial broadcasts, when he wanted to convey the gravity of the situation, he reduced his rate of speech to less than 100 words per minute so that everyone could understand. In this way, the fireside chat on the outbreak of war in Europe on September 3, 1939, was delivered at 98 words per minute and the Japanese attack on Pearl Harbor merited a speed of 88.[69] The president also emphasized important points in his talks by placing stress on some words and drawing others out— all part of vocal pacing, at which he proved a master. His slow speaking rate projected an air of calm assurance to which the American people, frightened by the Depression and the impending war, responded with gratitude.

FDR also increased public understanding of his speeches by "relating his issues to individual situations and using everyday analogies to illustrate his points."[70] Instead of citing complex figures and employing statistics in his June 28, 1934, chat on the revival of the banking system, the president framed his argument like this: "The simplest way for each of you to judge recovery lies in the plain facts of your own economic situation. Are you better off than you were last year?"[71] According to Sam Rosenman: "When his voice came over the radio, it was as though he were right [there] ... discussing their personal problems with them—the cattle or crops of the farmer, the red ink of the shopkeeper, the loans of the banker, the wages and hours of each worker."[72]

One of Roosevelt's most useful assets as a political broadcaster was the magnificent quality of his voice. Unlike many of his predecessors, Roosevelt lacked any kind of distinguishable regional accent. In contrast to the nasal tones of Calvin Coolidge, Roosevelt possessed an "all-American voice," which was "far more acceptable to the broad reach of Americans."[73] Part of his ability to communicate to all classes of society was due to the "neutral character of his voice, which gave no hint of his patrician upbringing."[74] In addition to this, "many of the wild fluctuations in volume that characterized Hitler's fiery tirades were similarly absent from Roosevelt's voice."[75] Whereas the German Führer worked himself and his audience into an impassioned delirium, Roosevelt "maintained a tight rein on the more excitable side of his personality" and was "skillful in communicating the subtle nature of his emotions to the public." John G. Carlisle, speech critic for CBS, observed that Roosevelt's "vocal cords were more sensitive and more susceptible to the influence of his emotions than the strings of a violin to the master's touch of the bow."[76] Sam Rosenman admired the "attractiveness of his voice; its fine shadings and nuances, [and] the infinite variety he knew how to give it—strength, sarcasm, humor, volume, charm, persuasiveness—all these would hold his listeners even when the content [of his speech] was dull."[77] Network engineers and technicians were pleased to find the "modulation and pitch" of his voice so smooth during broadcasts that there was no need to "touch the controls to remedy the usual peaks and valleys."[78]

FDR's voice was as polished as that of the most seasoned radio announcer. He "seldom faltered on a word, rarely cleared his throat on the air, and never gave the impression that he was reading a prepared text."[79] The "mechanical excellence" of Roosevelt's voice was such that the author of a book entitled *The Way to Good Speaking and Singing* wrote to the president expressing his admiration for "your individual way of speaking ... your volubility ... the naturalism in your vocal force, the perfection of your diction." The author went so far as to recommend FDR's voice as "an ideal pattern from which students may ... build their own vocal method."[80] *Broadcasting* hailed the president's voice as representing "a universal standard and an ideal of English speech."[81]

The most effective quality of Roosevelt's voice was its innate ability to inspire confidence among listeners. Prefacing every speech with the words, "My friends," Roosevelt "seemed to express a feeling of sincere concern for the problems facing the nation."[82] Through his "reassuring tone, FDR cultivated an image of himself as a fatherly figure who was genuinely interested in improving the lives of his people."[83] For a young Jimmy Carter, listening from his home in rural Georgia, "the resonant tones of the President of the United States slicing crisply through the static from faraway Washington, would remain and endure for him as an oral symbol of authority and strength, leadership and hope."[84]

The success of Roosevelt's broadcasting method can be ascertained by the number who consistently listened to him. The majority of his speeches and fireside chats were aired over a nationwide radio web that included as many as 600 stations. Through his own Rural Electrification Administration component of the New Deal, the expansion of "centrally generated electricity" into the countryside dramatically increased the size of the president's listening audience.[85] Many of his most important speeches were given worldwide coverage when they were translated into fourteen foreign languages and beamed out by shortwave.[86] For a typical fireside chat such as the one given on September 11, 1941, over 53,800,000 listeners (72.5 percent of the total American population) tuned in.[87] Throughout his broadcasting career, Roosevelt continued to set records by attracting the largest audience ever to listen to a single radio program. Numerous public opinion polls voted the fireside chats among the most popular radio programs on the air.[88] After the second or third time FDR had topped Jack Benny and Charlie McCarthy in the Hooper rankings, one advertiser queried: "How can my program achieve as high a rating as President Roosevelt gets whenever he is on the air?"[89] Radio critic and columnist John Crosby designated the president "the number one radio personality of all time."[90] Local stations airing competing programs during the time of the chats found no audience, and movie theaters were packed whenever they played a newsreel showing the president delivering a radio broadcast.[91] On Sunday nights when the president was on the air, theaters were vacant, and in the summer months when windows were open, one could walk the streets and not miss a word of the speech.[92]

When FDR delivered his second inaugural (January 20, 1937), the *Los Angeles Examiner* and CBS's Pacific Coast network ensured that every person in the city could hear the speech. Fifty radios were placed in department store windows, 200 in public and private schools, and "hundreds more in apartment houses, motion picture studios, places of business, restaurants and hotels."[93]

Roosevelt's drawing power was such that whenever he wanted to make a broadcast, Steve Early, had only to indicate the date and time to network officials and they would immediately arrange it. So eager were the nets to carry the president's voice that they were prepared to bring him to the air within ten minutes of any such request. When delivering an address, CBS, NBC and MBS employed duplicate equipment so as not to miss a word. Each network had two microphones on the presidential desk and two sets of transmitters to guard against technical failure. CBS and NBC technicians were constantly redesigning convenient microphones and speaking platforms to provide him with maximum comfort while broadcasting. In November 1935, a new portable mike that could easily be mounted and removed from train cars considerably facilitated FDR's touring schedule.[94]

Roosevelt made certain that he always had ready access to his radio entourage. Presidential announcers and engineers Carleton Smith and Albert Johnson (NBC), Walter Compton and William Cornell (MBS), and John Daly and Clyde Hunt (CBS) all followed Roosevelt on his official travels. All maintained regular facilities in the Oval Office, as well as the executive retreats at Hyde Park, New York, and Warm Springs, Georgia.

Because of intense public interest in the president's private life, network and press correspondents routinely reported on his daily activities. When on vacation, the president could rarely avoid the microphone. According to one observer: "If he goes out to San Diego or Charleston and boards a ship for a cruise, they follow him right up to the gangplank."[95] Veteran CBS announcer Bob Trout has recounted how he and his audience waited for several hours for the president to return to Portland after a fishing expedition, just to hear him say, "I'm glad to be back."[96] In another gesture signifying his immense radio appeal, the networks broadcast hour-long, celebrity-filled "birthday balls" for the president every January over combined hookups.[97]

Roosevelt was the greatest act on the air. But how could a political speech have competed with radio's popular entertainment programs? The answer was that FDR was not only a preeminent politician, but a talented actor as well. Realizing that listeners could easily turn the dial to Fibber McGee and Molly or Amos 'n' Andy, Roosevelt "had to seduce his audience with personality, and not with policy."[98] In an era when "the interruption of a comedy show by a political debate was resoundingly criticized by the public," a good politician was one who could entertain as well as lead. FDR continually demonstrated that the image a politician presented through an aural medium could be more important than the physical reality behind it.[99] Roosevelt accentuated and "perpetuated this illusion through his superb showmanship." Given the emphasis on image over substance, it is no surprise that the most prominent member of his writing staff was Robert Sherwood, one of the greatest Broadway playwrights of the day. Sherwood himself once remarked that he "never saw a better actor than Roosevelt,"[100] and *Variety* referred to him as "the Barrymore of the White House."[101] The president's "facility at enacting the script before him" stimulated countless listeners to write in asking that he read Dickens's *A Christmas Carol* over the air during the 1936 holiday season.[102]

The thought of having an entertainer in the White House unnerved some observers. During the 1932 presidential campaign, Herbert Hoover lamented that, because of Roosevelt's tactics, "efficient government does not interest the people as much as dramatics."[103] A writer for the *San Francisco Examiner* remarked, "A radio voice is only a phantom, as thin as the air in which it rides and as ephemeral as a New Deal campaign pledge. Voters have to decide: Do we want a showman or a statesman?"[104] FDR was a "master of stagecraft as well as statecraft, and was able to blur the line between the two." His techniques "in the dramatic art of make believe" would not be lost on his successors, especially Ronald Reagan.[105]

. Many critics warned of the dangerous precedent being established. In a situation where the image became paramount in the mind of the public, the issues received only secondary consideration. As the United States began to feel the impact of Europe's warlike rumbling in the 1930s, the "absence of intensive examination of foreign policy by the public might have led to U.S. involvement in situations where it had no vital interest, and even to war." Unfortunately, this probing criticism was beyond the realm of thought for many Americans. In an "electronic age where politicians sought them out and invaded their homes through the technology of radio," many people were content just to sit back and enjoy the show.[106]

Roosevelt had mastered the techniques of effective broadcasting. Through his command of such elements as timing, delivery, and voice, and his mutually beneficial relationship with the networks, FDR possessed all of the necessary ingredients of a successful "radio president."

2. Campaigning by Radio

The power of radio had a significant impact on the nature of political culture in the United States, and on the outcome of presidential elections. The introduction of wireless technology into the arena of political campaigning brought about many important changes. In past elections, a candidate had had to be physically present before his constituents in order to convey his message, and the size of his audience was limited by the capacity of the lecture hall. Now, radio allowed him to communicate to voters over vast distances and reach entire populations.[1] The *New York Times* noted:

> Radio has given a new meaning to the old phrase about a public man "going to the country." When President Wilson undertook to do it in 1919, it meant wearisome travel and many speeches to different audiences. Now President Roosevelt can sit at ease in his own study and be sure of a multitude of hearers beyond the dreams of the old-style campaigner.[2]

In this new style of political campaigning, vocal quality became one of a candidate's most vital assets,

> not only because the voice, through the all-covering power of radio, is reaching every American voter intimately and forcefully, but because the voice, more than anything else, is the most persuasive indicator of a man's personality, and to some extent, of his ability. A man's looks, his manner of dress—these are important—but more important are what he says, and the way he says it.[3]

For the first time, because of extensive network coverage, and the liberal extension of airtime to spokesmen of all persuasions, "voters were able to hear more candidates and political opinions, and to evaluate them more thoroughly, than ever before."[4] In the 1940 presidential campaign alone, listeners were briefed by no fewer than thirty major policy-makers.

Since candidates communicated over nationwide networks, "their appeals had to be directed more to diversified groups and less to sectional interests and local prejudices" than had previously been the case. They had to discuss issues of a "much wider import, at the expense of regional matters." Theoretically, "in the new broadcast setting, away from the rostrum, the politician was forced to be more direct, more analytical, and more concrete."[5]

No politician understood this changed situation better than Roosevelt. He was undoubtedly the first presidential candidate to grasp the true potential of radio as a vehicle for effective campaigning. Indeed, FDR's career and radio's development were inextricably linked, and many of his electoral victories were due largely to his masterful exploitation of the medium's power and possibilities. During his political life, the sheer pervasiveness of radio increased its importance as a tool for politicians. When he became governor in 1924, there were only three million sets in America. By the election for his third term as president in 1940, this number had jumped to nearly forty-eight million. FDR recognized the correlation between the "greater impact achievable in speaking to an entire nation," and success at the polls. By being able to "take his case directly to the people" in the presidential campaigns of 1932, 1936, 1940 and 1944, Roosevelt became the only man elected to four terms in the White House.[6]

Radio was not only instrumental in prolonging a candidate's time in office, it also had a much wider effect on American politics. Through the popularization of political debate in broadcast speeches and fireside chats, Roosevelt encouraged his listeners to take a much keener interest in the operation of the American political system. According to *Broadcasting*:

> Dispassionate discussion of public questions by candidates has a wholesome effect on listeners, arousing their interest in governmental affairs and public questions. The transmission of such intelligence to our people should prove most stimulating and add to the cultural progress of the nation by keeping the electorate fully informed on public matters.[7]

FDR accentuated this trend by making the people feel that they were an integral component of functioning government, and that he, as president, was merely their spokesman. In his May 7, 1933, fireside chat on the progress made during the banking crisis, Roosevelt underscored this element of accountability: "Tonight I have come ... to give you my report ... to tell you what we have been doing and what we plan to do."[8] In his broadcast of April 14, 1938, he stated: "I never forget that I live in a house owned by all of the American people, and that I have been given their trust."[9]

To further cultivate this sense of participation, the president originated a Sunday night interview series featuring his confidential secretary, Louis Howe. On the program, Howe was asked questions on governmental affairs by Walter Trumbull of the North American Newspaper Alliance. Trumbull acted "in the capacity of a private citizen" querying FDR's representative on matters of current interest. The radio audience was encouraged to use the newspaperman as its "interrogator" and urged to provide him with their written concerns.[10] In 1941, station WINX supplemented this with a weekly quarter-hour program in which listeners submitted their queries directly to the White House, and the responses were broadcast the following week.[11]

All of this translated into a marked increase in active participation at the voting booth. Many scholars believe that Roosevelt's use of radio was directly responsible for the 87 percent increase in the number of ballots cast in national presidential elections during the period between 1920 and 1940. This statistic is all the more striking when one remembers that the population only grew by 25 percent.[12] Roosevelt's radio appeals not only expanded the pool of voters in the 1930s, but also "persuaded an overwhelming number of these newcomers to cast their ballot for him." One former Republican voter commented, "All that man has to do is speak on the radio and the sound of his voice, his sincerity, and the manner of his delivery, just melts me and I change my mind."[13] FDR was such a formidable radio campaigner that when he took to the airwaves "his political foes quaked before his persuasive dominance."[14]

Roosevelt's opponents had good reason for such trepidation, for neither Herbert Hoover, nor Alf Landon, nor Wendell Willkie, nor Thomas Dewey, nor any other presidential candidate since 1920 could "approach his mastery of the microphone."[15] Among his predecessors, "there had been no attempt to develop special skills for radio or any great understanding of its persuasive powers." Only Roosevelt possessed a "voice and style perfectly tailored for the medium."[16]

While Woodrow Wilson was credited with having delivered the first presidential radio address to the American public in 1920, his message was brief, his delivery was "uninspiring, and the number of listeners [were] few." The following year Warren Harding broadcast his inaugural speech, and on June 21, 1923, he became the first chief executive to have his voice carried across the nation via a long-distance telephone relay system from WEAF in New York.[17] But Harding spurned radio and used it infrequently. His successor, Calvin Coolidge, held an equally negative view of the medium, and his "droning New England accent and unexpressive voice proved to be severe liabilities."

Herbert Hoover, on the other hand, did recognize some value in the new medium. As secretary of commerce in the Coolidge administration, he took a major hand in broadcasting's early development and regulation. In 1927, he served as president of the 74-nation International Radio Conference, and helped to write a series of treaties controlling global wireless traffic. In the same year, he was instrumental in securing the passage of the Federal Communications Act and in the establishment of a Federal Radio Commission. For the next two years, Hoover promoted legislation that sought to prevent government interference in radio through a system of voluntary regulation, and was a strong proponent of the maritime uses of broadcasting.[18] During his presidency, 1929–33, Hoover made about 95 radio speeches, only nine less than FDR delivered in his first term.[19] Despite his lifelong interest in radio and his frequent use of it, however, Hoover never became one of its abler speakers. He was completely bereft of all the vocal qualities needed to make his addresses effective.

Thus, FDR lacked any model to refer to when he began his career of political broadcasting. Despite this impediment, when compared to his predecessors and his future rivals, Roosevelt was unique "in being blessed with all of the characteristics that constitute an exemplary radio orator." To say that he made the most of his advantages would be an enormous understatement.[20]

Roosevelt's Early Political Career and Governorship

As early as 1924, Roosevelt had demonstrated an understanding of radio's potential use as a vehicle for political electioneering. During the Democratic National Convention of that year, FDR had been selected to present the nomination for New York governor Alfred E. Smith over the air. The 1928 convention, at which Roosevelt again delivered Smith's nomination, was the first to be transmitted nationally, and for most Americans it was a "novelty to be able to tune in and listen to the proceedings." Roosevelt was among the few of his party who "acknowledged this wider audience," and his nomination speech "was adapted for the listening public and not for the delegates who were assembled before him in Madison Square Garden." Despite his candidate's loss to Herbert Hoover in November, Roosevelt's performance "convinced not a few onlookers that the new electronic medium was rendering the old fashioned kind of campaign oratory obsolete."[21]

During his own four years as governor of New York, Roosevelt took full advantage of the broadcasting opportunities to which his office entitled him. From 1928 to 1932, he utilized WOKO of Albany and a wide-ranging state network to deliver no less than 75 radio talks.[22] Roosevelt frequently experimented with this "technological instrument of democracy" and tried various approaches to his audience. Much to his delight, the governor discovered that radio could be used to "overcome the power of private lobbies" and "move a reluctant legislature." By delivering his "reports to the people" two or three times each month; by employing "simple, direct and chatty" language to explain gubernatorial initiatives; and by making his policies appear "morally humane and socially responsible," FDR used radio as a valuable instrument for "mustering public opinion in his favor."[23] Sam Rosenman recalled:

> During his first term as Governor, the Republican leaders fought him bitterly on nearly every progressive measure he recommended—and wound up by grudgingly passing a good part of his program. There were several reasons for his striking victories ... But the most potent reason was Roosevelt's adept use of what came later to be known as the fireside chat. From time to time during each session of the Legislature he delivered a ... radio talk in which he told the people of the state what was currently going on in Albany, and appealed to them for help in his fight with the Legislature. He also did this after each session, reporting on the failures and accomplishments of the year. A flood of letters would deluge the members of the Legislature after each talk, and they were the best weapon Roosevelt had in his struggles for legislation.[24]

The success of this approach in helping him to pursue a variety of programs—the development of New York's natural resources, increased support for social services, heightened supervision of state business activities, and aid to farmers and unions—led Roosevelt to gloat: "Time after time in meeting legal opposition, I have taken the issue directly to the voters by radio, and invariably, I have met a most heartening response."[25]

Roosevelt used radio energetically in his 1930 bid for reelection. From Buffalo to Brooklyn, FDR broadcast speeches contrasting previous Republican misadministration of state affairs with his own strong first-term record. His "knack of homely exposition enabled him to get across to the people in forceful and understandable language" his two-year achievements in public works, labor legislation, regulation of public utilities, and prison and hospital reform. His broadcasts in favor of cheap electricity, in which he avoided "technical matters and kilowatt hours" and simply contrasted the amount Canadians paid to run home appliances with the eight times more required of New York residents, earned him "widespread support from the women of the state." In his final address over a statewide hookup from New York City, he "heaped ridicule on the [Republicans] for not discussing the real issues" of the campaign—prohibition, agricultural relief, hydroelectric power, and old-age pensions. Coming on election eve, the "speech had a telling effect." In his book *Working with Roosevelt*, Sam Rosenman argues that FDR's broadcasts were a major factor in securing him the highest Democratic plurality (725,000 votes) in New York since 1922.[26] When the governor set his sights on bigger political objectives in 1932, this fact would not be forgotten.

The 1932 Campaign

Among the bitter lessons learned by the Democrats after their defeat in the 1928 presidential election was that a more thorough exploitation of radio would offer the best chances for the future political success of the party. Toward this end, the position of "director of radio publicity" for the Democratic National Committee was created and a seasoned industry official, former secretary of the Federal Radio Commission Herbert L. Pettey, was selected to fill it. Pettey, with FDR's encouragement, formulated a clear agenda for utilizing "this new medium to promote a greater national consciousness of Democratic Party interests."[27] Deciding that radio would be their "primary publicity outlet" in the 1932 campaign, the Democrats allocated the bulk of their three million dollar budget for purchasing airtime. The fact that this represented over three times more than the Republicans were spending on broadcasting, and considerably less than the Democrats' own print campaign, led James G. Stahlman, president of the Southern Newspaper Publishers Association, to accuse DNC chairman James Farley of "favoritism towards radio."[28] Because Pettey resolved to again have the 1932 convention carried live, millions of eager listeners tuned in and were "captivated by the emotional verbal contest" between the supporters of Roosevelt and Al Smith. William Paley was one of the many prominent members of the radio industry who expressed their astonishment at how the debate "captured the imagination of the radio public."[29] On July 1, 1932, when the convention delegates had reached a decision, Roosevelt learned of his victory over the radio while at home in Albany's executive mansion. "With his flair for the dramatic," he contacted the convention hall by telephone and "asked the delegates to remain in session while he flew to Chicago to accept the nomination in person."* The traditional practice had been for a nominated candidate to delay his acceptance speech until after having been personally notified by party delegates one to two months later. According to Sam Rosenman:

> Roosevelt would have none of such prosaic arguments. He knew the value of drama in public office and in public relations, and he understood the psychology of the American people of 1932. He felt the dismayed, disheartened and bewildered nation would welcome something new, something startling, something to give it hope that there would be an end to stolid inaction. He wanted people to know that his approach was going to be bold and daring; that if elected he would be ready to act—and act fast.[30]

Delighted by this unusual breach of protocol, "millions of listeners waited expectantly by their radios for FDR to arrive." At 4:30 P.M. the next day, Roosevelt became the first presidential candidate in history to deliver his acceptance speech to the whole of the nation over a coast-to-coast radio hookup. "The words he delivered on this occasion were a historic indication to the public of the bold program he intended to implement upon gaining the presidential office." In a phrase that "heralded the revolution he envisioned for American society," he declared: "I pledge you, I pledge myself to a new deal for the American people!"[31]

Before he could set his plan in motion, FDR had to win the nation's highest office. For the next six months, Roosevelt campaigned tirelessly all around the country. Wherever he journeyed "there was a microphone on hand, and as he spoke his words were broadcast to the entire nation."[32] The result was some of the most effective campaign rhetoric ever spoken. Already on April 7, 1932, Roosevelt had taken an opportunity before the mike to denounce his opponent, Herbert Hoover, "criticizing the Republican 'trickle-down' panacea to the Depression as a fantasy, and asserting that only government intervention could produce a workable solution to the nation's problems." FDR argued that the "forgotten man" at the bottom of the economic pyramid must be given every

---

*This was another indication of Roosevelt's understanding of technology's role in modern politics. In addition to his unprecedented use of radio, FDR became the first presidential candidate ever to campaign by airplane.

manner of federal assistance possible in his great hour of need. Of Hoover's personal leadership, Roosevelt remarked: "If the old car, in spite of frequent emergency repairs, has been bumping along downhill on only two cylinders for three long years, it is time to get another car that will start uphill on all four."[33] In other speeches, Roosevelt "branded Hoover as a culprit for the country's economic woes, and implored the people to repudiate him."

In September, FDR stepped up his broadcast activities considerably, delivering four coast-to-coast speeches in that month alone (from Topeka, Portland, Salt Lake City, and Sioux City).[34] In an October speech in Pittsburgh, FDR offered something for everyone, including the traditional political promise to lower taxes and balance the budget. Roosevelt appealed to the listening audience to give him the chance to demonstrate that he was more capable than Hoover. His comments won wide approval, but they did not go unanswered by his opponent. After back-to-back speeches by the two candidates on October 31, 1932, the *Los Angeles Evening Herald* commented that "rather than being heard by a comparatively few persons, as was the case in past campaigns, the two candidates spoke to nearly 25 million Americans, or an unprecedented 75 percent of the listening population, making it the greatest debate in American political history."[35]

In the end, Roosevelt's rhetorical onslaught paid off. He soundly defeated Hoover after gaining 472 electoral votes to his opponent's 59.[36] Because of the "interest generated in the campaign by FDR's verbal digs at his opponent," more Americans went to the polls in 1932 than at any other time since the First World War.[37] Through his well-crafted radio speeches, FDR had succeeded in firmly establishing a link between Hoover and the Depression in the public mind. In so doing, he had repeatedly directed his vigorous attacks against "a vulnerable administration at its Achilles heel."[38] Hoover wrote: "Roosevelt's method was to pound incessantly into the ears of millions of radio listeners, by direct statement and innuendo, the total heartlessness of his opponent."[39]

Instead of adapting to the different style and techniques demanded by radio, Hoover endeavored to maintain the "outmoded image of stumping."[40] In his memoirs, Hoover referred to the days before radio's influence in politics as "those happier speaking times." In 1932 he refused the aid of ghostwriters, yet he was so inept at constructing his own radio speeches that it took him at least two or three weeks to prepare each one. Whenever broadcasting, he insisted that the microphone be hidden from public view behind the rostrum.

Hoover's unease before the mike stemmed from his awareness that his monotone speaking tone had a "soporific effect on listeners." Radio critic Ben Gross remarked that Hoover was "one of the dullest speakers" he had ever heard. Whenever he entered the studio network executives "shook their heads in frustration."[41] Listeners were frequently annoyed with the "hard, raspy" quality of the incumbent's voice, and the manner in which he articulated such words as "revenoo" and "constuhtooshun." After hearing one of his broadcasts, the *Ottawa Journal* warned its readers to be careful lest they become "contaminated by listening to such Americanese."[42] While Hoover's comebacks were hindered by his "prosaic style of delivery and seeming aloofness," Roosevelt was continually effective in "expressing the sentiments of an audience that was fed up with the status quo and desired change."[43]

While Roosevelt did win considerable political points by frequently contrasting his Depression-fighting record as governor of New York with Hoover's relative inactivity, the 1932 campaign was not conspicuous for its "thorough discussion of the issues or for the presentation of a comprehensive plan of action." Rather, FDR seemed satisfied with slamming his opponent, speaking in "optimistic generalities," and allowing his "energy and personality [to] contrast with the lethargic and colorless campaigning of Hoover."[44] Given the dreadful state of the national economy and the lack of easy remedies, it was natural that the contest would become largely one of personalities and not substance. In such a situation, Hoover's seeming remoteness and austerity, and his reliance on fear tactics, were certain to repel voters. FDR's use of radio to "work his way into the hearts of millions … with a smile, a gesture, and a promise of deep concern," on the other hand, seemed the perfect formula for success.[45]

After winning the 1932 presidential election, Roosevelt had no difficulty in "expanding his radio methods from the state to the national level." Having "mastered the techniques of political broadcasting from a limited state-wide hook-up" and periodic national exposure, he "sought to apply them to a permanent coast-to-coast network system." Such an entity was only then coalescing into its modern form, and thus had been available to no other chief executive. As early as March 12, 1933, Roosevelt had gained access to a network of 150 stations that reached approximately 20 million homes and a potential audience of 60 million people.[46]

The 1936 Campaign

In March 1936, *Broadcasting* observed:

> Democrats and Republicans alike believe that "radio sermons" will make the next president…and managers of both parties intend to fight out their campaign battles before the twenty-three million firesides to which the microphone has given them access."[47]

That radio was to be the "number one medium for reaching the electorate during this campaign" was admitted by all, "including the press."[48]

During the campaign season of 1936, the Republicans finally recognized the importance of conveying their political message through "modern radio techniques."[49] Faced with such a formidable oratorical rival, the GOP was forced to experiment with a number of innovative broadcasting devices. Party publicists took the necessary steps to have their convention broadcast over 200 stations, and candidate Alfred M. Landon allowed himself to be interviewed on radio at every possible opportunity.[50] Once the campaign commenced, Landon made a series of short commercials that emphasized the main aspects of his platform.

On October 17, Senator Arthur Vandenburg presented a "debate" on CBS in which he asked questions of a nonpresent Roosevelt, played selected recordings of the president's speeches in reply, and then ridiculed the answers.[51] While this approach was unique, the Republican party's effort was soon plagued by difficulty. Vandenburg's "fireside mystery chat" had violated a decade-old CBS policy against the use of recordings on the air, and consequently many affiliates either refused to carry the broadcast or terminated it as soon as its unfair character became apparent.[52]

Roosevelt's special relationship with the radio industry was immensely advantageous during this campaign. Despite a policy of "equal access to all qualified candidates," the major networks temporarily refused to donate or sell the Republicans airtime after the Vandenburg incident, leaving Landon with only one broadcast alternative, station WGN in Chicago. This decision immediately sparked Republican accusations of government monopoly of radio and demands for an investigation of network fair practice policies. Although listeners felt network airtime was being evenly distributed during the election, the GOP felt that section 315 of the Federal Communication Act was consistently interpreted and applied by the FCC in the administration's favor, and that loopholes in the law were routinely used to prevent prominent Republicans from broadcasting. Indeed, in January 1936, when the GOP requested free airtime in which to respond to the president's state of the union message, CBS and NBC declined.[53] In February, Henry P. Fletcher, GOP committee chairman, demanded equal facilities for rebutting another FDR speech, and the nets again refused. A few weeks later, in an attempt to appeal to an entertainment-hungry audience, Landon depicted his campaign promises in an allegorical radio play, "Liberty at the Crossroads," but once again the networks pulled the plug.[54] In September, NBC slightly modified its rigid position and stated that it would honor Republican requests "from time to time." CBS agreed to do so "only in accordance with its best editorial judgment."[55]

Unfortunately for the Republicans, Landon's unexciting style prevented him from taking full advantage of the few broadcasting privileges open to him. In a country where people were becoming accustomed to having a charismatic and eloquent radio president, "Landon was greatly outclassed by his Democratic opponent." He frequently shied away from the microphone and allowed several weeks to pass between radio appearances. While the Kansas governor was a "simple and sincere man," he was unable to "convey the strength of his character effectively to potential voters in the listening audience."[56] His "voice was weak, his timing poor, and his delivery awkward." He spoke at such a "rapid and uneven pace that he never left his audience time to applaud."[57] He also tended to become irritable after long spells on the campaign circuit. During a sojourn through Missouri, Iowa, and Wisconsin, he displayed a "curtness of manner" and a "grim militancy" that alienated many listeners.[58]

Unlike the GOP, the Democrats employed no special contrivances during their radio drive in 1936. With the outstanding rhetoric of FDR, they needed nothing more. At first, Roosevelt found himself in an uneasy situation where, as incumbent, he often had to defend the status quo against his opponent's criticisms of governmental interference, radicalism, and the infringement of personal liberties. Rather than continue to allow Landon the initiative, Roosevelt soon mounted a powerful counterattack. Through the means of radio, FDR answered charges that the New Deal had not yet mastered the Depression by saying another term was necessary to complete the many reforms already begun. He pointed to signs of economic recovery and contrasted them with the conditions that prevailed when first he succeeded Hoover. To blunt Landon's accusations of fiscal extravagance on the part of the government, FDR upheld relief spending as a "conservation of human resources" and contended that the "cost was balanced by rising national income."[59] On September 6, Roosevelt used the occasion of a fireside chat to convey an election appeal to two of the "largest and most politically potent groups in America": farmers and blue-collar workers. For the former, who had been devastated by drought and dust, he reviewed a list of various federal measures he had introduced to mitigate their plight, including soil and water conservation and public works projects. For the latter, FDR referred to the upcoming Labor Day holiday to praise the "brave spirit" with which so many workers were "winning their way out of the depression" (with considerable help from the Roosevelt administration and its employment policies, of course). In his Syracuse speech of September 29, he mocked the Republicans in an allusion to an old man who fell into a river while wearing a silk hat. A friend jumped in and saved him, said Roosevelt, but the hat was lost. Several years later, the old man could still be found reproaching his friend for having lost the hat. To at least one listener, Roosevelt's "finesse in making the Republicans appear ridiculous was indeed clever."[60]

In another late–September speech, he again belittled Landon. "Raising his voice to near falsetto and sarcastically arching his eyebrows,"[61] FDR said:

> Let me warn the nation against the smooth evasion which says: "Of course we believe in social security; we believe in work for the unemployed; we believe in saving homes. Cross our hearts and hope to die, we believe in all these things; but we do not like the way the present Administration is doing them. Just turn them over to us. We will do all of them—we will do more of them—we will do them better; and most important of all, the doing of them will not cost anybody anything.[62]

In his October speeches, FDR successfully defended his first-term record. At a cornerstone ceremony in New York he declared: "I have laid many cornerstones and ... none of the buildings have fallen down yet." In Pittsburgh, he confidently remarked:

> The government of this great nation, solvent, sound in credit, is coming through a crisis as grave as war, without having sacrificed the American dream or the ideals of American life.... Starvation has been averted, homes and farms saved, banks were re-opened, industry revived, and dangerous forces subversive to our form of government were turned aside.[63]

On October 31, Roosevelt again castigated the Republicans by referring to them as a "hear-nothing, see-nothing, do-nothing government."

> For twelve years this nation...looked to Government but the Government looked away. Nine mocking years of the golden calf and three long years of the scourge! Nine crazy years at the ticker and three long years in the bread lines! Nine mad years of mirage and three long years of despair! ... Powerful influences strive today to restore that kind of government with its doctrine that that Government is best which is most indifferent. For nearly four years you have had an Administration which, instead of twirling its thumbs, has rolled up its sleeves. We will keep our sleeves rolled up.[64]

At the height of the Depression, people relished the president's attacks on "economic royalism," government for the rich, and other "elitist components of Republican ideology." Roosevelt's ability to communicate the "stern indignation" of the people and a sense of "moral fervor" won wide praise from all quarters of the nation. Before a capacity crowd in Madison Square Garden, FDR defiantly proclaimed: "The forces of organized money are unanimous in their hate for me. And I welcome their hatred." After highlighting all he had already done for "farmers, consumers and home owners" FDR proclaimed: "We have only just begun to fight!"[65] The "determined and inspiring tone" in which the President advocated a war against indigence, which would include pensions for the aged, help to the unions, relief for the unemployed, and restrictions on business, stood in stark contrast to Landon's dry manner.[66]

As a broadcaster, Roosevelt successfully applied the lessons he had absorbed in 1932. Recognizing that the cancellation of popular entertainment shows for political speeches made listeners resentful and "lost more votes than it achieved," FDR never overspoke during scheduled periods. He also had discovered the counter-productiveness of booking a political talk on a station at the same time as another speech was being presented on his behalf, thus "dividing the attention of his audience."[67] The Republicans never grasped this, and often aired overlapping addresses.

Perhaps most importantly, the president recognized the necessity of having the last word on election eve. On November 2, 1936, the Democrats paid

$100,000 for "radio time in last minute appeals to vacillating voters." While Landon, William Lemke (Union party) and Earl Browder (Communist party) were given the opportunity to speak on election eve, FDR followed them all, during the 11:00 P.M. to midnight slot. While Landon and the others used the limited facilities of one network (NBC-Red) for their concluding remarks, Roosevelt utilized all four (NBC-Red, NBC-Blue, CBS, MBS), thus giving his message a significantly greater range of coverage.[68]

Again, as in 1932, Roosevelt's verbal onslaught overwhelmed his opponent. When the returns came in for the 1936 presidential election, FDR had won 27.5 million popular votes, while Landon had garnered only 16.5 million. The electoral count was even more impressive: 523 to 8. The only two states Roosevelt failed to carry were Maine and Vermont. With over 61 percent of the total votes cast, FDR enjoyed a margin of victory unprecedented in American elections (and topped only by Lyndon Johnson in 1964). The election of 1936 also witnessed a marked increase in the Democratic majority in Congress, with 331 seats in the House and 76 in the Senate (compared to the Republicans' 89 and 16 respectively).[69]

Roosevelt had been farsighted in realizing that the modern American politician would have to cultivate his radio "appearance" if he desired any chance of success at the polls. In the 1936 campaign, Roosevelt made it clear to a majority of his countrymen that his radio image was superior to all rivals. Owen D. Young appraised FDR's performance as follows:

> I have no hesitation in saying that yours were equal to the best and superior to most of the speeches which have been preserved to us from the political campaigns of the century. They were forceful like Teddy Roosevelt's, they were elevated in tone and diction like Wilson's, and they had that rare moving quality of which Bryan was so great a master. The radio has certainly restored the primacy of the spoken word and its service in this campaign was amply evident to me for all the efforts you have made in its behalf.[70]

Radio was indeed FDR's greatest asset in the 1936 campaign. Following Roosevelt's stunning victory at the polls, Harry Butcher underscored this advantage in a letter to Steve Early in which he noted the contrast between the "benevolent neutrality of radio and the 80–85% of the press which had opposed the President" throughout the campaign.[71] James Farley commented:

> The influence of radio in determining the outcome of the 1936 election can hardly be overestimated. Without that unrivaled medium for reaching millions of voters, the work of overcoming the false impression created by the tons of written propaganda put out by the foes of the New Deal would have been many times greater than it was, and, to be candid, it might conceivably have been an impossible job. Yet no matter what was written or what was charged, the harmful effect was largely washed away as soon as the reassuring voice of the President of the United States started

coming through the ether into the family living room. The full effect can be realized only by pondering on the fact that the Chief Executive was able to reach directly every voter in the land who had a radio and whose mind was sufficiently open for him to turn over the dial.[72]

Speaker of the House Sam Rayburn was even more direct in his praise for radio's contribution to Democratic victory. In a letter to FDR a few years after the election he wrote, "It was your nationwide radio speeches in 1936 which carried 46 out of 48 states."[73]

Imitating the Master

Because of Roosevelt's overwhelming success in exploiting radio for political ends, he inspired many other would-be politicians to emulate him. According to *Broadcasting*, after the 1936 election, office seekers from all over the country "recognized radio as the number one medium for reaching voters" and "demanded time on local stations in greater amounts than ever before."[74] Many individuals who were not even politically affiliated felt that they had a shot at office if they could gain access to the ether.

It was natural that station owners and industry executives would be among the most eager to attach their names to the ballot. The 1930s saw numerous successful attempts by such men as John Devaney (controlling stockholder of Minnesota's WLOL), who won a seat in the United States Senate.[75] In 1940, Frank Gannett, New York publisher and station owner, used the airwaves in his bid for the GOP nomination for president against Thomas Dewey, and James Noe (owner of WNOE of New Orleans), did the same for the Louisiana governorship.[76] A newscaster for WHO of Des Moines, H.R. Gross, astonished Iowa politicos when he ran a tight second in the governor's race against incumbent George Wilson. With no prior political experience, and "without making personal appearances and kissing babies," Gross waged his campaign almost entirely through paid commercials over WHO.[77]

In the 1938 radio campaign for the Texas governorship, a flour manufacturer, W. Lee O'Daniel, sponsored a country-music program that was broadcast throughout the state. During the program he delivered commercials in which he asked listeners if they would support his bid for political office. After 54,499 affirmative replies were mailed in, he undertook a breakneck campaign effort in which he "employed further radio appeals and sound trucks." In the end, his efforts paid off and he was soon elected.[78]

Another Texan, Lyndon B. Johnson, won a seat in Congress in 1937, largely through his effective use of airtime on KNOW, Austin, and KTSA, San Antonio. In the closing days of the campaign, Johnson made more radio appearances than the other seven candidates combined.[79] Constantly displaying a penchant for the unorthodox, on one occasion LBJ broadcast a populist appeal from a barbershop in Johnson City, Texas.[80]

Perhaps no one exemplified the Rooseveltian method better than New York mayor Fiorello La Guardia. Fed up with the persistent hostility of the city's press and their editorial distortion of his speeches, La Guardia "resolved to find a more direct line to his constituents." He once remarked: "I have learned that important public questions must be presented impartially, and the only way I know of doing that ... is by word of mouth."[81] In January 1942, he commenced a series of Sunday evening "Talks to the People," which presented informal political talks and personal advice in a style clearly modeled on FDR's fireside chats. While some criticized La Guardia for the way in which his squeaky voice, "feverish demeanor and earthy syntax, contrasted with the polished style of conventional radio announcers," his "caring expressiveness and fatherly tone" made him a favorite with over two million New York listeners.[82] The image of sincerity he projected in his broadcasts was vital when trying to sell his reform package to a city wracked by the strain of massive unemployment. His vast audience regularly tuned in to hear the mayor's views on a wide variety of topics, from religion to fashion. When a newspaper strike deprived metropolitan children of their Sunday comics, La Guardia went on the air and vividly reenacted the exploits of Dick Tracy for them.[83] The ratings for his weekly half-hour program were so high that opponents branded WNYC the "mayor's personal plaything."[84] La Guardia, like FDR, relished the intimate nature of radio, and he "spoke into the microphone as if there were only a few close buddies before him." By projecting the mayor into the lives of his constituents, radio helped to overcome the "barriers which had traditionally separated city government and its citizens."[85] Through his broadcasts, La Guardia assured himself of a devoted following which faithfully supported his bid for four terms in office.

Among the others who sought to follow FDR's example were the members of his own clan. Not long after their move to the White House, the first family earned the sobriquet of "the Radio Roosevelts."[86] In 1933, Jimmy Roosevelt signed on as a news commentator for Boston's Yankee Network. Elliot became vice-president of the Southwestern Radio Group and part owner of the Texas State Network. In 1940, he too tried his hand at newscasting, preparing stories for the popular *America Looks Ahead* program.[87]

Eleanor was by far the most energetic broadcaster after the president himself. Between 1934 and 1940, she made charitable donations of more than $100,000 in earnings from her sponsored commentary programs. Her show generally featured "discussions of pertinent problems facing women" and often included interviews with prominent guests.[88] In October 1940 she went on the air in a thirteen-part series for NBC, and in July of 1941 she began a popular quarter-hour Sunday program for Pan American Coffee.[89] *Broadcasting* described the manner in which she adopted the techniques of her husband:

She wrote and rewrote. She rehearsed constantly and faithfully.... She went over and over her script to make it fit the time allotted, down to the last second. She also took lessons in speech to learn how to breathe properly.[90]

As a sign of her dedication, she once delivered her weekly broadcast by long-distance telephone from a "remote farmstead" where her son had recently been married. As a small gesture to enhance the size of her growing audience, Mrs. Roosevelt purchased over one hundred radio sets a year and presented them as gifts.[91]

The 1940 Campaign

It was clear to both parties that victory in the 1940 presidential election would be determined by the candidate who made most effective use of the airwaves. Never before would "comprehensive political broadcast schedules [be] so completely arranged, so far in advance."[92] When Roosevelt and Wendell Willkie took to the air, their voices would be carried by over 500 stations to a potential audience of over 100 million people.

The proportion of individual Americans who now owned radios was nearing 75 percent.[93] Of these listeners, more than 52 percent now relied on the radio as their chief source of political information.[94] The findings of the Lynds in Middletown also supported this trend.[95] A series of surveys conducted during the campaign revealed that "most voters preferred radio's coverage of political events like conventions, rallies, and inaugurations to that found in newspapers." Also discovered was the extent to which "radio had the effect of strengthening voters' predispositions." Most of those queried "tended to listen most to the candidates they favored."[96]

With the country still in the economic doldrums, and with its role in the spreading world conflict uncertain, voter interest burgeoned to an unprecedented high. As a result, radio's coverage of the 1940 presidential race was placed on a full-time schedule. The entire broadcasting world eagerly anticipated the opening of the campaign: "Two great speakers selling themselves to America and competing for attention and votes. It's going to be a verbal battle of giants!"[97] As both FDR and Willkie endeavored to win votes through the influential power of radio, the "medium would again be employed in new and interesting ways."[98]

Willkie took the initiative and began a lightning radio public relations campaign that propelled him from a little-known utilities executive to a prominent GOP contender. Once he clinched the Republican nomination, he toured the nation by train, broadcasting speeches at almost every stop. To increase his national exposure, Willkie was featured on a popular quiz program, *Information Please*, and was a guest panelist on *America's Town Meeting of the Air*.[99] Such appearances "established him as a radio personality and gave the first fillip to his presidential quest." In the "fast-paced question and answer setting" of these programs, Willkie impressed all by his "amazing breadth of knowledge and facility of expression."[100]

Although this seemed like an auspicious beginning, Willkie's broadcast fortunes quickly soured. Although the networks got the ball rolling in July 1940 by carrying the GOP convention to a large audience of enthusiastic supporters, Willkie rapidly lost the momentum and allowed considerable time to lapse before again taking to the air.[101] When his next speech finally came, it was such a disappointment that Republican headquarters considered limiting the candidate's national microphone appearances to no more than six in the lead-up to November 5. When Wells Church, radio director for the Republican National Committee, realized in late September that record numbers of listeners were tuning in to political campaign broadcasts, and that the GOP would "win or lose the election on the air," he sharply increased Willkie's radio budget and greatly expanded his broadcast commitments.[102] From October 15 through 31, NBC carried eight of Willkie's speeches from such locations as St. Louis, Minneapolis, and Chicago.[103] On November 2, he was featured in a lavish Republican rally in Madison Square Garden, and on election eve, following Democratic precedent, he offered listeners an election-eve promotional broadcast entitled the "Willkie for President Rally," which featured such famous personalities as Clare Boothe Luce and Mary Pickford.[104]

Although millions of Americans heard Willkie's radio messages, many were unimpressed. When, during his nomination acceptance speech from Elwood, Indiana, he expounded on his platform promise to preserve many aspects of the New Deal and to defend Britain, he sounded not unlike his Democratic opponent. Although Willkie "was a magnetic personality who generated much excitement in person, much of his impact was lost over the airwaves." He possessed a raspy voice that "sounded shrill when compared to FDR's reassuring baritone."[105] His failure to satisfactorily articulate his ideas, and his tendency to "telescope three or four words into one or two," led to such distortions as "guhment" (government), "cabnut" (cabinet), and the more egregious one referring to the chief executive as the "Presen Unide-States."[106] He slurred his consonants, and his t's, d's and p's were "not pronunciated [sic] with what trained speakers would consider accuracy."[107] After the Elwood fiasco, which proved particularly detrimental since it received the highest rating for a political speech up to that point (21 million, 37.8 CAB), *Broadcasting* remarked:

> When it comes to vote-getting in this day of radio and audiences by the millions, teamwork among the organs of speech is vital. How the vocal chords mesh may be more important than how the Hatch Act* performs. An Adam's apple may win the election and determine the destiny of

The Hatch Clean Politics Act placed statutory limitations on the amount of campaign spending permitted by each candidate.

nations. We don't think how a thing is said should be equally as important as how it is thought, but in campaigning it is. Mr. Willkie should take heed of this problem and realize that he is up against the greatest epiglottis in the known world.[108]

Willkie's performance at Elwood was so bad, one New Dealer commented on how it "won us a couple of million votes." This speaker went on to say: "Willkie's microphone manner must be improved if he is to meet FDR on equal terms as a radio votegetter."[109]

Despite this critique of his vocal form, Willkie refused to consult a voice specialist, and he habitually neglected to rehearse his speeches. While a magnificent impromptu speaker, Willkie had serious difficulty coping with his scripts. The "printed page seemed to put a bit of a barrier between him and his audience." Willkie frequently appeared fatigued during his delivery, and often backtracked rather than coming directly to the point.[110] His "failure to acknowledge the nature of radio's amplifying power caused him to shout into the microphone at the top of his lungs, thus straining his voice into a croaky hoarseness." The man assigned by NBC to Willkie's campaign, Charles C. Barry, complained how he "suffered with him through dozens of speeches because of his failure to learn how to use his voice." Barry recounts how, in a speech in Peoria, Illinois, "the sounds he produced were so guttural and indistinct that the audience actually laughed."

On several occasions, Willkie's "gruff manner and inability to gauge the temperament of his audience" got him into trouble. While speaking to a large crowd in Cicero, Illinois, he opened his address by saying: "Now that we're in Chicago..." When the throng reminded him that he was in Cicero, the unthinking candidate retorted: "All right, to hell with Chicago!" According to Willkie biographer Mary Dillon, "This statement made front-page headlines throughout the country, alienating Chicagoans and the deeply religious.... It was one of the worst blunders of the election."[111] He also offended a large segment of women voters. Referring to FDR's female secretary of labor, Frances Perkins, Willkie told his Pittsburgh audience: "If elected I will appoint a Secretary of Labor directly from the ranks of organized labor ... and it will not be a woman either!"[112]

From the start, the GOP campaign was continually plagued by misfortune. On October 23, a speech by Senator Bruce Barton endorsing Willkie was preempted for a presidential address on national security. The next day, the Republicans secured time on NBC-Red for a Willkie talk from Erie, Pennsylvania, only to have the train late and the first fifteen minutes of the program filled by piano music.[113] Unlike FDR, Willkie "scorned the limitations of radio, allowing himself to run over a scheduled period by as much as a quarter hour." Once, Willkie's refusal to heed the cues to wind up his speech "cost the Republican National Committee $10,000 for extra air time."[114]

By contrast, Roosevelt made efficient use of his time, exploiting his special relationship with the networks to get the best coverage of his speeches. Because of the unusual nature of the 1940 election, FDR would have to be at his very best as a political persuader. To many Americans, the "no third term" tradition was sacred and inviolate. To convince voters of the rectitude of overturning this hallowed democratic custom, FDR would employ two new techniques: He would make "extraordinary use of the audiences that assembled to see him speak, and he would call upon the finest talent in Hollywood to endorse him over the air."[115]

Roosevelt wasted no time in applying his new devices. During the July 16 Democratic National Convention in Chicago, FDR strategically placed Tom Garry, the city's commissioners of sewers, and a "host of loyal followers" in the basement of the convention hall. An intricate array of microphones and sound equipment connected the room to loudspeakers in the hall above. These men could hear the ceremonies proceeding by radio, and with every reference to FDR they erupted in mighty cheers that were amplified into the convention hall and over the air. Upon hearing the sound of Garry's voice, Democratic stalwarts in the galleries took up the cry: "Roosevelt, Roosevelt, we want Roosevelt!" By means of this clever deception, delegates and the 25 million listeners at home heard a "boisterous enthusiasm that did not really exist in the convention room."[116] In contrast, whenever anti–FDR forces attempted to organize a demonstration, they were silenced by a thunderous wave of organ music.

After the convention, Roosevelt withheld his campaigning until the last weeks before the election. In so doing, he projected the illusion of being "drafted" into running by a public who felt him to be indispensable to the national welfare and by an otherwise helpless party. Responding to repeated Democratic efforts to prevail upon him, FDR finally declared in an October broadcast: "My conscience will not let me turn my back on a call to service."[117]

Except for one address to the Teamsters Union on the eleventh, FDR spent most of September in Washington, while various government officials, cabinet members, and Democratic congressmen did his stumping for him. On September 10, House speaker William Bankhead broadcast over 42 CBS stations, and on the twentieth, Senator James F. Byrnes used the facilities of NBC-Red. The president, however, was by no means idle during this period. Exercising his prerogative as incumbent, and circumventing the limitations imposed by his tight publicity budget, FDR used the occasion of a state of the union address to make his pitch for a third term.[118]

As election eve beckoned, FDR threw his campaign machine into high gear. On October 4, the Democrats used Mutual for a coast-to-coast talk by Federal Works Agency administrator John M. Carmody. On October 7, secretary of commerce Jesse Jones made an appeal over NBC-Blue, and on October 9, attorney general Robert H. Jackson took to the air on FDR's behalf. This was quickly followed on October 11 with an address by vice-presidential candidate Henry A. Wallace. From October 14 to 16, Senator Byrnes, secretary of state Cordell Hull, secretary of agriculture Wickard, and Senator George Norris were all heard.[119]

During this period, Roosevelt was able to rely on two of his campaign mainstays for vital support. His wife, Eleanor, herself an active broadcaster and accomplished speaker, endorsed FDR while appearing on various forums, panels, and interview programs. On September 27, she delivered a formal address over a nationwide hook-up. The president's old friend and New Deal soulmate Fiorello La Guardia was used extensively as his "tough proxy" and "spear carrier." In the fall of 1940, the New York mayor made dozens of on-air appearances around the country, attacking the Republicans as the "kept party of business" and Willkie as the "polished front for this shameful organization."[120] On September 12, Fiorello lent his national reputation to the Democratic cause when he broadcast a fifteen-minute endorsement for "our revered President" over a chain of 116 NBC-Red stations.[121]

In the run-up to the election, FDR personally took a more active role in his campaign, broadcasting daily from October 28 to November 2 to some of the largest audiences in history. On every occasion, his speeches topped Willkie's by almost 100 percent in the Hooper and CAB (Cooperative Analysis of Broadcasters) ratings. The widest spread in their numbers came on October 28, when Roosevelt attracted 37 percent of listeners while Willkie drew only 16 percent. The primary reason why FDR was able to reach far more voters in the last crucial days was that the Democrats spoke at prime evening hours. Also, the Democrats always used at least two networks to carry their appeals, while the Republicans usually relied on only one.[122] Overall, the Democratic Party spent $1.3 million* on radio publicity, $350,000 of which was disbursed in the month of October alone.[123] This figure not only topped GOP expenditures for this race, it far exceeded the Democrats' own extravagant radio budget of 1936.

A major issue of the election was whether the President would keep the nation out of the war in Europe. Willkie charged, "If his promise to keep our boys out of foreign wars is no better than his promise to balance the budget, they're already on the transports."[124] In response, Roosevelt collaborated with Robert Sherwood and Samuel Rosenman to produce a series of ingenious radio speeches that assuaged the fears of the American public and discredited the Republican accusations.[125] During one broadcast from Madison Square Garden on October 28, 1940, Roosevelt successfully "shellacked" some of his isolationist Republican opponents who blamed him for not adequately preparing American defenses, by inciting the crowd to chant their last names, "Martin, Barton, and Fish," in derision.[126] Contrasting his consistent policy of preparedness with the political opportunism and wavering of the Republicans, FDR stated:

*Approximately $500,000 went to NBC, $350,000 to CBS, $150,000 to MBS, and the rest to local stations and regional networks.

> There is the ... permanent, crystal clear record. Until the present politi-
> cal campaign opened, Republican leaders, in and out of the Congress
> shouted from the rooftops that our defenses were fully adequate. Today
> they proclaim that this Administration has starved our armed forces, that
> our Navy is anemic, our Army puny, our air forces piteously weak. Yes, it
> is a remarkable somersault. I wonder if the election could have something
> to do with it.[127]

He asked the audience to "support his rearmament policies, and to reject reckless Republican charges that he was leading the country down the path of war." "My policy has always been an affirmative, realistic fight for peace," he declared.[128] On October 30, 1940, he again assured the radio audience: "I have said this before and I shall say it again and again and again. Your boys are not going to be sent into any foreign wars."[129] Roosevelt used his clout with the networks to have many of his important speeches recorded and rebroadcast so that people who missed it the first time around had another opportunity to tune in.[130]

Perhaps the most effective Democratic campaign contrivance during the 1940 presidential contest was a two-hour election-eve gala program that featured speeches and endorsements from politicians and well-known Hollywood entertainers.[131] This rally was aired Nov. 4 over all four national networks during the choice period between 10:00 P.M. and midnight, and cost the party over $100,000.[132] Listeners at home were treated to the voices of secretary of state Cordell Hull, the famous authors Carl Sandburg and Alexander Woolcott, and the commentator Dorothy Thompson.[133] In addition to these, the cream of the stage, screen and radio worlds made brief appearances before the microphone to speak for the president. Audience ratings left little doubt that the program was successful, and given the public's preference for "politics dressed up as entertainment," it must certainly have resulted in an increase in the number of votes cast for the Democrats, particularly among the "last-minute unde-cided." The radio branch of the Democratic Party discovered this formula for success after listeners became outraged when a speech by Senator Robert F. Wagner at the National Convention cut into a boxing match.[134] In compari-son to this spectacular offering, Willkie's program later that evening was a modest affair that was aired so late at night that few stayed up to listen to it.[135]

While Willkie succeeded in keeping up with Roosevelt in the polls until late October, once the president launched his publicity campaign and mobi-lized his talents for radio, the Republicans' prospects for victory quickly van-ished. On election day, FDR won a spectacular landslide with 449 electoral votes to Willkie's 82.[136] FDR had successfully convinced the American people to allow him an unprecedented third term in office. Again, many observers agreed that the president's skillful manipulation of radio was the key to his vic-tory. In mid–November, *Broadcasting* noted: "FDR's astute use of radio prob-ably accounted as much as any other tangible factor for [his] re-election."[137] According to Sam Rosenman:

He had won in spite of the ancient third-term tradition; he had won in spite of the public irritations that had inevitably accumulated in eight years of office-holding; he had won ... in spite of the vast campaign funds against him, in spite of the pent-up hatred of conservatives and isolationists, and in spite of the opposition of the richest and most powerful industrialists and financiers.[138]

To others, Roosevelt's sweeping victory had demonstrated radio's position as the nation's dominant medium once and for all. *Variety* wrote:

> His election for a third term demonstrated as nothing else could, the power of American radio. More than a political contest, the 1940 election was a battle between newspapers and radio to test which medium exercised the greatest influence on the American public. When the papers lined up almost 90% solidly against the third term, Roosevelt took his case directly to the people by the airwaves. Newspapers denied that the victory had been a clear cut one, claiming that the Roosevelt voice and personality was as much a factor in the victory as the medium of radio.[139]

In any case, it had been to the mutual advantage of FDR and the radio industry to conduct the 1940 campaign in convenient alliance. Roosevelt won "another spell in office, and the networks achieved some of the highest ratings they would ever receive." Thus, in November, they had both gained considerably.

The 1944 Campaign

As the 1944 presidential campaign dawned it was again clear that "the welfare of the candidates depended to a major extent upon their radio appeal to the people."[140] Unfortunately for Roosevelt, victory in 1944 was not to be as easily attainable as it had been in the previous election. This was largely due to the fact that many of the broadcasting faculties that gave FDR an edge in past campaigns were also present in his new opponent, Thomas E. Dewey. *Broadcasting* noted:

> For twelve years now, presidential campaigns have been one-sided. As a radio personality there was no opponent who could remotely approach the effectiveness of Franklin D. Roosevelt. We had a feeling that things would go on like that indefinitely. But now we have been listening to Governor Thomas Dewey.[141]

Louis Foley, professor of English at Western Michigan College, observed: "Not since radio became a first-class medium for political campaigning has there been a Republican leader who approached Dewey's caliber as a broadcaster."[142] Another observer took this praise one step further: "Considered all around, Dewey represents about the best vocal equipment displayed on the air by *any* political leader in this country in recent years."[143] While most broadcast insiders felt the two candidates to be "evenly matched in speaking prowess,"[144] one commentator writing in the *Weekly Digest of Radio Opinion* actually gave Dewey the edge.[145] At age sixty-two, the president was "no longer the rugged campaigner of other years."[146] As a result, FDR was to face the most formidable rival of his political career, and the outcome of the presidential race was never completely certain until all the votes were counted.

By the time he became governor of New York, Thomas Dewey had already acquired an array of impressive oratorical skills from his many years of experience as a criminal prosecutor. Once he set his sights on the White House, he sought the professional advice of the popular radio commentator Lowell Thomas. Through regular coaching sessions, Dewey emerged as a "powerful rough and tumble orator."[147] According to Professor Foley:

> Dewey has a fine, manly voice that is a pleasure to hear. Its clear, ringing tones are not marred by rough edges or fuzzy overtones. It is strong without any evidence of strain or overexertion, and he uses it wisely so that it will hold up under frequent public speaking. It is not a lulling or soothing voice, but it is one that is steadily exciting.[148]

Unlike Willkie, Dewey possessed both "clean-cut enunciation" and "perfect syllabication." He was a master of the vocal pause and had a highly refined penchant for dividing sentences in the right place and spacing the pieces "so that [they] are distinct, yet coalesce smoothly into the larger thought group to which they belong." Like FDR, Dewey's voice conveyed the impression of one who was "thoroughly well-bred and poised, but without the exaggeration of refinement and certainly without weakness or indecision." Dewey's diction revealed no trace of a sectional or regional dialect. He was not only free from any kind of "Hahvud" accent, he also avoided the "well-known mid-western linguistic peculiarities which sound almost barbaric to people from other parts." Overall, Foley concluded, Dewey's voice was "just good American."[149]

Dewey was also a savvy broadcaster. The night before a scheduled address, the governor was known to go through as many as four drafts and stay up until early morning "polishing phrases."[150] His "radio consciousness" prevented him from running overtime while on the air, thus earning him the respect of network officials and saving his party from considerable expense. Dewey deployed his radio resources shrewdly, concentrating his speeches in areas where he had a good chance of winning, and refusing to squander airtime on stations in FDR's "solid south."[151]

As a lawyer, Dewey was well-versed in the art of improvisation. On his way to Springfield, Missouri, where he was supposed to wave as the train passed through, Dewey heard a KWTO broadcast describing the crowd of 8,000 that had gathered to see him. Not one to lose a publicity opportunity, Dewey decided to halt the train and deliver an unannounced speech.[152]

The governor gave the public ample opportunities to become acquainted with him, appearing on a range of programs from the *New York Herald-Tribune*

Forum to the thoroughly Democratic *Farm and Home Hour*. As a means of reaching as many potential voters as possible, Dewey helped Republican women organize a nationwide chain of "neighborhood listening parties" to keep families without radios informed of GOP policies.[153] From October 16 to November 6, the governor made over eight major broadcast speeches, and his vice-presidential running mate, Gov. John W. Bricker, made three.[154]

But Dewey did have his limitations. To many commentators, the strength of the governor's vocal abilities manifested itself only in settings that allowed him to play off of or respond to another's remarks, such as question-and-answer sessions or debates. When compelled to deliver a monologue into a microphone, he was not quite as effective. Perhaps Dewey's most conspicuous shortcoming was his lack of the bedside—or rather, fireside—manner that so endeared FDR to his listeners. According to *Broadcasting*, Dewey needed to recognize the difference between a radio address and a lecture-hall oration. "He needs to come closer to the private conversational tone adapted to members of a radio audience who are listening as individuals." Like Willkie, Dewey was robbed of the element of sincerity that is conveyed when speeches appear to be read.

Professor Foley felt that Dewey's delivery possessed a "certain monotony of rhythm that failed to excite his audience in any meaningful way."[155] In addition, his lack of humor, "super efficiency" (verbally punctuating each sentence with a "period" as if dictating), and "boy scoutishness" (overuse of such expressions as "Oh Lord" and "Good Gracious" when excited), tended to put off many listeners.

Another of Dewey's major problems was that, like Willkie, he could never present himself and his platform in a manner that clearly and compellingly distinguished himself from his Democratic opponent. He constantly railed against the New Deal in his speeches, and yearned for a life unburdened by the restrictions it provided; yet, as a reporter for *Time* noted,

> he [never] sufficiently dramatized the conditions that made such a free life attractive to the average American. Nor did he ever clearly differentiate the way of life which he saw from that which had been created under three terms of Mr. Roosevelt. Somehow, the case against the New Deal [had] not been made.[156]

Sensing the challenge to his radio dominance, FDR was inspired to make even greater efforts at refining his broadcasting skills. He drew upon all of his inherent strengths: "carefully choosing his speech settings to obtain favorable audience response, adopting an aggressive defense in verbal sparring with Dewey, and generally employing the typical Rooseveltian brand of humor that was so successful in winning the hearts of his listeners." At first, FDR found himself in an uncomfortable defensive position. But even in a purely reactive posture, the president's "defensive tactics were the equal of the offensives he had laid down against three prior opponents." Throughout September, one of his principal strategies was to underscore his indispensability to the war effort by emphasizing his role as commander-in-chief. This scheme presented Dewey with one of the "greatest disadvantages that ever faced a presidential candidate," and saved Roosevelt from a "slashing, all-out attack" by his opponent.[157]

As in 1940, FDR conserved his strength until the weeks just before the election. On September 23, in one of his first campaign speeches, he scored a major publicity coup that reassured listeners of their president's position as undisputed radio king. Responding to Republican allegations of prodigality in the executive branch, FDR sarcastically replied:

> These Republican leaders have not been content with attacks on me, or my wife, or my sons. No, not content with that, they now include my little dog, Fala. Well, of course, I don't resent attacks, and my family doesn't resent attacks, but Fala does resent them. You know, Fala is Scotch, and being a Scottie, as soon as he learned that the Republican fiction writers in Congress and out had concocted a story that I had left him behind on the Aleutian Islands, and had sent a destroyer back to find him—at a cost to taxpayers of two or three, or eight or twenty million dollars—his Scotch soul was furious. He has never been the same dog since.[158]

The audience "erupted in laughter, and Dewey's credibility dipped sharply." When he concluded his broadcast, Sam Rosenman remarked, "the applause and cheers ... were startling, even to those of us who had seen him out campaigning in 1932, 1936 and 1940. Never had there been a demonstration equal to this in sincerity, admiration and affection."[159] According to another observer, "FDR was at his best ... even the stoniest of Republican faces around U.S. radios cracked into a smile."[160] *Time* called it one of the best campaign speeches ever, one that was made with "an unsurpassed sense of delivery and timing."[161] The editor of the *Atlanta Constitution* stated that, with this one speech, "Roosevelt had effectively defended his title as the world's most effective radio speaker." Coming in the wake of Republican accusations of FDR being overtired and sick, the "Fala Speech" "reinvigorated the Democratic campaign and gave the country the impression of Roosevelt as a dynamic, jovial, and confident leader."[162] *Time* declared:

> The old master still has it.... He was like a veteran virtuoso playing a piece he has loved for years, who fingers his way through it with a delicate fire, a perfection of timing and tone, and an assurance that no young player, no matter how gifted, can equal.... With a voice that purrs softly and then strikes hard [FDR] kept his audience with him every minute he was on the offensive.[163]

Newsweek proclaimed: "The 1944 campaign is on and Franklin Roosevelt is off to a flying start!"[164] Public opinion polls indicated a marked increase in the president's popularity after the speech.

Dewey could never approach the kind of impact FDR produced with such broadcasts. In a September 22 speech in the Los Angeles Coliseum to an audience of over 93,000, the governor delivered a "dry exposition" about expanding old age pensions rather than the "slam-bang type of speech" that was winning the Democrats so many adherents.[165] "However earnest and sincere the speech may have seemed," *Time* noted, "it was not the firebreather [the audience] had hoped to hear." Far from helping him to wrest control of California from FDR, the broadcast was considered by most observers to have been a "total flop."[166]

Roosevelt gave Dewey no time to regain his balance after this stunning blow, and on October 5, 1944, he used a full-network fireside chat to broadcast an election appeal directed at the large block of independent voters. Later that night, speeches were heard by Charles W. Tillett, vice-chairman of the Democratic National Committee, and Harry S Truman, vice-presidential candidate.[167]

Two weeks later, on October 21, FDR again took the offensive, broadcasting a vow that a vote for him would mean a speedy return of all soldiers after the war, and their full employment; unequivocal American support for the new United Nations; and a continuation of the nation's "miracle of production." In addition to shoring up the expectations of those who had endured three years of prolonged conflict and chronic shortages, FDR promised that the benefits of the New Deal would be maintained and he would not "turn back the clock."[168] "The fruits of victory this time," he declared, "will not be apples sold on street corners."[169] His assurance that a defeated Germany would not be dealt with too harshly did much to soothe the anxiety of German-American voters. By drawing attention to successful war measures that prominent Republicans had opposed, and specifically citing Dewey's obstructionist record, Roosevelt again "put the Governor in the frying pan."[170] During this speech, FDR was interrupted 42 times for applause, and observers remarked that it was "as good as it had to be."

By the end of October, the president's declining health was becoming an increasingly prominent issue of the campaign. To prove his fitness to a growing number of uncertain and nervous voters who were coming to believe he might not survive another term in office, FDR "donned his blue-black navy cape and campaign hat" and embarked upon a lengthy tour of several United States cities. Said Democratic National Committee chairman Robert Hannegan: "After the people have seen [and heard] the President, they can make up their own minds about his vigor and health."

His first stop was New York City. Bareheaded and without overcoat, Roosevelt traveled for four hours along a 51-mile motor route through the city with the top down in a hard, steady rain. With his characteristic grin and customary animation intact, FDR completed the journey and decisively "allayed [public] fears that he had lost his ability to take it." That autumn being unusually inclement, Roosevelt repeated the experience in Wilmington, Philadelphia, and Camden, New Jersey.[171]

As in 1940, the Democrats spent the final weeks of the fourth-term campaign intensifying their broadcast activities. In the beginning of November, party spokesmen, including vice-presidential candidate Truman and former Ohio governor Cox, were on the air almost daily. On November 2, Roosevelt made another strategic broadcast when he singled out America's women voters and praised them for their contribution to the war effort. On the Saturday before the election, virtually the whole night's programming was purchased for Democratic propaganda, with multi-network broadcasts airing at regular intervals each hour.[172]

As in the past, Roosevelt's network alliance proved vital. NBC and CBS not only gave the president carte blanche in the selection of time slots, they frequently recorded and rebroadcast his speeches for "early rising farmers and late-shift workers." In order to allow the Democrats to maintain their radio schedule, MBS conducted a "Pledge a Dollar to Put Your President on the Air" campaign in collaboration with New York's *P.M.* newspaper, and collected over $9,000 on the first day alone.[173]

One of the Democrats' most valuable assets in the 1944 campaign was their use of "spot" broadcasts. Whereas the Republicans favored using their airtime in long, thirty-minute segments that included excerpts from Dewey's speeches, the Democrats preferred the more effective five-minute vaudeville-style broadcasts featuring politicians, celebrities, veterans and war mothers.[174] In the "campaigning by proxy" that was created through the large-scale use of transcriptions and disk recordings of Democratic speeches and slogans, FDR was able to broadcast his appeal to far more voters than in a live campaign address. Whereas live pitches were limited by the number of stations tied in to the network airing them, transcribed spots could be reproduced in unlimited quantities and mailed to any station for broadcast, many of which were either unaffiliated or too remote to be on a regular network circuit. As developed by J. Leonard Reinsch, radio director of the Democratic National Committee, spots were broadcast whenever major Democratic addresses were not already scheduled, thus giving the party "a voice on the air nightly from the beginning of October to election day." Reinsch avoided scheduling full half-hour "period[s] of politicking" as the Republicans were doing. He felt more people were apt to listen to a pitch if it was inserted at the end of a regular evening program. Through network good graces, Reinsch arranged time on the most popular entertainment and music shows of the day: *Your Hit Parade, Information Please, Kay Kyser,* and *Ginny Simms.*[175]

While most spots consisted of general messages of praise for FDR's experience and skill, many were tailored for a specific audience. At the end of September 1944, the *Roosevelt Sunrise Hour,* a special transcribed radio series directed at farmers and highlighting the benefits they had received from the Roosevelt Administration, was aired in rural areas from New York to Wisconsin.[176] For the daunting logistics involved in this task, Democratic state committee proved invaluable in mobilizing local stations for intensive state-by-state coverage. Another audience that FDR hoped to capture was the 4.3 million servicemen whom Congress had recently made eligible to vote. Since they were portable, disks could be sent to any part of the world where Americans were stationed and broadcast over the Armed Forces Radio Service (AFRS).[177]

Republicans virulently opposed this type of campaigning, but practical necessity compelled them to begin producing their own one-minute plugs just before the election drew to a close. Finally, and belatedly, the GOP had recognized what the Democrats had known all along: It was "production value and not the issues" which mattered most to the American electorate.*

At 10:00 P.M. on election eve, November 6, Roosevelt expanded the spot format and staged his greatest campaign triumph yet. In an effort that dwarfed the Democratic Rally program of 1940, the president broadcast a spectacular propaganda exhibition that aired over all four networks and included the biggest names the film, radio, and stage industries had to offer. For the script, the Democrats recruited Norman Corwin, radio's most innovative dramatic playwright. Critics objected that as an entertainer, and not a politician, Corwin was an inappropriate choice, but the Democrats realized that Corwin's talents were precisely what was needed. They understood that a cumbrous political speech would make listeners tune out. "Only by enacting a script that was abundant in human interest material could one hope to seize and maintain the audience's attention for any length of time."[178]

Roosevelt was concerned with the ten million independent voters, whose ballot might be crucial if the race was as close as the pollsters were predicting. With this in mind, the object of the program, as outlined by Paul Porter, Democratic National Committee chairman, was to generate a "sense of urgency that would activate this large body of uncommitted voters and get them to the polls." FDR felt that if they believed the outcome of the contest had already been decided by the night before election, they would have been disinclined to vote.

To stimulate the interest of the apathetic voter, FDR's program concentrated not on the needs of the war that had so wearied much of the country, but on the postwar situation and the need to press forward with reforms that had been deferred for the duration. For this purpose, network goodwill was again essential. While the Republicans had been chastised for defying a rigid ban on the use of dramatized political messages in 1936, when their *Liberty at the Crossroads* program was removed from the air, NBC and CBS allowed the Democrats almost complete creative freedom.[179] For the script of the 1944 gala, CBS released Corwin from the strict terms of his contract and allowed him to do the program for free.

---

*Reinsch, writing in 1988, felt that FDR's spots were the "genesis of the five-minute political inserts that we accept as a common campaign tool today" (p. 16).

The first device used in the program was to assemble before the microphone a representative sample of Americans, all of whom had supposedly gained from FDR's policies, either as a result of the New Deal or during the war. Among the speakers were "a TVA farmer, a union member, a soldier and sailor returned from action, a World War I veteran who had sold apples on the street during the Depression, an industrialist, a housewife, a small businessman, an old man who voted in fourteen elections, and ... a young girl who was about to vote for the first time." As the "cavalcade of voices paraded past the microphone, listeners could feel the momentum building."[180]

If the public was not convinced by the comments of ordinary folks like themselves, they might be persuaded if a famous star endorsed the president. This was the logic that prompted Corwin to amass the greatest concentration of talent ever to appear before the microphone at one time. "Never before or again," the writer later remarked, "would radio see such an open commitment to a political candidate by so many top-ranking stars on one show."[181] Among those who voiced their support for the president were: Humphrey Bogart, Judy Garland, Claudette Colbert, John Garfield, Paul Muni, Lana Turner, John Huston, Linda Darnell, Paulette Goddard, Ed Wynn, Joseph Cotten, and James Cagney. For the next half-hour, listeners at home heard a long procession of entertainers board the "Roosevelt Special" on its way to the White House:

CHORUS:	All Aboard for tomorrow!
L. BALL:	This is Lucille Ball. I'm on the train.
CHORUS:	Vote!
T.B:	This is Tallulah Bankhead. So am I.
CHORUS:	Vote!
J.B:	Joan Bennett for the champ.
CHORUS:	Vote!
I.B:	Irving Berlin—
M.B:	And Mrs. Berlin
CHORUS:	For Roosevelt![182]

In another skit, James Cagney, Groucho Marx and Danny Kaye formed a barbershop trio to satirize the Republicans in song. The broadcast created an "extraordinary bandwagon effect, and by the time the long introduction was over and the president came on to speak, many Americans had been persuaded."

At 11:00 P.M., the Republican program was to be aired, and many people wondered if it could top Roosevelt's extravaganza. Many Democrats feared their "star-studded effort" might only serve "to build an audience for Dewey's last word." But either through unexpected circumstances (entertainer Jimmy Durante canceled his appearance at the last minute) or by calculation, Roosevelt ended his speech a few minutes early. The networks, adhering to a precise time schedule, were compelled to play a musical interlude to fill the time until the Republican program came on at the beginning of the hour. After a few minutes of drab organ melodies, Roosevelt merrily remarked, "no one will keep their sets on for the Republicans."[183] Many listeners, not expecting Dewey's program to follow, retired.

Perhaps it was all for the best, for when Dewey finally came on, he didn't give listeners any reason to remain awake. Failing to take note of FDR's successful formula, he stated his aims in the beginning of the program: "We will present no campaign songs, shows or entertainment to distract the American people from the issues." While Dewey's intentions are to be admired, he completely "failed to gauge the mood of the public" as Roosevelt had so effectively done. The result was a "resounding success for the President," and for Dewey, "a program [that] droned on and on, even putting Fala to sleep."[184]

One analyst claimed that the Democrats' broadcast effort gained several million votes for Roosevelt.[185] The president wrote Corwin that even he had not been prepared for the results of such an "incredible performance."[186] Political experts had forecast that the outcome of the election would "depend to a large extent on each party's performance during the broadcast winding up the campaign."[187] The extra votes that FDR obtained were certainly instrumental in sealing his victory in the popular vote. In a close finish, Roosevelt secured 25,602,505 votes, while Dewey had 22,006,275. In the electoral count, FDR's success was far more decisive: 432 votes to Dewey's 99.[188] A survey conducted shortly after the election discovered that 38 percent of those questioned said that their votes had been influenced by radio. This figure is remarkable when compared to the 23 percent for newspapers.[189]

J. Leonard Reinsch felt those who had forecast a tight race need only "have looked at FDR's radio ratings" to discover which candidate was the safest bet. Although Dewey had made far more personal appearances at the mike during the campaign (8 hours and 30 minutes, compared with FDR's 3 hours and 39 minutes), the president had consistently enjoyed higher ratings for each of his broadcasts.[190] His best, the Fala Speech, had attracted 82.6 percent of the listening audience, while Dewey's jewel in Oklahoma had garnered only 65.3 percent.[191] Even the lowest rating the president received exceeded the best Dewey could command.[192] Throughout the campaign, Dewey never developed the kind of support that FDR enjoyed. Whereas the president's CAB ratings generally increased from speech to speech between September and November (from 60 percent to 83 percent), Dewey's sharply declined (from 65 percent to 35 percent). During the course of each individual address, the trend was similar. Roosevelt's audience grew as he spoke; Dewey usually lost listeners as his talk progressed.[193] To those observers who had failed to recognize it during the past three campaigns, the "correlation between a candidate's speech ratings on radio and voter support" was now unmistakable.[194]

While Roosevelt's approach to radio during the 1944 election had been remarkably successful in attracting voters, it was furiously criticized by some observers who saw a pernicious trend developing in broadcasting. In a campaign where personalities and style were more important than the issues, "it was natural for the level of political debate to devolve into a mudslinging contest." Throughout the campaign, "with the microphone used as a sort of verbal bazooka ... radio had been called upon to deliver into American parlors a devil's brew of bitter invective."[195] Right from the start, with FDR's Fala Speech and Dewey's Oklahoma City reply:

> The gloves were off. Not in any of Mr. Roosevelt's three previous campaigns had his rival for the presidency lashed away as did Dewey. In a dozen major speeches, the Republican nominee punched directly at the President's own record. In half that number of addresses, Mr. Roosevelt counterjabbed, employing a caustic style that helped to raise the campaign's already-raging temperature.[196]

While Dewey persistently assailed the president's health and competence, FDR retaliated by characterizing his Republican opponent as an "unmitigated liar" and comparing him to Hitler. According to Sam Rosenman, almost every one of FDR's speeches was "spiced with biting sarcasm,... ridicule, and bitter denunciation."[197] Near the end of October, the Democrats produced a series of five-minute spots featuring a prominent party speaker, followed by a *Democratic Reporter* bit in which conflicting statements made by Dewey were reported and criticized. The program concluded with the remark: "This is to show that sometimes the elephant *does* forget." Another series of talks, *Unmasking Dewey*, was distributed to various Democratic state committees for local broadcast. The GOP replied with a few one-minute segments focusing on the supposed communist support for FDR's reelection.[198] The *Washington Post* condemned this type of "political bushwhacking" at a time when "spiritual leadership of a high order was urgently needed."[199] Another revolted observer exclaimed: "If the millions of American soldiers who were fighting and dying to save the world for democracy had witnessed the contest, they would have been disgusted."[200]

Network officials regretted their role in the campaign. With specific reference to the election eve program, *Broadcasting* remarked:

> We have elected a President with pledges set to music by some of the most talented boogie-woogie librettists in the business. We have elected a President with singing commercials, with jive and jabberwocky, and with profound exhortations on the issues of the day by such thoughtful statesmen

as Orson Welles and Humphrey Bogart.... As we look ahead, radio, which four years from now must lend its great voice to the espousal of other causes, may hope that it will not again need to carry the burden of such contraband.[201]

To ensure that such theatrical offerings would never again "place the discussion of vital political and national issues on the basis of dramatic license rather than upon a basis of responsibly stated fact or opinion,"[202] the networks revised their broadcast policies to make a repeat of November 6, 1944, impossible.

Fortunately for Roosevelt, however, only a handful of people felt his broadcasts to have offended "wartime sensibilities and traditions of presidential decency." For a majority of Americans, the candidates' "mutual sniping, the five minute sound bites, and the dramatic propaganda galas" had provided the best show on radio to date.[203] Gallup polls constantly revised upward the estimated voter turnout after each bitter exchange was broadcast.[204] Roosevelt's example had shown to subsequent generations of campaigners that, as in the case of the Roman Caesars, the American politician who could best entertain the masses was assured of the greatest political success.

The 1944 campaign produced no dearth of valuable lessons for later politicians. Dwight Eisenhower's Madison Avenue television ads were directly inspired by FDR's spots, and there is little doubt that Richard Nixon had Fala in mind when he delivered his famous "Checkers Speech." While Dewey paid the price of discouraging "foo-faraw, bands, parades and demonstrations,"[205] his Republican successors certainly would not. A new kind of political campaigning had been born.

* * *

Roosevelt's political broadcasting career marked a watershed in the development of radio. According to *Broadcasting*, Roosevelt was the "only president of whom it can truly be said that radio elected him."[206] James Farley remarked: "Under the conditions pertaining today [with radio], Franklin Roosevelt stands without a peer or a close rival as a political campaigner and it may be decades before the country ever sees his equal again."[207] By circumventing an unsympathetic press and delivering his campaign appeal directly to the people via radio, FDR was the only person to sit in the White House for twelve years. According to Gil Troy, much of Roosevelt's success was based not only on his extraordinary oratorical qualities, but on his exploitation of the illusions that radio created in the minds of its listeners. While the "intense personal exchanges between an old stumping candidate and his audience" had irretrievably passed, and the politician was now merely "a voice coming over a loudspeaker," Roosevelt was able to maintain the impression of proximity by the sheer "intimacy of his personal appeal." Understanding, like no other politician of his age, that the "needs of a speaker's immediate audience had to be subordinated to those of the unseen masses" in living rooms and parlors throughout the nation, and that the coverage of a political event was more important than the event itself, Roosevelt had used the audience "witnessing his speeches as props" in order to achieve the maximum effect and entertainment value for the millions of potential voters in the listening audience. Finally, Troy argues, by concealing his aural "sleight of hand techniques" and the work of his many ghostwriters "behind the facade of an omniscient, caring president," Roosevelt used radio to inaugurate the new era of the "modern spectral candidate."[208] James Farley has observed that because of the frequency with which FDR made his radio appeals, the "day of the 'front-porch' candidate, the man who stays at home and says nothing, while others carry the burden of campaigning for him, [was] over." Because of Roosevelt's precedent, modern voters expect to "[hear] the candidate for office, and make their own estimation of his qualifications, before marking the ballots."[209] Presidential candidates since Roosevelt who fail to cultivate their media image, or who neglect opportunities to "appear" in the public mind's eye, do so at their own peril.

3. Selling the Domestic Agenda

The Voice of Confidence

When Roosevelt took office in 1933, the country was in the grip of the worst economic disaster it had ever faced. Nothing "since the onset of industrialization had so soundly shaken the entire western world at its very foundation." Americans who could not remember the depression of the 1890s were utterly unprepared for the catastrophe that came crashing down on them after the Wall Street failure of October 1929. As a result, many Americans experienced a debilitating loss of confidence, "not only in the current political leadership, but in the very political and economic system itself." As spending was severely curtailed, orders for new goods diminished, businesses closed, workers were laid off, and wages and prices fell, the country sank deeper into the quagmire of the Great Depression. Between 1929 and 1933, the gross national product was almost halved, from $100 billion to $55 billion.[1] During this same period, corporate profits fell from $10 billion to $1 billion. As banks collapsed, life savings disappeared overnight. Over 100,000 businesses failed, and industrial production declined by over 51 percent, causing the unemployment figure to leap from 4 percent in 1929 to 25 percent in 1933.

The economic calamity certainly had an adverse effect on the prevailing mood of the country. It seemed that capitalism had failed, and a large part of the population could no longer attain even a minimum standard of living. "Opportunities for profitable capital investment, and safety for personal savings, seemed non-existent."[2] To many Americans cognizant of the wider spiritual and moral import of the crisis, some of the "oldest and strongest faiths ... underwent their severest test." Such traditional beliefs that America was a "land of limitless opportunity" where any able body could find work, that the "capitalist system was the most efficient economic arrangement in the world, and that the democratic system was capable of dealing with complex problems," were being "questioned by Americans as they had never been before."[3]

The social consequences of the Great Depression were staggering. From January to November 1930, the number of jobless rose from four to six million.

By the time the Depression reached its peak in 1933, 12.8 million people—one out of every four Americans—were jobless. Many people went from middle-class comfort to menial jobs or even destitution. Minorities, the elderly, and workers in consumer durables industries were particularly hard hit. For a generation of youths, career paths were disrupted and the prospect of college disappeared. Others suffered shattered lives as hopes of retirement or of starting a family evaporated. For the already impoverished, America became the inhospitable land of the "Oakie" and the "Arkie," the "hobo," the "Hooverville," and the soup kitchen.

As labor income dipped by over 40 percent, the average citizen could no longer sustain a sufficiently nourishing diet. As everyday necessities like eggs and vegetables became increasingly scarce, malnutrition became rampant, and the underfed fell prey to numerous diseases (including tuberculosis, typhoid, dysentery, and heart disorders). In 1932, New York City authorities reported over 95 deaths from starvation. Pregnant women and children suffered most from the dearth of nutrients. In many communities, milk grew so scarce, it was actually used as a medicine. The inability to afford fuel to cook and heat magnified the discomforts of the indigent. Many families had to double-up in crowded apartments, and those who could no longer pay their rent were often mercilessly evicted. Ramshackle packing-crate dwellings sprang up in urban areas across the country, while many homeless slept in the park.

In a countryside already accustomed to privation, hardship deepened. From 1929 to 1932, agricultural prices dropped by 60 percent and farm income declined by over one half. Dust, drought, and insect swarms loomed as ever-present menaces during the depression years. In 1933, 45 percent of rural homeowners fell delinquent on their mortgages and suffered foreclosure.

In communities that were most severely affected by unemployment (Detroit at 50 percent, Chicago at 40 percent), the resources of local government and charitable relief were soon exhausted. In 1933, excessive demand for relief compelled 1,300 local governments to default on their debt obligations.

Throughout the country, marriage and birth rates dropped. The self-esteem of many former male breadwinners was seriously undermined. With scarcely anyone immune to the economic, social and psychological dislocation that accompanied the Great Depression, it is no wonder that the national suicide rate climbed precipitously. The American people were in desperate need of a savior to lift them from their miserable circumstances and restore their personal and national dignity.

This is the situation that Franklin Roosevelt observed when he assumed power in 1933. Through the use of Keynsian notions of "pump priming" or deficit financing, the new president sought to navigate the United States out of the depression. By infusing billions of federal dollars into the economy, FDR hoped to stimulate business enterprise and consumer purchasing power, and to boost employment. As integral components of his New Deal, FDR proposed

FDR at the microphone.

a series of laws designed to assist blue-collar workers, farmers, bankrupt local governments, businesses, the elderly, and even needy artists and writers.

Before Roosevelt could proceed with his bold legislative agenda, he had to win the confidence of his despairing countrymen. During this period of grave uncertainty, nothing did more to help him accomplish this than radio. According to a contemporary psychologist:

> In times of politico-social disruption, the radio voice of someone in authority, speaking to millions of citizens as "My friends," tends to decrease their sense of insecurity. It diminishes the effects of rumor and allays the dread and apprehension of what is unknown.[4]

Through his broadcasts, FDR was able to "speak directly to the American people, explain to them the economic issues at hand, and offer them adequate assurances that the economic, psychological and spiritual crisis facing the country could be successfully overcome."[5] Through radio, Roosevelt was not only able to explain and justify various New Deal programs that would "serve as a panacea to the nation's economic woes"; he could successfully disarm his opponents on both the right and left, who advocated even more radical measures. By convincing many Americans of the necessity of his legislative initiatives, FDR consistently secured their support behind those programs he had presently before Congress.[6] In a series of inspiring fireside chats, Roosevelt "projected the image of a concerned leader and assured his flock that the economic crisis that was generating so much adversity was being dealt with sensibly and effectively." By speaking confidently, he was enormously successful in restoring the public's hope and self-esteem. According to one historian: "If he could not cure the disease that was gripping the nation, he was successful in soothing some of the pain."[7]

Roosevelt delivered four fireside chats in his first year in office, and each time "his voice entered American homes, millions found in his calm statements some assurance that he was their friend." Because of the hopeful appeal of his broadcasts, the "public developed a sense of trust in Roosevelt, in the same way they have confidence in a good doctor without knowing much about the science of medicine."[8]

The success of this approach was amply illustrated in the White House mailrooms after each broadcast. On average, each time the president went on the air, he could expect to receive at least 500,000 letters and telegrams from listeners.[9] Much of the correspondence was similar to the letter that follows:

> My wife and I are two typical American citizens, so I think I can speak for my fellow citizens. We were sitting in front of the fireplace, where a couple of chunks of fir bark were throwing off a comforting heat, when your voice came to us from the White House. We went into the next room and got in front of the radio, and for twenty minutes listened to you as though you were visiting us in our house and talking over our problems, and the problems of our friends and neighbors.
>
> One cannot listen to your frank, straightforward discussion … without being inspired with faith in your intentions, and hopes for your success. It means so much in the banishing of fear, doubt, worry and unrest. There is a new spirit of courage and willingness to endure, a new spirit of Americanism and brotherhood. We are no longer Republicans or Democrats, we are Americans standing with our President, who is doing all he can to help make this land we have a land where fear is banished and faith in the future restored.[10]

Millions of responses like this gave Roosevelt "an incalculable political advantage." The fireside chats and the favorable response "helped propel through Congress," with astonishing speed, "a broad legislative program" that included such landmark bills" as those establishing the Agricultural Adjustment Administration (AAA), the National Recovery Administration (NRA), and the Federal Emergency Relief Administration (FERA), as well as numerous other "New Deal innovations." Whereas "Hitler had once said, without motor cars, sound films, and wireless, there might have been no victory for National Socialism, FDR could have very well said the same about radio and the New Deal." While Roosevelt was not to accomplish all of his goals with the New Deal, and it was only with United States entry into World War II that unemployment was decisively overcome, his domestic policy innovations left an indelible mark on the American political and social landscape. Largely as a result of his capable leadership as communicated through radio, America emerged from the Depression with her economic and political institutions preserved. The progressive movement and the Democratic Party had been revitalized and the way prepared for a vastly expanded role of the federal government in society.[11] In social security, the Federal Deposit Insurance Corporation, old-age pensions, and unemployment insurance, the basic infrastructure of FDR's welfare state is still alive today.

Roosevelt's First Inaugural

Roosevelt wasted no time in employing radio to address the problems arising out of the economic crisis. When he went on the air in his first inaugural address, "millions of Americans anxiously listened to hear how the man they had just elected planned to lead the country out of the Depression." By this time, as prices for agricultural and manufactured goods continued to plummet, thousands of factories had shut down, many banks had closed, and stores had been deserted. Businesses and local governments were forced into bankruptcy, and hunger marches were becoming increasingly common. Americans were "apprehensive of the future, many were desperate, and some were almost without hope."[12] Because of the extraordinary circumstances, all four American networks made their entire facilities available to the new president so "that there shall be throughout the country, a clearer and fuller understanding of the great tasks which must be performed."[13]

On March 4, 1933, before a microphone on the Capitol steps, FDR began to speak for the first time as president, and as he did an enormous sigh of relief was audible throughout the country. Among the president's first words were those informing the people that he intended to face the crisis before them "frankly and boldly." Despite pessimistic rumors, he dispersed all doubt that "this nation will endure as it had endured, will revive and will prosper." To those who were frightened and insecure, he offered confident assurance that "the only thing we have to fear is fear itself—nameless, unreasoning, unjustified terror which paralyzes needed efforts to convert retreat into advance."[14]

The president then went on to describe the problems that were plaguing the nation: rising taxes, falling prices, a failure of the financial system, and most importantly, unemployment. Roosevelt made it clear that he regarded the economic emergency as the equivalent of a foreign invasion in its threat to the nation's existence. He outlined a program in which the government would undertake to revive the stagnating economy through the creation of vast public works projects and the raising of the value of agricultural products. He also sought to "improve the government's relief effort, prevent future home and farm foreclosures, provide federal supervision of communications, utilities, and transportation, and rigorously regulate banking and investment activities."[15]

Since this program was a radical departure from traditional government policy, Roosevelt realized that mass public support was essential. The president endeavored to obtain this backing by "invoking military metaphors and by declaring a figurative war on a serious economic condition." Appealing to a generation of Americans that had participated in the national effort of the First World War, he declared: "The nation asks for action, and action now.... We must act and act quickly. We must move as a trained and loyal army willing to sacrifice for the good of common discipline, because without much discipline no progress is made, [and] no leadership becomes effective."[16] Continuing the martial imagery, he asserted: "If need be, I shall ask Congress for the one remaining instrument to meet the crisis—broad executive power to wage a war against the enemy, as great as the power that would be given to me if we were, in fact, invaded by a foreign foe." Given the unprecedented amount of power Roosevelt would assume in such a situation, he reassured listeners that he had no dictatorial designs: "Action to this end is feasible under the form of government which we have inherited from our ancestors. Our constitution is so simple, so practical, that it is possessed always to meet extraordinary needs by changes in emphasis and argument without the loss of essential form." FDR closed by calling upon all Americans to fulfill their "patriotic duty to support his quasi-military leadership in his symbolic war on the Depression."[17]

The reaction to the president's address was electrifying. Many observers compared FDR's rhetoric to that of Lincoln in 1861. The president's personal secretary, Harry Hopkins, noted that "with that one speech, and in those few minutes, the appalling anxiety and fears were lifted, and the people knew that they were going into a safe harbor under the leadership of a man who never knew the meaning of the word fear."[18] Radio commentator Edwin C. Hill spoke for many Americans when he said in his news broadcast a few days later:

> That voice, with its supreme confidence and courage, still resounds in my ears. That was the inspiring, heartening, thrilling fact—not this man—Roosevelt, taking command in one of the darkest hours the nation has seen for more than 70 years, seized the helm of the leaky, drafty ship of state with a hand that revealed no slightest trace of indecision or of uncertainty, but with the most buoyant confidence in himself and in the American people.
>
> Something had happened to the cross section of the American people within the hour, something that had given them confidence, new fortitude to face problems and troubles of the hour. For they had looked upon, and they heard the voice of a man who was willing to lead.[19]

The success of the speech was due in large part to FDR's unique oratorical skills. The *New York Times* remarked, "The human voice ... does reflect man's mood, temper, personality, and ... character. President Roosevelt's voice reveals sincerity, goodwill, kindness, determination, conviction, strength, courage, and abounding happiness."[20] A well-known speech professor who had listened to the address felt that the "cues in FDR's voice were so uniquely capable of inspiring confidence that, if Herbert Hoover had spoken the same words into the microphone, the stock market would have fallen another notch, and public confidence with it."[21]

The day after his inaugural speech, President Roosevelt used his mandate from the people by calling Congress into an emergency session to cope with the crisis, commencing the famous "hundred days." At no other time in American history would "such far-reaching social and economic legislation be enacted in so short a time."[22] Roosevelt had made it absolutely clear to Congress, in his speech, that if they were not cooperative in passing his bills, he would resort to emergency executive powers to implement them. Many political analysts believed, "If Congress fails him, the country will strongly back him in his demand for virtual war powers."[23] By winning the confidence and support of the masses during his first radio address, Roosevelt knew he could count on the "full force of an overwhelming public opinion" to back up his reform legislation.[24] From now on, *Broadcasting* noted, "whenever Roosevelt spoke into the microphone, he spoke not only as the President, but also as the 'voice of the people.'" So that the public was continually aware of the progress of the president's bills, NBC began to broadcast the complete debates from the floors of both Houses on a regular basis.[25] Sensing this pressure, Congress responded with a host of significant decisions that included the Emergency Banking Act (March 9), the Civilian Conservation Corps (March 31), and the Emergency Farm Mortgage Act (May 12).[26]

The Banking Crisis

Quickly following upon the success of his inaugural address, Roosevelt again took to the airwaves on March 12, 1933, to discuss the collapse of the banking system. The president felt the need to deliver this first fireside chat in order to stem the "wave of uncertainty" that had led thousands of Americans to withdraw their savings from financial institutions all over the country. By using radio on this occasion, FDR wanted "to make clear to his constituents the various facts that might otherwise have been misinterpreted, and in general to provide a means of understanding which would restore confidence."[27]

The significant decline in the value of stocks, bonds, mortgages and other financial assets pushed many banks and savings institutions toward insolvency. From 1929 to 1932, some 5,000 banks with insufficient funds were compelled to close their doors. In February, Michigan and Maryland had suspended banking operations completely, and by March 4, thirty-six other states followed. In the process, nine million individual savings accounts, totaling over $2.5 billion, had been lost. Generations of Americans who had come to believe in saving as a virtuous and practical habit found their accounts had vanished.

As a means of halting the flood of withdrawals, which were exacerbating the financial straits of an already fragile economy, FDR issued a proclamation on March 6 which declared a four-day banking holiday. Three days later, the president's action was legalized in the Emergency Banking Act. This legislation provided Reconstruction Finance Corporation funds to be made available to banks that were sound but needed a temporary infusion before they could reopen. Insolvent banks were to remain closed, and emergency currency was issued to meet demands.

On March 12, Roosevelt went on the radio to explain to 60 million listeners the steps he had taken.[28] He wanted to elucidate how, by issuing the proclamation, the "first step in the government's reconstitution of our financial and economic fabric" had been accomplished. He also sought to mitigate fear by answering some of the questions that had been troubling listeners. He defused suspicions about banks not immediately reopening by explaining that they had not gone bankrupt, but were merely in the process of reorganization.

FDR wanted to win the confidence of the people so that they would return their currency and gold deposits to the distressed banks. He accomplished this in a number of ways. First, he deflated the myths of hoarding and told his listeners that their money was safer in a reopened bank than "under the proverbial mattress."[29] Secondly, he "enhanced his persuasive credibility" by speaking frankly and honestly to his listeners. He openly told them that not all of the banks would reopen. By "not promising more than he could deliver," he encouraged many people to give their assent to his proposals.[30] Another way he won the confidence of depositors was by simplifying the complex issues involved in such a manner that the great bulk of his listeners, with "little or no experience of the technicalities of banking, would be relieved of their anxiety as to whether they would ever see their money again."[31] Sam Rosenman recalled:

> The Treasury Department prepared a scholarly draft of the speech. The President saw that it would be meaningless to most people, tossed it aside without any attempt at rewriting, and proceeded to write his own instead. He dictated it in simple, ordinary language—he looked for words that he would use in an informal conversation with one or two of his friends. He found the kind of language that everyone could understand. And everyone did understand.[32]

Once he had given listeners a better understanding of the situation, he persuaded them to "unite with the government in concerted action to rectify it."[33] In his speech, he attempted to form this "partnership for action" by saying, "You people must have faith. Let us unite in banishing fear.... it is up to you to support and make it work. It is your problem no less than it is mine. Together we cannot fail."[34]

Roosevelt's plea to his people was enormously successful. The *New York Times* reported:

The fear and panic which led to the banking moratorium appears to have almost entirely passed. This happy result must be due in part to the calm and reassuring radio address which President Roosevelt made on Sunday evening. His simple and lucid explanation of the true function of a commercial bank; his account of what had happened, why it had happened, and the steps taken to correct the mischief were admirably fitted to cause the hysteria, which had raged for several weeks before the banks were closed, to abate if not entirely to subside.[35]

Radio commentator Edwin C. Hill noted:

It was as if a wise and kindly father had sat down to talk sympathetically and patiently and affectionately with his worried and anxious children, and had given them straightforward things that they had to do to help him along as the father of the family. That speech of the President's over the air humanized radio in a great governmental, national sense as it had never been humanized before.[36]

According to psychologist Hadley Cantril, Roosevelt was able to gain a "swift appraisal" of popular feeling after the broadcast. A few minutes after his chat ended, "the White House was inundated with telegrams that were unequivocally favorable to the President's action."[37] One listener remarked: "The people trust this administration as they distrusted the previous one."[38]

The morning after the speech, countless Americans ceased their withdrawals and began depositing their savings again. Consequently, 90 percent of those banks that had closed during the holiday were able to reopen.[39] The public had been so moved by the president's words that they applied pressure on Congress to pass the Glass-Steagall Banking Act in June, a "measure which empowered Federal Reserve Bank to regulate its members and to prevent the fiscal irresponsibility which had created so much instability in 1929." By establishing the Federal Deposit Insurance Corporation to insure deposits up to $2500, this bill went far to provide an "effective, long term solution to a complicated financial problem."[40] As a result of these actions, less than one-tenth as many banks failed in the rest of 1933.

Evaluating the First Two Months of the New Deal: The Fireside Chat of May 7, 1933

Halfway through the first "hundred days," Roosevelt decided to give another fireside chat. The purpose of this talk was twofold. First, the president used the opportunity to acquaint the American people with the "encouraging progress" that had been made during the first two months of the New Deal. Secondly, and more importantly, FDR sought "to establish a momentum for crucial bills that he had proposed, but that Congress had not yet acted upon."[41]

Roosevelt opened his discussion by pointing to the important measures that had already been accomplished by the administration. He drew particular attention to the Civilian Conservation Corps (March 31). The CCC had been one of the several relief efforts designed to aid the 2.5 million unemployed Americans between the ages of 18 and 25 by giving them meaningful work: planting trees, restoring historic sites, clearing camping areas, and building dams and bridges.* FDR also used the occasion to assure the country that despite the intensive activity of the past two months, "nothing drastic or extreme was occurring in the White House." Reemphasizing his appeal for a "partnership of the people" and the president, Roosevelt stated, "It is wholly wrong to call the measures we have taken, government control of farming or government control of industry, or government control of transportation. It is rather a partnership—a partnership between government and industry, government and transportation, government and farming."[42]

Roosevelt's main reason for the May 7 chat was to familiarize the public with a number of the president's bills that were then under consideration by Congress. FDR hoped that the people would become convinced of the necessity of these measures and urge their congressmen to adopt them. The president mentioned the Federal Emergency Relief Act (authorizing $500 million in aid to state and local governments) and the Tennessee Valley Authority (TVA), an unprecedented effort to enlarge the economic well-being of the depressed Tennessee River Valley through the construction of a series of dams for flood control and electricity production. In addition to this, there was the Home Owner's Refinancing Act and the Farm Credit Act, both designed to reduce the number of mortgage foreclosures. The president also pushed the Railroad Bill, an effort to rejuvenate the national railroad system through government regulation.[43]

FDR devoted the most time to two of the most important and controversial pieces of legislation in the early New Deal. The first was the Agricultural Adjustment Act (AAA), a federal program to restore the purchasing power of American farmers and protect them from the uncertainties of the market through subsidies and yield controls designed to curtail overproduction. The second was the National Industrial Recovery Act (NIRA), which attempted to stabilize prices and wages, and limit production, through cooperative "codes of fair competition" that involved government, business and labor. NIRA also tried to reduce unemployment through federal public works programs (Public Works Administration) and guaranteed workers the right of collective bargaining.

The president concluded his chat by thanking the people for supporting him thus far, and imploring them to continue to do so:

> You have been patient, granted us wide powers, and encouraged us with
> a widespread approval of our purposes. Every ounce of strength, every
> resource at our command, we have devoted and we are devoting to the end

By the time of its termination in 1942, the CCC assisted over 3 million young men and 250,000 veterans.

of justifying your confidence. We are encouraged to believe that a wise and sensible beginning has been made. In a spirit of mutual confidence, in the present spirit of mutual encouragement, we go forward.

Roosevelt's speech was widely praised. NBC president Merlin Aylesworth remarked, "On last Sunday night your intimate talk to the American people ... was in my opinion, most effective. I can honestly say that I have never known a public official to use radio with such intelligence."[44] The flood of mail that poured into the White House so taxed the energies of the staff that it was unable to acknowledge individual letters and had to ask the press to publish a general notice of the president's appreciation.[45] His appeal was enormously successful in securing for him the requested legislation. Five days after the chat, Congress passed the Federal Emergency Relief Act. One week later, the Tennessee Valley Authority became a reality, and on June 13, the Home Owner's Refinancing Act was passed. Continuing the momentum, on June 16, both the Farm Credit Act and the Railroad Bill became laws. Most importantly, the president's two legislative centerpieces were approved: the Agricultural Adjustment Act on May 12, and the National Industrial Recovery Act on June 16.[46]

The Record of the First "Hundred Days": July 24, 1933, and October 22, 1933

The AAA and NIRA were so vital to Roosevelt's plans for national recovery that he devoted the whole of the next fireside chat to explaining and justifying them to the American people. Even though the measures had already passed Congress, they required popular support in order to become effective. By detailing the virtues of the two programs, and by showing how they served as the "foundation upon which [the entire] program of recovery was built," the president sought to drum up enthusiasm for them.[47] This was particularly true of the National Recovery Act (NRA), a central component of NIRA. Marshaling his best salesmanship skills, Roosevelt explained to the public how the NRA had already made gains in stabilizing the economy by reducing unemployment and by paying decent wages to workers so that they could purchase goods. Efforts had also been made to eliminate harmful competition and reduce overproduction so that prices would rise to a more remunerative level. Employing his military metaphors again, FDR urged the public to embrace the NRA and make it succeed.

As a result of the president's "frank and vigorous" entreaty, hundreds of thousands of employers and millions of their workers flocked to subscribe to FDR's emergency industrial code.[48] The *New York Times* described the dramatic success of Roosevelt's appeal:

Hardly had he finished before telegrams and long-distance telephone calls came pouring into the White House acclaiming his speech and pledging

cooperation. The testimonials came from all branches of industry and all
walks of life; from the big employer of labor to the day worker and the
"white-collar slave." One and all pledged his utmost cooperation with the
President in his organized campaign against the forces of depression. A
half hour after the President finished speaking, he was notified that 350
telegrams were awaiting his pleasure, all pledging support of his program
... At eleven o'clock, [this figure] was nearing 5,000.[49]

Roosevelt presented another "report card" on what had been accomplished
by the New Deal on October 22, 1933. The purpose of this fireside chat was
to "offset a recent wave of disappointing economic news by reporting steady
advances in many fields, and by assuring the American people that things were
on track and steadily moving forward."[50] The president discussed the heartening progress that he had made in reducing unemployment, abolishing sweat-
shops and child labor, and directing relief to needy families. He told how
farms had been saved from foreclosure, how banks were becoming more sound,
how public works projects had employed thousands, and how commodity price
levels were on the rise.

According to Sam Rosenman, FDR's optimistic appraisals in his four fireside chats of 1933 moved the public firmly behind his New Deal efforts.

> These chats not only informed; they cemented the relationship between
> the people and their President. They created confidence in Roosevelt's
> leadership; they explained his objectives so clearly that the people as a
> whole were ready to forgive the mistakes he made in his "bold experi-
> mentation" to reach those objectives.... By 1934 there were no traces of
> the panic and fear of March 4, 1933. There was complete realization, as
> the President himself put it, "that the Legislative and Executive branches
> of their government were willing and ready to use all the power and
> resources of the nation to alleviate suffering, prevent further disaster, and
> rebuild the structure of economic life upon firmer foundations of social
> justice." And with it had come a general acceptance and approval of his
> program of reform.[51]

Fending Off Attack: June 28, 1934

The primary motivation behind FDR's next fireside chat was to use the
radio as a means of responding to the critics who were becoming more vocal
in their condemnation of his policies. While many on the left criticized the
president for not going far enough in helping the down-and-out, many conservatives accused him of seeking to accumulate too much power in his own
hands, while using the federal government to penetrate areas of American
economic and social life where it had previously played no role. There was too
much taxation and government regulation, conservatives charged, and liberal
expenditure on welfare programs had sapped individual initiative and self-
reliance. Roosevelt was imposing on the country a "maelstrom of centralized
order giving," similar to fascism or communism.[52]

On June 28, 1934, the president took to the airwaves to answer these accusations. In a stirring speech, he declared that the criticism being levied against his administration was originating with "plausible self-seekers and theoretical die-hards" who were frustrated over no longer being accorded "special political and financial privilege" and tried to mislead the public by attaching "new and strange names" to what the New Deal represented. According to FDR, these people constituted the "comparative few who seek to retain or gain position or riches, or both, by some shortcut which is harmful to the greater good." He added that his program would proceed even though "the toes of some people are going to be stepped on." Defending the accomplishments of his administration, FDR asked his listeners to compare their own economic situation with what it had been a year earlier: "Are you better off? Are your debts less burdensome? Is your bank account more secure? Are your work conditions better? Is your faith in your own individual future more firmly grounded?"*

Next, Roosevelt sought to assure the people that democratic traditions were not threatened by his actions. He asserted that his administration had moved strictly within the limits of government that Americans accepted as their tradition. American freedoms were as safe as they had always been. He entreated listeners to reread the Bill of Rights and ask themselves "whether [they had] personally suffered the impairment of a single jot of these great assurances." He queried: "Have you lost any of your rights or liberties or constitutional freedom of action and choice?" As a "matter of fact," FDR declared, "what we are doing today is a necessary fulfillment of what Americans have been doing—a fulfillment of old and tested American ideals." While other nations might sacrifice democracy, "we are restoring confidence and well-being under the rule of the people themselves." Through the use of his particular brand of logic and his patriotic imagery, the president was able to disarm his detractors and convince the public that his intentions were honorable and his objectives necessary. In Roosevelt's hands, radio had become a most effective political weapon for diverting criticism and overcoming opposition.

Fireside Chats of April 28, 1935, October 12, 1937, and April 14, 1938

Roosevelt used the airwaves to solicit popular and Congressional support for his policies on three more notable occasions.

In his fireside chat of April 28, 1935, the president eagerly utilized the medium to explain and defend the mammoth program of public works that had recently been passed by Congress. As part of Harry Hopkins's Works

*There are no recorded copies of FDR's June 28, 1934, fireside chat. The other two "missing chats" were delivered on July 24 and October 22, 1933. For printed texts of the speeches, see Rosenman, Public Papers and Addresses of FDR, vols. 2 and 3.

Progress Administration (WPA), thousands of parks, bridges, public buildings, airports, and roads had been constructed, and 8.5 million laborers, artists
and musicians had been employed.* In his radio discussion, FDR lobbied hard
to convince the public that this enormous effort was absolutely essential for economic recovery. This was a clear attempt by Roosevelt to head off the mounting criticism that the WPA was inefficient, wasteful, and nothing more than
an easy outlet for idlers "leaning on their shovels."[53]

The second purpose of the chat was to familiarize the public with a series
of bills that were then being taken up by Congress. In an effort to get the people to goad Congress into action, Roosevelt stressed the importance of the
Social Security Act (providing unemployment insurance and pensions for the
elderly), the renewal of the NRA, and the adoption of the Banking Act of 1935.
In addition to this, he endorsed the contentious Public Utilities Holding Company (Wheeler-Rayburn) Act that reduced monopoly in the energy industry.

Again the president's approach yielded impressive political dividends.
The WPA received a new pledge of support from the people, and Congress
passed, in quick succession, the Social Security Act (August 14), the Banking
Act of 1935 (August 23), and the Public Utilities Holding Company Act
(August 28).[54]

A similar flurry of legislation followed the October 12, 1937, fireside chat,
in which the president used the radio to describe and explain the most important measures he would introduce to Congress in the coming weeks. According to Sam Rosenman:

> He thought he could get the people to bring pressure on their Congress-
> men, who were then home in their own districts. He hoped that by the
> time they met in Extraordinary Session, they would have been convinced
> that their constituents wanted action.[55]

Roosevelt opened his speech by contending that most citizens were
encouraged by the progress of the economy but wanted legislation to ensure
that progress continued. As a result, certain new measures were needed. FDR
recommended laws to restrain agricultural surpluses, to step up conservation,
to designate a minimum wage, and to place a cap on the number of working
hours. At first Congress proved reluctant, but the president's compelling
appeal, and the onset of a new recession, generated the popular encouragement
needed to move them in his favor.

The sudden worsening of economic conditions also inspired Roosevelt's
next fireside chat. After an unemployment census had revealed that between
eight and eleven million Americans were still out of work,† and the industrial

*By the time of its termination in 1943, over 650,000 miles of highways, streets, and roads,
125,000 public buildings, and 8,000 parks had been built by the WPA.

†FDR's November 14, 1937, chat was enormously successful in getting Americans to participate in the census.

index fell by over one third, FDR sent a message to Congress on April 14 requesting over $3.7 billion in fresh public spending. At 10:30 that same night, the president addressed the American people and presented his case so persuasively that hundreds of thousands of Americans pressed his cause on their Congressional representatives. Sam Rosenman remarked:

> I heard Roosevelt deliver this speech. His voice seemed to reach out right into every home in the United States. Those paragraphs, spoken badly, could have sounded very "corny"; but, as he delivered them, they expressed the deep, sincere, warm emotions of a leader who was terribly concerned about the millions of human beings whose welfare was so greatly affected by the policies of the government he led.[56]

Many legislators, "already facing a bleak campaign in the fall because of the tottering economy, sought to appease their constituents, and therefore assented to the President's requests." As a result, numerous temporary measures were enacted. The WPA was reinstated, farm appropriations were enlarged, and credit was once again loosened. In addition to this, Congress was persuaded to increase the number of work projects, and to pass the Agricultural Adjustment Act of 1938 and the Fair Labor Standards Act of June 1938, which established a minimum wage and set limits on the number of hours in the workday.[57]

Domestic Success

Thus radio was instrumental in enabling Roosevelt to effectively battle the Depression. Through it, he was able to speak directly to the American people and "dispel the mood of fear and uncertainty that had immobilized them." Using the familiar setting of the fireside chat, FDR was able to explain to his listeners the measures his administration had undertaken to deal with the economic situation, earn their confidence, and enlist their support behind future efforts. This popular sanction was a formidable instrument with which to coerce an often immovable Congress into accepting his policies. The result was a "series of reform initiatives that had the effect of putting people back to work, reviving the stagnant economy, and ensuring greater equity in the capitalist system by providing federal regulation of many crucial aspects of it." While many of the New Deal programs were ephemeral solutions to singular problems, many others irrevocably transformed the political, economic and social life of the country. In an age when the federal government was enlarging its role in day-to-day affairs, Roosevelt's radio talks had a way of "mitigating presidential power by establishing a personal relationship between the people and their leader." Rather than being "passive onlookers in a time of tremendous change, Roosevelt encouraged the people to join with the government in a partnership dedicated to waging a determined war against the problems plaguing American society."[58]

Throughout FDR's anti–Depression crusade, the cooperation of the major networks and industry officials was vital. Soon after Roosevelt's fireside chat of July 24, 1933, National Association of Broadcasters president Alfred H. McCosker declared:

> The President's re-employment program has the complete cooperation of the NAB.... The NRA has been offered free run of the ether over all member stations, and the networks have promptly agreed to the practically unrestricted use of their facilities to further the campaign.[59]

By carrying the president's fireside chats and the speeches of other federal representatives over full nationwide hookups, and by blanketing the airwaves with spot ads, government commercials, transcription announcements, and other promotional material, the nets participated in a massive radio campaign to sell the New Deal, which reached as many Americans as the "ubiquitous Blue Eagle in every department store window." To streamline the process by which its message was disseminated over the air, the administration sought to centralize all government broadcast operations in a single agency. Before this, nets and stations had to contend with more than 120 separate bureaus seeking airtime. To comply with all of these requests, it was felt, was "bad radio and worse economics." In 1939, Roosevelt concluded that to have all placements cleared through one source, "professionally handled and with due regard for time limitations and program balance, would ease the burden and be conducive to more effective programming."[60] For this purpose, the president created the National Emergency Council (NEC) and appointed Robert I. Berger, former radio director of the Democratic National Committee, to head it.

As a sort of public relations bureau and information agency for the administration, the NEC was responsible for booking airtime for federal functionaries and for developing official government programs. One of its first acts was to produce a series of fifteen-minute transcriptions entitled *The U.S. Government Reports*. In these presentations, Lowell Mellett, one of the NEC's executive directors, interviewed the president and various members of his cabinet on the progress of New Deal policies.[61] With this production clearly designed to "sell the whole government establishment to the people," the Roosevelt administration had assumed complete control of its message content, thus circumventing the editorializing tendencies of the newspapers, and even, to a minor extent, of radio as well.

Roosevelt's example encouraged many local stations to mobilize their resources against the Depression. In the spring of 1939, WMT of Cedar Rapids carried a thrice-weekly series, *Opportunity Knocks*, to fight the city's high unemployment. In this quarter-hour program, those citizens without jobs were given an opportunity to appear before the microphone and state their qualifications for potential employers in the listening audience.[62]

While cooperation usually could be relied on, pressure sometimes had to be applied in order to ensure compliance with the president's economic initiatives. Following reports that some companies and businesses were violating the terms of the National Recovery Act, Federal Radio Commission secretary Herbert Pettey issued a circular to every licensed radio station in the country stating: "It is the patriotic, if not the bounden legal duty of all licensees of radio broadcasting stations to deny their facilities to advertisers who are disposed to defy, ignore, or modify the codes established by the NRA."[63]

4. Domestic Challenges

A balanced account of Roosevelt's political use of the radio must analyze not only his successes, but also his failures. In two notable cases—the president's attempt to change the composition of the Supreme Court and his effort to reorganize the Democratic Party—Roosevelt failed to employ his radio resources adequately, and consequently was denied the popular and Congressional approval that he had come to expect.

The Plan to Pack the Supreme Court

In the spring of 1937, the president hatched a plan to radically alter the composition of the Supreme Court by personally appointing additional judges for each one who had already served ten years and failed to retire within six months of reaching the age of seventy. Had this plan been implemented, it would have meant the designation of six new justices to the highest court of the land, and forty-four to lower federal tribunals, all presumably sympathetic to the administration. Roosevelt felt compelled to resort to such drastic action because his reform agenda had been encountering extreme difficulty in the Supreme Court. While FDR had been successful in gaining the support of the American public and the Congress for most of his anti–Depression measures, the Court seemed determined to overturn them. Justices Pierce Butler, George Sutherland, James McReynolds and Willis Van Devanter felt that the New Deal had not only been hastily or incoherently enacted, it delegated far too much power to the executive branch. In reaching this conclusion, the "Four Horsemen" were joined by Chief Justice Charles Evans Hughes himself.

On May 27, 1933, the justices struck down the National Recovery Act. Shortly afterward, the Frazier-Lemke Bankruptcy Act, the Municipal Bankruptcy Act, and the Railroad Retirement Act of 1934 were targeted for destruction. In the celebrated May 1935 case of *Schecter v. U.S.*, the Court unanimously invalidated NIRA. In January 1936, much to the president's chagrin, the Court torpedoed the Agricultural Adjustment Administration (*U.S. v. Butler*). In the ruling for this suit, the judges decided that agriculture was a local concern, and thus, as covered under the tenth amendment, was subject to state rather than central authority.

As Roosevelt viewed the political situation in February 1937, it seemed that his industrial and agricultural recovery programs were dead and that the crucial Social Security Act and the Wagner Act were being readied for the Court's chopping block. As a result, the president felt that he needed to take action at once in order to restrain the "obstructionist tendencies of the Court, and if only to preserve the gains of the New Deal and continue his legislative experiment."[1] While the Court had succeeded in eliminating much of the work of the first hundred days, FDR was determined that it would not do the same with the second. Given the enormous sticking power the judges had demonstrated during his first term, there was little prospect of a vacancy on the bench in the near future.

On February 5, Roosevelt set his plan for judicial reorganization rolling when he submitted his controversial bill to Congress. While his plan was logical and his argument persuasive, numerous mistakes in the method of delivery undermined the effectiveness of his appeal and prevented it from gaining public acceptance. According to Samuel Rosenman, the reorganization "need not have been a disaster if it had been presented to the people correctly, instead of the way it was."[2]

The first step Roosevelt should have taken, but did not, was to adequately prepare public opinion for his scheme, as he had done successfully on numerous other occasions. A perfect opportunity for this would have been his second inaugural address. Here the president could have delineated the political principles that were compelling him to attack the Court, at the same time making it clear that he did not intend to overstep his executive boundaries.

After presenting his bill to Congress on February 5, the president used the occasion of a press conference to announce his plans for retiring the older judges. In so doing, he made an important blunder. Released to the press rather than to the public at large, his message not only reached a smaller number of people, but was filtered through the interpretation of unfriendly newspaper editors.

Only when it became obvious that the bill would have to be sold to the country did FDR take to the air. In a crucial tactical error, Roosevelt waited over a month after the initial announcement of his plan to deliver his follow-up attack. In his Democratic victory dinner address, which was broadcast on March 4, 1937, FDR highlighted the progress-blocking quality of the Court by listing the vetoes of important New Deal legislation that it had handed down during the previous three years. The president said: "As yet there is no definite assurance that the three-horse team of the American government will pull together. If one horse lies down in the traces or plunges off in another direction, the field will not be plowed."[3] FDR then went on to explain to his listeners that the judges needed to be removed because "excessive age and waning mental vigor" had rendered them grossly inefficient. The president seemed to be starting off in good fighting form, but soon the issue began to be poorly handled.[4]

Failing again to develop any kind of momentum, Roosevelt waited five days after this speech to deliver the final blow for the cause of judicial reorganization. Due to his "lack of success with other channels," the president resorted to the consistently effective fireside chat on March 9, 1937.[5] Although his presentation was convincing, FDR indulged in overly caustic references to the "nine old men, who stood opposed to the democratic will of the people speaking through their president and elected representative."[6] The president declared that he had no intention of packing the Court with "spineless puppets." Rather, he merely proposed to return that legal body to its "rightful and historic place," and rescue the Constitution from "hardening of the judicial arteries."[7] Again, he hacked away at the theme of judicial unproductiveness and mental exhaustion. According to historian Halford Ryan, Roosevelt's accusation "planted in the audience's mind a misrepresented fact and an ill-defined issue that [was] difficult to dislodge rhetorically." Some days later, Chief Justice Charles Evans Hughes assured Americans that the court was not behind in its work, severely weakening the president's assertion that he was trying to improve the body's performance. A more enlightened strategy would have been for FDR to avoid issues of health and to explain that he was attacking the justices' continuing hindrance of New Deal measures. This was not only the truth, but the majority of Americans who supported the New Deal and derived some benefit from it might have come out in support of the president's plan.[8]

Despite these weaknesses, Gallup polls revealed a noticeable shift of opinion toward FDR's cause immediately following the March 9 chat. Asked "Are you in favor of President Roosevelt's proposal regarding the Supreme Court?" 48 percent responded in the affirmative. But again Roosevelt allowed considerable time to pass and failed to use his radio resources to capitalize on this trend. The next week, support for FDR fell below 40 percent. According to historian Kenneth Davis, this downward movement represented the "cost ... for his self-imposed silence during this period."[9]

The administration made another tactical error when a speech by Harry Hopkins in support of FDR's bill was scheduled opposite the popular Charlie McCarthy program and few tuned in. "Even though it was a nationwide hookup," the presidential secretary recalled, "I don't think many people listened to it. There is no chance of drawing any considerable audience held by McCarthy. I will never do that again."[10]

Other events beyond the control of the president were conspiring against him. Facing an already hostile Congress, Roosevelt was unable to compensate for the sudden death of Joseph Robinson of Arkansas, who, as majority leader, had been the most ardent supporter of the bill in the Senate. His demise "took much of the steam out of the president's crusade."[11]

Another powerful factor behind the failure of FDR's bill was that for the first time in his career he was outdone by his opponents in successfully employing the radio to achieve a political objective. Throughout the months of February and March 1937, congressional and judicial critics frequently went on the air to condemn the president's proposal. In such programs as *Congressional Opinions on the Proposed Changes in the Federal Judiciary*, *Why Pack the Supreme Court?* and *Mass Meeting of Opponents to the President's Supreme Court Plan*, Roosevelt's opponents applied his own tactic of presenting their case directly to the public. In an attempt to appeal to the average American, the congressional opposition presented a series of man-in-the-street interviews on the dangers of FDR's plan.[12] In addition to this, numerous congressmen themselves took to the air over a twelve-day period to speak out against the bill. These individuals included such political heavyweights as Gerald P. Nye, Burton K. Wheeler, and Frederick Van Nuys.[13] To millions of listeners, Wheeler declared before the Senate Judiciary Committee investigating the matter:

> The bill is a needless, fruitless and utterly dangerous abandonment of constitutional principle...without precedent or justification. If passed, the bill would subjugate the Court to the will of Congress and the President, and thereby destroy the independence of the judiciary, the only certain shield of individual rights.[14]

Quoting from a book written by FDR in 1933, *Looking Forward*, Wheeler employed the president's own words to support the case against juridical enlargement. In another March 1937 broadcast, Senator Kenneth Burke manipulated one of Roosevelt's catchphrases to assert that under the Court scheme "constitutional democracy was facing a rendezvous with death." Senator Copeland warned that if the president succeeded, his next target would be an assault on religious freedoms.[15]

The National Committee to Uphold Constitutional Government sponsored two broadcast lectures against FDR's plan. In the first, Louis Taber discussed how enlargement would harm agricultural interests. The second was an address by noted historian James T. Adams entitled "The Supreme Court: Bulwark of Liberty."[16] So frequent were the attacks of FDR's opponents that one listener wrote to the White House wondering why the president "did not go on the radio and defend himself."[17]

In the end, the American majority was unswayed by the president's appeal and made no attempt to pressure Congress into adopting the bill. After 168 days of debate, the Senate finally rejected FDR's judicial reorganization proposal on July 22, 1937. Many Americans felt the president had misinterpreted his recent landslide electoral victory as a blank check and had dramatically overstepped the limits of presidential authority. Many were unnerved by the fact that his own vice-president, John Garner, and several of his closest advisors were adamantly opposed to his plan. For most citizens, the Constitution "had stood the test of time ... long, and the system of checks and balances was something too sacred, to be tampered with." The president "not only attempted to sell the American public an impossible bill of goods, but his many errors in strategy and presentation did nothing to help persuade them." As a consequence of his poor radio showing, FDR allowed himself to be "upstaged by opponents who employed the medium more skillfully on this occasion than the old master himself."[18]

Some historians have argued that Roosevelt did not in fact fail. Russell Buhite maintains that while the president was denied support for this proposal, his move "might have had its desired effect." Perhaps Roosevelt never really believed that he could get his unusual bill passed, and used the radio not to pressure Congress but the Court itself. Subscribers to this theory point to the fact that only two months after the fireside chat, the conservative septuagenarian Justice Willis Van Devanter announced his retirement. There is no doubt that the Supreme Court Roosevelt faced after waging his reorganization campaign was much more amenable than the body he had encountered only months before. In a "sharp departure from prior decisions," the Court overcame much of its reluctance and delivered pro–New Deal rulings upholding the constitutionality of both the Social Security Act and the National Labor Relations Act. Quite unexpectedly, it even validated a state minimum-wage law that was a virtual carbon copy of one it had defeated only months before. Furthermore, the Court tended to "reinforce the New Deal gains already on the books." FDR ultimately received his original wish. By 1945 the normal course of resignations* and death gave him the opportunity of naming eight new justices to the bench.[19] These included the distinguished magistrates Felix Frankfurter, William O. Douglas and Hugo Black, all of whom continued to exert a progressive influence for decades after.

Purging the Democratic Party

While disagreement over Roosevelt's failure in March 1937 persists, historians universally agree that the outcome of his next great initiative—the reorganization of the Democratic Party along more liberal lines—was an unmitigated disaster. The president's considerable radio blunders not only prevented him from attaining his immediate objective, but helped to create an adverse legislative environment that would continue to plague him for many years after.

During the Seventy-fifth Congress, a conservative Democratic bloc had joined with Republicans to prevent the president from realizing many New Deal programs. In 1937, this coalition's opposition to any increase in executive authority had made them come out strongly against FDR's Supreme Court plan. In his June 24, 1938, fireside chat, the president drew attention to the obstructionist character of this body:

*In August 1937, FDR increased the attractiveness of this option by making generous pensions available to departing judges.

Never in our lifetime has such a concerted campaign of defeatism been thrown at the heads of the president and senators and congressmen as in the case of this Seventy-fifth Congress. Never before have we had so many Copperheads—and you will remember that it was the Copperheads who, in the days of the War Between the States, tried their best to make Lincoln and his Congress give up the fight, let the nation remain split in two and return to peace—peace at any price.[20]

FDR declared that he would be actively involved in the upcoming Democratic congressional primaries. He targeted nine conservative Democratic senators whom he wanted to unseat and replace with southern progressives. He endeavored to justify this position to listeners:

As head of the Democratic Party, charged with the responsibility of carrying out the definitely liberal declaration of principles set forth in the 1936 Democratic platform, I feel that I have the right to speak in those few instances where there may be a clear issue between candidates for a Democratic nomination involving these principles, or involving a clear misuse of my name.[21]

After stating his intention to campaign against the senators, Roosevelt made various speeches endorsing their opponents. The president was particularly energetic in condemning Walter George of Georgia, Millard Tydings of Maryland, and Ellison "Cotton Ed" Smith of South Carolina. Two days after his chat, in a radio address commemorating the third anniversary of the Social Security Act, FDR publicly thanked four members of Congress whom he credited with carrying this landmark bill through both houses. One of those representatives was David J. Lewis of Maryland, the White House candidate for Tydings's senate seat.

In presenting his case to the radio audience, Roosevelt made some crucial mistakes. He told listeners that he was troubled by the nine Democrats' uncooperative "general attitude" and "yes, but" stand on New Deal legislation that had been "overwhelmingly reaffirmed by voters in the election of 1936." His attack approach was disorderly, framing his accusations in vague terms and "not dealing with issues or differences in policy between himself and the nine renegade senators." Because of his failure to clearly define what he regarded as "conservative," the public had no reason to believe that the president was not merely trying to purge some of his political rivals from the party. The *Philadelphia Inquirer* observed: "The President has called not for a Democratic Congress but for a hand-picked, completely subservient ... Roosevelt Congress. It's not what the constituents want, or what the country wants. It's what Mr. Roosevelt wants." The *Baltimore Sun* called FDR's decision "arrogant self-righteousness," and the *Hartford Courant* wrote: "The whole tenor of the President's address betokens his belief that he is and ought to be the government."[22] Roosevelt's image suffered considerably when critics began comparing his "high-handed tactics" with the forcible purges that had taken place in Hitler's Germany and Stalin's Soviet Union.[23]

In attacking his own party members, Roosevelt violated one of the basic doctrines of a sound "rhetorical presidency." While the public would accept a politician campaigning for a candidate in his own party against an opponent from another party, many people found it distasteful when the leader of a party tried to turn voters against a fellow member. According to Sam Rosenman, "resentment ... is nearly always aroused when a national figure interferes in a local political situation in a state where he does not live and vote."[24] Many local voters regarded FDR's action as an "unwarranted intrusion ... inappropriate to his high office." Others believed that "the high role of president does not seem to include dividing the party over picayune partisan politics."[25]

Again, as in the attempt to purge the Court, Roosevelt's opponents became adept at employing "his" medium against him. When Roosevelt and his candidate Lawrence Camp assailed the character of Walter George, they failed to arrange for adequate radio exposure throughout the senator's home state of Georgia. By contrast, George conducted an intensive tour of the state in which he addressed the radio audience from every stop. The same was true of Senator Tydings, Frederick Van Nuys, Howard Smith and Guy Gilette. While FDR appealed to the nation in his fireside chat, these congressmen shored up their support and assured their positions at home via statewide radio hookups. Since the election was to be decided within the states themselves, this was certainly a shrewd move. Tydings was particularly adept at rousing his fellow citizens against Roosevelt's plan, opposing such blatant "outside interference" in his state's internal affairs. Maryland would never permit "her star in the flag to be 'purged' by FDR and his carpetbaggers."[26]

In the few areas where pro–New Deal Democrats did utilize radio, the president had considerable success. Veteran broadcasters Claude Pepper of Florida and Alben Barkley of Kentucky both soundly defeated their conservative challengers. This was also the case with Robert Bulkley (Ohio), Lyndon Johnson (Texas), Elmer Thomas (Oklahoma) and Hattie Caraway (Arkansas). But in the majority of primaries, where there was no effort to contest the airwaves with illiberal candidates (Augustine Lonergan of Connecticut, Alva Adams of Colorado, Bennett Champ Clark of Mississippi and Pat McCarran of Nevada), conservatives usually prevailed. The fact that most of the Northeast and virtually all of the South and Midwest were neglected in this way was a major reason for the failure of the president's realignment effort. In the end, because of his lethargic broadcast campaign, all but one of the candidates he personally stumped for failed to win election. Of the nine originally targeted senators, only John O'Connor was defeated. In the November elections, the number of Republicans increased by eight in the Senate and doubled in the House. The New Deal was in for a rough time.

Thus, with the relative failure of his efforts at judicial and Congressional reorganization, Roosevelt discovered that his effectiveness in manipulating the ether to influence public opinion was not always certain. When he was at

Populist Louisiana senator and Roosevelt opponent Huey Long.

his best, FDR was irresistible, but when he neglected to use his well-developed talent for formulating an appeal and persuasively delivering it, his attempts to achieve his domestic political agenda could be seriously jeopardized. This was doubly true when he faced an adversary who could mobilize radio in a manner and on a scale that rivaled his own. Perhaps Roosevelt had temporarily forgotten the fundamental lesson he had derived from his many presidential election campaigns: The individual or party that most effectively utilized broadcasting had an incalculable advantage over any rival. He was determined never again to allow this advantage to pass from his hands. But such control would be possible only after he faced two other, more formidable, challenges to his dominance of the airwaves.

Huey Long

The first such challenge came from another politician, Huey Long. Like Roosevelt, Long recognized the potential value of radio as a political instrument and employed it frequently during his early career. While campaigning for the Louisiana governorship in 1928, Long had been the only candidate to understand and utilize radio's unique ability to reach large numbers of potential voters. During a broadcast appeal over WCAG in New Orleans, the station manager revealed that there were only 8,000 sets in the city. Confidently,

Huey replied that if only half of them were tuned to his program, with five listeners per set, he could reach over 20,000 people.[27] Long's burgeoning dominance of the airwaves in his home state provided the rhetorical edge that propelled him first into the governorship and then the United States Senate.

In the early thirties, Long had been a faithful supporter of the New Deal, and his frequent broadcasts to his constituents on the subjects of reform and wealth distribution earned him a faithful following of hundreds of thousands. Before very long, the networks, recognizing Huey's ability to draw listeners, hastened to offer him free airtime.[28] When Long first went on the air as a senator in 1935, Roosevelt immediately recognized in him a kindred spirit. Like the president, Long appealed to a broad reach of Americans because of his populist philosophy and the informal manner in which he addressed his listeners. Like FDR, he would open all of his radio talks with the intimate greeting, "My friends." He would then go into a discussion of some issue in which he used "pure vernacular that carried with it no hint of condescension." His ability to frequently quote scripture earned him the devotion of thousands of pious southerners.[29]

Always seeking to attract the maximum number of voters to his listening audience, Long would routinely begin his broadcasts by saying, "While I'm talking ... I want you to go to the telephone and call up five of your friends and tell them that Huey is on the air." He would then ramble on for a few minutes, allowing others to tune in before he proceeded to elucidate his central points. This device proved enormously successful in putting him on the top of the rating charts for months on end. Another factor which contributed to his popularity with listeners was his gift of showmanship. Overcoming an initially nervous and bombastic vocal style, Huey rapidly developed into a masterful broadcast speaker who never turned his head away from the microphone, learned "every shade of inflection and emphasis of voice," and never conveyed the impression of reading from a prepared script.[30] Radio critic Ben Gross favorably compared him with the best radio humorists of the day, Will Rogers and Ed Wynn. The senator himself enjoyed being called the "Kingfish," after a main character in the immensely popular comedy show *Amos 'n' Andy*.[31]

While Long began his political career as a Roosevelt supporter, in the fall of 1933 he suddenly turned viciously against both the president and his New Deal reform package. He found the NRA too conservative, and felt that the president had fallen into the pocket of big business. As soon as Long began using his radio access to broadcast anti-administration propaganda, the president became concerned.

In 1935, Long mounted a violent attack on FDR over the airwaves. He told listeners that under Roosevelt's direction, the country was "going straight to hell." In his correspondence with NBC president Merlin Aylesworth, he often referred to Roosevelt as "that son-of-a-bitch anarchist." In one anti–FDR broadcast in March 1935, Huey drew over 25 million listeners.[32] As an alternative to

the New Deal, Long offered his listeners a program that promised every citizen a $5,000 home, free college education, $2,000 in annual income, government storage of agricultural produce, and limitations on working hours.* To
gain popular approval for his bills against concentrated wealth in Congress,
Long purchased national airtime from NBC. By arranging a coast-to-coast
hookup, he did something unprecedented for a United States senator: He
"placed himself on a level with the President."[33] Long declared that in his "Share
the Wealth" society, "the rich would become poorer but even the poorest would
live like a king!"†

After one year in existence, the Share the Wealth Association boasted
clubs in over 8,000 cities across the nation, with a membership exceeding 7
million.[34] There was little doubt that Long intended to use the club's organization as the core of a political movement that could sweep him into the
White House. Radio commentator Raymond Swing felt that Long's "fine oratorical skills, his radio connections, and his ever-expanding army of devoted
adherents" made him a serious political threat to FDR.[35] But the president
never had to face this. On September 10, 1935, Huey Long's ambitious career
was cut short by an assassin's bullet. Before FDR could draw a sigh of relief,
however, another hostile voice invaded the air. To his surprise, this new challenge to his command of the ether came not from a savvy politician, but from
a shrewd Catholic priest.

Father Coughlin

Father Charles L. Coughlin began his radio career in the late 1920s,
broadcasting Sunday sermons over station WJR in Detroit. Because of the
enormous number of letters that regularly flowed into his parish office from
enthralled listeners, more stations (WLW, Cincinnati, and WMAQ, Chicago)
offered to carry his broadcasts. Eventually, even CBS recognized the audience
appeal of this eloquent clergyman, and they too extended him weekly airtime.
Soon after Coughlin received this national exposure, his audience grew to an
estimated 10 million.[36]

As the Depression intensified, Coughlin's speeches began to assume a more
political character. Like Long, Coughlin began his career an ardent supporter

*Long's plan was in some ways similar to that of another radio demagogue, Dr. Francis
Townsend. In the mid–1930s, Townsend took to the airwaves on behalf of his "Old-Age
Revolving Pensions Plan," under which the government paid $200 a month to every citizen
over sixty on condition that the funds were spent within a month. Townsend claimed this
method would not only assist the elderly, but by infusing considerable purchasing power into
the economy, would mitigate one of the worst problems of the Depression. Though the project
was fiscally unsound, it did address a genuine need at a time when social security had not yet
been established and many localities lacked any kind of relief.

†Some contemporaries have argued that Roosevelt's 1935 Wealth Tax Act, imposing greater
income and inheritance levies on the rich, was merely an attempt to steal Long's fire.

of the Roosevelt administration, but soon became disillusioned. The priest particularly resented the AAA's price-boosting practices of slaughtering livestock and destroying crops when millions of Americans went hungry. In late 1936, Coughlin began to direct his attacks toward the president, whom he felt to be personally responsible for the country's malaise. Blasting the fiscal policies of the New Deal, Coughlin told millions of American voters that a ballot cast for the president was a vote for "Roosevelt and Ruin."[37] Coughlin went so far as to openly urge his listeners to "purge the man who claims to be a democrat from the Democratic Party. I mean Franklin Double-Crossing Roosevelt."[38]

Coughlin showed Roosevelt that he was not the only broadcaster who could use the radio to gain mass support. When he delivered a speech condemning J. P. Morgan and Andrew Mellon, over 600,000 letters flooded into the little post office in Royal Oak, Michigan, where the radio priest delivered his "sermons."[39] This number leaped to an amazing 1.2 million after another speech denouncing Roosevelt's monetary policies.[40]

Like the president, Coughlin attempted to use his influence with listeners to apply pressure on Congress. In 1934, when the issue of American participation in the World Court came before that legislative body, more than 200,000 letters were sent in by Coughlin's supporters denouncing the idea. Those letters were instrumental in convincing senators to scrap the plan for participation.[41]

Much of Coughlin's radio success was due to his extraordinary vocal qualities and his speaking prowess. Many listeners felt that his voice was of "such mellow richness, such manly, heart-warming, confidential intimacy, such emotional and ingratiating charm, that anyone tuning past it almost automatically returned to hear it again."[42] So formidable were his oratorical powers that *Broadcasting* remarked: "He is a man who could have led his Hippodrome Theater audience in New York recently to march downtown and literally tear down the portals of the House of Morgan."[43]

Not only did the radio priest possess many of FDR's coveted vocal qualities, he had one advantage that the president did not. Given his position in the church, Coughlin was able to present his political views as if they had the sanction of holy faith. The language he often employed highlighted this presentation. In his campaign against Roosevelt's bid for a second term, he informed his listeners, "My friends, this is the most important crusade which we have ever undertaken. It is a contest between Christ and chaos."[44]

Coughlin's dual role as cleric and radio personality also generated considerable financial rewards. Coughlin's appeals to his listeners for monetary contributions swelled the coffers of his little parish, enabling the priest to build an extravagant broadcasting tower next to his church and making him the forerunner of the modern televangelist. In 1935, the staff at the Shrine of the Little Flower had to be expanded from 81 to 200 in order to handle the growing number of incoming contributions.[45] As his fame grew, Coughlin milked it for all it was worth. As tourists flocked to his church, he built a "Super Shrine" gas station to serve them.[46]

Despite his official church affiliation, Coughlin's appeal was by no means purely denominational. In fact, the great bulk of his followers consisted of non–Catholics.

The extent of Coughlin's popularity impressed many prominent observers. A December 1938 poll by the American Institute of Public Opinion found that 15 million Americans had listened to one or more of his broadcasts, and that 7.5 million tuned in on a regular basis.[47] *Fortune* referred to the radio priest as "the biggest thing on radio," and Coughlin's superior, Bishop Gallagher of Detroit, asserted, "If Coughlin had lived in Russia before the revolution, and had possessed radio facilities, the revolution may have never taken place."[48] CBS affiliate WCAU in Philadelphia conducted a poll asking listeners who they would rather hear on a Sunday afternoon, Coughlin or the New York Philharmonic. The clergyman received 187,000 votes and the orchestra only 12,000.[49] Coughlin was such a spectacular draw that *Broadcasting* once remarked: "No single radio feature on the air, with the exception of the President himself, is met with greater expectancy than the Sunday broadcasts from the Shrine of the Little Flower."[50]

Coughlin's popularity gave him tremendous leverage with his network critics who felt that the father's oratory was a bit too inflammatory.* When CBS ordered him to cease his attacks on the president, Coughlin appealed to his listeners: "Should CBS be allowed to muzzle me?" The network was so overwhelmed with letters of protest (1.2 million) that it dropped the subject. When he defied an order to submit his scripts to network censors prior to airtime, the nets tried unsuccessfully to push him off the air.[51] When WMCA of New York and WDAS of Philadelphia tried to enforce this code, listeners erupted in violent protest, forming picket lines before the two stations and urging fellow citizens to boycott their advertisers.[52]

The president was also eager to revoke Coughlin's radio privileges, not only because of the corrosive effect he had on the administration's image, but because of the genuine political threat that many felt that he posed. In the spring of 1936, Coughlin merged his political organization, "The Organization of the Little Flower," with Huey Long's Share the Wealthers to form the Union party. With some polls giving Long's party 10 percent of the popular vote, and Coughlin promising to deliver nine million additional ballots to the coalition, many observers believed that "together they might just be able to topple Roosevelt" in the 1936 presidential race. Luckily for the president, Long's death two months before the election took much of the steam out of

---

*Coughlin's immense popularity inspired a host of evangelical imitators. One of these was the Baptist "Radio Preacher" of Ranger, Texas, Reverend John Lovell (*Broadcasting, March 15, 1939, p. 32*).

the Union party movement. In November its candidate, William Lemke, received only about one million votes. While this figure was nowhere near FDR's 27.8 million, it did represent a considerable total for a fringe organization.[53]

After the demise of the Union party, Coughlin's new political organization, the Christian Front, began to assume a strongly anti–Semitic and fascist character. In speech after speech, Coughlin blasted the "Communists, Jews, socialists, capitalists, and international bankers" who he claimed were responsible for the country's economic crisis.[54] In 1938, following the excesses of the Kristallnacht in Germany, bands of Christian Front hoodlums all over the country assaulted Jews and desecrated their property. When, during a February 20 meeting of the German-American Bund, Coughlin declared that all America's efforts should be directed at stopping the spread of communism, and that Hitler was a bulwark against Russian bolshevism, he was vigorously applauded.[55]

Historian Irving Fang has analyzed many of Coughlin's most notable speeches of this period and demonstrated how similar they were to addresses given by Nazi propaganda minister Josef Goebbels. Indeed, one German newspaper, *Der Sturmer*, proclaimed, "Father Coughlin has the courage to speak his convictions. His conviction is that National Socialism is right."[56] Such comparisons persuaded many members of the Catholic Church to use the airwaves to "counteract Coughlin's propaganda." On February 16, 1939, Father W. C. Kiernan of Trinity Episcopal Church in New Jersey inaugurated a new series, *Free Speech Forum*, in which he invited distinguished guests to refute the radio priest.[57] In July, Reverend Harry Ward of Union Theological Seminary also began a series of addresses, *Answering Father Coughlin*, on WHBI, Newark.[58] In response to this campaign, Coughlin supporters made arrangements for stations like New York's WWRL to transcribe his speeches and distribute them more widely.

Many observers became convinced that Coughlin was scheming to become a dictator. The influence of his radio appeals and the loathsome message they contained certainly made Coughlin a menacing demagogue. His "acrimonious invective" sparked a bitter controversy within broadcasting circles over how far a speaker should be "permitted to use the airwaves as a vehicle for inciting racial and religious hatred."[59] In a 1939 meeting of the National Association of Broadcasters to discuss this concern, it was decided that the radio industry should "exercise its duty of self-regulation" on this issue, "if only to forestall the heavy hand of government censorship." That the latter was becoming an increasingly attractive option in 1939 was evident in the comments of Elliott Roosevelt, who stated: "Even [government] censorship might not be too high a price if it will help insulate us against the radio priest's anti–Semitic oratory."[60] NAB president Neville Miller declared Coughlin's bigoted statements to be "an abuse of the privilege of free speech" and an "evil unworthy of American radio."[61] As a result, CBS and NBC agreed that Coughlin would be gradually forced from the air by applying the long-standing network policy of denying airtime to "spokesmen of controversial public issues."[62] Anxious not to lose their broadcasting licenses, many of the stations that had regularly transmitted Coughlin's program now declined to do so. Roosevelt took the "final step that sealed Coughlin's fate by applying pressure on the radio priest's clerical superiors to silence him."[63] In the end, the president, like Shakespeare's Henry II, succeeded in ridding himself of a most "troublesome priest."

While the "increasing use of radio by politicians and office seekers clearly demonstrated radio's power and growing importance,"[64] it also illustrated a potent danger that is inherent in the medium itself. In a society that is deeply enmeshed in economic chaos, where public uncertainty and dissatisfaction is pervasive, it is not difficult for a demagogue utilizing the airwaves to gain popular support for "implementing wild schemes, and in targeting certain groups for persecution." Indeed, to a clever manipulator, radio and the Depression presented "twin blessings" that could be exploited for personal and political ends.[65] Radio commentator General Hugh S. Johnson recognized this when he warned the administration: "If you don't think Long and Coughlin are dangerous, you don't know the temper of the country in this distress."[66] The radio careers of Huey Long and Father Coughlin brought many Americans to the startling realization that while "broadcasting could be a mighty weapon for good, at the disposal of those appealing to the base emotions of prejudice, it could be one of the most powerful media for evil ever devised."[67]

5. Selling the Foreign Policy Agenda

After devoting the first half of his radio presidency to mitigating the effects of the Great Depression, Roosevelt in the late 1930s was increasingly preoccupied with the expanding international crisis in Europe and Asia. Between 1937 and 1941, the president concerned himself with two tasks. First, he had to craft a "suitable policy for dealing with the breakdown of the post–World War I peace structure," and the danger to American interests that this implied. Once this had been accomplished, FDR had to use his rhetorical strength to "convince the American people of the rectitude of his approach."[1]

As an initial response to the rumblings of conflict in Africa, Spain, the Rhineland, and China between 1935 and 1937, Roosevelt sought to ensure United States noninvolvement by strict adherence to Congress's neutrality legislation. By forbidding the export of American arms and capital to belligerents, Roosevelt hoped to keep the United States from becoming embroiled in the world's disputes. On August 14, 1936, the president spoke for the nation at Chautaqua when he declared: "I have seen war. I have seen war on land and sea. I have seen blood running from the wounded. I have seen men coughing out their gassed lungs. I have seen the dead in the mud ... **I hate war.**"[*2] But after 1937, when these distant feuds threatened to destroy the post–Versailles status quo that Americans had fought a world war to achieve and upon which the security of the United States depended, the president had to reevaluate his country's position.

In October 1937, with Italy enlarging her empire in Ethiopia, Germany openly assisting Franco's rebels in Spain, and Japan battling to the gates of Peking, FDR modified his strict noninterventionist stance and began to voice his opposition to the perpetrators of aggression. In his famous "Quarantine Speech" of October 5, the president decried the spreading "epidemic of world lawlessness."

During the First World War, FDR served as assistant secretary of the navy. Despite the fact that his position did not involve front-line duty, his somber and sincere tone convinced listeners that he had witnessed firsthand the graphic images depicted in his speech.

> Without a declaration of war and without warning or justification of any
> kind, civilians, including vast numbers of women and children, are being
> ruthlessly murdered with bombs from the air. In times of so-called peace,
> ships are being attacked and sunk by submarines without cause or notice.
> Nations are fomenting and taking sides in civil warfare in nations that have
> never done them any harm. Nations claiming freedom for themselves,
> deny it to others...[3]

Drawing upon a medical analogy, he asserted that the war and aggression were
like communicable diseases that continued to spread until the uninfected "join
in a quarantine of the patients in order to protect the health of the community."[4]

Despite verbal denunciations of Axis expansionism, public passivity and
American military weakness severely limited the president's response options.
His deep engagement in legislative battles over domestic issues at this time
made bold international initiatives unlikely. After the German annexation of
Austria in March 1938, America's only action was to suspend its commercial
treaty with the latter. When Hitler threatened the territorial integrity of the
Sudetenland in October 1938, Roosevelt declared: "The government of the
United States has no political involvement in Europe, and will assume no
obligation in the conduct of the present negotiations." Similarly, after the German absorption of Czechoslovakia in March 1939 and Italy's attack on Albania, the president's only response was to ask the Axis leaders for assurances
that 31 specified countries would not be invaded within the next ten years.

By mid–1939, with news about the mass arrest, deportation, and virulent
persecution of European Jews, Americans increasingly perceived Hitler's
anti–Semitism as a threat to all civilized values. As far as FDR was concerned,
when Axis challenges to the peace structure were "abstract," the United States
was not compelled to react. But when changes in the international strategic
balance of power presented the country with direct threats to its security, firm
action became necessary.[5] With Germany and Japan endeavoring to forge hostile empires on her flanks, and attempting to dominate the seas in between,
the peril to America was becoming all too real. Between 1939 and 1941, with
her allies besieged or overcome, diplomacy foundering, and armed incidents
occurring with distressing frequency, the United States was increasingly drawn
toward active resistance against Axis aggression.

As a result, the president devoted much of his later radio presidency to preparing the American public for the adequate defense of the nation. This involved
not only sending moral and material aid to Hitler's enemies, but also attempting to "prepare America itself both psychologically and materially for a war that
might eventually engulf them." Roosevelt firmly believed that the public had
to be "informed of the efficiency of the defense effort and urged to participate
in it." The fireside chat would prove an effective vehicle for "increasing public
awareness of the national crisis, while building faith in its ability to deal with

it."[6] Thus the Roosevelt administration carried forward its program to confront the Axis through such measures as Cash-and-Carry, Destroyers for Bases, Lend-Lease, and in the "shoot on sight" order against German U-boats in the Atlantic, during the period up to actual American participation in the war. Given the official neutrality of an American government preoccupied with the internal economic crisis, and the lingering isolationist sentiment of the nation, securing approval of these measures and enacting them called for a persuasiveness and level of salesmanship that could only be accomplished through the influence of radio.

Cash-and-Carry

On September 3, 1939, for the second time in twenty-five years, Europe was again thrown into ruinous conflict when German troops invaded Poland. Making good their promise to guarantee Polish territory, Britain and France declared war on Germany after appeals to Hitler to withdraw his troops had failed. Sensing the impending crisis, and clearly sympathetic to the Allied position, Roosevelt had been trying since May to obtain congressional agreement for altering the United States's neutrality legislation. When he went on the air three hours after the Anglo-French declaration, his aim was to convince the American people and Congress of the need to assist "those countries now resisting Axis aggression." In particular, Roosevelt wanted Congress to repeal the arms embargo of 1935 and allow belligerents access to American war material on a Cash-and-Carry basis. By stipulating that any nation seeking such a transfer of arms must pay ahead of time and then transport the arms themselves, the president ensured that only Britain and France, with their extensive merchant fleets, would be in a position to take advantage of the offer.[7] To persuade listeners of the necessity of taking such action, and to make them more amenable to it, FDR presented his case in a skillful mixture of interventionist and isolationist language. Given the "pacifistic mood" of the country, Roosevelt was careful to avoid allowing his policy to appear "unneutral."[8] If Congress assented to Cash-and-Carry, he promised to support legislation prohibiting American warships from convoying Allied supply vessels into the Atlantic's danger zones.

On the evening of September 3, FDR began his chat by underscoring his own anti-war feelings. He lamented, "Until 4:30 this morning, I had hoped against hope that some miracle could prevent another devastating war in Europe and bring to an end the invasion of Poland by Germany." The president warned his listeners that America should not delude itself into thinking that the far-away conflict did not affect the United States.

> Passionately though we may desire detachment, we are forced to realize that every word that comes through the air, every ship that sails the seas, every battle that is fought, does affect our American future. It is our national duty to keep those wars out of the Americas.[9]

Next, Roosevelt reaffirmed the official neutrality of the United States, but left no doubt in the minds of listeners where the sympathies of the administration were being directed.

> This nation will remain a neutral nation, but I cannot ask that every American remain neutral in thought as well. Even a neutral has a right to take account of the facts. Even a neutral cannot be asked to close his mind or close his conscience.*

The president's September 3 fireside chat "effectively moved his country from words to deeds" in the effort to counter Axis belligerence, and prepared the American public well for the actions taken by the administration later that month. On September 8, Roosevelt responded to the escalating conflict in Europe by proclaiming a "limited national emergency," in which troop levels were raised and the reserves activated.[10] On September 21, he summoned Congress into an extraordinary session, and formally made his request for the elimination of the restrictions on arms transfers to Britain and France.[11] As FDR presented the merits of his proposal to Congress, millions of listeners tuned in and followed the proceedings.† The cascade of telegrams that poured into offices on Capitol Hill were vivid proof of the speech's persuasive impact.

A *Fortune* poll indicated that 50 percent of Americans favored repeal in early September, 57 percent after the president's September 3 address, and over 60 percent immediately following the speech of September 21.[12] The results of this survey revealed a growing spirit of sympathy with the Anglo-French allies. *Time* commented on the precarious implications of this attitude shift: "While Roosevelt's formula was realistic, in that it recognized a real threat to U.S. interests, it was also dangerous." By openly declaring for the Allies and "inviting Americans to condemn Hitler as loudly as they liked," the president was inadvertently placing his country on a collision course with Germany.[13] Despite continued affirmations of American neutrality, future events would do little to ameliorate this strained relationship. For the present, the "tide of public opinion that now flowed into the House and Senate" was instrumental in securing the passage of FDR's revised Neutrality Act on November 4.

"The Development of Our Defense Program"

During the winter of 1939–40, Western Europe was relatively quiet as the German and French armies waged a "phoney war" of inaction. But the peace was suddenly broken in April and May 1940 when Hitler launched his powerful

---

According to Time: *"To all ears this was the most striking sentence of the broadcast ... for no thinking man can fail to have his convictions about the causes which plunge the world into war."*

†*The Repeal of the Arms Embargo speech received one of the highest ratings for a foreign policy address up to that time, 26.8 percent of the total audience (*Broadcasting, *July 1, 1940, p. 75).*

blitzkrieg against Scandinavia, the Low Countries, and France. German attacks on Norway and Denmark increased American anxiety over the fate of Danish-controlled Iceland and Greenland, which lay within the western hemisphere. With German panzers sweeping across France, Roosevelt felt the need to prepare the American public for the eventuality of a French defeat, and the vital necessity of supplying the British in their continued resistance to Hitler. The president had in mind a plan to provide Britain with the arms and equipment it would need to withstand the Nazi assault that was certain to come. As a small island nation, Britain was heavily dependent on foreign imports for 50 percent of its food requirements (especially North American wheat), most of its metal and machine tool needs, and all of its oil. In 1939–40, Britain had to import 55 million tons of goods in order to sustain its wartime way of life. While the British economy expanded by over 60 percent during the war, military expenditure exhausted 50 percent of the total GNP. According to John Keegan:

> Had Britain attempted to sustain its military outlay from domestic resources, its economy would have been broken.… Despite all the sacrifices made, in the extension of working hours, the liquidation of foreign and domestic capital, the reduction of living standards, the utilization of marginal farming land, the substitution of ersatz for accustomed commodities, conscription of women to the workforce, and a dozen other emergency measures … the British economy could not have borne the strains of war without external assistance.[14]

Since sales from private stocks were proving insufficient, the American government recognized the need to open its warehouses and arsenals, and "extend the [full] material resources of the nation." Roosevelt dubbed this policy of heightened aid to Britain, "dynamic non-belligerence."[15]

On May 26, 1940, a "grim … but very determined" Roosevelt took to the airwaves in a fireside chat designed to prepare the American people for this "expanded commitment to the British."[16] He also sought to "reassure Americans of the current state of military readiness, and of his determination to increase the nation's preparedness by increasing its military production."[17]

Because developments in Europe had so increased the importance of FDR's speech, NBC scrapped all of its prior programming commitments to carry it. In order to assure the president the undivided attention of the listening audience, A. A. Schecter, NBC's director of news and special events, arranged to have the time of the Ambers-Jenkins Championship fight, which the net was to broadcast, moved up an hour so as not to conflict with the message from the White House.[18]

Roosevelt opened his talk by discussing the plight of those who had been attacked, and the need for America to remain alert.

> There are many among us who in the past have closed their eyes to events abroad—because they believed in utter good faith what some of their fellow Americans told them—that what has taken place in Europe was none

of our business; that no matter what happened over there, the U.S. could always pursue its peaceful and unique course in the world.[19]

According to the president, a defense policy based on this naive assumption would only "invite future attack." Therefore, America must begin to prepare its own defenses, while helping the enemies of Hitler to shore up theirs. He said, "It is our purpose not only to speed up production, but to increase the total facilities of the nation in such a way that they can be further enlarged to meet the emergencies of the future." The president announced that he would be submitting to Congress a request for the largest appropriations bill in the peacetime history of the army and navy. He would use this money to enlarge preexisting war plants, build new factories, and develop other sources of supply for the growing number of tanks, planes, ships, artillery and small arms that would be needed.[20] Only in this way could the United States hope to exist in a world "threatened by the forces of destruction." Drawing upon the public-government partnership that had worked so well in addressing the problems of the Depression, FDR declared: "It is my resolve and yours to ... meet the present emergency."

New York City cinema and theater owners recorded an 80 percent drop in attendance during the hour of FDR's speech. When a worker at Radio City tuned one of the hall's sets in to the president's talk, the first floor was soon jammed with eager listeners. According to the May 29 *New York Times*, "this audience indicated its approval of the President's words."

Judging from the mail response, Roosevelt's speech was successful in assuring Americans that the country was adequately fortifying itself. One listener wrote in saying, "As I was sitting and listening to your fireside chat last night, it seemed to me that an iron-clad cloak of fear lifted itself off my shoulders."[21] The president also succeeded in convincing the public that further safeguards were necessary. According to Sam Rosenman:

> Telegrams poured in offering personal services, plants, factories etc.... To most Americans, [FDR's] statements ... were enlightening. The war in Europe seemed much closer as the President spoke. The American people were no longer interested spectators. Their attitude of sympathetic aloofness began to drop away quickly.[22]

Time remarked: "The cry changed to action ... only a few people expected antiaircraft guns to sprout from every rooftop, but the U.S. as a whole [now] wanted assurance that individuals, firms, labor, and politicians would all fuse in a national mobilization for defense."[23] In a survey conducted after the broadcast, 90 percent of those questioned felt that the U.S. should increase the size of its armed forces, and 86 percent believed that another billion dollars should be expended on the military.[24] Soon after the May 26 speech, Congress responded to the president's request and voted him $1.6 billion in defense spending.[25]

As the French campaign continued, Roosevelt was extremely concerned about the possibility of Italian intervention. On June 10, while the French army was in total disarray, Mussolini invaded France and declared war on both allies. While the war had been hitherto confined to central and northern Europe, Italy's action now expanded its scope to the Mediterranean and North Africa. On the same day, Roosevelt delivered a commencement address at the University of Virginia, Charlottesville. Using vivid imagery to condemn Il Duce's treachery, the president declared: "The hand that held the dagger has struck it into the back of its neighbor."[26]*

The Crossly Service estimated that over 45 percent of all United States homes had tuned in to this broadcast. Such figures were typical of the consistently high ratings that FDR's foreign policy speeches enjoyed during this period of anxiety. Other American public officials seldom attracted an audience greater than 23 percent, and foreign statesmen even less. Hitler and Neville Chamberlain's declarations of war each drew only 16.3 percent and a worldwide broadcast by the Duke of Windsor on the beginning of hostilities only garnered 10.1 percent.[27] Exactly one month after his "Stab in the Back" speech, Roosevelt sent a request to Congress for an additional $4 billion defense subsidy. Sam Rosenman wrote: "The isolationists still shrieked; but the preponderance of American public opinion was rallying in back of the president ... as leader of the free world he could look over his shoulder and see a nation following him."[28]

On July 18, Roosevelt introduced his plan to dramatically expand the size of United States armed forces by imposing the first peacetime draft in the nation's history.[29] To sell this controversial bill to the public, the administration mounted the "most intense radio campaign ever conducted." With the cooperation of the NAB and network representatives, the president's radio drive "flooded the country with conscription messages." In preparation for the October 16 Registration Day, Capt. Ernest M. Culligan, public relations officer at National Selective Service headquarters, booked network time for numerous government speakers, and sent recordings of their speeches and fifteen-minute interview scripts to state Selective Service branches for distribution to local stations. In addition to this, one-minute announcements reminding men between the ages of twenty-one and thirty-five where and when to register were sent over the airwaves thousands of times, and enrollment information was supplied to network commentators and sponsors for use in their programs.[30] To promote a clearer understanding of the technical and legal aspects of the Selective Service Act, the National Defense Advisory Council produced a series of half-hour question-and-answer discussion shows. The United States Army played a large role in the effort to augment its ranks, with its own

---

Sam Rosenman felt this memorable statement was representative of "the way in which the president could dramatize an event in a few words ... that would stick in the public memory long after the rest of the speech had been forgotten" (p. 198).

radio recruitment drive. Under the direction of Lt. Herbert Chase, special pleas for recruits by FDR, secretary of the navy Frank Knox, assistant secretary of war Robert Patterson, and commentators Raymond Swing and Dorothy Thompson were recorded and aired at regular intervals in the broadcast day.[31] In New York, Lt. George J. Doeir and Col. Frank Lamb of the Army Air Corps gave weekly talks on WHN and WINS to encourage enlistment, and WMCA presented a special offering of concerts by the 16th Infantry Regimental Band.[32] Such devices were enormously successful. By the end of October, over 16,400,000 young American males had registered for service.

To make the draft more palatable to a reluctant public, on October 29 the president himself drew the first registration numbers during a lottery in the State Department Auditorium in Washington. As millions tuned in, Roosevelt announced the first capsule and a woman in the back of the hall shrieked; it belonged to her 21-year-old son. A few minutes later, while describing the ceremony for Mutual, Stephen McCormack, chief engineer at member station WOL, saw his own number selected. From midnight to 3:00 A.M., NBC reiterated all 8,500 numbers drawn in a special program. Later the next day, the network broadcast interviews with many of the new trainees, and discussed expectations of life on active service.[33]

In his speech, the president deliberately refrained from using the terms "conscription" or "draft," and avoided the "beating drums" and martial fanfare associated with troop-raising rituals in less democratic states. According to Sam Rosenman, "the atmosphere was that of a mustering of the human resources of the nation in a righteous cause."[34] Invoking patriotic images of the colonial past, the president declared:

> You who will enter this peacetime army will be the inheritors of a proud history and an honorable tradition. You will be members of an army which first came together to achieve independence and to establish certain fundamental rights for all men. Ever since that first muster, our democratic army has existed for one purpose only: the defense of our freedom.[35]

On November 1, 1.2 million new recruits and 800,000 reservists reported for duty. Under Roosevelt's persuasive guidance, the United States, in spite of its official neutrality, was increasingly assuming the guise of a country primed for war. Roosevelt's victory in the November presidential election was a strong indication that the majority of Americans understood "the dangers of [his] policy," and accepted them.[36]

Lend-Lease

By the fall of 1940, the war situation had considerably worsened for those opposing Hitler. France had been overrun and ignominiously occupied, while England was engaged in a life-and-death struggle with the German Luftwaffe for command of her skies. British citizens in many large cities were experiencing nightly bombing attacks that proved very costly both in human life and materiel. On "Eagle Day," August 12, the Germans flew 1,786 sorties against various targets in Britain. On August 17, a total blockade of Britain was declared and many contingents of the Home Fleet were driven from the Channel. From September 7 to November 13, the Luftwaffe sent an average of 300 to 600 bombers (dropping 100 tons of high explosives) over London daily. At any moment, the Germans were expected to spring across the English Channel in an all-out effort to conquer England.

Britain was in desperate straits, and Winston Churchill informed President Roosevelt that in order to prevent his country from succumbing to German pressure, a dramatic increase in the quantity of material aid was immediately required. Unfortunately for the prime minister, the supply of British dollar credits and gold reserves had been seriously depleted, and present resources were not expected to last more than a few months.[37] While Roosevelt recognized that some expedient would have to be found to keep America's "first line of defense" in England operating, he knew that he would have to act carefully because American public opinion would not support a complete repeal of the Neutrality Act. The Johnson Debt-Default Act of 1934, which forbade loans to belligerents and restricted trade except on a cash basis, meant that Britain lacked the means to purchase American weapons.

In September 1940, Roosevelt formulated an unusual plan. He arranged to trade Britain fifty World War I–era destroyers for 99-year rights to air and naval bases in Newfoundland, British Guiana, Bermuda, and the Caribbean. The British urgently needed these vessels in their convoy escort service. FDR made a bold gamble when he completely bypassed Congress and authorized this transfer by executive order. The president felt that he had public sentiment behind him because he had carefully tested the waters beforehand and found it was favorable to such a move. One such way this had been accomplished was by allowing his secretary Marvin McIntyre to appear on a radio forum show and make the topic under discussion a theoretical situation in which the United States "swapped some old U.S. destroyers for certain British bases."[38] The favorable mail reaction to this particular program seemed to give solid assurance to the president that he "could proceed to negotiate such an exchange."[39]

While the "Destroyers for Bases" deal was successful, it proved to be only a temporary expedient. Given the poor state of Britain's defenses, and the meagerness of its monetary reserves, a "more considerable and enduring solution had to be found." Roosevelt discovered it in the form of the "Lend-Lease" plan. Once adopted, the United States could "produce implements of war and 'lend' them in massive amounts to the British," who would compensate the American government after the war.[40] This was an ideal way of circumventing the various obstacles inherent in the neutrality laws. But before it could become effective, Roosevelt would first have to sell this policy to a public that was still heavily isolationist.

On December 17, the president officially introduced Lend-Lease in a radio-press conference. In it he employed a vivid metaphor to rationalize the plan in the minds of his listeners.

> Suppose my neighbor's house catches fire and I have got a length of gar-
> den hose.... You would not haggle about wanting fifteen dollars for the
> hose. You would tell your neighbor to take the hose and put out the flames
> and give the hose back later.[41]

Roosevelt's message was given wide currency on the week's radio news programs. "As complicated and grandiose a scheme as Lend-Lease turned out to be," Sam Rosenman recalled, "it could never have been more simply or effectively placed before the American people."[42]

In order to drive the point home, and sustain public opinion for the Lend-Lease bill when it would be formally submitted to Congress at the end of the month, FDR delivered a fireside chat on the subject. In his famous "Arsenal of Democracy" broadcast of December 29, the president endeavored to persuade listeners of the vital necessity of granting him the broad discretionary power to "sell, transfer, title, exchange, lease, lend, or otherwise dispose of" articles of war to any nation deemed central to American security. He would accomplish this by "showing how serious the danger was to the United States" and "how disastrous it would be for us if Britain were to fall."[43]

The main device FDR employed to bring Americans to this realization was playing upon their feelings of vulnerability. According to Halford Ryan, the December 29 chat was "laced with fear appeals."[44] The president commenced his speech with a stark warning:

> Never before since Jamestown and Plymouth Rock has our American civ-
> ilization been in such danger as now.... The Nazi masters of Germany
> have made it clear that they intend not only to dominate all life and
> thought in their own country, but also to enslave the whole of Europe,
> and then to use the resources of Europe to dominate the rest of the world.[45]

He then went on to describe how only the stalwart resistance of Britain had kept the Germans from our shores:

> Does anyone seriously believe that we need to fear an attack anywhere in
> the Americas while a free Britain remains our most powerful naval neigh-
> bor in the Atlantic?... If Britain goes down, the Axis powers will control
> the continents of Europe, Asia, Africa, Australia, and the High Seas—and
> they will be in a position to bring enormous military and naval resources
> against this hemisphere.

Using powerful images of American helplessness, Roosevelt explained that if Britain was not prevented from falling, "it is no exaggeration to say that all of us in all the Americas will be living at the point of a gun, a gun loaded with explosive bullets."

Roosevelt then drew attention to the fact that the oceans could not protect the United States if Britain capitulated. He pointed out the frightening reality that the distance from Africa to Brazil was less than that from Washington to Denver. As a result, many targets on the East Coast would be only five hours' striking distance from the latest bombers. According to the president, if the Axis gained bases in the Western Hemisphere, practically any American city could be easily attacked. The Germans had justified the occupation of Belgium to save it from Britain; "would the Germans hesitate to say to some South American city, 'We are occupying you to protect you from aggression by the U.S.?'" Certainly, FDR warned, the vast resources and wealth of the Americas "constitute the most tempting loot in all the round world."

The second device FDR employed to gain public acceptance of his proposal to aid Britain was to discredit the prominent isolationists who branded it as an act of war. Ridiculing those who advocated nonintervention, Roosevelt quoted a telegram that begged, "Please, Mr. President, don't frighten us by telling us the truth." He explained that the danger abroad must be faced and "cannot be escaped ... by crawling into bed and pulling the covers over our heads." To those who believed that Lend-Lease would push America nearer to actual war, Roosevelt replied:

> There is far less chance of the U.S. getting into war if we can do all we can now to support the nations defending themselves against attack by the Axis than if we acquiesce in their defeat, submit tamely to an Axis victory, and wait our turn to be the object of attack in another war later on.

According to the president, America was only being asked to pay a small price for her security. The people of Britain were not asking the United States to do their fighting; they were asking for the implements of war, "the planes, the tanks, the guns, the freighters, which will enable them to fight for their liberty and for our security." Roosevelt exhorted his countrymen to get these weapons to them, "in sufficient volume and quickly enough so that our children will be saved the agony and suffering of war which others have had to endure." The struggle against world conquest would be greatly aided by all manner of munitions and supplies that the United States could send to those on the front lines. In short, FDR proclaimed, America "must be the great arsenal of democracy," for the nation was involved in an "emergency as grave as war itself."[46]

Many listeners were impressed with the "forceful brilliance" of Roosevelt's Lend-Lease broadcast. Over 50 million Americans, or 59 percent of all United States radio homes, had tuned in to hear the president speak.[47] The successful manner in which he explained his proposal to the country "with simplicity and in a way that would capture its imagination—and obtain its approval" was revealed in numerous public opinion polls.[48] One such survey, conducted immediately after the broadcast, found that of those who had heard the address, 68 percent had agreed with FDR, while only 28 percent registered disapproval.[49] It was clear that as a result of Roosevelt's "skillful persuasion," public sentiment was now moving overwhelmingly towards support of Great Britain. Of those polled, 79 percent said England should not accept a favorable peace with Germany, but should keep on fighting until the Axis had been soundly defeated.[50] Before the speech, of those asked whether the United States should aid France and Britain, short of war, only 50 percent had responded in the affirmative. Immediately after the chat, this figure increased to 70 percent.[51] One typical expression of public feeling stated, "I am in complete agreement with you [FDR], and I, too am convinced that, if England is defeated, we will be left to fight alone. Let us, before it is too late, give all-out aid to Great Britain."[52]

With hundreds of thousands of such statements of approval, most congressmen had little trouble making up their minds. On February 8, 1941, the Lend-Lease Act was passed 250–165 in the House, and on March 9, 60–31 in the Senate.[53] Accompanying the bill was a $7 billion appropriations amendment to implement it.*

With the enactment of Lend-Lease, "any pretense of American neutrality effectively disappeared." The United States had not only chosen sides in the conflict raging in Europe, "but through its own declaration was now actively committed to seeing Great Britain prevail over its enemies." With the vast assistance that the United States would contribute to Britain's war effort, the "Germans now had a *casus belli* that could justify a declaration of war on America." While the United States was "not personally engaged in battle, by this bold move, she was, by proxy, at war with Germany."[54]

Unlimited National Emergency

The first five months of 1941 saw America edge even closer to open conflict with Germany. During this time, the Nazi war machine became engaged in Yugoslavia, Greece, Crete, and North Africa. In February, American and British commanders met in Washington (the ABC Conference) to discuss joint strategy in case America was next on Hitler's list. At the same time, German submarines were sinking American vessels with alarming frequency in the Atlantic. From January to May, almost 2 million tons of American and Allied merchant shipping, along with inestimable quantities of beef, butter, wheat, rubber, oil and military equipment needed in Britain, were sent

*By the end of the war, total Lend-Lease expenditures reached $50 billion ($30 billion of it went to Britain alone). Over 38 countries ultimately became eligible for some type of aid. As a precursor to the foreign assistance programs of the post–World War II era, Lend-Lease was another of FDR's most enduring creations.

to the bottom by U-boat wolfpacks and surface raiders. Since the new construction of Anglo-American commerce vessels was averaging less than 175,000 tons a month, the rate of sinkings far surpassed any effort at replacement. Meanwhile, U-boat production exceeded 200, and total losses since the onset of war had been only 50.*

Because of Axis interdiction of Lend-Lease supplies, the British government had to impose a program of food rationing that provided for no more than a minimum level of subsistence. FDR recognized that Britain's survival depended upon maintaining an uninterrupted flow of American foodstuffs and war materials through its Atlantic lifeline. In early May, the president proclaimed that a state of "unlimited national emergency" existed, requiring the immediate strengthening of American defenses on the high seas. Roosevelt extended the neutrality zone around the United States to the mid–Atlantic, and prohibited U-boats from entering there. Next, he ordered an American air and sea patrol to seek out interlopers and radio their positions to British warships operating in the area.[55]

On May 27, 1941, FDR used a fireside chat to explain to listeners the "facts that made necessary the declaration of unlimited emergency," and to justify the measures he had taken "to ensure that American-made supplies reached the battlelines of Britain." Public safety, he insisted, was dependent "upon these drastic steps—even though they might increase the danger of our becoming [directly] involved in the war."[56] As some indication of the importance Roosevelt attached to this speech, it was the only fireside chat to which a formal audience was invited. Crowding around the broadcast table in the majestic East Room of the White House were the diplomatic representatives of Canada and the South American republics, and an array of cabinet members and other high officials.

Roosevelt opened his address by describing what American life would be like in a Nazi-dominated world.

> They plan to strangle the United States of America and the Dominion of Canada. The American laborer would have to compete with slave labor in the rest of the world. Minimum wages, maximum hours? Nonsense! Wages and hours fixed by Hitler. The dignity and power and standard of living of the American worker and farmer would be gone. Trade unions would become historical relics, and collective bargaining a joke…. The whole fabric of working life as we know it—business and manufacturing, mining and agriculture—all would be mangled and crippled in such a system…. Even our right to worship would be threatened. The Nazi world does not recognize any God except Hitler….[57]

He told listeners that the key to preventing such a terrible scenario would be to deny Germany domination of the seas. Once the Nazis obtained absolute

---

*In his six-volume history of the Second World War, Churchill confessed: "The only thing that really frightened me during the war was the U-boat peril."

control of the Atlantic, nothing would stop them from establishing bases in Greenland, Iceland or the Azores, from which they could launch an attack on the United States. In a gesture that implied a firmer American policy, Roosevelt stated that although he did not know when the Axis would attack the Western Hemisphere,

> it would be suicide to wait until they are in our front yard. When your enemy comes at you in a tank or a bombing plane, if you hold your fire until you see the whites of his eyes, you will never know what hit you.... Our Bunker Hill of tomorrow may be several thousand miles from Boston.

Moving from words to action, he declared, "We shall actively resist wherever necessary, and with all our resources, every attempt by Hitler to extend his Nazi domination to the Western Hemisphere or threaten it." Even at the risk of war, the United States would "not hesitate to use [its] armed forces to repel such an attack." To the nearly 66 million Americans (an unprecedented 70 percent of all United States radio homes), and countless foreigners* who tuned in to this broadcast, this sounded like a "summons to war."[58]

Numerous polls indicated a striking transformation in public opinion before and after the president's speech. From the evidence, it was clear that most Americans believed their country should assume a more active role in the war against Hitler. On May 8, 52 percent of Americans surveyed felt that the United States should not carry war materiel to England† in American vessels. This figure had fallen to 38 percent by June 9.[59] While 80 percent of those polled on May 22 believed that the United States should stay out of a war against Germany and Italy, on June 2, 62 percent preferred that America enter the fighting rather than see Britain forced to surrender to the Axis.[60] Overall, Steve Early found that nine out of ten Americans strongly approved of the president's speech.[61] One listener expressed the sentiment of many when he wrote FDR: "You have made a brave and wise move, and I will support you in every way I can."[62]

The Greer Incident

The strong vote of popular approval Roosevelt secured with his May 27 address emboldened him to move further down the road to open belligerency with Germany. In response to the Nazi invasion of the Soviet Union in June, the president ordered the freezing of all German financial assets in the United States. To deny Hitler any strategic outposts in the Arctic, FDR arranged in

---

*NBC shortwaved the president's speech to South America, Europe, and Australia (Broadcasting, June 2, 1941, p. 47).

†The majority of Americans were unaware that at the very time FDR was delivering his speech, Erich Raeder, chief of staff of the German navy, was also addressing the issue of freedom of the seas. He considered America's action "most unneutral," and warned the president that American convoys to Britain would constitute an act of war (Time, June 2, 1941, p. 6).

July for Greenland and Iceland to be brought into "our sphere of cooperative defense" and established American garrisons there. The dispatch of United States Marines to Iceland allowed the British divisions stationed there to join Field Marshal Claude Auchinleck's forces opposing Rommel in North Africa. During the Placentia Bay meeting with Churchill in August, Roosevelt covertly commanded American warships to begin escorting Lend-Lease convoys as far as Reykjavik. If any Axis submarines interfered with these missions, the navy was instructed to sink them. Since this violated all of America's neutrality laws, and created a situation of undeclared war on the high seas, Roosevelt needed an incident upon which he could "pin an appeal to the American public" for support.[63] This need for an excuse was particularly acute since FDR had given his naval orders without first consulting Congress. On September 4, 1941, an incident in the Atlantic involving the American vessel *Greer* provided Roosevelt with exactly the pretext he needed.

The old American World War I–era destroyer was completing a routine mail run a few hundred miles west of the Iceland when a British reconnaissance plane notified it that a German submarine was in the area. The *Greer* tracked the underwater craft and relayed its position to a British bomber, which dropped depth charges on it. The U-boat retaliated by firing torpedoes at the *Greer*, which countered by dropping eight depth charges of its own. The German torpedoes failed to hit their target, and the *Greer* proceeded with its mission.[64]

When he went on the air in his September 11 fireside chat, Roosevelt sought to use this affair to his advantage. By cleverly manipulating certain aspects of the story, he presented a distorted picture of events to the American public, so as to arouse their "sense of patriotism and feelings of indignation."[65] FDR neglected to inform his listeners that the American ship had provoked the sub into firing upon it. What he did tell them was that the *Greer* was clearly distinguished as an American vessel, and despite this fact, the "Germans initiated two unwarranted torpedo attacks on her." Despite what the isolationists might say, Roosevelt declared, "the German sub fired first upon this American destroyer without warning and with deliberate design to sink her."[66] The president went on to describe three other American vessels that had been sunk by the German "pirates"—the *Robin Moor, Sesa,* and *Steel Seafarer*—without offering any details of the incidents. These "were not isolated occurrences," he continued, but part of a conscious "Nazi design to abolish freedom of the seas and acquire absolute control and domination over the seas themselves." Once this had been accomplished, the way would be clear for their next step, the "domination of the United States ... by force of arms." For the incredulous, FDR pointed to recent Nazi attempts to seize control of the governments of Uruguay, Argentina, Bolivia, and Colombia.

Adopting a more warlike tone, Roosevelt declared that Germany's unrestricted submarine warfare created a situation where "normal practices of diplomacy ... are of no possible use in dealing with international outlaws who sink our ships and kill our citizens." The president reassured his listeners that the United States government desired no shooting war with Germany, but "neither do we want peace so much that we are willing to pay for it by permitting [Hitler] to attack our naval and merchant ships while they are on legitimate business." Employing another colorful metaphor to underscore his argument, the President said:

> When you see a rattlesnake poised to strike, you do not wait until he has struck before you crush him. These Nazi subs and raiders are the rattlesnakes of the Atlantic.... Their very presence in any waters which America deems vital to its defense constitutes an attack.

Proclaiming that "the time for action is now!" Roosevelt then informed the people of the measures he had taken "to ensure American security and freedom of the seas." In so doing, the president swept away any last "vestige of formal American neutrality, and pledged his country to act as a belligerent power in the Battle of the Atlantic."[67]

> In the waters which we deem necessary for our own defense, American naval vessels and American planes will no longer wait until Axis submarines lurking under the water, or Axis raiders on the surface of the sea, strike their deadly blow first.
> Upon our naval and air patrol falls the duty of maintaining the American policy of freedom of the seas—now. That means ... that our patrolling vessels and planes will protect all merchant ships—not only American ships but ships of any flag—engaged in commerce in our defensive waters.... From now on, if German or Italian vessels enter [this area] ... they do so at their own peril.

This broad commitment on Roosevelt's part was almost "certain to precipitate a full-blown war between the United States and Germany." Though the president cited numerous historical examples in which the United States had fought to preserve the freedom of the seas, he could "not conceal the fact that he was placing America on a new collision course with Germany." The issuance of his "Shoot on Sight" directive, as his policy came to be called, ensured that naval clashes would be both "frequent and unavoidable."[68]

Nevertheless, the American people had been convinced that Roosevelt's actions were essential for American defense. Again the White House was inundated with favorable letters. One representative listener commented: "You clearly showed the American people the serious problem facing our country, and told them what you were doing to protect our interests."[69] Once again, public opinion polls mirrored the effectiveness of the speech. A Gallup poll taken shortly after the president's chat indicated that 56 percent of those surveyed approved of the United States having to fire on German submarines. By the end of the month, this figure had climbed to over 62 percent. Largely as the result of Roosevelt's thorough preparation of the public for war, an October 5 poll revealed that 70 percent of Americans felt that it was more important to defeat Germany than to keep the United States out of the war.[70]

Using the mass approval generated by his speech, Roosevelt asked Congress on October 9 to revise the Neutrality Act "to permit the arming of American merchant ships and to remove all restrictions on sending American vessels and cargoes into belligerent ports."[71] American efforts to deliver supplies to the Allies were being severely hampered by the navy's inability to enter combat zones east of Iceland. The extension of this operating area to include the waters around Great Britain and Russia,* the president argued, would in no way increase the risk of war. The October 17 loss of the United States destroyer *Kearney* 350 miles southwest of Iceland had proven that Germany would continue to sink American ships regardless of their location.

In an effort to prod Congress into accepting his recommendations, Roosevelt chose Navy Day (October 27) as the occasion of his next broadcast. The president began his speech by again "impressing upon the American people the great peril which civilization faced if Hitler were to win" the war.[72] He revealed two official German documents, recently come into his possession, that contained graphic evidence of the Führer's ungodly scheme to carve up the world. The first was a map illustrating Nazi plans for the reorganization of Central and South America after they had been conquered and for denying the United States access to the Panama Canal. The second document "was even more startling in its implications."[73] It provided for nothing less than the complete abolition of all existing world religions. "In place of the churches of our civilization," Roosevelt observed, "there is to be set up an International Nazi Church—a church which will be served by orators sent out by the Nazi government." The president again emphasized the vital necessity of supplying Britain and Russia with American war supplies, and stated his intention to "deliver the goods" no matter what.

> In open defense of that will, our ships have been sunk and our sailors have been killed. I say that we do not propose to take this lying down.... Our American merchant ships must be free to carry our American goods into the harbors of our friends.... It can never be doubted that the goods will be delivered by this nation, whose Navy believes in the tradition of "Damn the torpedoes; full speed ahead!"

In the "strongest [foreign policy] speech" he was to deliver before Pearl Harbor, Roosevelt "made a flat declaration that we were [already] in the fight."[74]

> America has been attacked. We have wished to avoid shooting. But the shooting has started. And history has recorded who fired the first shot. In the long run, however, all that will matter is who fired the last shot.... Today in the face of this newest and greatest challenge of them all, we Americans have cleared our decks and taken our battle stations. We stand

*On June 24, the Soviet Union was formally accorded Lend-Lease assistance.

ready in the defense of our nation and in the faith of our fathers to do
what God has given us the power to see as our full duty.

Subsequent events suggested that the president's call for increased protection in the Atlantic had been well-advised. Four days after his Navy Day speech,
on October 31, the American destroyer *Reuben James* was torpedoed by U-552
and the entire crew was killed.[75] Following this tragedy, veterans' organizations
throughout the country declared themselves strongly in favor of FDR's policy.
In a November 11 broadcast by the American Legion, one speaker remarked:

> This is the twenty-third Armistice Day and we are at war in the Atlantic
> Ocean with German submarines. A large part of our fleet is guarding the
> sea lanes to Iceland and convoying merchant ships a part of the way to
> the British Isles. Our destroyers have been fired on ... and American naval
> officers and sailors have been killed in pursuit of their duties. This is not
> a one-sided affair in the North Atlantic. The only reason you have not
> heard of German subs sunk by American depth bombs and gunfire is
> because it is the policy not to announce these sinkings ... so that the Ger-
> man Admiralty will wonder for a time which subs are afloat and which
> are in Davy Jones' locker. It is the fixed policy of the U.S. government to
> supply Great Britain and Russia with the airplanes, guns and other equip-
> ment necessary to defeat Germany.... Let our merchant fleet fight back
> and keep German subs' heads underwater and sail on any waters to deliver
> their cargoes of munitions and food. Wouldn't you like to be present in a
> British port when the first American escorted convoy comes steaming in?
> What a welcome there will be by the sorely-pressed British, who have so
> gallantly defended their island for these two years. The Stars and Stripes
> have once again taken their place beside the Union Jack in a war to defend
> civilization itself.[76]

On November 14, Congress acceded to the president's wishes and repealed
most of the remaining neutrality restrictions.

Thus did Roosevelt score another considerable political victory. Through
his "rhetorical persuasiveness, he was finally able to overcome the last illusion
of neutrality, and make American participation in the crusade against Hitler
a reality." With overt and energetic American assistance, it was now certain
that Britain would not fall and the cause of freedom extinguished. Roosevelt's
success had been largely due to radio. Only through its pervasive influence
could the president "have circumvented congressional authority and presented
the controversial issue of intervention" in a manner that won the resounding
approval of the American public.

It should be emphasized that in the fall of 1941, this approval had not been
earned in an entirely honest fashion. In using fear and distortion to turn a
minor episode on the seas into a major international incident, Roosevelt had
"exploited the trust he had earned from the people during the Depression, and
used it to his advantage in one of the greatest deceptions of all time."[77] According to historian Robert Dallek, FDR's conduct during the *Greer* incident "created

a precedent for the manipulation of public opinion," and a legacy of mistrust "that would be both emulated and abhorred."* Just as Roosevelt's "aural sleight of hand" had helped to get the United States farther into the European War, so did another American president a quarter of a century later consciously mislead the public about a supposed naval attack in order to get the nation involved in yet another conflict. There can be little doubt that Lyndon Johnson had Roosevelt's *Greer* speech in mind when he delivered the Gulf of Tonkin address in 1964. It can be said that by helping to prepare American defenses for an inevitable conflict, FDR's "deviousness was in a good cause"; LBJ, however, would demonstrate that this device could also be used against the best interests of the nation.

Struggle with the Isolationists

In attempting to implement his "preparation short of war" measures, Roosevelt frequently encountered considerable opposition from the nation's isolationists. This well-organized political lobby dedicated itself to keeping America out of another costly world war by adhering to a policy of absolute neutrality. Prominent isolationists included the conservative senators Robert Taft (Ohio) and Arthur Vandenberg (Michigan), who adamantly opposed any "entangling European alliances" that could lead to a "repeat of the 1914–18 bloodbath." The two senators believed that American sovereignty should be unfettered, and American freedom of action always guaranteed. Other members of the "peace bloc" in Congress included liberals like William E. Borah (Idaho), Burton K. Wheeler (Montana), Robert La Follette, Jr. (Wisconsin), Gerald Nye (North Dakota), Arthur Capper (Kansas), and Edwin C. Johnson (Colorado). These men became staunch isolationists because of their belief that the First World War had impeded the progress of much-needed social reforms and violated many of the freedoms Americans were supposed to be defending.

Perhaps the most notable member of the isolationist bloc was its figurehead and main speaker, the aviation hero Charles A. Lindbergh. Lindbergh's pacific sentiments stemmed from an admiration for Germany's growing military and air might, and his belief that Nazism represented Europe's "wave of the future." These views were combined with a strong distaste for the cowering, decadent Anglo-French democracies, and the Allied cause in general. Lindbergh believed that war between the United States and Germany would be disastrous, and hinted that American national interests would be better

*Because of Roosevelt's chicanery during the Greer incident, many members of Congress were incredulous when he reported the Japanese attack on Pearl Harbor a few months later. In the House, one representative who voted against a declaration of war, Jeanette Rankin, warned: "This might be another Roosevelt trick. How do we know Hawaii has been bombed? Remember the Kearney [Greer]!" In the Senate, Gerald Nye remarked: "I can't somehow believe this.... There's been funny things before" (Time, December 15, 1941, p. 19).

served cooperating with Hitler against the Russian menace. Other anti-war luminaries included John T. Flynn, Gen. Hugh S. Johnson, Henry Ford, Eddie Rickenbacker, Mrs. Alice Roosevelt Longworth, and Louis Taber.

The isolationists opposed FDR's attempts to ready the country for a foreign war, particularly his efforts to send aid to Britain at the risk of America's own involvement. As a vehicle for resisting such measures as Cash-and-Carry, Lend-Lease and American convoys to Britain, Lindbergh established the America First Committee (AFC). In contrast to the administration's "Defend America by Aiding the Allies" organization, Lindbergh declared that the government should look after America's own defenses in the Western Hemisphere and not send supplies to Britain that could be used for America's protection.

> Defend America first.... That is the slogan of the America First Committee, which is working tirelessly now to keep America's armaments for herself that we may build strong our own defense. Any aggressor will think twice before striking a prepared nation.[78]

With the clash of isolationist and interventionist opinion, it was natural that the opposing sides would use the most efficient means of communication of the day in an attempt to sway public opinion in their favor. As a result, between 1939 and 1941, radio became a veritable battleground upon which both the Roosevelt administration and its isolationist antagonists hotly debated the pros and cons of America's involvement.

Recognizing early on that the battle for public support would be determined by whichever side was more clever in exploiting the airwaves, the "peace bloc" mustered all of its political strength and mobilized its radio resources on a scale that rivaled the president's. Members like Martin Dies went on the air at the time of the Cash-and-Carry speech to speak out against any revision of the neutrality laws.[79] At the same time, Wheeler, Taft, and Vandenberg conducted an intensive radio campaign that included appearances on many forum and round table programs.[80] During the debate over Lend-Lease, the America First Committee utilized a forty-station network in a series of self-sponsored, fifteen-minute programs that seriously criticized FDR's foreign policy "giveaway."[81] This was the issue against which the isolationists concentrated their main attack. Observing how FDR's exchange had depleted America of vitally needed war materials, Sen. Wheeler remarked:

> We have transferred 5/7 of all combat planes produced in the U.S. in 1940 to England and other countries. We have transferred so many that the American air force does not have a single completely modern plane equipped with ... adequate firepower. We have traded so many destroyers to England ... our naval strength seriously lags behind the Axis.[82]

The America Firsters believed that Britain was trying to maneuver the United States into the war. They cited the increasing tide of shortwave propaganda broadcasts being beamed into the United States from England as unmistakable proof of this conspiracy. Wheeler warned the American people that aid to Britain was another step in FDR's plan to "plow under every fourth American boy."[83] In an early America First broadcast, he denounced the dangerous manner in which the administration was misleading public opinion into approving its interventionist policies. He declared:

> Every agency of mass communication has been and is being utilized to excite the passions and the emotions of the American people. Are we Americans to eternally dedicate ourselves and our children to the preservation of the British Empire?[84]

Despite their criticism, the isolationists proved themselves equally adept at employing strong language and graphic imagery to stir people and manipulate their emotions. In a stark warning against Roosevelt's warmongering, Wheeler declared in one broadcast: "We are so close to war, that on January 30, 1941, the War Department announced that they were seeking bids on 1,500,000 caskets, for your son and for mine."[85]

By far the most effective spokesman for the isolationist cause was Charles Lindbergh. The beloved hero of the 1920s still retained his immense popularity with much of the public. When he spoke over the radio, his voice was carried over all four networks to an audience almost as large as the president's. For his May 23, 1941, speech in Madison Square Garden, over 20,000 people packed the auditorium, and another 10,000 gathered around car radios and portable sets outside.[86] With his "boyish sincerity and vibrant voice, Roosevelt knew he was being formidably challenged in an area of mass communication of which he had long been the master."[87] Lindbergh's message against the repeal of the arms embargo in September 1939 stimulated a flood of letters that poured into congressional offices.[88] While this prompted only one senator to come out against revision, "many others began to waver." Not until FDR delivered his fireside chat on the subject did most of these senators acquiesce to the administration's position.

Lindbergh continued to deliver speeches on "Keeping America Out of the War" until American participation became an accomplished fact at Pearl Harbor.[89] By making his plea directly to the people in his broadcasts, Lindbergh had brought tremendous pressure to bear on Roosevelt by "arousing isolationist sentiment among the public at a time when the President was trying to quell it."[90] If Roosevelt wanted to win the public over to his interventionist position, he would have to play his radio card even more skillfully than his opponents.

Directly from the onset of hostilities in Europe, Roosevelt sought to delegitimize the isolationist cause in his broadcasts. In his arms embargo repeal message to Congress on September 21, 1939, the president disarmed his critics when he stated: "Let no group assume the exclusive label of the 'peace bloc'—

we all belong to it."[91] When the isolationist-dominated Senate Foreign Relations Committee advised against repeal, FDR declared: "I think we ought to introduce a bill for statues of [Senators] Austin, Vandenburg, Lodge and Taft ... to be erected in Berlin and put the swastika on them."[92] This "guilt by association" tactic, which identified noninterventionist activity with treason, was extremely effective. In his December 1940 "Arsenal of Democracy" talk, the president remarked:

> There are some Americans, many of them in high places, who ... are aiding and abetting the work of [enemy] agents. I don't charge these citizens with being foreign agents. But I do charge them with doing exactly the kind of work that the dictators want done in the U.S.[93]

Roosevelt and his aides were "absolutely certain that Lindbergh was a Nazi" and made an enormous effort to convince the public that this was so. In a May 1940 broadcast rebuttal of a Lindbergh speech, secretary of the interior Harold Ickes openly accused the America First chairman of being an Axis sympathizer. Treasury secretary Henry Morgenthau, Jr., remarked that Lindbergh's address could have been "written by Goebbels himself." In his third inaugural address (March 1941), FDR made a disparaging reference to an isolationist work by Anne Morrow Lindbergh, *The Wave of the Future*:

> There are men who believe that democracy, as a form of government and a frame of life, is limited or measured by a kind of mystical and artificial fate—that, for some unexplained reason, tyranny and slavery have become the surging wave of the future—and that freedom is an ebbing tide. But we Americans know this is not true.[94]

In April 1941, administration spokesmen compared Lindbergh to the Copperhead Clement Vallandighan, who criticized government policy in a most unpatriotic way before the Civil War.

Lindbergh's own conduct did nothing to counter FDR's fascistic image of him. In a September 1941 address, his assertion that "the Jews" were the group most eager to push the U.S. into war "dealt the America First Committee and himself a staggering blow."[95]

Discrediting the opposition was not enough. In order to sell his policy of intervention to the public, the president mounted the greatest propaganda campaign the radio industry had ever seen. As in the case of the 1940 and 1944 presidential elections, FDR recruited to his cause the best talent the radio and film worlds had to offer. By conveying his pro-involvement message through the vehicle of the radio drama, Roosevelt assured himself of a sizable listening audience. According to Sherman Dryer: "Factual dramas had the advantage of emotional appeal, something that no amount of talking by one man, no colloquy by two men, no roundtable discussion" could duplicate. When in capable hands, dramatic presentations "could not only inform and clarify, they could also inspire."[96]

Aviation hero Charles A. Lindbergh, a staunch isolationist, drew large audiences for his radio broadcasts condemning Roosevelt's interventionist policies.

In 1940 the National Council for the Prevention of War complained vigorously after one of its pro-peace discussions was immediately followed by "an emotional half-hour dramatization" of the capture of German spies who had been infiltrating the American army. One administration spokesman delightedly observed that this production was "just the kind of thing to increase the tempo of war hysteria, and certainly the kind of programming likely to offset the words of even the most gifted spokesman for isolationism." The administration found this approach particularly effective because most people "did not generally identify entertaining material as propaganda." In addition to this, the "war-related subject matter was easily adapted into popular drama and could be insinuated into the existing storylines of many well-known programs without great difficulty."[97]

In the first seven months of 1940, NBC broadcast over 627 programs that were labeled as "defense-related." Many of these were produced in collaboration with the executive office of the president. Again, FDR's close working relationship with the radio industry yielded important political fruits. Neville Miller, NAB president, remarked:

> A free radio can do, and is doing, no greater patriotic service than to lend generously of its time and facilities to do those things necessary to preserve the freedom of the American people.... The broadcasting industry

is proud to cooperate with the Army, Navy, National Defense Council, and all other proper agencies of government in the furtherance of the national defense program.[98]

In August 1940, all four networks broadcast a special half-hour program in which all seven members of the National Defense Advisory Commission discussed the work of their department and the goals of the administration's preparedness campaign.[99]

Many government propaganda programs were transcribed and distributed to local facilities nationwide for broadcast at all hours of the day. Stations also agreed to air short, interventionist spot announcements. In the first half of 1941 more than 1,000 such messages were transmitted.[100] According to one observer:

> From sun up to midnight, the American listener is peppered with frequent announcements carried free and freely by some 800 stations. He hears professionally-acted network programs. He hears locally-acted programs built from scripts furnished by numerous federal agencies. He tunes in transcriptions of programs provided by government departments.... The dictatorial governments have an able rival in the art of contracting the citizen by air.[101]

The "marriage of interventionist propaganda and entertainment" gave birth to a host of new programs. Such shows as *America Looks Abroad, I Am an American*, and *Speaking of Liberty*, while "not overtly warmongering," nonetheless "surpassed anything that had been aired on radio to that date."[102] Many established shows proved eager to plug the war for the administration as well. Listeners to the extraordinarily popular *Fibber McGee and Molly* or *Eddie Cantor* sitcoms often heard anti–Hitler jokes and commercial pleas for British war relief.[103] One observer noted that "no one listening to the radio in 1940–41 could fail to understand that the nation was embarked upon a great and critically important endeavor involving the participation of millions of their fellow Americans."[104]

The administration spent exorbitant sums producing its programs, hiring the best playwrights, directors, sound effects men, and dramatic actors in Hollywood. Not only did the president produce more hours of programming than his isolationist rivals (20 hours vs. 8 in July 1940), their overall quality could not be matched.[105] In *Defense for America, Treasury Star Benefit, Spirit of '41*, and *America Preferred*, one was treated to the moving performances of such film greats as James Cagney, Irene Dunn, and Humphrey Bogart. In addition to variety and musical numbers, such programs also featured speeches by government officials and notable figures like Sgt. Alvin York (a World War I hero) and scientist Marie Curie, "appeals for defense bonds, and reports on trends in war production."[106] Other dramatic offerings, such as *America Marches On, The Free Company, Our America, Lest We Forget, America Calling, Americans All, Immigrants All* and *American Challenge*, were intended to "unify listeners" and "offset repulsive foreign ideologies" by "praising the achievements of past patriots and instilling a deep sense of appreciation in the American way."[107]

No doubt the most remarkable example of this type of pro-administration production was the four-network broadcast of December 15, 1941, *We Hold These Truths*. This special hour-long program commemorating the 150th anniversary of the Bill of Rights was produced by the Office of Facts and Figures and written by Norman Corwin. It featured Lionel Barrymore, Edward Arnold, Walter Brennan, Walter Huston, James Stewart, Orson Welles and Rudy Vallee. Bernard Herrmann composed the musical score, and dramatic sequences originated from New York, Hollywood and Washington. The program concluded with an address by FDR and a rousing rendition of the national anthem played by the New York Philharmonic Orchestra under the baton of Leopold Stokowski.[108] The Crossly service estimated the listening audience to have been over 60 million.[109]

Some programs were produced on behalf of one specific policy or piece of legislation. To gain mass approval for his Cash-and-Carry initiative, FDR commissioned such informational novelties as *Uncle Sam Makes and the World Takes*, *Yankee Ships and Yankee Trade* and *U.S. Foreign Trade Comes of Age*.[110] To promote his policy of "hemispheric unity," Roosevelt engaged Orson Welles in a fifteen-part series that focused on the cultural and linguistic heritage of *The Other Americas*.[111]

Many of the programs were blatantly pro–British. In popular variety shows like the *White Cliffs of Dover* and *Bundles for Britain*, listeners heard appeals from Basil Rathbone, Cedric Hardwicke, Lynn Fontaine and Ronald Colman, on behalf of the British-American War Relief Agency.[112] On *Friendship Brigade* and *Hospital on the Thames*, Americans learned of the exploits of ambulance drivers, nurses and other medical personnel on the frontlines in Britain's bomb-torn cities. *England Expects* chronicled the daring activities of Nelson and other British military heros.[113] In *Young America Wants to Help*, Mickey Rooney, Judy Garland, and other American adolescents offered moral encouragement to their young counterparts in Britain.[114] Alexander Woolcott's *Town Crier* program regularly made space between critiques of new books to report on conditions in England,[115] and one session of the quiz show *Information Please* had its regular panelists—Franklin P. Adams, John Kiernan and Oscar Levant—in London answering questions from the studios of the British Broadcasting Corporation (BBC).[116]

In the fall of 1939, the United States networks ceased rebroadcasting foreign shortwave programs, citing the "adverse effect repeating foreign propaganda in this country might have on American neutrality." While transmissions originating in Germany and Italy were the first to go under this new policy, British broadcasts were unaffected.[117] In July 1940, listeners with world bands on their sets began tuning in to J. P. Priestly's "talks to the American people" on *Britain Speaks*. The setting for this program was often a "bombproof shelter somewhere in England." More than 33 American stations regularly carried BBC newscasts, in addition to those broadcast nightly over Mutual.[118]

As early as May 1939, some American observers began to criticize the unhindered ease with which prominent Englishmen could "disseminate their propaganda over U.S. airwaves."[119] Commenting upon the compassionate bond that had been formed between American listeners and British broadcasters, one citizen remarked:

> Last September, emphasis was placed on the maintenance of our own neutrality, and every word and move [was] weighed in the light of whether it could give "aid and comfort" to any belligerent. Today, there can be no doubt as to the sympathies of the United States.[120]

The networks also staged elaborate productions in support of other anti–Axis combatants. Prominent among these efforts were a ninety-minute extravaganza for Greek War Relief featuring Ronald Colman and Clark Gable and a 1941 fund-raiser for Nationalist China.[121]

While many Americans were able to separate fact and fiction in the propaganda dramas, most could not apply this same critical sense to the many news programs that purported to report with complete objectivity, but were "firmly and consistently in support of Roosevelt to the exclusion of any other point of view."[122] In his book *The News and How to Understand It*, commentator Quincy Howe made no effort to conceal the fact that he and many of his colleagues were "benevolently disposed toward the administration and strongly anti-isolationist."[123] In October 1939, *Broadcasting* observed:

> Many biased newscasters, through inflections of the human voice, are reading meaning into their own reports. If favorable to the Allies, as most of them are, they read Berlin dispatches with an "Oh yeah" tone that belies their personal viewpoints.[124]

CBS reporter Eric Sevareid noted how he developed a reputation as a "prejudiced propagandist":

> Every journalist, since time and space are limited, must select the facts he will present, the quotations he will emphasize. He is not a machine, and does not work in a vacuum.... I was supposed to be doing an "objective" job of reporting the crisis ... in the Capitol.* No matter how much I tried to be objective, I would never be neutral in my mind, and neutrality is a different thing.... Almost every broadcast, no matter how cautious, brought some manner of protest from an angry Congressman or a worried radio station director somewhere on the network.... I was denounced by many isolationists....[125]

In his analysis of the six most influential commentators, David Culbert found that four of them were "conscious and reliable agents" of the government

---

The February–March 1941 congressional debate over Lend-Lease.

who volunteered for the role of disseminating official propaganda.[126] Others, like Walter Winchell, worked out an agreement by which, in exchange for scoops, they would put their airtime at Roosevelt's disposal, "to develop any angle of foreign affairs the administration deemed worthwhile."[127] So biased were Winchell and H.R. Baukhage in FDR's favor that several stations refused to carry them until "programs with countervailing points of view" were offered.[128]

Much to the president's delight, commentators were eager to point out the frequent contradictions in statements made by American Firsters. For example, Senator Edwin Johnson condemned Lend-Lease in one broadcast and then admitted, "Of course it is to our advantage for England to win" on another.[129] Whenever a public official criticized the isolationists, newscasters were certain to pick up on it and report it widely. They also regularly compared the statements of the AFC to the pseudo–Nazi German-American Bund whenever the latter took to the air.[130]

Commentators considerably aided the president's preparedness campaign. In the summer of 1941, John B. Hughes regularly set aside large blocks of time on his *News and Views* program to present "on-the-scene defense reports" from the Lockheed aircraft plant in Burbank, California, and other centers of war production in Detroit, Portland, San Francisco and elsewhere.[131] During the same period, Fulton Lewis, Jr.—who began his broadcasting career as an ardent New Deal opponent, but strongly supported FDR's rearmament efforts after 1939—originated so many broadcasts from shipyards and munitions factories, and featured so many interviews with military officials, that he temporarily changed the title of his program to *Your Defense Reporter*.[132] Both men gave comprehensive coverage to all of Roosevelt's speeches promoting increased war production, including his September 27, 1941, full-network broadcast on the launching of the liberty ship *Patrick Henry* in Portland,[133] and his November 6, 1941, address to the International Labor Conference.[134]

Because of radio's influence in American society, FDR felt that "criticism from this medium was much more damaging than similar remarks in printed form." The few commentators, like Upton Close and Boake Carter, who proved hostile to the president and his international policies were either forced to change their ways or thrust from the air.* While Close's audience was relatively negligible,† Carter was heard on "85 stations, five days a week at prime time." In August 1938, the administration lobbied hard to get Carter removed from CBS. With his departure, there remained no popular commentator who

*A February 14, 1939, article in Look *magazine entitled: "Do You Want Radio Censorship?" displayed a picture of Boake Carter, Alexander Woolcott and other administration detractors, with the caption: "The FCC kicked them off the air."*

†*Close's newscasts were heard only once a week (Sundays on NBC), and his Hooper rating never rose above 6.3 compared to Kaltenborn & Winchell's 25, Davis's 24.5, and Lowell Thomas's 19 (Fang, p. 126).*

opposed the president's foreign policy objectives. Culbert has argued that "Carter's fate ... deterred others considering presenting the news from an isolationist perspective," and it deprived the movement "of an important source and symbol of legitimacy."[135] One newscaster observed, "It proved impossible to discuss what was happening to Great Britain after 1939 without letting one's information or analysis betray what America's foreign policy should be."[136] Despite the industry's "fairness doctrine," which promised equal airtime to those with conflicting political notions, the networks refused access to isolationists and "secretly conspired with the administration to allow Roosevelt to dominate the airwaves."[137] Countless stations, such as KYW and WCAU in Philadelphia, routinely disallowed requests by Lindbergh and the AFC to purchase airtime. In August 1940, Rep. Martin Dies, chairman of the House Un-American Activities Investigating Committee and a strong opponent of internationalism, was cut off in mid-speech while delivering an address over a thirty-station Mutual hookup.[138] In December 1944, Upton Close's persistent criticism of FDR's wartime leadership compelled NBC to replace him with the far more amenable AP correspondent Max Hill.[139]

Even some esteemed forum programs were occasionally "distorted by biased, prowar interlocutors." In frustration, isolationist spokesman Norman Thomas complained:

> We are dealing with a situation on the radio in which practically all commentators are on one side, in which people who talk on public affairs or sponsored programs are almost always, without exception, interventionists.[140]

Indeed, the radio industry "greatly aided Roosevelt's campaign to create a popular majority favorable to full scale intervention in Europe."[141] The extent of this sympathy for the president's foreign policy is suggested by the accusation of America First member John T. Flynn. In October 1941 he declared:

> When this country is plunged into war, the heaviest and darkest stain of guilt will rest on the hands of the radio companies, whose chiefs are interventionists and who have gone all out on the air to entangle this country in Europe's war.[142]

By the fall of 1941 Roosevelt's clever exploitation of radio had enabled interventionism to win the battle for America's ear. A few months later, his efforts would no longer be needed, for events in the Pacific had ensured that public sentiment would soon be turned overwhelmingly in favor of war.

War with Japan

The period that saw the deterioration of United States–German relations also witnessed a growing diplomatic crisis with Japan. In July 1937, the

Japanese Kwantung Army commenced a full-scale invasion of mainland China. Within a year, much of the coast had been occupied, the Chinese Nationalist government had twice been compelled to relocate its capital, and the Japanese air force had begun a ruthless and indiscriminate bombing campaign against civilian population centers. In 1940 Premier Konoye and his war minister Hideki Tojo began extending Japan's Far Eastern empire to the resource-rich areas of Indochina.

As the colonial powers were too fully committed in Europe to offer anything in the way of resistance, the United States was the only nation in a position to check this relentless advance. With strong strategic and economic ties to the western Pacific and east Asia, and a long tradition of missionary activity in China, America responded negatively to Japan's aggression. The tension in American-Japanese relations was exacerbated by the 1937 sinking of the United States gunboat *Panay* on the Yangtze River, the bombing of the international settlement in Shanghai, and the conclusion of the Tripartite Pact with Germany and Italy in 1940.

In order to get Japan to comply with his demand for the immediate evacuation of its newly acquired territories, Roosevelt imposed a series of economic sanctions. These included cancellation of the 1911 trade treaty; a ban on the export of scrap iron, steel and aviation gasoline; a freeze on all Japanese financial assets; and a complete embargo on oil. Because her economy and war machine were almost completely dependent on American imports, Japan responded by trying to negotiate "an empire-wide modus vivendi" throughout the late summer and fall of 1941.[143] When all attempts at compromise failed, diplomatic ties ceased. On December 7, 1941, the Japanese military launched a devastating surprise raid on the American naval base at Pearl Harbor. The United States was now officially at war.

On December 8, President Roosevelt went before Congress and requested a declaration of war against Japan. As millions of Americans tuned in at home, the president sought to convey the seriousness of the situation and prepare the nation for the taxing job that lay ahead. He opened his broadcast speech with the now-famous words, "Yesterday, December 7, 1941—a date which will live in infamy—the United States of America was suddenly and deliberately attacked by naval and air forces of the empire of Japan."[144]

Due to a delay in the transmission of the text of Japan's declaration of war from Tokyo to its Washington embassy, its contents were not formally delivered to the United States State Department until a half-hour *after* the opening of hostilities. After having framed his beginning remarks to underscore such "Japanese perfidy," FDR contrasted this with the "purity of American motives."[145]

> The United States was at peace with that nation and ... looking forward to the maintenance of peace in the Pacific. One hour after the attack the Japanese ambassador to the U.S. delivered to the Secretary of State a

formal reply ceasing diplomatic negotiations but containing no hint of war
or armed attack.

Next, the president further highlighted Japanese deceit.

> It will be recorded that the distance of Hawaii from Japan makes it obvi-
> ous that the attack was deliberately planned many days or even weeks in
> advance. During the intervening time, the Japanese Government has
> deliberately sought to deceive the United States by false statements and
> expressions of hope for continued peace.

To arouse within the American people a profound sense of moral indignation, Roosevelt related the details of the attack with "heavy voice" and in
the "blackest manner."[146]

> The attack yesterday on the Hawaiian Islands has caused severe damage
> to American naval and military forces. I regret to tell you that very many
> American lives have been lost. In addition, American ships have been
> reported torpedoed on the high seas between San Francisco and Hono-
> lulu…. Last night Japan attacked … Malaya, Hong Kong, Guam, the
> Philippine Islands, Wake Island…. This morning—Midway Island.

The president then presented an optimistic declaration of the nation's
resolve to shoulder the challenge that had been thrust upon it, and see it
through.

> As Commander-in-Chief of the American Army and Navy, I have directed
> that all measures be taken for our defense. But always will our whole
> nation remember the character of the onslaught against us. No matter how
> long it will take us to overcome this premeditated invasion, the American
> people in their righteous might will win through to absolute victory.

With a "rising cadence" the president proclaimed:

> With confidence in our armed forces, with the unbounding determina-
> tion of our people, we will gain the inevitable triumph—so help us God.
> I ask the Congress declare that since the unprovoked and dastardly attack
> by Japan … a state of war has existed between the United States and the
> Japanese Empire.

Roosevelt "concluded his speech to the thunderous ovation of an inspired citizenry."[147] The president had spoken for only six minutes. While secretary of state
Cordell Hull had recommended that he deliver a full account of Japanese-
American relations and America's persistent attempts to find a peaceful solution, Roosevelt knew that his message would be more dramatic if it was kept
short. Thirty-three minutes after he finished speaking, Congress declared war
on Japan. The "Day of Infamy" speech attracted the largest audience in radio
history, with over 81 percent of all American homes tuning in to seek guidance
from the president, "now turned Commander-in-Chief."[148]

Due to the unprecedented nature of the situation that now confronted the nation, and the relative brevity of his congressional address, Roosevelt deemed it necessary to address the American people again the next evening. In his fireside chat of December 9, 1941, the president "reviewed the long record of Axis aggression" and went to enormous lengths to "prepare the country for the bad news" that was filtering in from American outposts all over the globe.[149] In the process, Roosevelt projected the image of the sympathetic leader. "I deeply feel the anxiety of all the families of the men in our armed forces and the relatives of the people in the cities which have been bombed."[150] He regretfully acknowledged that the public would have to learn to accept such losses: "It will not only be a long war, it will be a hard war." Clearly modeling his words on Churchill's "Blood, Toil, Tears and Sweat" speech of the previous year, FDR informed his listeners that there would be demands for even greater sacrifices in the months to come: higher taxes, keener shortages, longer and more rigorous work, and hazardous military service. But, he continued, "the U.S. does not consider it a sacrifice to do all one can, to give one's best to our nation, when the nation is fighting for its existence and its future life." Roosevelt warned of the danger of rumor-mongering, and called for a major increase in the nation's volume of war production. Drawing his chat to an end, Roosevelt declared that the United States would exert all of its effort "to make very certain that this form of treachery shall never endanger us again." He concluded with stirring remarks on the American people's moral fiber: "We don't like it, we didn't want to get in it—but we are in it and we are going to fight it with everything we've got."

There can be little doubt that Roosevelt's two Pearl Harbor speeches had their desired effect of unifying the nation and strengthening its resolve. Sam Rosenman described the scene in the Capitol:

> It was a most dramatic spectacle there in the chamber of the House of Representatives. On most of the President's personal appearances before Congress, we found applause coming largely from one side—the Democratic side. But this day was different. The applause, the spirit of cooperation, came equally from both sides.... The new feeling of unity which suddenly welled up in the chamber on December 8, the common purpose behind the leadership of the President, the joint determination to see things through, were typical of what was taking place throughout the country.[151]

Telegrams poured into the White House in unusually "large batches."[152] One listener wrote to FDR: "On that Sunday we were dismayed and frightened, but your unbounded courage pulled us together."[153] On December 9, recruiting stations were jammed and had to go on twenty-four-hour duty. New York City reported twice as many volunteers as it had received in 1917. *Time* observed:

> To a greater extent than at any other time since he first took command during the choking depression eight years ago, the President could [now]

act with complete authority, and with perfect assurance that the country was solidly behind him.[154]

Even the administration's bitterest and most persistent critics now fell into line. One listener wrote: "I have always been a Republican and have opposed your policies ... but now I realize that you have been right in your analysis of the situation ever since Hitler began overrunning the various European states"[155] Charles Lindbergh declared:

> We have been stepping closer to war for many months. Now it has come and we must meet it as united Americans regardless of our attitude in the past toward the policy our Government has followed.... Our country has been attacked by force of arms, and by force of arms we must retaliate. We must now turn every effort to building the greatest and most efficient Army, Navy and air force in the world.[156]

Foreign Policy Success

From 1937 to 1941, the United States was confronted with a serious challenge to its security by the aggressiveness of the Axis powers. In his fireside chats, Roosevelt succeeded in alerting the American people to "the dangers that threatened from beyond the seas" and prepared them for a war that seemed destined to engulf them.[157] CBS correspondent Eric Sevareid observed:

> We were in a race; it was the rate of America's growing understanding versus the rate of the Fascist's physical advance.... Was the President to withhold action ... and so risk arriving too late, when the few remaining bastions of the shrinking world would already lie in enemy hands?... Roosevelt knew that he must act, and that only in the test of action would the people rally and this democracy become more than a debating society in a world of violent action.[158]

As the president prudently adapted his foreign policy to meet the mounting threats from Asia and Europe, and the position of the United States changed from strict neutrality to sympathy and aid to the democracies and finally to active belligerency, Roosevelt acted with the "overwhelming might of public opinion behind him." By using radio to present his interventionist message simply, directly and compellingly to the whole of America, Roosevelt was able to overcome isolationist opposition and congressional reluctance, and secure the implementation of a host of highly controversial measures: Cash-and-Carry, Lend-Lease, Destroyers for Bases, a "shoot on sight" directive, and economic sanctions. Hadley Cantril has established a direct link between FDR's broadcasts and the creation of a favorable body of public opinion. After "one or more speeches had been given" on a particular topic, polls indicated that popular support was strong. Conversely, when no speeches were delivered for an extended period of time, surveys revealed a shift against Roosevelt's position."[159]

Despite the fact that the dominant mood of America in 1940 was isolationist, every presidential radio address in support of assistance to England produced a steady increase in public favor for the proposal, from 51 percent in March 1940 to almost 70 percent in April 1941.[160] From 1937 until American entry into the war in December 1941, there was a consistent level of support (between 60 percent and 80 percent of Americans polled) for higher spending on the armed forces, "even if this meant paying more taxes." The number of those who favored unconditional American participation in the European war rose from 19 percent in June 1940 to 47 percent a little over a year later. As a result of his radio addresses, when war finally came, Roosevelt found himself leading a nation "psychologically and materially prepared, and united in the certainty of an American victory."[161]

As American forces became engaged in combat all over the globe, and the home front experienced the hardships of total war, radio was to serve a useful function for the new commander-in-chief. Throughout World War II, FDR continued his fireside chats in order "to offer hope and encouragement during times of defeat, inspire the public to give to the war effort, explain his war strategies and policies, and prepare the nation for its new international responsibilities in the postwar world."[162] During the years 1941–45, radio audiences almost never fell below 50 million, and "public support for the President's wartime leadership seldom waned."[163] FDR's "radio pow-wows and pep talks" were considered so effective that many people believed the Axis deliberately timed major attacks to dilute the potency of the president's words.[164] One frequently cited example is the Japanese shelling of the California coast during Roosevelt's February 23, 1942, chat on combatting defeatism. Understanding radio's power to sway mass audiences themselves, Axis strategists recognized in FDR a "formidable adversary, whose oratorical talents constituted one of America's greatest wartime weapons."[165]

6. The Death of FDR

Unfortunately, Roosevelt would not survive the war for which he had toiled so hard to prepare his country. At 3:35 P.M. on April 12, 1945, the president died of a massive brain hemorrhage at his retreat in Warm Springs, Georgia. At 5:47 P.M., the news that the war had claimed one of its greatest casualties was flashed all over America via radio.

The networks were so rapid in getting the International News Service bulletin "Flash Washington—FDR is dead" over the air that Sam Rosenman, Winston Churchill, Joseph Stalin and countless others were apprised of the tragedy long before they were informed through official sources or by members of the Roosevelt family. The only individuals who knew of the event before radio made it public knowledge were Eleanor, her children, and Vice President Harry Truman.

The medium that had been such an integral part of Roosevelt's political life was now present to serve him in death. As a mark of respect for one of radio's most esteemed broadcasters, networks, independent stations, and short-wave facilities (both commercial and government owned) eliminated all advertisements and canceled regular programming for days so that news of the president's passing could be transmitted to the world. The only programs that were allowed to go on the air as scheduled were newscasts and other types whose subject matter could easily be altered "to conform to the present state of national mourning." The *American Album of Familiar Music* and other popular musicals presented special renditions of "Home on the Range," "Home Sweet Home," "Swing Low, Sweet Chariot," and many of the president's other favorite songs.[1] The *March of Time*, *Cavalcade of America*, and *These Great Americans* featured biographical dramatizations of Roosevelt's life and career which utilized recorded extracts from his best remembered speeches.[2] As filler between shows, the airwaves were alive with the somber strains of Barber's "Adagio for Strings" and various hymns and spirituals. From 5:49 P.M. Thursday, April 12, when the first flash was given, until sign-off Sunday night, NBC aired more than 72 broadcasts dealing with the tragic news.[3] It was an unprecedented effort by the broadcasting community. FDR's death was accorded more airtime coverage than either the Pearl Harbor attack or D-Day.

Tributes from political and religious leaders, foreign dignitaries, businessmen, media figures and statesmen flooded the airwaves. Among those offering eulogies were Edward J. Noble (ABC* chairman and former under-secretary of commerce), James A. Farley (Democratic national chairman), General George Marshall, James Byrnes, Herbert Hoover, Thomas Dewey, Senators Connolly, Barkley and Biddle, Justice William O. Douglas, Rep. Rayburn, Harold Ickes (secretary of the interior), and now President Harry Truman. At station WNYC, Fiorello La Guardia told his audience in a quaking voice: "Franklin Roosevelt is not dead. His ideals live on.... Centuries from now, as long as history is recorded, people will know FDR loved humanity...."[4] From abroad, Radio Tokyo interrupted a P.O.W. broadcast to "introduce a few minutes of special music to honor the passing of this great man."[5] When the Armed Forces Radio Service delivered the news of Roosevelt's death to American fighting men in Germany and on Okinawa, the guns suddenly went still, and a moment of silence was observed in honor of the fallen commander-in-chief.

On Sunday night, April 15, the entertainment world paid its final respects in a series of reverent memorial broadcasts. On ABC, Orson Welles was heard praising FDR's domestic accomplishments and "stressing the need for continuing [his] work." CBS featured seasoned literary figure Archibald MacLeish on *This Living World*, discussing the president's international contributions. Three minutes into his dialogue, MacLeish was so overcome with grief he had to terminate the broadcast. When he got to the words "our great president who is now so tragically dead at the moment of greatest need," the writer's voice faltered and the network had to switch to a musical interlude.

The most impressive mark of respect was paid by NBC. From Hollywood, a seemingly endless parade of film and radio personalities stepped before the microphone and offered thoughts on their fallen leader. Among those present were James Cagney, Amos 'n' Andy (Freeman Gosden and Charles Correll), Fibber McGee and Molly, Kay Kyser, Ed "Archie" Gardner, Dick Powell, Ronald Colman, Eddie Cantor, Harold "The Great Gildersleeve" Peary, Jack Benny, Ingrid Bergman, Bob Hope, and Edgar Bergen. Charles Laughton opened with a reading of Walt Whitman's tribute to Lincoln, "O Captain! My Captain!" Robert Young and Bette Davis followed with a heartwarming skit (written by Carleton E. Morse) about how FDR's postwar vision sustained a young pilot during a difficult mission, and Bing Crosby rounded out the two-hour pageant singing "Faith of our Fathers."[6]

Through the reports of correspondents stationed at strategic points, listeners were able to follow Roosevelt's funeral procession from the "Little White House" in Warm Springs, through Washington, D.C., and on to the final resting place at Hyde Park.[7] As Gunnar Back, Bill Henry, Bob Evans, Arthur

---

On October 12, 1943, anti-monopoly legislation forced NBC to divest itself of its Blue network. The chain was sold to Lifesaver candy tycoon Edward J. Nobel's American Broadcasting System, Inc., and thereafter became ABC.

Godfrey, and Cliff Allan described the passage of the presidential caisson down Pennsylvania Avenue, millions of Americans who had weathered the hardships of the Depression and the trying experience of war somberly realized that the "warm, reassuring radio voice, with its heartening, 'My friends,'" would be heard no more. The most vivid account was Godfrey's, who was also the most clearly moved by the spectacle he was witnessing.*

> As far as we can see [are] the people from all over the country who have come to pay their last respects to the man who was their leader, their commander-in-chief, and their friend, standing 15, 20, and in some places 30 or 40 deep to get a glimpse. Overhead 24 B-24 Liberator bombers are flying across slowly, and at a still higher altitude are 50-60 P-47 fighters.... The crowds stand mutely, quietly, dazed expressions on their faces, still unable to believe, won't believe until the caisson itself passes.... Now, just coming past the Treasury, I can see the horses drawing the caisson, flanked on either side by 6 or 7 motorcycles ... God give me strength to do this. And there is the flag-draped coffin resting on the black caisson.... The men in uniform salute and behind, in the car, is the successor to the late president, President Harry S Truman—the man on whose shoulders now falls [*sic*] the tremendous burdens and responsibilities that were handled so well and to whose body we are paying our last respects now...[8]

At this point, a grief-stricken Godfrey unexpectedly signed off, leaving the network with no choice but to pipe in organ filler.

From all over the broadcast community, personal statements of homage poured forth. NAB president J. Harold Ryan remarked: "The passing of Franklin D. Roosevelt brings a sense of deep personal loss to the broadcasters of America. He gave historic evidence of the effectiveness of this medium of communication in the solution of national and international problems."[9] CBS newscaster Bob Trout commented on how FDR "was the first statesman to use radio as a vital instrument of social power. He saw, clearly, the power of radio before any man in the government had seen it. He was the first to take problems to the people simply and directly by speaking to them all at once over radio."[10] NBC presidential announcer Carleton Smith declared:

> Franklin D. Roosevelt was the first radio president. It was through radio—through those famed visits to the White House fireside—that Americans came to know him best. Around that fireside he gathered the greatest listening audience in the world. They listened and they listened well—but never to just a voice.... It was Roosevelt, the man, who brought to radio much of the importance and dignity it has today. He used it wisely and carefully. He used it well.[11]

---

*FDR's funeral coverage was Godfrey's first national exposure. Network executives were so impressed with his performance, he was given a program of his own less than two weeks later. On April 28, 1945, he left his position as a morning deejay on WJSV (Washington) and began work on Arthur Godfrey Time.

Even the ordinarily hostile newspapers lamented on how this "feeling of close contact with the seat of government" was now gone.[12] One editor wrote:

> ...I never saw him—
> But I knew him. Can you have forgotten
> How, with his voice, he came into our house,
> the President of the United States,
> Calling us friends...[13]

Sam Rosenman observed:

> All throughout the United States there was a sense of personal loss. Millions of people in America, and in the rest of the world, seemed to have lost a close relative or dear friend—even though they never laid eyes on him.[14]

A prominent member of the press once remarked that Roosevelt's spectacular political success was 80 percent attributable to his adept use of the airwaves. *Broadcasting* declared:

> FDR's meteoric career was inextricably linked to the development of radio itself ... and the history of the medium is sprinkled with Roosevelt firsts. It was only during the eventful last twelve years that radio really achieved its maturation.[15]

By exploiting the possibilities of radio technology on a scale that dwarfed Polk's use of the telegraph and Wilson's handling of the motion picture, and through his special relationship with the networks, Roosevelt had been given the opportunity to become the "modern Cicero, leading his beleaguered nation in time of crisis."[16] Using simple language and impeccable delivery, FDR was able to reach out to the American people and restore their confidence through the most direct and efficient means available.* While Roosevelt manipulated the medium for his own personal ends, to answer critics and win an unparalleled four elections, he also successfully employed it to help the nation surmount two of its greatest crises, the Great Depression and the Second World War. By redefining the role of the electronic mass media in political campaigning and in selling foreign and domestic policies, FDR established a precedent that all subsequent chief executives would endeavor to follow. According to *Broadcasting*: "Roosevelt has placed upon radio, in his communion with the people, an emphasis which cannot be ignored. It is up to those who follow him to train themselves in the medium's use."[17] FDR's imposing radio presence was an integral part of the "large shadow" he cast on the White House after his demise. Remarking on his enduring influence, William Leuchtenberg has written:

*It is only fitting that when designers unveiled the first Franklin D. Roosevelt memorial in Washington, D.C., in 1997, it included a sculpture depicting a family gathered around the radio during one of the president's fireside chats.

Critics asked not whether Roosevelt's successors dealt adequately with contemporary problems, but whether they equaled FDR. They were required not merely to quote from Roosevelt and replicate his policies but to do so with conspicuous ardor, not only to put through a program of similar magnitude but to carry it off with the same flair.... When they ran for office, it was asked why they fell so far short of the Great Campaigner, and at the end of each successor's first hundred days, observers compared the score with FDR's.[18]

Harry Truman was the first to be held up to this impossible yardstick, and to most observers he fell considerably short. The unfavorable comparison was immediately evident when the former Missouri senator first addressed the nation as president on April 16, 1945.[19] *Broadcasting* noted that Truman's "microphone technique was ordinary" and "grass-rootish," and that many who heard him "shook their heads" in disappointment.[20] During the 1948 election, Democratic chairman Robert Hannegan told Truman to "stay out of sight" while the party sought to arouse voters through recordings of FDR's voice.[21] No president since has ever "attained the oratorical heights which marked [Roosevelt's] career."[22] The very few that have come close, John F. Kennedy and Ronald Reagan, did so only through a conscious and intensive cultivation of the master's methods.

Part II

"We Take You Now To…"

7. Early History of Broadcast News

The power of broadcasting was demonstrated in another important way in the 1930s. As the most technologically advanced electronic agency of the day, radio emerged as the dominant means of disseminating information for mass consumption. Originating first as a novelty, the medium developed rapidly into the most effective means of "enhancing public awareness and understanding of current events at home and abroad" during the turbulent Depression era. Through the vehicle of radio news broadcasting, the average American listener was put in intimate contact with the important events of his time as soon as they happened. By spanning the distance between the listener and the event, whether in New York, London, Berlin, or Tokyo, radio news greatly accelerated the process of tying the world closer together. In a nation previously limited to local printed dailies, radio itself became a type of "national newspaper" that was a major factor in the homogenization of American culture.[1] Indeed, by the late 1930s, radio was to rival and then surpass the traditionally dominant "fourth estate" as "America's number one informational source."[2] Through the living room loudspeaker, Americans could hear the latest news reported more "directly, personally, concisely, and full of human energy" than in printed matter.[3] Many times, the listener was able to witness a news event firsthand through the voices of actual participants or the sounds from the scene. In addition to this advantage, radio provided a host of news commentators and analysts who interpreted the news for the average listener and made it more comprehensible.

As Americans became more conscious of the world around them (a trend that radio both encouraged and reflected), they grew increasingly reliant on radio for the latest news. Since the vast majority of people comprehended "facts and abstract material better when heard than read," radio's educational appeal was much stronger than that of the printed media.[4] As an "aural phenomenon," radio news could reach many of those who were untouched by newspapers. In contrast to the tendency of newspaper writers to "prolong rumors and heighten the suggestion of conflict" in order to boost circulation, radio news was increasingly seen as a "reliable and objective service" that provided

131

"crisp and conclusive reports."[5] Furthermore, broadcasting possessed no "headlines with which to skew or color reports" and was less prone to editorializing.[6] In an increasingly fast-paced society, listeners could obtain far more current information through radio then "someone who put in twice as much time reading a newspaper.[7] Because radio demanded less concentration than a printed medium, one could occupy himself with other activities while listening in. With no more effort than the turn of a switch, radio was delivered directly into the home and was totally gratis.[8] A Bureau of Applied Social Research study revealed that radio was instrumental in stimulating the "less educated and the illiterate" to take a keener interest in current affairs. In doing so, radio [had] "done a great service to democracy's need for an informed population."[9] By the end of the decade, many of the fundamental tools associated with today's televised news reporting had been developed.[10]

Radio News Is Born

The origins of radio news were firmly tied to the early development of the medium itself. The "broadcasting pioneers of the 1920s" habitually chose newsworthy events as the occasion in which to launch new stations. As early as November 7, 1916, the first words to emanate from Lee De Forest's experimental transmitter were a brief rundown of the Wilson-Hughes election figures. A few years later, on August 31, 1920, the Michigan primary returns were heard by hundreds of Detroit-based amateur wireless operators.

Where it did exist, broadcast news coverage was confined to local and regional matters, and the material for it was usually acquired from individual newspapers or one of the national press services. As a supplier of news, radio was not envisaged as a serious challenger to the printed daily. Instead, these early years witnessed the formation of a symbiotic relationship between the two media. In return for free radio advertising, the newspapers printed radio program logs, reviewed new shows, and provided news material for broadcast. WWJ's *raison d'être* was to increase subscriptions to the *Detroit News*. KDKA in Pittsburgh was operated by Westinghouse Electric in order to advertise the new line of $125 radios that the company had just put on the market, and to generate entertainment for those who purchased a set. This station had the honor of scoring many radio news "firsts,"* such as its coverage of the 1920 Cox-Harding election returns. As the *Pittsburgh Post* received the figures over its ticker, they were telephoned to KDKA, where a station "publicity man" copied them down and then read them over the air. By midnight, radio listeners

*There still exists some debate as to whether KDKA was the first commercial station on the air: WBZ (Springfield, MA), WWJ (Detroit), KCBS (San Francisco), and WHA (Madison) have all made similar claims. Given the haphazard nature of broadcasting in the 1920s, and the total lack of regulation, it is difficult to pinpoint the precise time and location of the first formal transmission.

throughout western Pennsylvania were aware of Harding's landslide victory. The next day, the station received a large number of telegrams and letters by impressed listeners "asking for more." In another demonstration of the benevolent relationship between radio and the press at this time, the *Pittsburgh Post* gave the broadcast "full story and picture treatment" in its morning edition.[11]

Elsewhere, on March 4, 1921, the full text of Warren Harding's inaugural address was re-read over the air, and on July 2, the Dempsey-Carpentier fight was transmitted to some 200,000 listeners. In 1923, the details of Harding's unexpected death and the opening of Congress were broadcast over a seven-station hookup. In November 1924, over ten million listeners learned of Calvin Coolidge's triumph over John W. Davis hours before the newspapers reached them. In March of the next year, Coolidge's first speech as president was carried by 26 stations.

While many newsworthy items were broadcast over early radio, reports were ordinarily used to fill gaps between phonograph records or during unused airtime. Radio's commitment to the coverage of current events was slight, and bulletins rarely exceeded one minute in length. The notion of a regular schedule of 10- to 15-minute newscasts was inconceivable. Most early stations were content to "lift information from the newspapers and read it over the air," despite the warnings of the Associated Press to cease such "pirating."[12]

In 1927, the Federal Radio Act encouraged the development of news broadcasting by demanding that stations reserve several hours a day for public interest programming. Although those who controlled commercial broadcasting still felt there to be "little interest in the small drawing potential of news," the public appetite had been whetted. In 1928, radio's coverage of the Smith-Hoover presidential contest stimulated the growing desire for regular news programming even further. To fulfill this desire, station KFAB in Lincoln, Nebraska, commenced two daily "radio newspaper" broadcasts. In 1930, KMPC in Beverly Hills began to air a series of three 15-minute news shows on a daily basis. While the growth of early radio news was significantly facilitated by the sympathetic cooperation of many newspapers, "who alone possessed the requisite capital and news-gathering infrastructure," this remained the case only insofar as radio news operations "were on a scale small enough to offer no competition to the pre-eminent position of the printed media."[13]

The "Crime of the Century"

In 1932, electronic news journalism suddenly burst onto the national scene. When Charles Lindbergh's infant son was kidnapped from the family residence in Hopewell, New Jersey, on the night of March 1, radio mobilized its resources, however fledgling, to cover the "crime of the century." Newark's WOR was the first station to carry the news, with a statement by Col. Norman H. Schwartzkopf*, head of the New Jersey State Police. Immediately, NBC and CBS dispatched a corps of announcers and engineers to Hopewell, Princeton, Trenton, and other nearby points. Once there, they commandeered restaurants and hotel rooms to serve as provisional studios. WOR was perhaps the most strategically located, having established its "remote station" in Trenton police headquarters.

After laying wires and setting up their considerable transmitting equipment, network correspondents Don Higgins, Herb Glover, Douglas Gilbert, and Mack Parker flashed updates every half-hour as news items trickled in from the Lindbergh estate. Both nets employed "mobile transmitting stations mounted on trucks" to relay information to a receiving point in Princeton, and hence to the main studios in New York for rebroadcast to the American public. Also in New York were powerful short-wave units waiting to beam the latest news to an interested world audience. CBS and NBC remained on the air almost continuously for the first 150 hours after the kidnapping, "keeping the nation apprised of every detail in the case."[14]

In early 1935, when Bruno Richard Hauptmann was apprehended for the kidnapping,† network news staffs from around the country converged on Flemington, New Jersey, to cover the court proceedings. As new evidence was uncovered and tension mounted, tuning in to the latest news of the case became a national event. The broadcasters' widely disseminated coverage of the trial greatly increased the unifying tendencies of radio. Only through this medium could the entire nation "experience the Lindbergh's agony" as the details of the kidnapping and the child's gruesome death were revealed.[15] In its ability to capture the drama and pathos of the situation, radio distinguished itself from the more sedate reporting found in the press. In the "natural expectation" that Hauptmann's accomplices were, like millions of others, listening to the radio reports of the case, Charles and Anne Lindbergh frequently made emotional on-air appeals for the criminals to "come clean."

From Flemington, all three networks broadcast Press-Radio bulletins at regular intervals. These were supplemented by the perceptive commentaries of Boake Carter (CBS), Lowell Thomas (NBC) and Gabriel Heatter (WOR), all of whom had taken up residence in the poolroom across from the courthouse. Through countless hours of coverage, these individuals became celebrities to the millions who anxiously followed the course of the trial through their broadcasts. Since microphones were not admitted into the courtroom, correspondents observed the proceedings, then dashed out to convey to listeners what they had just seen. On the first day of the trial, when Lindbergh

---

*Father of the Persian Gulf War general of the same name.

†On May 12, 1932, the decomposing body of the child was discovered, and later Hauptmann was arrested for possession of some of the ransom money.

himself testified, Boake Carter vividly described the setting inside the court-room and repeated the aviator's words almost verbatim.

To simulate the actual conduct of the case, NBC used three announcers: one for narration and two others who read the day's testimony in question-and-answer form. Highlights were repeated on the *Five Star Final* program later in the evening. Transradio maintained two men in the courtroom and three correspondents "covering other angles" elsewhere in New Jersey. On an average day, the news agency provided its radio subscribers with over seventy special bulletins and enough additional material for four regular news sessions. WNEW was the most energetic independent station in Flemington, with correspondent A. L. Alexander delivering over three hours of commentary and two hours of "summarized testimony" every day. Having placed a microphone in the local sheriff's office, WNEW was always privy to the hottest bits of new evidence. The station scooped its larger rivals when it brought listeners an exclusive interview with Edward J. Reilly, Hauptmann's principal lawyer.[16]

At 10:28 P.M. on February 13, 1935, Hauptmann was found guilty of the kidnapping and murder of Charles Augustus Lindbergh, Jr. Fifteen minutes later the networks flashed the Press-Radio bulletin revealing the sentence: Hauptmann had been given the death penalty. Earlier, a false decision (life sentence) was supplied by an overzealous AP correspondent and broadcast over the air. This caused considerable embarrassment for network executives and served to "widen the breach between papers and radio." One observer called it the "greatest journalistic boner since the false armistice report of 1918." At 10:45 P.M., NBC conveyed the sentence correctly and apologized for having not sought confirmation before broadcasting the mistaken report.[17]

On April 3, 1936, Hauptmann went to the electric chair. Outside the Trenton State Prison, Gabriel Heatter prepared to deliver a five-minute broadcast for Mutual. When the execution was delayed unexpectedly, the commentator was compelled to ad-lib for almost an hour. One writer observed:

> Soaked in sweat, Heatter began desperately to improvise. He reviewed the highlights of the trial, philosophized, moralized and speculated on the possibility of a reprieve; then did it all over again, with variations. This went on until 8:48, when the word that Hauptmann was dead came from the penitentiary gate. When it was all over, Heatter was near collapse, but his marathon ad-libbing had made him, and he has had a waiting list of sponsors ever since.[18]

With this event, radio news coverage had made its spectacular debut, and for the first time began to attract a sizable audience. From all over the world, the networks were praised for the "fine restraint in handling the news and their careful consideration of the facts."[19] The Hauptmann trial was America's first national courtroom thriller, and many of the technical, methodological, and journalistic devices that broadcasters employed to cover it laid the ground-work for all subsequent media-legal sensations, including the O. J. Simpson case.*

The Press-Radio War

During the Lindbergh episode, the newspaper industry began to take notice of its emerging electronic rival. To stem its growing influence and limit its access to the sources of news, the Associated Press denied the networks use of its facilities in the 1932 presidential election. Undeterred, the ever-resource-ful broadcasters set up their own news-gathering apparatuses in the Democratic and Republican conventions and carried the nominating ceremonies live. These were quickly followed on September 22 by a news event "that only radio could cover." As William Beebe descended 2,200 feet below the Atlantic off Bermuda in a bathysphere, millions of listeners in America heard him through a special microphone installed in the submersible. On February 15, 1933, radio again scooped the newspapers by providing a full account of the attempted assassination of President Roosevelt in Miami a mere one and one-half hours after the event.[20]

While most of these broadcasts were newsworthy, the networks consid-ered them "special events" rather than straightforward news programs and presented them only as the occasion warranted. Nevertheless, such broadcasts were instrumental in helping to establish radio in the popular mind as a legit-imate "purveyor of news and an alternative to the traditional newspaper." Because of the "increased listenership to these broadcasts and the intense interest the public expressed in them, the radio industry was given a tremen-dous boost of confidence in its ability to disseminate news over the air."[21]

In 1933 the number of regular news programs began to rise. In an effort to impede this trend, the Associated Press tightened its ban on allowing sta-tions access to its news wire. This policy had little effect, however, because many stations were able to seek the data they needed from the United Press (UP), the International News Service (INS), or other agencies that continued to cater to them. Gradually, many of the larger newspapers, including the Hearst chains, the *Chicago Tribune*, and the *Milwaukee Journal*, became infu-riated with broadcasters who pilfered news from them and "put it on the air before the printed editions reached the streets."[22]

In a move to eliminate radio's competition for news stories and advertis-ing dollars, the American News Publishers Association (ANPA) agreed in April 1933 to terminate the sale of news material to the networks. The American

---

Among its many precedents, the trial was notable for the enactment of the American Bar Association's Canon 35, which attempted to "alleviate the circus-like atmosphere" of cases by "severely limiting access to the courtroom by radio and photographers" (and later, television). While this law is still officially on the books, it does not appear to have been systematically applied in recent years (Sterling, p. 179).

Press Association (APA) also responded by refusing to print radio listings and program schedules. Frank Noyes, president of the AP, justified this move in this way:

> We recognize that radio needs advertising to support itself, but when it enters the news field on a strictly competitive basis with us, we propose to pursue a policy of not advertising our competitors.[23]

CBS replied aggressively by setting up its own news-gathering service, the Columbia News Service, under the able direction of Paul White. With over 800 correspondents nationwide, the CNS had a main office in New York and small bureaus in Washington, Chicago, Los Angeles, and London. Foreign news was provided by the British Exchange Telegraph news agency and financial information from the Dow Jones wire service. All of these sources were utilized to create two daily 15-minute newscasts by Boake Carter and H. V. Kaltenborn. NBC, meanwhile, used the Consolidated Press for service, and resorted to the "scissors and pasting" of newspaper accounts.[24]

Tension between the newspaper and radio industries erupted into an all-out "Press-Radio War," in which both sides engaged in numerous legal battles for control of the news business. After many costly and inconclusive court bouts, the networks agreed to the Press-Radio Plan (Biltmore Agreement) of December 11, 1934. In exchange for a promise to refrain from news gathering of their own, the networks were to be supplied by the wire services with two daily five-minute news reports. The nets were to broadcast these only on a sustaining basis and could not sell them to advertisers. The agreement also stipulated that the contracting station had to credit the AP or other agency at the beginning and end of each newscast in this way: "This news is furnished by the Associated Press as a public service. For further details, read your AP newspaper."[25]

While the plan worked well for a while, neither of the two parties was completely satisfied. Since the networks served only a third of all broadcasting stations in 1934, the plan did not preclude independent news gathering by the other large, unaffiliated station blocs across the country. As a result, the Yankee Network of New England, the Radio News Service of America, the American Broadcasting News Association, and the Transradio Press Service were able to offer their services to large broadcasting areas. Together they provided far more material than the expansive wire services—enough for more than four 15-minute broadcasts a day. Many broadcast chains also had access to the newly created Radio News Association, which supplied news material specially adapted for radio. Seeing that their arrangement was failing, the UP and INS broke ranks and announced that they would resume news service to the networks, effectively destroying the Press-Radio Bureau. The AP continued to withhold its wire service from CBS and NBC until 1940, a "testament to the deep animosity the newspaper profession harbored towards its burgeoning electronic competitor."[26]

Nevertheless, with the end of the Press-Radio War, the networks were guaranteed a regular and much-enlarged supply of news material. From 1936 to 1941 there was a steady increase in the number of stations enrolled with some type of news service. In 1936, there were 325; 1937, 443; 1938, 541; 1939, 611; 1940, 743; and 1941, 843.[27] In addition to the larger news supply, NBC and CBS received a "significant overall improvement in the quality of service." In 1936 the UP installed a modern teleprinter system in network newsrooms that produced material designed for immediate use over the air. The networks also retained their own news-gathering agencies that had been created during the height of the Press-Radio War.

To some observers, the relationship between radio and press did not necessarily have to be antagonistic. In many respects, news broadcasting "helped rather than hindered" the sale of newspapers.[28] In April 1939, members of the American Newspaper Publishers Association's Bureau of Advertising agreed that "people who have heard the highlights of any news story on the air were *more* anxious to read the full details in their newspapers than those who had no knowledge at all of what had occurred." As evidence, they cited the fact that in 1922 there was no broadcast coverage of the Pope's election and only 1,000 newspaper extras were sold. In 1939, by contrast, there was detailed reportage on the air and over 5,000 additional papers were purchased. "Radio reports both before and after the event," the panel concluded, "seemed to whet the public's interest in the color and background of the election and to create a desire for more extended accounts and comment published in the press."[29] In recognizing radio's ability to enlarge the audience of print readers, Guy Hamilton, general manager of McClatchy Newspapers, Ltd., told members of the California Newspaper Publishers Association: "Radio can be made an important adjunct to newspaper expansion and promotion."[30] At an ANPA meeting on April 23, 1940, discussions centered not on competition between the two media, but on ways in which publishers could acquire financial stakes in station operations. Following this advice, 275 of the 829 stations licensed during the remainder of 1940 were either partially or completely owned by newspapers.[31]

Thus by 1937 the basic infrastructure of radio news had been firmly established. Although the Press-Radio War would continue for a few more years and the tension between the two media would linger, the 1937–41 period would see the great development and flowering of radio news broadcasting. As the nation "sank deeper into economic depression, natural and technological disaster struck, and war loomed across the oceans," events conspired to increase public interest in radio news as never before. The networks would successfully mobilize their resources to cover a wide variety of news events for the American public, more quickly, thoroughly and intimately than the newspapers could. "Responding to unique situations and an ever-expanding scope of events," radio would consistently prove its value as the "most effective purveyor of news in 1930s America."[32]

8. Radio Covers Domestic Events and Crises

Natural Disaster

Throughout the 1930s radio proved its usefulness in reporting the news of great disasters to a concerned public. Already newsworthy in themselves, "local disturbances had a way of becoming national calamities" as a result of radio's wide coverage. This phenomenon was demonstrated as early as 1933, when the networks apprised the country of the devastation wrought by an earthquake in Long Beach, California.[1]

On an even larger scale was radio's coverage of the Ohio and Mississippi River floods in January 1937. This was perhaps radio's most outstanding performance during a domestic crisis, not only in the medium's detailed reporting of the event, but in its cooperative role in aiding the nation's relief effort. Frequent news broadcasts kept the whole of America informed of the progress of the flood and the measures taken to contain the rising waters.[2] Far from being merely a interested spectator, radio took an active hand in serving the public interest. Numerous stations scrapped their regular program schedules and "remained on the air day and night in order to direct flood victims to areas of food and shelter" and to reunite separated family members.[3] Through radio, public officials were able to issue emergency orders for the conservation of electricity and drinking water and to coordinate the various agencies engaged in combating the swelling rivers. Many other stations conducted fundraising efforts to relieve the suffering of those who had been dispossessed by nature.[4] American Red Cross appeals brought an "instant and generous response to the stricken" in the form of clothing, food, bedding, and medicine, which poured into local studios. In one day, WKRC of Owen City raised over $100,000 in financial assistance. Radio also served a "much-needed communications function" as it provided a "point-to-point broadcasting message service" for government and aid agencies that no longer had access to telephones. When a crumbling dike threatened to topple several Ohio River bridges, a WKRC appeal for volunteers attracted "54 men bearing shovels and sandbags" less than an hour later. In Louisville, radio was used to direct Coast Guard cutters to the relief of the marooned. The networks mobilized all of their resources for this daunting task, sending out scores of courageous microphone crews who "fanned out" over the entire stricken area and provided a continuous stream of news from strategic vantage points in the air, on land, and on the water. During the first week alone, NBC transmitted over 100 special broadcasts from the scene. WREC of Memphis established a record when it remained on the air for 574 continuous hours.[5] In one NBC broadcast, FCC chairman Anning S. Prall declared:

> I humbly salute radio for its tremendous contribution in this hour of need…. Sufficient reports have been received to indicate that in the saving of lives, the safeguarding of property, and in the raising of funds, radio, and the splendid men and women associated with it, played a major role…. Radio has done a magnificent job.

The February 15, 1937, issue of *Broadcasting* quoted the commendation of U.S. House members O'Connor, May, and Woodrum: "We are prone to look on radio with a take-it-for-granted attitude, and it is only on such occasions that we fully understand and appreciate [its] untold value."[6]

During the Ohio and Mississippi flood coverage, radio's "immediacy and portability" were abundantly demonstrated.[7] So too was its dynamism, which stood in sharp contrast to the relative inactivity of the press during the crisis. Compared to radio's "carpet-soaking realism," printed accounts of the disaster appeared tedious and impersonal. The newspapers themselves recognized the "tremendous work radio had performed." They joined with countless flood victims and their families in exclaiming, "Thank God for Radio!"[8]

As in the Lindbergh case, radio's extensive reporting of the tragedy helped foster a strong sense of national solidarity. The *Bluefield* (West Virginia) *News and Times* observed:

> The radio has been mostly responsible for making people visualize the enormity of the flood disaster and sympathize with the victims, and hence making the response to appeals for relief so prompt and unstinting. Thus, thanks to radio … the nation as a whole has had its nerves, its heart, its soul exposed to the suffering and the needs of its unfortunates. And that is well, for disaster in one region means grief to all regions. We are a nation integrated and interdependent. We are "our brother's keeper" … through economic necessity as well as by compulsion of human sympathy.[9]

The networks repeated this commendable performance on September 21–22, 1938, when severe winds and flooding wreaked havoc all over the northeast coast. Again radio cast aside its commercial commitments and launched into its public service activities. WBZ and other New England stations made their facilities instantly available to state, police, rescue, and Red Cross agencies, and assured an anxious public that relief efforts were proceeding satisfactorily. It was a Herculean effort for broadcasters to remain on the air amidst frequent power failures and damage to transmitting equipment. In Rhode Island, WJAR of Providence was the only station in the state whose tower was left standing. The damage from this storm was not as bad as it had been in Ohio in 1937, partly because radio had "forewarned people in seven states of the impending deluge" many days in advance so that they could adequately prepare.[10]

The Hindenburg *Explosion*

In May 1937, radio again demonstrated its ability not only to inform listeners of important events, but to actually transport them to the scene through on-the-spot coverage. This was facilitated by the advent of a light backpack type of recording apparatus that enabled a reporter to transcribe his words and the sounds around him directly onto a magnetic disc. This recording could be taken back to a studio and played for listeners thousands of miles from the scene of action. The resulting broadcast conveyed all of the drama and immediacy of an event so effectively that the listener felt he was an actual "ear-witness." Furthermore, since disc recorders were relatively inexpensive and did not require multiple supporting devices (antennae, unwieldy transmitters, etc.), even the most resource-conscious of local stations could use them to cover newsworthy events.

On May 6, 1937, correspondent Herb Morrison and engineer Charles Nehlsen were assigned to record their observations of the landing of the German zeppelin *Hindenburg* at Lakehurst, New Jersey. Since the flight of dirigibles had ceased to be thrilling news, only one station, WLS in Chicago, bothered to cover the *Hindenburg's* arrival. To mark the "first anniversary of the inauguration of trans–Atlantic air service," the station decided to record the landing, preserving it for the sound effects department and the transcription library of WLS.[11]

As Morrison began to record his observations of the ship as it began its descent, the routine landing suddenly turned into disaster. As those on the ground gaped in horror, the enormous hydrogen-filled vessel caught fire and exploded. In less than a minute, the *Hindenburg* had been reduced to a flaming wreck that slammed into the ground, instantly killing 37 of its 97 passengers and crew.

Despite the emotional impact of the event he was witnessing, Morrison continued to relate a complete account of the disaster around him as rescue workers braved the smoke and heat to remove the unfortunate passengers. Immediately after the recording had ceased, Morrison rushed back to Chicago and broadcast a 15-minute excerpt to thousands of bewildered listeners at 3:30 A.M. Later that morning, at 11:45, the complete 40-minute transcription was aired for the whole of America, over the four major networks.[12] Morrison's vivid reporting made listeners feel they were actually witnessing the disaster firsthand. Capturing the intense drama of the situation, Morrison reported:

She is practically standing still now. The ropes have been dropped and they have been taken hold of by a number of men on the field. It is starting to rain again. The rain has slacked up a little bit. The back motors of the ship are holding her just enough to keep her.... She burst into flame!

Get out of the way! Get this, Charlie! Get out of the way please! She is bursting into flames! This is terrible! This is one of the worst catastrophes in the world. The flames are shooting five hundred feet into the sky. It is a terrific crash, ladies and gentlemen. It is in smoke and flames now. Oh, the humanity! Those passengers! I can't talk, ladies and gentlemen. Honest, it is a mass of smoking wreckage. Lady, I am sorry. Honestly, I can hardly—I am going to step inside where I cannot see it. Charlie, that is terrible. Listen folks, I am going to have to stop for a minute because I have lost my voice.[13]

Morrison's coverage was considered so newsworthy and unique that the major networks temporarily suspended their ban on playing recordings in order to allow the American public to hear this momentous transcription.* The listener heard not only the impassioned description of Morrison, but also the sounds of the explosion and the terrified responses of the spectators. The blast was so violent that it knocked the recording needle off the machine. (The needle was quickly replaced by the vigilant engineer.) Morrison's broadcast was interrupted five times as he laid down the microphone to help retrieve the survivors, many of whom he later interviewed for the radio audience. The *Hindenburg* recording was so realistic that to this day writers often mistake it for a live broadcast.

Certainly, this type of immediate and moving reporting could not have been replicated by any other medium.[14] Both the newspaper accounts and the newsreel footage of the event "lacked that intimate sense of personal participation that could only be conveyed through the human voice." Again, the newspaper world could not contain its admiration for radio's superlative performance. One writer for the *Chicago Tribune* called Morrison's account "the most dramatic broadcast of all time," and a group of reporters proclaimed it "the most gripping thing they ever heard." The *Chicago Herald-American* referred to it as "one of the best pieces of word-eye broadcasting" ever aired.[15] Herbert Morrison himself recognized the enormous impact his performance had on the development of radio news. In an interview some years later he stated, "The broadcast gave me the confidence that radio indeed was the method of bringing news to the public in the quickest possible form right from the source."[16]

Radio's account of the airship disaster was a major scoop over the newspapers, not only in the quickness of its reporting but in the quality and thoroughness of its coverage. Morrison's report was only one of several examples

*Because the Hindenburg *episode highlighted the shortcomings of regular network policy, NBC and CBS became far more willing to forgo their anti-recording bias after 1937. MBS, regional chains, and local stations, who had been routinely employing news-bearing disc material prior to Morrison's broadcast, now began to do so on a much larger scale.*

of radio's outstanding efforts at broadcast coverage on this occasion. The dirigible exploded at 7:23 P.M. on May 6, and in less than eight minutes, the news was being flashed over station WHN in New York. At 7:45, NBC broadcast the official Press-Radio bulletin and five minutes later conducted a man-in-the-street interview to gauge the popular reaction. As soon as the news had been received, an army of radio announcers, engineers, special events men, and reporters flocked towards Lakehurst by whatever means possible. At 9:07 that night, NBC aired the first eyewitness account by telephone of someone who had witnessed the spectacle, and at 10:30 P.M. a member of the ground crew transmitted a 16-minute description of what he had seen. By 11:30 network representatives arrived in Lakehurst and set up remote broadcasting facilities to report live from the scene. An NBC correspondent interviewed eyewitnesses over the air, and Mutual broadcast the personal stories of nurses and priests who had attended the dying victims.

These live transmissions were possible only because of technological advances the year before. In 1936, remote broadcasting became portable through the use of hand-held and "top-hat" transmitters. These "smallest practical radio broadcasting stations" liberated the reporter from restricting wires and freed engineers from the necessity of having to transport larger and heavier sending units.[17] Whereas earlier, live broadcasts required the services of at least four men (two to hold the antenna aloft, one to manipulate the beaming mechanism, and one to carry the microphone), these new sets were completely self-contained and could be operated easily by an individual (usually the correspondent himself).[18] Now a reporter had greater freedom to wander about and cover a story from multiple perspectives and from many areas that had previously been inaccessible. At Lakehurst, the correspondent's words went into microphones and through the compact transmitter to a relay set atop a nearby vehicle or building. From here they were electronically dispatched to a larger receiver at Forked River, New Jersey, and thence by wire to Radio City in New York, where they were put over the air for public consumption.

This relay system was highly efficient and resulted in a flood of eyewitness reports direct from the scene. As the number of reporters and mobile broadcast units covering the ground area increased, CBS began to describe the wreckage site from an airplane flying overhead. Throughout the evening hours and well after sign-off time, the airwaves were alive with last-minute news from the wire services and other sources. Early the next morning, the networks presented a remote pickup from Paul Kimbel Hospital in Lakehurst, where survivors told of their experiences and announcers reported the names of those passengers who had made it to safety.

By the time the last *Hindenburg* broadcast left the air a few days later, it was clear that radio had accomplished something remarkable. Through its immediate and comprehensive coverage, "radio had not only reported history, it had made it." Radio had gained a tremendous advantage over all competitors and had firmly established itself as a leading news medium. For those who had previously questioned radio's usefulness as an informational device, its "ability to cover any important news story rapidly, carefully, and completely was never better demonstrated" than during its reporting of the *Hindenburg* tragedy.[19]

Explorer *and* Squalus

Radio's on-the-spot coverage of major domestic events scored a third impressive victory in 1937 with the broadcast of the *Explorer* disaster. In another dramatic presentation, radio correspondents were on hand to describe the course of the damaged stratosphere balloon *Explorer* as it plummeted earthward with some of its stranded crew aboard. Shortly after the outer skin of the observation craft was punctured at 60,000 feet, the radio audience was privy to the actual two-way conversations between the occupants of the airship and radio men on the ground.

Transcending its role of merely reporting, the radio industry attempted to use its facilities to intervene and resolve the difficulty. Though the balloon was beyond the reach of physical assistance, radio contact was established between the chiefs of the Air Corps at the War Department in Washington and the stricken balloonists. Offering "advice and encouragement," the voices in the capital were sent out over NBC network lines to shortwave transmitters which, in turn, projected them out into space. From there they echoed through the metal structure of the *Explorer*. Within hours of receiving the first distress call, special broadcast equipment was installed at fourteen strategic points across the country, ready to pick up messages from the balloon and transmit them to Washington. From 3:00 P.M. to 6:55 P.M. the networks remained on the air, charting the airship's course and broadcasting the complete dialogue between the crew and rescuers on the ground. Millions of listeners all over America were glued to their sets, anxiously awaiting the outcome of this tense situation. Eventually, as the nation held its breath, the crew contained the tear until they had descended low enough to bail out. In the end, the three men arrived safely on the ground and America drew a collective sigh of relief. Radio had again successfully covered an event while performing an act of public service. As in the case of the *Hindenburg*, many of those who tuned in were treated to an auditory spectacle that "while genuine and historical was nonetheless as exciting as the best radio fiction."[20]

Radio again came to the public assistance on May 23, 1939, when it helped to rescue the crew of the submarine *Squalus*, stranded on the bottom of the Atlantic. Through radio communication between the sub and the naval base at Portsmouth came the first indication that the underwater vessel was in trouble. Once this became known, nearby radio stations immediately interrupted programming to send out appeals to crews ashore to return to ship. Because of radio's speedy mobilization, the rescue vessel *USS Brooklyn* was underway within an hour. The broadcast appeal brought rescue craft from over a dozen locations converging on the sight of the disaster. In response to requests by the navy, many New England stations went on the air to instruct relatives of *Squalus* crew members not to jam the switchboards of the naval offices with their phone calls and thus hinder the rescue operation. The networks promised the public the latest news as quickly as it became known.

To expedite the flow of information, many stations chartered fishing boats and broadcast direct from the scene. WLAW, Lawrence, Massachusetts, was the first to arrive with a portable transmitter. MBS sent Dave Driscoll, its special events announcer, in an Eastern Airlines plane to survey the situation from above. These correspondents informed the world of the successful diving operation that established contact with the crew of the sunken vessel and commenced efforts to extricate them from their watery tomb. As Americans tuned in, reporters described the three successful trips of the navy's "miracle bell" that transported the crew to the surface. As soon as the survivors were known, their names were promptly transmitted to expectant relatives in the listening audience. The networks remained at the scene until it was certain that the 26 men in the aft compartment had drowned and the rescue operation was officially terminated. By that time, CBS had originated 21 separate broadcasts from the disaster area.[21] NBC returned to Portsmouth two years later to give an on-the-spot account of the navy's futile attempts to rescue the 33 officers and men trapped aboard the submarine *O-9*.[22]

The humanitarian efforts of the radio community won the kudos of the nation. Radio had once again demonstrated its ability to transcend distances, whether in remote areas of the country, in space or under the sea, by bringing the listener into immediate and intimate contact with important news events.* As in the cases of the Ohio and New England floods and the *Explorer* disaster, radio's performance during the *Squalus* episode demonstrated the medium's unsurpassed ability not only to inform but even to save lives.[23]

Covering the 1940 Campaign

Radio also proved its usefulness in covering domestic political events. As Roosevelt's bid for a third term and the darkening international situation ensured unprecedented voter interest in the 1940 presidential campaign, network news staffs endeavored to make radio coverage of the nomination and balloting processes the "most extensive and elaborate of any election in history."[24]

NBC and CBS got off to a quick start with their comprehensive reporting

---

During 1939, the nets also covered, with equal thoroughness, the crashes of the Imperial Airways seaplane Cavalier *(January 21) and a Boeing Stratoliner near Tacoma (March) (*Broadcasting, *February 1, 1939, p. 30, and April 1, 1939, p. 99).*

of the June 24 Republican Party Convention in Philadelphia and the July 15 Democratic gathering in Chicago. On both occasions, the networks had access to microphones in special broadcast booths overlooking the speaker's platform, on the convention floor, and on the tables of each state's delegation. As a result, listeners at home were able to "hear each vote cast as if they were present in the hall themselves."[25] The nets also maintained transmitting facilities in all of the committee rooms and in the headquarters of each candidate. Special studios located in the hall aisles enabled correspondents to conduct interviews with important political personalities and convention officials. Suspended above the floor were parabolic microphones which allowed listeners to hear the chants of the excited crowds and music from the band. Using four-pound pack transmitters and hand-held "beer mug" units, correspondents made various pickups from points all around the auditorium.[26] The ever-present nature of the microphone, while improving the quality of the coverage, also led to some embarrassing situations. At one point, when the Wisconsin delegation was called upon to comment on one of the ballots, listeners heard one unprepared member exclaim: "No, to hell with it!"[27]

Both nets employed a large staff of announcers and correspondents to handle the convention proceedings: Raymond Clapper, George Hicks, Charles Lyons, Carleton Smith and Herluf Provenson for NBC; Bob Trout and John Daly for CBS; and Arthur Henning, Wythe Williams and Gabriel Heatter for Mutual. All facets of the convention were aired: remarks by party leaders and campaign managers, roll calls, and nomination and acceptance speeches.

When voters went to the polls in November, the networks scrambled to bring listeners a "ballot by ballot report from the moment the first returns came dribbling in, until the final result was announced." For this task, NBC and CBS employed about 100 announcers, newsmen, correspondents and engineers. NBC turned the world's largest broadcasting facility, studio 8-H in Radio City, into a temporary newsroom, equipped with a huge election chart and a "battery of teletype machines" for delivering press association returns from points around the country. CBS's arrangements included "10 special long-distance telephone circuits, 6 private-line connections with remote points, 4 special Morse wires, and 9 AP, UP and INS printers for bringing election news to the streamlined copy desk." From there, editors passed the returns on to tabulators stationed at a colossal tally board, and to Bob Trout for dissemination over the air. To interpret the returns and situate them within the overall context of the presidential race, the nets turned to political experts such as Albert Warner, Quin Ryan, and Arthur Evans. Dr. Elmo Roper compared the state-by-state results to his own forecasts and those of other public opinion surveys.*

---

*Among the many modern features of broadcast election coverage in 1940, the large-scale use of political pundits and the obsession with a blow-by-blow type of coverage foreshadowed the more resent medial preocupation with the presidential "horse race" (Patterson, Out of Order).

In addition to compiling returns, the networks also presented an array of special election features. Mutual stationed its correspondents in both national party headquarters (Chicago and Washington) as well as in other key cities: Los Angeles, Boston, New York, Baltimore, Detroit, San Francisco, Denver, Kansas City, Hartford, Columbus, Indianapolis, Des Moines, and Minnesota, where frequent pickups were made during the course of the election. NBC sent its mobile unit to Times Square to gauge the views of "typical voters," and CBS interviewed the youngest and oldest of those going to the polls. Listeners were given the opportunity to debate the merits of the two candidates through a new call-in format. At Mutual, Fulton Lewis, Jr., made dozens of calls to political figures for comments on the progress of the contest.[28]

Throughout November 5, the nets made "election news the order of the day." During the evening, with returns filtering in, NBC, CBS and MBS increased the length of their coverage and preempted sponsored programs as the occasion warranted. An effort was made to transmit the results during musical numbers and station breaks, but as more information became available, many shows were canceled outright.* On the popular *Fibber McGee and Molly* sitcom, producers prepared for this eventuality and redesigned their script in such a way as to integrate the election into that week's storyline. While the McGees spent a quiet evening home at 79 Wistful Vista, Fibber gestured toward his set at frequent intervals and said: "Let's listen to the election returns."[29]

Shortly after the polls closed, the nets carried the news of the outcome. Many eastern stations had already reported state results while polling was still occurring in the western half of the country. NBC and CBS had direct lines into Hyde Park and Rushville, Indiana, where FDR and Willkie (respectively) had been anxiously listening to the returns. Sam Rosenman recalled:

> The President seldom got his returns much earlier than any citizen who paid close attention to the radio. There was ... an AP ticker, a UP ticker and extra telephones in the dining room ... but I found that I would get quicker and more satisfactory information by going upstairs to join a small group which gathered...around a radio.[30]

Immediately after they had been notified of the public's verdict, both candidates were interviewed over the air.

On November 6, FCC chairman James Lawrence Fly applauded the network's adept handling of a very heated election. He favorably compared radio's "dispassionate and analytical discussions" to the "acrimonious" coverage of newspaper commentators and editorialists.[31] In 1939, Roosevelt had observed: "Only a well-informed electorate can discharge the duties of citizenship, and the cause of democracy is advanced by every means which carries correct information

---

*This stands in marked contrast to the previous two elections, when the nets either waited until returns were completely in, or broadcast them only "periodically" (Broadcasting, November 1, 1932, p. 8).

about public affairs to the farthest ends of the country."[32] Through frequent interviews with candidates and party officials, complete broadcasts of major speeches, and insightful commentary by political experts, NBC and CBS ensured that the voter who went to the polls in November 1940 was thoroughly familiar with the "issues of the campaign and the position of each candidate on them."[33] By using these devices, network news bureaus established a precedent for election coverage upon which the modern electronic media would build. Although computers, video, and satellites would eventually transform the processing and dissemination of political news, methods for gathering information would linger on from their inception in 1940.

Radio Discussion Programs

But listeners needed more than radio news broadcasts in their quest for information on current topics. There was a clear need for a program that "presented both sides of the great controversies then raging, such as Prohibition repeal, the causes of the Depression, and isolationism."[34] Radio fulfilled this need by means of a unique innovation, the national discussion program. The purpose of radio forums such as *America's Town Meeting of the Air*, *University of Chicago Roundtable*, *People's Platform*, *Wake Up America!* and *American Forum of the Air* was twofold. Such programs were designed to "increase public understanding of major issues and problems while, at the same time, educating the listener in the democratic way of free speech."[35]

In one of the most popular forums, *University of Chicago Roundtable*, the goal was to "make truth felt and influence men to act rationally." First aired nationally in October 1933, this program was usually presented by a panel of university professors, researchers, scholars and accomplished artists discussing a wide range of educational and cultural topics from poetry and science to economics and history. Producer Allen Miller emphasized spontaneity in his broadcasts and forbade any kind of written preparation by his guests. A few days prior to airtime, Miller selected a topic and chose three authorities that he felt were qualified to debate it. Prominent invitees frequently included T. S. Eliot, William Allen White, and Eleanor Roosevelt. The program originated from a studio on the University of Chicago campus, but often traveled to news centers around the country. It enjoyed a large following, and on one occasion, over 21,000 listeners requested written transcripts of a particular broadcast.[36] Given that broadcasts usually revolved around the "most provocative and timely national issues," it was no surprise that air sessions regularly became heated.[37] At one point, Miller arranged to have the studio table covered with two inches of felt to muffle the poundings of enthusiastic speakers.[38]

Another popular discussion program that attempted to get "behind the issues to the fundamentals of the news" was *America's Town Meeting of the Air*. The producers of the show stated, "Through the honest clash of authoritative

Debating the issues on one of America's most popular forums of the 1930s, *America's Town Meeting of the Air.*

opinions, it is our hope that our listeners will be stimulated to do more thinking, studying, and discussing of the questions, and will emerge from the experience with objectively reasoned opinions."[39] The program began on March 30, 1935, in a 60-minute format hosted by George V. Denny, Jr. More than any other forum, *Town Meeting* confronted listeners with a wide variety of opposing political opinions and ideologies. Arguing their points of view on a show entitled "Which Way for America?" (May 30, 1935) were a capitalist (Raymond Moley), a socialist (Norman Thomas), a communist (A. J. Muste), and a fascist (Lawrence Dennis).

Attempting to revive the traditional town assembly of old, the program opened with a town crier tolling a bell and proclaiming: "Hear ye! Hear ye! Town Meeting tonight!" After introducing the topic, the featured personalities "would tear into one another and then pit their wits against 4,500 heckling citizens gathered to question them in the Town Hall audience."[40] The show regularly received about 9,000 letters a week and proved so popular that it was carried by NBC for over 23 years.[41] *Town Meeting* enjoyed such a large following that over 1,000 discussion clubs were formed to hear each broadcast and "then carry on the debate after."[42] The program's contribution to "furthering the democratic process" earned it the Women's National Radio Committee Award in 1938 and the distinguished Peabody Radio Prize in 1940.[43]

Because of its enormous prestige, the show usually attracted the most notable guests: Eleanor Roosevelt, Fiorello La Guardia, Wendell Willkie, and Carl Sandburg.[44]

Other well-known forums included Theodore Granik's MBS series, *American Forum of the Air*, and NBC's *Wake Up, America!* Both encouraged listeners to call in or telegraph questions, which would be answered during the second half of each program.[45]

Some forums focused exclusively on a specific theme or issue of public concern. On January 28, 1939, CBS commenced its *What Price America?* series, which explored efficient ways to manage the country's national resources, and featured Sterling Fisher, national director of talks and education, introducing FCC chairman Frank McNinch, secretary of the interior Harold Ickes, and other government officials.[46] Other symposia had direct applications to the classroom. The CBS *American School of the Air*, which began in February 1930, was required listening in over 200,000 schools nationwide. Over 15 million children relished the opportunity to close their texts every day for "thirty minutes of stimulating and imaginative fun."[47] To assist instructors in their lesson planning, CBS printed a series of teaching manuals to accompany each week's schedule of broadcasts. Because of the show's success in facilitating learning, it ran for 18 years and "helped to distinguish CBS as a leader in the field of educational programming."[48]

Judging from the popular response, the discussion programs more than fulfilled their noble intentions. On October 26, 1939, in a *New York Herald-Tribune Forum* broadcast, President Roosevelt praised the fact that through forums, "radio listeners have learned to discriminate over the air between the honest advocate who relies on truth and logic, and the more dramatic speaker who is clever in appealing to the passions and prejudices of his listeners."[49] In a letter to the *New York Times*, postmaster-general James Farley wrote:

> I have been thoroughly convinced that one of the greatest benefits provided by radio is the nation-wide communication and discussion of public questions that have been made possible by this modern instrument. As a result, our people are now kept completely informed at all times on national matters, a situation which has brought about a keener interest in public affairs than ever before existed in this country.[50]

"Time Marches On"

Another new type of offering was the radio news drama, or docudrama. Begun in March 1931 as a publicity vehicle for *Time* magazine, the *March of Time* developed into one of radio's most popular and best-remembered shows. The program was billed as, "a new kind of reporting the news, the reenacting, as clearly and dramatically as the medium of radio will permit, [of] some scenes from the news of the week."[51] These aural recreations were accomplished through the efforts of a host of highly gifted vocal impersonators: Dwight Weist, Carl Frank, Arlene Francis, Jack Smart, Paul Stewart, Ed Jerome, Everett Sloane, Martin Gable, Clayton Collyer, and Frank Readick. Up until 1937, the show focused primarily on domestic matters—the Depression, gangsterism, and New Deal politics. After Hitler's reoccupation of the Rhineland, stories were increasingly foreign affairs–oriented. During the course of its 14-year run, virtually every prominent newsmaking personality had the honor of being mimicked on the air at one time or another: Huey Long, FDR, Hitler, Mussolini, La Guardia, Edward VIII, Stalin, William Randolph Hearst, Gen. Franco, Willkie, and many more. In one typical broadcast, listeners heard a "conversation" between undersecretary of state Sumner Welles and Japanese foreign office personnel about aerial bombing atrocities in China; J. Edgar Hoover "speaking" to Princeton police about his plans to foil a kidnapping; and Harry Hopkins defending the WPA.[52]

March of Time was highly touted for its ability to remain on top of fast-breaking events. "Right up to the minute this program goes on the air," it was proudly announced, "the news of the day is flashing into the studios of New York where the program originates."[53] To accomplish this task, MOT writers had access to the news bureaus of *Time* and *Life* and their globe-trotting armies of correspondents. The show was structured around the rapid-fire "Voice of Time" narrator, who introduced each story. This position was filled successively by Harry von Zell, Ted Husing, and Westbrook van Voorhis. The latter, who also provided the commentary of *March of Time* newsreels, is perhaps the most famous.

A high point for the show came on October 5, 1934, when Bruno Hauptmann was "interrogated" for the radio audience:

PROSECUTOR: Bruno Richard Hauptmann, you are indicted for extortion, suspicion of kidnapping and murder.

HAUPTMANN: I am innocent.

PROSECUTOR: The handwriting on the ransom note left on the window sill of the baby's room on the night of the kidnapping has been identified ... as your handwriting.

HAUPTMANN: I do not know anything about it.

PROSECUTOR: In your house was found a German-American dictionary with the pages turned down where appeared the most difficult words of that note found on the crib.

HAUPTMANN: I am innocent.

PROSECUTOR: The ladder used to enter the Lindbergh nursery was constructed from lumber taken from the lumberyard in which you once worked.

HAUPTMANN: I do not know. I was never in Hopewell.[54]

Frank Smith, the show's producer, declared that such half-hour presentations were even "more dramatic than history itself." Indeed, the *March of Time* provided broadcasting's most effective "fusion of news and entertainment, fact and fancy." A July 1939 Kansas State College poll found that 95 percent of those surveyed preferred "dramatized news in the MOT style" to straightforward reporting. In another indication of America's partiality for style over substance in the presentation of their news, a Los Angeles study conducted at the same time revealed that when choosing a news period to follow regularly, the personality of the commentator or announcer was far more important than the type of coverage he offered.[55]

While this certainly foreshadowed the image-centered habits and "polished techniques" of later television newscasting, there were important benefits to this sort of format.[56] By recasting otherwise complex issues of the day into "more hearthside drama," *March of Time* programs increased public interest and understanding in a way that is difficult to overstate. According to J. Fred MacDonald, by adding "theatricality and educative value to the reporting of the news, [the program] helped emphasize the importance of matters that needed to be considered by an informed citizenry."[57]

March of Time's "dressed-up news" formula inspired a new genre and a host of imitators. In 1935, CBS presented "dramatic accounts of leading events told by the people who were there." Using the first-person singular, *I Was There* brought to life such sensational stories as the assassination of Austrian Chancellor Dollfuss, the Spanish Civil War, and Edward VIII's marriage. To further lend credibility to their efforts, CBS drafted one of its regular news commentators, Knox Manning (and later Chet Huntley), to provide the narration. In many respects, this program served as the prototype for the later and far more sophisticated docudrama, *You Are There*.

9. Radio Covers the World

Just as radio provided the most effective means of covering news events of national interest, it proved equally capable of reporting on occurrences in faraway lands. In the 1930s, when the "challenge to American isolationism and to world peace" increased, radio kept listeners continuously abreast of the latest political and diplomatic developments from global trouble spots, and in the process greatly stimulated the public's interest in foreign affairs. Whether for a crisis report or forum discussion, a speech by a European leader or a shortwave pickup from a far-off battlefront, radio was employed by a new breed of broadcast journalists and commentators to bring current world events to listeners in a manner that was "more vivid and immediate" than the printed media.[1] As public interest peaked, the networks devoted more and more time to news programs, from 850 hours in 1937 to over 3,450 in 1941. Many of these programs began to be featured in prime evening spots, and by 1941 almost every station scheduled some type of daily newscast, with some "providing summaries every hour" to keep up with the fast pace of events in Europe.[2]

Through extensive coverage of the events leading up to World War II, radio helped to create an informed populace that was "kept up to date on the expanding world conflict and America's emerging role in it." In contrast to the confusion that prevailed among Americans in 1917, public sentiment by December 7, 1941 was largely consolidated, thanks to radio's contributions.[3] By enlightening listeners about the issues involved in the impending struggle, radio "helped to forge a national foreign policy consensus that unified the nation prior to our own involvement."[4]

Early Foreign News Reporting

As early as 1924, the networks had begun experimenting with broadcasts originating from abroad. In January of that year, the first transatlantic wireless communication was established between Maine and Chelmsford, England, but the results were so discouraging that the project was hastily terminated.[5] Due to poor shortwave transmissions which caused overseas voices to fade out in the middle of a program, subsequent foreign pickups were severely limited. When Charles Lindbergh made his historic flight from New York to Paris in

May 1927, "international broadcasting played no part in spreading the news of the event."[6] The few items that were aired usually consisted of musical programs or noninformational audio curiosities. In 1933, a series of contacts were made with the Byrd Antarctic expedition, and listeners were enchanted to hear the ringing of churchbells in Bethlehem on Christmas Day.[7] Possibly the most notable example of this type of offering was CBS's costly arrangement on March 25, 1932, to have American listeners hear a 30-minute singing recital by an English nightingale from a "forest somewhere in Surrey." Perhaps indicating network priorities at this time, this program received the radio editors' award for the most interesting program of the year.[8] CBS executive William Paley declared, "International broadcasts … have retained the character of novelty broadcasts in the minds of most people."[9] NBC vice-president Frank Mason added, "[Radio] does not feel it has a responsibility to its listeners to supply the news…. Radio is an entertainment medium."[10]

Despite the popularity of such amusing material, the networks occasionally flirted with the notion of using the shortwaves to convey foreign news. In 1932, CBS presented 93 programs from 17 different sources, many from the scene of the Geneva Disarmament Conference.[11] When Wiley Post and Harold Gatty flew from New York to Berlin, NBC was on hand to interview the pilots when they landed at Templehof Field.[12] In 1934, NBC's wide-ranging correspondent Max Jordan broadcast a report from Vienna describing the assassination of Austrian chancellor Engelbert Dollfuss.[13] There were also sporadic broadcasts from foreign centers made by newspaper reporters who happened to be on the scene when a significant event occurred.

"Ten Days That Shook the Ether"

Given the enchantment many Americans felt with royalty, it was no surprise that the first European event to be elaborately covered by the networks was the abdication of King Edward VIII of Great Britain. In December 1936, Edward's decision to marry American divorcee Wallis Simpson sparked a major political and constitutional crisis in Britain. When Prime Minister Stanley Baldwin advised the king that popular opinion would not support such a match, Edward arranged to make his marriage a morganatic one (in which his wife would not become queen). While Edward did have a small party in Parliament ("King's Friends"), most of the public, all three major political parties, the Church of England, and the Dominion prime ministers strongly resisted the suit. They warned that if he persisted with his marital plan, Edward he would have no choice but to vacate the throne. As all sides endeavored to negotiate a settlement, CBS news director Paul White instructed Caesar Saerchinger to set in place the personnel and the technical means necessary for covering "the most sensational news story since the Armistice of 1918."[14] Writes Saerchinger:

Nothing else mattered; the Conference in America, the war in Spain, the Pope's illness, some of the worst airplane disasters in years—only the love story of a king and an American woman, and their struggle for happiness, against the effulgent background of the greatest throne and the oldest tradition in the world.[15]

For the next ten nights, the three American networks sent over eighty 15-minute reports (20 hours total) from across the Atlantic. Broadcasts from London averaged eight a day, "an all-time record for any single subject or event since international broadcasting began." Coverage was so intense that the networks "seemed to be originating as many programs from London as New York or Hollywood."[16] Of the American public's insatiable appetite for news from abroad, Saerchinger remarked:

Radio caught the big story at its flood, and from now on millions of eager people in the U.S. and Canada literally hung on their sets with bated breath as of unravelled, chapter by chapter, a story which raced with increased momentum to its dramatic close.... Hardly had we given the latest available news in a midnight talk, when they wanted another one at 4 am—even if there was nothing new! The public was wild and we were going mad. New York rang up to confirm every wild rumor; conservative but reliable information merely aroused suspicion that I was "slow." Day after day, night after night, we kept it up—with almost no sleep—hunting news, hounding speakers....[17]

In reporting the events of the crisis, radio at all times displayed a thoroughness and level-headedness that sharply contrasts with the manner in which the affairs of the Windsors are portrayed in today's media.

It wisely confined itself to the bare outward facts. To mere speculation and sensation-mongering, it opposed authoritarian analyses of the points at issue. It gave the historical background to the crisis; interpreted the traditional aspects and the political implications.... Lawyers and historians, sociologists and statesmen, nobles and commoners, parliamentarians of every shade, were drafted to this task of explanation and interpretation.[18]

The crisis reached its peak on December 11. The king had met the rest of the royal family at Windsor to discuss the issue. Meanwhile, Baldwin convened his cabinet in an emergency session and promised a statement for the next day. It was expected that he would introduce a bill in Parliament requesting Edward's abdication and conferring the succession on his brother, the Duke of York. When this was exactly what happened on December 12, radio was the first medium to report the news. Saerchinger remembers:

At 3:30 pm, Mr. Baldwin, a sealed document in his hand, rose from his seat [in the House of Commons], bowed to the Speaker and said: "A message from His Majesty the King".... At precisely 3:32 pm in London, my telephone outside our Broadcasting House studio rang, and a voice ... announced the fact of abdication.... The moment I got my signal,

I was able to announce to the waiting millions that King Edward VIII had abdicated, announce it from the very studio from which he had introduced himself to the Empire as King. In the meantime, over another telephone, the bulletin giving the actual text of the King's message had begun to come in. This, and Mr. Baldwin's moving recital of the whole story leading up to this tragic end, we read direct to the American listener at the very moment that the story was barely arriving in the newspaper offices in New York. Listening to the open circuit from New York I heard the announcer reading the Press-Radio bulletin announcing the King's abdication twenty minutes after I had announced it to the listeners direct. For twenty minutes the world outside knew through my words alone that King Edward was King no longer. For once, radio had "scooped the world."[19]

The next day, Edward confirmed what had happened in his own words. To listeners in the "four corners of the world," Sir John Reith introduced Prince Edward from Windsor Castle. After making some final corrections to his typewritten speech and requesting that all staff, engineers, and visitors leave the room so that he could be alone, the profoundly saddened former king spoke:

You all know the reason which has impelled me to renounce the throne.... You must believe me when I tell you that I found it impossible to carry the heavy burden ... without the woman I love. The other person concerned has tried to the last to persuade me to take a different course ... And now we have a new King. God bless you all. God save the King![20]

When his successor was crowned King George VI on May 12, 1937, the networks mounted another spectacular effort, spending three months preparing to cover the first coronation ever aired. While CBS and NBC relied heavily on the facilities and staff of the BBC, they also had to put together their own "small army of announcers, engineers and correspondents," and to purchase 7 tons of batteries and 472 miles of wire.[21] In the week before the royal pageant, network representatives in London presented a series of daily talks and interviews with many "informed experts": Hector Bolitho, Alistair Cooke, Lords Elton, Ponsonby and Strabolgi, Lady Astor, the marquis of Lothian, and others. During the ceremony itself, radio "brought all of the old world's pomp and circumstance into the ordinary lives of Americans" in an unprecedented six hours of live coverage. Some fifty or sixty microphones were installed at strategic points along the royal procession route, from Buckingham Palace, through Piccadilly Circus and Marble Arch, to Westminster. In order to present the most "complete and vivid picture possible," one microphone was placed "under the throne itself."[22] As listeners waited for the king to arrive in the Abbey, one correspondent described the spectacle inside:

A magnificent sight those bishops look with their golden and green coats.... The procession is gradually beginning to move up. All is quiet now and all eyes are turned toward the royal entrance. The banners are moving up slowly toward the west door. Everybody is in line and everybody's fairly quiet. The rustling you hear is the movement of the standards, which are at this moment just passing our microphones.... They are an absolutely magnificent sight—the splash of color against the deep blue of the carpets. And around the walls, the King's Company, the Grenadier Guards, form a guard of honor. And here she is, Her Majesty the Queen, with her magnificent purple and gold train.... Now below us, the gentlemen at arms have divided, and they have formed a broad avenue down which His Majesty will pass.... We see a blue stream running between two crimson banks—the most tremendous sight you could ever want to see. And behind the left-hand rank of the gentlemen at arms are the Yeomen of the Guard with their Tudor bonnets and carrying their halberds....[23]

An NBC spokesman was so proud of his network's achievement that he proclaimed, "You don't have to join the Navy to see the world!"[24] The abdication and coronation broadcasts were significant in that they marked the first time in broadcast history that "listeners in large numbers paid close attention to a foreign crisis as it happened."[25]

The trend of high American listenership during broadcasts depicting European royalty persisted throughout the 1930s. In 1939, NBC transmitted the duke of Windsor's speech from the Verdun battlefield (May 8) and covered the arrival of George VI in Quebec (May 17) for record audiences.[26]

Unfortunately, network executives were still slow to recognize radio's potential for bringing outside events home to the American public. By the end of 1937, CBS representatives in Europe stated that "none but the most urgent or important news could displace temporarily a program designed to entertain."[27] As a result, network news directors busied themselves with the task of scheduling concerts and special events broadcasts that often included publicity stunts like the "Great Singing Mouse Contest."[28]

It was only the tremors of war in Europe that stirred the networks out of their lethargic attitude toward regular foreign news broadcasting. When the Spanish Civil War erupted in 1936, the networks discovered a golden opportunity for American radio to thoroughly cover a major conflict. While broadcasts originating from the Iberian Peninsula were infrequent, radio correspondents like H. V. Kaltenborn were successful in transporting the war into millions of American living rooms. Kaltenborn recognized that merely "describing an event second-hand," as most news reporters had done, "failed to utilize one of radio's prime advantages over other mediums of mass communication." Through the use of "portable broadcasting facilities," it was possible to transport the listener to the scene of war and allow him to hear the genuine sounds of battle.[29] In July 1936, at the Battle of Irun, Kaltenborn broadcast from a haystack located near the Franco-Spanish border as Loyalist and Republican forces clashed around him. Through a sophisticated hookup that connected Kaltenborn's microphone to a telephone line in a nearby farmhouse, his words were sent to Bordeaux and then to Paris, London, Rugby, and by shortwave to New York.[30] As bullets whizzed past, and shells exploded nearby, Kaltenborn's account provided the "first time in history [when] people sitting in the safety of their homes an ocean away, could hear a war actually happening."[31] For a nation that valued its geographic isolation, the conflict in Europe no longer seemed a distant affair. According to one observer, the Old World, which used to be thousands of miles away, was now "only a kilocycle away."[32]

Anschluss

In March 1938, American listeners got their first indication of the aggressive designs of the German Führer, Adolf Hitler. When the Wehrmacht rolled into Austria on March 12, CBS had correspondent William L. Shirer on hand in Vienna. When he tried to contact the network with an account of what he had witnessed, he was bullied out of the studio by bayonet-wielding Nazi soldiers. Undeterred, Shirer immediately hopped a flight to London and delivered his story there.

> With the announcement that the plebiscite was off, the Nazis suddenly poured by the tens of thousands into the old inner city.... I saw a strange sight: twenty men bent down, formed a human pyramid, and a little man—I suppose he was picked for his weight—scampered over a lot of shoulders and, clutching a huge swastika flag, climbed to the balcony of the Chancellery.[33]

Shirer went on to describe how Hitler's armies, understanding the propaganda value of radio, made the Vienna station one of their primary strategic targets. Commenting on an integral component of blitzkrieg tactics that would be employed by the Germans in every subsequent invasion, *Broadcasting* noted:

> The technique of the modern invader, we have learned in this brutal era of mechanized and parachute troop warfare, is first to grab all lines of communication, particularly broadcasting outlets. The captured transmitters can then blare forth the conqueror's propaganda. Radio is the nerve-center in modern warfare.[34]

Coming on the air only hours after the actual event, Shirer's vivid account was the first broadcast in a nearly continuous stream of coverage that would last for the next six days. On March 13, CBS news director Paul White developed a new broadcasting technique. In the first multiple-pickup international broadcast, reporters in several European capitals "stood by microphones connected to shortwave transmitters and discussed the events of the day from their various vantage points." In an incredible "feat of logistics and planning," each correspondent gave his account live, "thousands of miles away from each other, yet able to hear and comment on their colleague's reports."[35] In this first "European News Roundup," American listeners learned about the Anschluss from the perspectives of Pierre Huss in Berlin, Edgar Mowrer in Paris, William Shirer in London, and Frank Gervasi in Rome. From Washington, Senator Lewis B. Schwellenbach supplied the American point of view. Coordinating all of this was Bob Trout in the CBS studio in New York, "in simultaneous telephone contact with all six speakers."[36] During the next six days of the Austrian crisis, CBS presented sixteen such roundups.[37] For the first time in history, the "peculiar magic of radio" had placed all of Europe within immediate reach of a listener's fingertips.[38] At the turn of a dial, Americans could instantly receive the latest news emanating from the main centers of Europe "by English-speaking correspondents on the spot."[39]

On the evening of March 13, listeners heard the first monologue by a reporter whose voice would become familiar to all Americans within the next two years. As Edward R. Murrow delivered his account of Vienna's fall, he gave a hint of the "descriptive genius, poetic insight and sensitive touch" that would soon distinguish him as one of the most talented newscasters in the history of broadcasting.[40]

> This is Edward R. Murrow speaking from Vienna. It is now nearly 2:30 in the morning and Herr Hitler has not yet arrived.... From the air, Vienna didn't look much different than it has before, but, nevertheless, it's changed. The crowds are courteous as they've always been, but many people are in a holiday mood; they lift the right arm a little higher here than in Berlin and the "Heil Hitler" is said a little more loudly. There isn't a great deal of hilarity, but at the same time there doesn't seem to be much feeling of tension. Young storm troopers are riding about the streets, riding about in trucks and vehicles of all sorts, singing and tossing oranges out to the crowd. Nearly every municipal building has its armed guard, including the one from which I am speaking.... There's a certain air of expectancy about the city, everyone waiting and wondering where and at what time Herr Hitler will arrive.[41]

The success of radio's coverage of the Anschluss forever altered the character of foreign broadcasting by the American networks. Until March 1938, shortwave newscasting had been very much an improvised affair. Bob Trout relates how CBS responded to the Austrian situation by "rigging up a studio" in its Madison Avenue suite and "hanging curtains on the walls to deafen [extraneous] sounds."[42] When informed of the scheduled pickup from Vienna, Shirer fretted:

> The truth is I didn't have the faintest idea how to do it. We had done one or two of these, but there had been months of fussing over technical arrangements before each one.... Now we had to put one together in eight hours.[43]

So dubious was Trout about the possibility of establishing contact with the Alpine capital that in "anticipation of pure static," he prepared an apology for listeners stating that the Vienna transmitter had been closed down.[44]

Because the networks had shown no inclination to maintain their own correspondents in Europe on even a semi-permanent basis, the Anschluss broadcasts had been possible only through the considerable assistance of various newspapermen, especially those from the AP, INS and *Chicago Tribune*. Ten days after the Vienna reports, Murrow sought to rectify this shortcoming. Immediately upon his return to London, he began to construct a full-time news organization that could capably serve America's growing appetite for international news. At first, Murrow was so anxious to assemble his staff, he neglected to screen applicants for such obvious criteria as "diction, phrasing or manner of speech."[45] Despite this oversight, Edward was nevertheless able to attract individuals who effectively combined both news-gathering savvy and considerable vocal ability.[46] With reference to his new team of correspondents—Bill Downs, Winston Burdett, Cecil Brown, Howard K. Smith, and Richard C. Hottlet—Murrow remarked prophetically, "I think this [radio journalism] thing may develop into something."[47]

Whereas technical facilities had previously been scarce, and transatlantic broadcasts infrequent, now European radio bureaus and news roundups would become a permanent component of the daily operation of radio news broadcasting.[48] Observers in the world of journalism hailed radio's achievement during the Anschluss as the "most complete coverage of a historical crisis ever achieved."[49] It was indeed a noteworthy performance—yet it pales in comparison to the coverage of the next great European predicament, the Czech crisis.

Munich Crisis

After swallowing Austria in March 1938, Hitler turned his sights on Czechoslovakia. In a fervid speech at Nuremberg on September 12, 1938, the German chancellor demanded the immediate cessation of the rich industrial Sudetenland to the Reich. The Czechs refused and requested the military assistance of Britain and France to back them in their position. As Europe braced for war, the leaders of the western democracies feverishly sought a nonviolent solution to this menacing dispute. For 18 days, between September 12 and 29, the American radio networks reported, minute-by-minute, the rapid course of diplomatic activity to an anxious audience. Providing the most comprehensive news coverage of a foreign event to date, radio reported every phase of the Czech crisis, from its beginning with the mobilization of German troops, through the negotiations at Godesberg, to its peaceable resolution at the Munich Conference of September 29.

As a result of network preparations during the Anschluss, radio was ready to give unprecedented coverage to this new emergency. CBS news director Paul White instructed his European director in London, Ed Murrow, and his continental representative, William Shirer, to expand their staffs of expert journalists and commentators in every European capital. All were to be prepared to broadcast the latest news to America on a moment's notice. A similar effort was mounted by NBC, where news director Abe Schecter augmented his personnel in London, Paris and Geneva. In America, communications were established with the White House and State Department, and a special "Studio Nine" was constructed as the center of operations for NBC's correspondents around the world. With this intricate system of coverage, the networks sought to bring home the events in Europe to a "distant America that still remembered 1917."[50]

The first way this was accomplished was by providing the American public the most up-to-date news as soon as it had occurred. Americans soon became accustomed to regular programming being interrupted by news flashes and bulletins at any hour of the day or night. During the 18 days of the crisis, NBC alone sent some 440 of these brief news transmissions.[51] In a rapid-fire stream of communiques, radio delivered a "complete blow-by-blow account as Europe teetered on the brink of war." Some of these tense announcements included:

September 12

ANNOUNCER: This morning the entire civilized world is anxiously awaiting the speech of Adolf Hitler, whose single word may plunge all of Europe into another world war…

September 15.

ANNOUNCER: Chamberlain has just left Munich for Berchtesgaden … Hitler demands the surrender of the Sudeten border area by Czechs as the price for peace in Europe…

September 17

ANNOUNCER: Prime Minister Chamberlain and his Cabinet are at this moment gathered round the polished oak table at No. 10 Downing Street, deciding whether to surrender to Hitler's demands or send Europe to war … Hitler is waiting impatiently … it must come soon if hostilities are to be averted…

September 18

ANNOUNCER: Daladier and Foreign Minister Bonnet have arrived in London … Mussolini speaks from Trieste, "If it comes to war there is no question which side Italy is on" … Czechs refuse the plebiscite…

September 20

ANNOUNCER: France and Britain tell Czechs that her answer is unsatisfactory … and that unconditional acceptance of Germany's demands must be delivered within 24 hours or Czechoslovakia will bear the consequences of invasion … Sudeten Army mobilizes…

September 21

ANNOUNCER: Czechs accept terms and will surrender Sudeten territory to Germany…

September 23

ANNOUNCER: Godesberg meeting has been postponed … Germany has 22 divisions on the border … French troop movement reported … Clash between Czech and German troops reported … Beneš orders full mobilization of Czech Army … Daladier pledges to come to assistance of Czechoslovakia if Germany invades … Negotiations stall between Chamberlain and Hitler…

September 23

ANNOUNCER: Negotiations have broken off entirely in Godesberg … All Europe is preparing for a threatened invasion of Czechoslovakia…

September 24

ANNOUNCER: Heavy German troop movements observed … Partial mobilization of the French Navy and Air Force … Great Britain prepares to mobilize all of its armed forces…

September 26

ANNOUNCER: French Chief of Staff arrives in London to discuss mobilization and joint defense plans between Britain and France … Antiaircraft guns have been mounted in Berlin … Americans in France advised by American Embassy in Paris to leave the country … British Parliament to meet in emergency session … FDR appeals for peace to Hitler…

September 27

ANNOUNCER: Russia has mobilized … King George has just declared a state of emergency … Everything is now ready for war … Second Roosevelt appeal to Hitler…

September 28

ANNOUNCER: Hitler announces Four Power Conference in Munich…[52]

In addition to these short summaries, American listeners received more comprehensive reports from direct shortwave pickups and commentaries from correspondents who were on the spot.* These transmissions were instrumental

---

*In the year leading up to Munich, the networks had been fine-tuning their shortwave techniques. At the end of 1937, NBC sent George Hicks 7,000 miles around the world to Canton

in keeping the world informed of the situation in Czechoslovakia, particularly since cable and telephone service out of that country had been extremely unreliable. Throughout the month of September, CBS and NBC together sent almost 300 special foreign broadcasts (CBS-151, NBC-147) to America from 70 correspondents.[53] In all, the nets generated over 73 hours of shortwave material from some 16 different continental centers, in addition to many hours of bulletins, commentaries, and other broadcasts. One observer noted: "It seemed as though newsmen were almost continuously on the air."[54] These reports originated with Murrow and Stephen King-Hall in London, Shirer in Prague, John Whittaker in Paris, Max Jordan in Munich, as well as from sources in Godesberg, Nuremberg, Geneva, Baden, Padua, Trieste, and Budapest.[55] NBC gloated, "This couldn't happen in 1914, but today through the miracle of radio, all America hears history being made ... and follows it across Europe's seething map!"[56] American listeners routinely prepared to be transported across vast distances every time the magic phrase was uttered: "We take you now to..."

At times these reporters had to surmount the greatest difficulties in order to get their stories on the air. One time, Shirer had to travel more than a thousand miles by air, sail, truck, and horse-driven carriage to file a report. Once a correspondent reached the microphone, he faced the most formidable obstacle of all: censorship. Because of a lack of efficient shortwave facilities in Prague, programs had to be conveyed by landwire to Berlin, where there were transmitters powerful enough to beam them across the Atlantic. To prevent the broadcast of material that might create an unfavorable impression of Germany, Berlin authorities regularly denied access to their equipment or "imposed a tight censorship that would entirely isolate Czechoslovakia from radio communication with the outside world."[57] Reporters filing their stories from the German capital had to submit three copies of each script for approval (propaganda office, military censor, foreign office) before it could go over the air.[58] (The Paris censors were only slightly less stringent, requiring two copies to be surrendered in advance of airtime.) Shirer quickly learned how to circumvent the rigors of official scrutiny:

> Using my wits ... to indicate a truth or an official lie by the tone and inflection of my voice, by a pause held longer than is natural, by the use of an Americanism which most Germans, who learned their English in England, would not fully grasp, and by drawing from a word, a phrase, a sentence, a paragraph, or their juxtaposition, all the benefit I could.[59]

The fact that the landwires of all central and eastern European nations

Island to report on the longest total eclipse in over a millennium. In early 1938, U.S. Egyptologists broadcast from within the pyramids of Giza. In 1938, NBC made 556 shortwave pickups from points all over the globe. The success of such presentations led one industry official to declare: "Ten years ago shortwave was news...today it supplies news!" (Broadcasting, February 1, 1939, p. 35).

converged in Berlin meant that an ejected American correspondent could not go elsewhere to dispatch his story. The only solution was to construct a transmitter in Prague capable of reaching the United States directly. By September, Czech officials had installed such a machine, and CBS immediately pressed it into service.

Another major problem for radio reporters was inhospitable weather (including high winds, sunspots, and electrical storms, among other problems), which frequently prevented signals from emanating from Prague and other cities.[60] There was no way of predicting the weather over a 4,000-mile zone. Conditions could change rapidly and overwhelm a program with static midway through transmission.* But for the most part, listeners enjoyed reception as clear as if the correspondents' voices originated not from distant centers but from "the home of any one of the Americans gathered around a loud speaker."[61]

Many Americans appreciated the "comprehensible and intensely human nature" of these broadcasts. No reporter communicated the plight of the Czech people more effectively than CBS correspondent Maurice Hindus. From Prague, he observed:

> The spirit these people are displaying in these crucial times is beyond belief ... One man said to me this morning: "I'm a very old man now.... Today I am seventy. Well, after all, seventy is not such a bad age at which to die."[62]

During the Munich Crisis, radio achieved many firsts that were beyond the reach of other media. Some examples included CBS's exclusive broadcast of British foreign minister Anthony Eden's Stratford-upon-Avon speech and Mutual's live interview with Chamberlain at Croydon Airport in Paris.[63] On September 29, NBC's Max Jordan scooped the world by reading the complete text of the Four-Power Agreement over the air, only minutes after it had been signed.[64] Because of the Herculean efforts of such men as Jordan, the American people knew the details of the accord two hours before the citizens of France, Britain, and Germany.† Using radio's power to convey emotion, Shirer commented on the Munich conference in this way:

> There is to be no European war after all! There is to be peace, and the price of that peace is, roughly, the ceding by Czechoslovakia of the Sudatenland to Hitler's Germany.... And that's the end, after just five and a half hours of talking here in Munich today, of Bohemia's 1,000-year-old frontiers. And of course, what is left of Czechoslovakia becomes another kind of state altogether.[65]

Many network correspondents were also able to communicate their views in the daily European roundups. By the time of Munich, this device was

---

*This is precisely what happened to Dorothy Thompson during her May 10, 1940, broadcast from Paris. To make matters worse, on the same program, atmospherics completely prevented contact with NBC's Stockholm correspondent (UMP #0235).

†American broadcasters consistently scooped their European counterparts. Early morning newscasts usually opened with the words: "London awoke to the news which you in the U.S. heard last night..." (CBS News, September 28, 1938, UMP #0233).

rapidly becoming a standard feature of news broadcasting. CBS alone aired fourteen transatlantic roundtable talks in September. In a situation where "the diplomatic positions of the major negotiating powers were constantly in flux, radio kept Americans up-to-date."[66] In a typical international broadcast of this sort, when Americans were eager to learn how the world would respond to Hitler's demands, the nets presented views from New York, Prague, Paris, London, Rome, and Berlin during their daily five-minute European tours.*

Although Mutual did not possess a news-gathering service comparable to CBS and NBC, it was no less successful in fulfilling its obligation to keep the public informed. Many foreign governments broadcast news in English to the United States by shortwave in order to provide their own interpretations of the day's events. MBS decided to bring to its audience the "last-minute news from Paris, Prague, and Berlin exactly as it came through from these foreign centers."[67] The shortwave signals were picked up by New York–based listening posts and channeled, unedited, through MBS's normal transmitters for public consumption in the United States. During September, the network rebroadcast more than 130 such programs.[68]

Mutual did have its own reporters in Europe, John Steele in London and Louis Hoot in Paris, but they rarely went on the air. To avoid the high costs of maintaining transoceanic phone communications, these correspondents usually telegraphed their copy to New York, where it was read by an announcer. By making do in its own economical way, MBS was able to "maintain its place in the scramble for news coverage with its wealthier rivals."[69]

Popular interest in shortwave swelled during the Munich Crisis. By providing shortwave tuning guides entitled "War News from the War Capitals," industry periodicals "encouraged listeners to tune in to trouble spots directly."[70] Responding to widespread demand, radio manufacturers began equipping most units with multiple foreign bands.

Network use of shortwave also made it possible to broadcast the actual voices of the principal players in the Munich drama. By the time the crisis was over, American listeners had the opportunity to experience firsthand all of the important speeches by Hitler, Mussolini, Chamberlain, Daladier, Konrad Henlein, and Edvard Beneš.[71] Other prominent figures such as Czech ambassador Jan Masaryk, Anthony Eden, Josef Goebbels, Premier Hodza of Hungary, Russian foreign minister Maxim Litvinoff, and Pope Pius XII were also heard.[72] From Hitler's address in Nuremberg on September 12 to Chamberlain's "Peace in our Time" speech at a London airport on September 30, radio had made it possible for Americans to "witness history in the making as it poured through their loudspeakers."[73]

In many respects, American listeners were as well-apprised of the European

While shortwave pickups occasionally emanated from other locales during the crisis, these were the permanent network anchors in the round-up system.

situation as their foreign policy leaders. Indeed, President Roosevelt and his cabinet regularly tuned in during the crisis. The "on-the-scene familiarity that radio provided, formed the basis from which they made many of their decisions."[74] In many foreign policy meeting photographs, a radio is located on the table next to the president.

Presiding over all of this activity was Hans von Kaltenborn in CBS's Studio Nine. Here is Kaltenborn's description of this state-of-the art facility:

> [It] is furnished with three desks, on each of which rests a microphone. One of the walls is hung with a sound-absorbent curtain to control acoustics. The room's one window looks into the 'control room', where the engineer sits behind his panel of instruments. The room has two entrances— one through the control room, the other through a small chamber where teletype machines pound out the cable news from the three great press associations. Adjoining the ticker room on the opposite side is Paul White's office, where telephone calls are put through to the various cities in Europe, and the various departments in the network—all of which must function together as smoothly as clockwork.[75]

As the great stream of bulletins, speeches, two-way conversations, and eyewitness accounts came pouring in from across the Atlantic, Kaltenborn attempted to make sense of them for the average American listener. Rarely was an overseas broadcast not followed by some type of comment or interpretation. Kaltenborn promised his audience:

> Following every important new development, whether reported directly from abroad or through a cabled news dispatch, you can take it for granted that I [will] come on the air with an analysis of the news, fitting it into its place in the whole picture and thus prepare you for the next eventuality.[76]

Much of the broadcasting community noted how Kaltenborn's "processing of the facts into an understandable picture of the situation" significantly "enhanced the public's overall comprehension of the complex issues involved in the Czech crisis."[77] Kaltenborn's frequent analyses earned him a large following, and throughout Munich he monopolized the radio spotlight. For eighteen consecutive days, the "Dean of Commentators" was on the air in over 85 separate broadcasts.[78] To keep up with the continuous flood of information reaching him from overseas, Kaltenborn remained awake for days on end, sleeping on a studio cot only between news flashes. Recounting his ritual every time the teletypes "clanged their bells and pounded out" a fresh release, Kaltenborn wrote:

> Before the ticker has completed the bulletin, Paul White has rushed into Studio Nine. "A flash Hans," he says, and pushes the button on [a] little box. Immediately, all other programs are cut from the air, and all stations are connected with my microphone, and that of the announcers at my side. While the announcer tells listeners where they are, an attendant brings me

H. V. Kaltenborn commenting on fast-breaking developments.

the bulletin, which I read and on which I comment. Then the engineer is given the cue to restore the network once more to normal operations.[79]

Because of his facility with several foreign languages, particularly German, Kaltenborn was uniquely equipped for this task. Many times, he could translate speeches by foreign leaders instantaneously as they came through his headset. Kaltenborn provided running commentaries for Hitler's Nuremberg (September 12) and Berlin (September 26) speeches. In contrast to his report from Irun two years earlier, which had been held up until airtime could be arranged for it, "CBS now gave Kaltenborn's broadcasts priority over all commercial obligations." In this way, Columbia lost some $25,000 in advertising refunds.[80] But this was "trifling compared with the widespread respect the network had won through its fifty hours of Kaltenborn's news commentary."[81]

Because of the "extraordinary quality of the reportage and its speed in reaching the listener," radio's coverage of the Munich Crisis was an unqualified success for American broadcasting.[82] One international affairs expert wrote:

> The European news service of CBS showed as never before how a population can be given immediate understanding of events distant in space, breathless in speed, and of ultimate effect on the life and thought of almost every American. Those who are on the European scene are not so well informed about the meaning of current events as the American people thousands of miles away.[83]

Another observer explained, "This great feat of speedy and comprehensive news reporting elevated the prestige of broadcasting as an industry as has no other single event or series of happenings since its advent sixteen years ago."[84] William Paley congratulated his newsmen on "the best job of its kind ever done in radio broadcasting."[85]

Despite the fact that the press had again been outdone, spokesmen for the printed media did not conceal their praise. H. O. Bishop, speaker of the National Press Club, declared: "Radio has leaped ahead ten years in the last three weeks," and other newspapermen called it "the most remarkable feat of coverage in history."[86] Acclaim was also offered the networks from across the sea. In the British weekly news journal *Cavalcade*, one author noted:

> The best information on the development of the international situation for many days past has come from American shortwave stations. Vivid on-the-spot relays from foreign capitals, plus expert commentaries by students of foreign affairs, have kept Americans abreast of events. Fortunate are those Britons who had receivers which brought in the Columbia broadcasts.[87]

This view was supported by the British ambassador to the United States, Lord Lothian, who remarked, "Anyone who wanted to know the truth about the Czech situation should have tuned in to the American stations."[88]*

In a September 30 press conference, President Roosevelt praised the "fine way in which … the radio kept [its] feet on the ground" during the crisis.[89] To industry officials who lived in constant "fear of federal control of communications," radio had so proved its value as a privately owned medium by its remarkable public service that "advocates of government censorship … have been decisively thrown back."[90]

As a consequence of radio's extensive coverage, the Munich Crisis was the best-known event in European history at the time.[91] The American people had never been so moved by a situation occurring beyond their own country's borders.[92] Lord Lothian observed, "There is no country in the world in which public opinion today is more interested in foreign affairs and more universally informed by radio than in the U.S."[93]

Sensing the "urgency in events taking place overseas," Americans now began turning in significant numbers to their radios as their major source of news. Public interest in radio news expanded considerably during the crisis. Many polls indicated that 69 percent of all listeners to network broadcasts during September had tuned in to news shows.[94] A Kansas State College survey found that less than 8 percent of Americans did not listen to at least one newscast a day. The same poll revealed that news shows were the "most consistently popular

---

*On several occasions during New York–Prague transatlantic interviews, Kaltenborn surprised Maurice Hindus with news items "of which the entire Czech people were still in ignorance" (Kaltenborn, p. 4).

program on the air today." It also noted a 39 percent increase in the number of listeners during 1938.[95] In the midst of the crisis, "more radio sets were sold than during any previous three-week period in the industry's history."[96] The fact that many of them were the new line of portable units that had just hit the market ensured that people were listening in places where radio had not previously penetrated.[97] The new fashion for listening to foreign news from early morning to late at night was reflected in the large number of telegrams that were received by network newsrooms.[98] Since a majority of the country's affiliate stations had carried the Munich broadcasts, listeners on farms and in isolated rural communities were able to tune in for the first time.[99] A reporter for the *Chicago Herald-Tribune* remarked that even "in the far western states, quite removed from the populous centers, I found businessmen who bought extra radios for their offices and even for their bathrooms, so they could be in constant touch with new developments in Europe." Because of the new mass interest in foreign affairs that radio had stimulated, "network news operations transformed from a marginal activity relegated to undesirable time slots, to a prestigious, sponsored enterprise aired during peak hours."[100] Shirer observed:

> It was the Czech Crisis which made daily coverage a permanent thing on American radio. Reluctant at first to allot its correspondents in Prague and elsewhere so much as five minutes of time a day, CBS within a week now carries a dozen broadcasts from European capitals.[101]

Some observers felt that radio had not only proved a "capable spectator" during Munich, but had been active in finding a solution to the predicament. H. V. Kaltenborn remarked in his book *I Broadcast the Crisis* that in bringing the nation a coverage "so swift, so sure and so complete, radio became of itself one of the most significant events in the crisis." It had demonstrated that "in every great crisis in which it played a part, the "ultimate issue of peace or war would be decided ... [through] the great forum of the air." Kaltenborn wrote:

> In September, war came closer than it has come since the Armistice. We were saved from war, I am convinced, by the mobilization of world opinion for peace. When the crisis came, we had mastered a force of which we knew almost nothing in 1914. Through it, and because of it, the peoples of the world demanded and got an exact accounting of every important move by their leaders. The people heard not merely from their own leaders, but, even in countries where censors may try to plug up the ether itself, from the leaders of all nations involved in the crisis. The medium worked both ways, and through it, the people carried back to their leaders their response to every move. Their response was a demand for peace which even the most hardened dictator could not but obey. The medium was radio.[102]

This view was reinforced by President Roosevelt's comments in his September 30 press conference. When asked if he thought radio had hastened the end of the imbroglio, the president replied, "Because of radio and easier communication ... the meeting of the situation was speeded up ... and [could] be tided over more quickly.... As we all know, in this particular crisis, a very large portion of the earth's surface took some part in an expression of government opinion and public opinion."[103] FDR, with his characteristic ability to gauge the popular mood, clearly understood the "dual role of technology and public opinion in influencing foreign policy." He recognized, as did others, that the "barrage of broadcast statements" by world statesmen had added an utterly new dimension to diplomacy. Now, "for the first time, history [had] been made in the hearing of its pawns."[104]

Apparently Hitler had not understood this. Recent archival research has revealed that the success of Germany's original Sudeten invasion plan depended upon moving quickly and presenting the western powers with a fait accompli before the action became public knowledge. Radio's intensive coverage of the event ensured that public opinion was well-informed of Hitler's intentions and aroused against it right from the start. Nazi party heads and the German general staff certainly listened to the output of American short-wave stations. According to James Rorty: "What they heard was ... the voice of world opinion rising in pitch and volume, and becoming more articulate and more menacing."[105]

While the German Führer might have been able to ignore international sentiment, he had to take into account the feelings of his own people. Widespread listening to Allied shortwave newscasts, either openly or clandestinely, was instrumental in diminishing the zeal with which many Reich citizens embraced the Nazi cause in Czechoslovakia.* This was a vivid demonstration of the way in which radio had profoundly transformed the conduct of conventional warfare. In an advertisement for one of its products, RCA boasted:

> The Battle of New Orleans would never have been fought had radio communications been developed in 1815. Andrew Jackson met and defeated the British at New Orleans two weeks after peace had been signed in Ghent, Belgium. Today, via RCA communications, news travels at lightning speed ... Radio would have saved over 2,000 lives![106]

Radio pioneer Lee De Forest also predicted that radio would serve to shorten the length of modern war. In an article for *Broadcasting*, he asserted: "The masses of the warring nations [can] acquire hourly knowledge of how the battle is going on all fronts. Therefore, radio conditions exist making for an earlier termination of the awful slaughter by the suffering masses themselves, the ones who always pay with their blood."[107] Unfortunately, for the 55 million soldiers and civilians that were about to die in the longest and most destructive world conflict in history, this confident forecast would prove woefully untrue.

*For a fascinating examination of this topic, see Ian Kershaw, Popular Opinion and Political Dissent in the Third Reich: Bavaria 1933-45 (Oxford, 1983).

As the American public listened to the Munich reports, it began to draw some important conclusions. By "creating a mass interest in foreign affairs" and by "drawing the world closer to home," radio broadcasting was emerging as a "principal means of combating isolationism."[108] Through coverage that "fostered a greater familiarity and understanding" of Europe's difficulties, "the blind, head-in-the-sand isolationist view of foreign affairs was no longer tenable."[109] At last, a previously ambivalent American public was becoming painfully aware that Germany, "alone among the big powers, was playing for keeps."[110] The unmistakable anti–Nazi tones in the voices of announcers and corespondents clearly suggested that if the "U.S. wished to avoid the fate of Austria and Czechoslovakia, it had better begin preparing its own defenses."[111]

One of the most significant and enduring results of Munich was the rise to prominence of the modern news analyst. Kaltenborn had performed a valuable service for Americans by making sense of the overwhelming amount of complex news that was rapidly emanating from Europe. This achievement set a notable precedent, and henceforth regular news commentary was "desired by all those bewildered listeners who could hear the sounds of distant places but could not always understand what it all meant."[112] A contemporary poll discovered that 62 percent of those sampled preferred radio news programs which combined straightforward news with interpretation, and twice as many favored radio commentary over newspaper editorials.[113] As a result, "the radio commentator acquired popular status as the vehicle through which the public's hunger for knowing the 'why' behind the news was thoroughly satisfied."[114] The fact that the European situation was becoming more foreboding ensured that the need for radio commentary would become much keener.

In response to this requirement, the broadcasting field witnessed the sudden proliferation of over 400 commentators. Not only did the networks expand their staffs of analysts, but local stations also began to employ them. Many of these commentators began to attract a significant audience for the first time, and many received their own daily programs that were sponsored. Whereas the solitary voices of Boake Carter, Gabriel Heatter, and Lowell Thomas had dominated network news slots a few months earlier, after Munich they had to share air space with General Hugh S. Johnson, Baukhage, Walter Winchell, Hugh Gibson, John Gunther, and many others.[115] Even Mutual was able to enroll the services of two prominent commentators: Quincy Howe and Raymond Gram Swing. Swing became a familiar presence not only in the United States, but also in Britain, where numerous "Swing Clubs" were formed by Winston Churchill, King George VI, and various members of Parliament.[116]* Whereas Mutual's news broadcasts had been infrequent before September 1938, it now presented Swing in a regular feature, five times a week.[117]

---

*Broadcasting *calculated Swing's audience in Britain to consist of 30.7 percent of the adult population (April 1, 1940, p. 26).*

As a consequence of radio's laudable performance during the Munich Crisis, the electronic medium "irrevocably displaced the traditional newspaper as the dominant source of foreign news." Through rapid communication, "radio was able to reach larger audiences more quickly and more often with the high spots of relevant news."[118] While newspaper reporters had to wait until the full text of a speech was available and then "put it on the wire for cabling or radioing across the ocean," the nets had been able to broadcast the words of Hitler, Chamberlain, and the others as they were actually being said.[119] By continually scooping the newspapers day after day, radio had "signaled the death knell for the morning extra."[120] In relaying to the public the actual sounds of foreign events, radio demonstrated a "personal, dramatic appeal" and a "sense of participation" that was "completely lacking in the cold, stale printed media."[121] By transmitting its coverage to the entire nation, radio "had completely repaired the failure of the press in many rural areas where the war news in local papers might average between a half and three-quarters of a column."[122]

Many of the most gifted press reporters, seeing the ascendancy of the electronic medium during Munich, exchanged typewriter for microphone and flocked to join the ranks of its burgeoning news staffs. In this way, the radio community obtained the services of Floyd Gibbons, Edwin C. Hill, and many others.[123] Publishers, too, attempted to join the radio bandwagon. By the end of 1938, more than 250 stations had been purchased by newspaper concerns.[124]

American radio's Munich record also stood in stark contrast to the "timid and unenterprising" conduct of its European counterparts. Given the significant measure of government control, British and French broadcasting outlets usually served as "instruments of the cautious and uncertain policies of their respective Foreign Offices." Czech radio was even further from the comparatively balanced and dispassionate programming characteristic of the United States, with most of its energy devoted to "meeting and countering Germany's propaganda air campaign."[125]

Numerous public opinion polls taken after Munich revealed the true extent of radio's triumph. One survey in October 1938 found that 70 percent of those questioned had relied on radio as their principal news source during the European crisis.[126] Some months later, a poll by *Fortune* magazine discovered that 68 percent of Americans felt that radio was the most important news carrier, and 58 percent believed it to be "more accurate and freer from prejudice than newspapers."[127] When faced with "conflicting versions of the same story, a majority of Americans indicated that they would be more inclined to believe radio than newspaper reports, editorials, or columns."[128]

Because of their experience during Munich, the radio networks were adequately prepared to deal with the next great European emergency. With the increased public dependence on the medium for news, more and more Americans found themselves "tuning in to the events" that drew the world inexorably toward war.[129]

Closer to the Brink

By the middle of 1939, these events were occurring with an unsettling rapidity. Enlarging upon their Sudeten victory, the German army seized control of the rest of Czechoslovakia on March 15, 1939. Having anticipated this move for some time, the networks were on the scene. On March 17, NBC, CBS, and MBS transmitted a speech by Chamberlain condemning Hitler's act as a flagrant violation of the Munich Pact, and that evening NBC carried a two-way conversation between John T. Flynn in New York and Howard Marshall in Berlin discussing the next phase of the crisis. Two days later (March 19), CBS broadcast the first of its four-way hookups from London, Paris, Prague and Chicago,* with correspondents replying to questions from H. V. Kaltenborn. Paul White had streamlined this system by using the five minutes before airtime to apprise his speakers of what American listeners had already been told, and to coordinate their presentations so that "repetition was avoided and the full broadcast could be devoted to new news only available from each particular city in the hookup."[130] Also on the nineteenth, the former Czech prime minister delivered the first address since resigning his post. On March 26, NBC, CBS, and MBS broadcast a speech by Mussolini before the Fascist Guard in Rome delineating Italy's position in Europe's precarious balance of power. Il Duce's words were immediately interpreted for American listeners, and afterwards a complete translation and summary were provided. On March 29, Premier Daladier was heard responding to Italy's demands for a slice of France's African empire.[131]

On April 28, all nets carried Hitler's address before the Reichstag in which he abrogated the Polish-German Non-aggression Pact of 1934. The Führer also scornfully dismissed a recent appeal by President Roosevelt to preserve the peace of Europe. Two days earlier, Hitler had renounced the 1935 Anglo-German Naval Treaty to his world audience.[132] To many observers, it appeared that nothing would stop Hitler short of full-scale war.

With this inescapable conclusion in mind, the networks further augmented their news-gathering resources. In the late spring of 1939, White, Murrow, Trout, and Kaltenborn discussed the logistics of such expansion in a broadcast forum, "What Next Europe?" In July, White instructed Murrow in London to recruit 26 more full-time correspondents for CBS's European Division.[133] Among those now established in Europe's capitals were the promising young "air journalists" Eric Sevareid, Thomas Grandin, and Larry LeSeur.[134]

---

*While multiple points were contacted during a normal round-up program, each correspondent was usually heard in succession rather than simultaneously, in a conference-like manner. As developed by A. H. Peterson, assistant traffic manager of CBS, the four-way system allowed each speaker to hear the voices of the other three and respond to them directly, while the audience heard all four. Before this innovation, most transatlantic talks were conducted bilaterally.

NBC also enlarged its European staff, with the addition of Fred Bate in London and William C. Keirker in Berlin. To accommodate this growing army of radiomen, well-equipped newsrooms were installed in stations all over the continent, and transmitters were completely rewired.[135] In many of these studios, efficient AP news tickers became available after the wire service lifted its years-long ban on selling news to radio.

As a sign of radio's status as a "full-fledged news-gathering and disseminating medium," radio reporters were finally admitted into congressional press galleries and White House press conferences, and accorded facilities comparable to those of the press. In the ceremony bestowing these privileges upon the networks, Senator Bankhead remarked: "With the establishment of radio galleries, contact between people and their Government is now made even closer and more immediate."[136] In addition to this, Columbia University's School of Journalism introduced into its curriculum a new course on radio news writing.[137]

In another indication of the networks' increasing preoccupation with events abroad, most of the radio discussion programs began concentrating on issues of foreign policy. A listener tuning in to the *University of Chicago Roundtable* in the summer of 1939 could hear subjects like "Hitler's Economic Motives," "America and the Next War," and "If Europe Had Paid Its Debts," debated by such internationally prominent figures as President Edvard Beneš and Maxim Litvinoff.[138] It was also around this time that the *March of Time* turned from domestic stories to programs about the conquest of Austria and Czechoslovakia.[139]

In a further attempt to diminish the distance between America and events across the sea, the networks greatly improved their system of receiving international pickups. To accomplish this, CBS established a shortwave listening facility on Long Island to pick up European broadcasts and quickly relay them to American listeners.[140]*

As a means of testing this efficient news machine, NBC broadcast a unique live report direct from within the cement and steel casemates of the Maginot Line. As fascinated Americans tuned in, Max Jordan toured the defensive monster with a French officer who boasted of its invulnerability to German attack.[141] In the fall of 1939, *Broadcasting* noted:

> The Munich Crisis had shown broadcasters the weak spots in their European coverage plan and started them experimenting with various means of reporting the news from abroad. The annexation of Czechoslovakia by

*On June 17, to further refine its system of shortwave relays, CBS broadcast direct from the Pan-American Airways Atlantic Clipper during its transoceanic flight from Port Washington, New York, to Lisbon, Portugal. When the aircraft was midway across the Atlantic, the network presented a two-way conversation between Bob Trout on board and William L. Shirer, who was observing the flight from the vessel Mauretania below (Broadcasting, July 1, 1939, p. 187).

Germany in March gave American radio a chance to try out and further perfect its methods, with the result that when the next crisis arose it found radio ready and willing.[142]

The Polish Crisis

The true test of radio's power to inform came in August and September 1939 when Europe was seized by an emergency in which war was virtually unavoidable. On August 22, the world was startled to hear the news by radio that Germany and Russia, previously implacable enemies, had concluded a non-aggression treaty. The official reactions of the British and French governments, who had hoped to secure an alliance of their own with the Soviets, were aired later that evening.* When it became clear that Hitler's move was a diplomatic prelude to his invasion of Poland, the networks went all-out to satisfy the public's hunger for news during this critical hour.[143] Network correspondents were on hand in Europe's danger spots, ready to take to the air as soon as hostilities began. At home, announcers, special events departments, and engineers at New York network headquarters went on round-the-clock duty. Newsmen

> moved into studios, erected cots between desks, hovered over news tickers or talked to co-workers in London, Paris, Berlin, or Warsaw. Shortwave operators strained their ears to catch the news broadcasts of [foreign] state radio stations. Transmitters stayed on all night, broadcasting summaries and intermittent bulletins with recorded messages in between, or if stations did sign off, were kept warm and ready to start again at a moment's notice. All remained on duty—waiting, watching, listening for the word that would send them leaping to their posts again.[144]

As the Polish Crisis reached its most intense phase with German demands on the port city of Danzig, radio brought the voices of Daladier, British foreign minister Lord Halifax, and Pope Pius XIII expressing their desires for peace.[145] In a growing tide of news from abroad, the networks aired the views of the British cabinet on the situation, and regularly rebroadcast the Polish news in English.[146]

On August 31, at the height of world tension, the networks relayed one of the most dramatic broadcasts of all time. From London, a BBC correspondent described the mass evacuation of children "as thousands boarded trains for unknown destinations throughout England where they would presumably be safer than in the metropolis in case of air raids." Shortly after, Shirer went on the air in Berlin during an air raid alarm, and was able to give

*NBC found itself uniquely well prepared for this task, having begun, weeks earlier, a regular series of talks by Anglo-French statesmen: Churchill, Lord Duff Cooper, Yvon Delbos, Pierre Flandin, and Eduoard Herriot, all of whom would assume prominent positions on their respective countries' war cabinets in the next few days.

Americans a firsthand description of the scene and the reactions of the German people.[147]

On September 1, 1939, it became clear that war was imminent. When Adolf Hitler addressed the Reichstag in what was equivalent to a declaration of war against Poland, American listeners followed every word through H. V. Kaltenborn's accompanying translation.[148] All four networks and many of their affiliates immediately went into 24-hour emergency schedules, and throughout Europe, radio's finest broadcast journalists assumed action stations close to the front:

> In a London office with windows screened with black paper for air raid blackouts, a Berlin building with an air raid shelter in the basement, a Warsaw street shadowed by bombers, a hundred scattered outposts too small to be found on most maps.[149]

While it would take over 24 hours for the first photos of the German invasion to reach the newspapers and three days for the first newsreels, radio again distinguished itself "as the fastest agency yet devised to flash world-shaking events into every home with a receiver."[150] Between August 21 and September 2, NBC and CBS together aired over 400 programs from abroad in 150 hours of near-continuous coverage. Even the unprecedented eight new editions of the major newspapers, put out at half-hour intervals, "could not compete with radio's swift and instantaneous coverage."[151] On September 2, the *Warren Tribune-Chronicle* declared: "This [newspaper] believes that because of the rapidity with which events are occurring abroad, extras are not needed, because radio ... is keeping the public well-informed of events as they take place."[152]*

Complete coverage of the Polish invasion was possible only because the radio and newspaper industries laid aside their usual competitive impulses and collaborated as never before to bring the American public an unhindered supply of news. Radio, as usual, depended for much of its information on the regular news services (UP, INS and Transradio), where many of the flashes and bulletins that were read over the air originated. As a public service, the large press associations waived all restrictions on the broadcast of their news from Europe, "which they continued to serve to stations on an around-the-clock basis regardless of contractual time restrictions." In addition to this, in the hot spots where there were no network correspondents, newspapermen regularly took the microphone and described the scene for listeners. In exchange for such assistance, the nets routinely passed along their scoops to pressmen, along with copies of speech texts and other material gathered from the airwaves. According to *Broadcasting*: "Evidence of the services of radio could be seen on

---

*Shortly after the Polish crisis, the networks underscored their advantage of rapidity with a weekly news show entitled Ahead of the Headlines. The major press associations responded with a series of broadcast news programs of their own: Press Association News, United Press Reports, United Press Is on the Air, and later, Soldiers of the Press and Behind the Front Page.

front pages, where lead stories were frequently credited to a particular network or station." When Max Jordan delivered a running translation of Hitler's September 1 Reichstag address, newspapers noted: "NBC issued the following summary of Adolf Hitler's speech as released in Berlin by the German Government and read over the air by Max Jordan."

Another major source of network information came from material broadcast by foreign stations. Because international programs often contained information not given to foreign correspondents stationed abroad, network listening posts monitored the shortwaves on a 24-hour basis. Mutual's monitors scored an impressive scoop early in the morning of September 1. Over DJL, Berlin, word had been received that Hitler was to address the Reichstag at 5 A.M. (New York time). While awaiting confirmation, Mutual heard a German announcer giving Hitler's official "orders to the German people" warning "airplanes against flying over Germany and ships against entering German or Polish ports." Realizing that this was the "signal for an invasion," the networks immediately rebroadcast the German message to American listeners and provided a translation. After this, many wire service members decided to "sit with the broadcast monitoring crews to wait for another such break."

As during Munich, the cost-conscious MBS nightly rebroadcast the foreign news in English by "state-controlled European stations." According to *Broadcasting*, this service made a unique contribution to international news coverage:

> In addition to showing how other states color news to suit their own purposes, it showed better than any other way how much better the average American was informed of happenings abroad than were the people living in the centers where the events were taking place.[153]

Not satisfied with keeping those at home apprised of events transpiring in Europe, the nets likewise mobilized their international divisions on a round-the-clock basis to keep European listeners informed of "events uncolored by the political censorship of their own countries, and of the world reactions to these events." In an effort to provide Europe's citizens with the same quantity of data that was available to United States listeners, every CBS newscast that went out over the domestic network was also beamed abroad. From the earliest stages of the crisis, the nets kept their shortwave transmitters on the air continuously, with WCBX (CBS) and WRCA (NBC) sending to Europe, and WCAB (CBS) and WNBI (NBC) to South America. In addition to French, Spanish, Italian, German, Portuguese, and English, CBS added Polish to its list of foreign language newscasts. Total network shortwave programs generally exceeded 175 per day (40,000 words). With NBC and CBS receiving European propaganda and responding in their own broadcasts, the shortwaves became a battleground for the "war of words," waged to win the sympathies and loyalties of entire peoples. In this respect, radio added a fourth dimension to the developing war. Henceforth, the conflict would be waged not only on land, on the sea, and in the air, but also over the airwaves. Hitler so feared the morale-damaging effects of foreign propaganda broadcasts that on September 2, he issued a decree attaching the death penalty to any Germans who "listened to and repeated what they had heard" over the shortwave.[154]

On September 3, American listeners had the opportunity to witness an unparalleled event. At 11:33 P.M., anyone in front of a receiver heard history being made as Prime Minister Chamberlain solemnly issued to the world the British declaration of war against Germany.[155] After Munich, statesmen had recognized the value of using the airwaves as an instrument of diplomacy. While Germany understood her failure to respond to Britain's ultimatum meant a de facto situation of war, Chamberlain's broadcast served as the formal vehicle through which such information was conveyed. Almost immediately, reports began to pour into network studios from all over Europe. In London, Edward R. Murrow broadcast:

> Forty-five minutes ago, the Prime Minister stated that a state of war existed between Britain and Germany. Air raid instructions immediately were broadcast, and almost directly followed by air raid sirens screaming through the quiet calm of the Sabbath morning. The crowd outside Downing Street received the first news of war with a rousing cheer, and they heard that news through a radio in a car parked nearby.[156]

This was just the beginning stages of what proved to be the "most stupendous day of all time for radio listeners." After Chamberlain's declaration, in "rifle-shot sequence," Americans at home heard Premier Daladier's war announcement, an address by King George VI informing the British Empire of hostilities, President Roosevelt reasserting American neutrality, Canadian prime minister MacKenzie King pledging the support of the dominions, and news of one of the first actions of World War II, the sinking of the British ship *Athenia*.[157] The networks aired speeches by former French premier Leon Blum, Anthony Eden, Jacques Keyser (French Socialist Party president), King Leopold of Belgium, Queen Caroline of Albania, British foreign secretary Lord Halifax, Lord Maugham (Lord High Commissioner, House of Lords), Count Jersi Potocki (Polish ambassador to the United States), Lord Snell (British opposition leader, Lords), novelist H. G. Wells, Prince Felix of Luxembourg, and liberal leader Sir Archibald Sinclair.[158]

Kaltenborn's extraordinary success in analyzing and interpreting the news during Munich led to the extensive use of commentators by all the networks in the September crisis. With Kaltenborn on assignment in London, CBS hired Elmer Davis and Albert Warner to illuminate the international situation from their perspectives in New York and Washington. In addition to its main analysts, John B. Kennedy and John Gunther, NBC engaged Dorothy Thompson to do a "special series of 15-minute interpretive broadcasts," and appointed Earl

Godwin to its Washington bureau. At Mutual, Raymond Gram Swing was "never more busy," working double-time and transmitting over 4,000 words a day.[159] Fulton Lewis, Jr., expanded his Washington commentaries to three times a day.[160]

The quantity of news-related material coming over the airwaves during the Polish crisis far surpassed anything of its kind, even the recent Munich coverage. While 14 percent of all daytime and 19 percent of all night programming during Munich had been news, a Cooperative Analysis of Broadcasters report found that the figures for the August 24–29 period alone was 19 percent and 27 percent, respectively. News listenership peaked on August 26, when one out of every three programs heard was a news broadcast. Between August 20 and September 4, MBS delivered 196 separate broadcasts on the situation abroad (66 hours), while NBC generated 255 for the August 21–September 14 block. CBS, as usual, topped them both, with 726 transmissions between August 21 and September 8. Reports from Europe were so frequent that WJSV Washington announcer Arthur Godfrey "instituted a new technique in commercials" during his early risers *Sun Dial* program: "We now interrupt a war news broadcast to bring you a spot announcement."[161]

Once again, the networks earned widespread respect for their "wholesale cancellation or abbreviation of paid commercial programs to carry special announcements on current developments in Europe."[162] NBC lost over $33,000 in sponsor rebates. Despite this loss, the greatly enhanced public interest in news broadcasting found advertisers "grabbing up such time as fast as it could be obtained." In order to "cash in on increasing American news-consciousness," nine of the seventeen network news programs that began after September 1— including *Paul Sullivan Reviews the News*, *Bob Garred Reporting*, and *Bob Trout News*—found immediate sponsors. In addition, most existing news periods were now commercialized. These included *Kaltenborn Edits the News*, *Human Side of the News with Edwin C. Hill*, *Jergens Journal* (Walter Winchell), *Four-Star News* (H. R. Baukhage), *Richfield Reporter*, and the programs of Lowell Thomas, Raymond Gram Swing, Rush Hughes, and Fulton Lewis, Jr.[163]

Industry spokesmen assured the public that they were getting the news as quickly as it could be put on the air. As a result of the vivid reporting from the scene of action, CBS representatives proclaimed to listeners, "You are closer to the front in Europe's war than anyone has ever been in any previous war."[164] During the prologue of his fireside chat later that evening, President Roosevelt complimented radio for its superb efforts. Referring to the "continuous stream of information" the public was receiving, he commented:

> You the people of this country are receiving news through your radios …
> at every hour of the day. You are, I believe, the most enlightened and best
> informed people in all of the world at this moment.[165]

On October 26, after the crisis had momentarily subsided and a full assessment of radio's accomplishment could be undertaken, FDR remarked: "I would like to throw bouquets at … radio. Through a period of grave anxiety, [it] has discriminated between fact and propaganda and unfounded rumor, and has given its listeners an unbiased and factual chronicle of developments."[166]

The Phoney War

For six months after the end of the Polish campaign, there was a lull in radio war reporting due to the military inactivity of the "Phoney War." By the third week in September, with no major engagement on the Western Front, the networks decided to prepare for the long haul and returned to regular program schedules as much as possible, with only occasional news meriting the interruption of normal operations. Despite the temporary cessation of the minute-by-minute coverage maintained since August 24, public interest in the European situation remained high, and the nets stayed in regular contact with their foreign correspondents. CBS kept up its twice-daily European round-ups and commentaries by H. V. Kaltenborn and Elmer Davis. It also held two 15-minute time slots in the morning and evening open for special news from abroad. Paul White explained: "It may be a different kind of war, but it's still worth covering." NBC continued its three daily shortwave pick-ups and stood ready to go full-time if "news of transcendental importance" should occur. Mutual dramatically curtailed its continental coverage, carrying only John Steele's ten-minute reports every Friday, Waverly Root from Paris on Saturday, and Sigrid Schultz from Berlin every other Sunday. With no hot news occurring, network reportage generally consisted of accounts detailing the ways in which European citizens were dealing with wartime conditions and reviews of popular films and books in Paris, London, and Berlin. CBS routinely broadcast reports from its correspondents at the front: Bill Henry (stationed with the British Expeditionary Force in France) and Thomas Grandin (who joined the French army in the Maginot defenses). Mutual also had Arthur Mann and Victor Lusinchi on the scene.

On December 17, 1939, NBC scored a major coup when it broadcast an eyewitness account of the scuttling of the German pocket-battleship *Graf Spee* from Montevideo. Immediately after the vessel's December 15 arrival in the harbor, where it had sought refuge from pursuing British battleships *Ajax*, *Exeter*, and *Achilles*, James Bowen, MGM representative, and Bill Clark, RCA advisor in Buenos Aires, set up transmitting equipment and microphones and established direct wires to the network's New York headquarters. For two days, the two radiomen described the ship's activity as the world awaited Hitler's decision: would the vessel fight its way out of the harbor, or allow itself to be interned for the duration? At 5:55 P.M., as the *Graf Spee* seemed to be firing its boilers and gathering steam, Bowen roared: "Give me the air! The ship has exploded!" NBC immediately cleared its lines and broadcast Bowen's dramatic description of the chaotic situation in the harbor.[167] A short time later, Harold

Inside the NBC newsroom.

K. Milks of the AP was heard relating his trip around the smoldering ship in a launch and the efforts of Uruguayan officials to evacuate the wounded. Contributing to NBC's exclusive was the fact that at the very moment of detonation, the other networks' telegraph lines to Montevideo suddenly went dead.[168]

On Christmas Eve 1939, NBC broadcast a program direct from the

Siegfried and Maginot lines. Max Jordan gave an account of Yuletide cele-
brations in the German trenches, and *New York Sun* reporter William Boyd
sang carols with French soldiers and attended underground mass. The next
morning, during an NBC round-up, Larry LeSeur was at the Royal Air Force
main base in France, William Shirer reported from a German tanker in the
Baltic, and William Allen White broadcast from Finnish general headquarters in Viipuri. The latter program was cut short by heavy Russian shelling.
From London and Paris came a heartwarming broadcast in which various
radio and press correspondents "exchanged over-the-air greetings" with wives
and children assembled in NBC's New York studio.

On December 30, CBS dramatized the top twelve news stories of 1939
in an hour-long program entitled *Twelve Crowded Months*.[169] The stories,
selected by a poll of 1,000 network stations and UP editors, were

1. Allied declaration of war against Germany
2. Invasion of Poland
3. Russia's invasion of Finland
4. Nazi-Soviet Non-aggression Pact
5. George VI's United States visit
6. Death of Pope Pius XI
7. *Squalus* disaster
8. September 21 neutrality session
9. Annexation of Czechoslovakia
10. Sinking of the *Athenia*
11. Munich Beer Hall explosion
12. Sinking of the *City of Flint*

It had certainly been an eventful year, and the net's presentation struck
listeners as less a news review than a report card. In every case, CBS had been
on hand to cover these world-shaking events as they occurred, and had covered them in the most efficient manner possible. Such a feat by his network
led William Paley to declare 1939 the "greatest year in the history of American broadcasting."[170]

France's Agony

In April 1940, the peace on Europe's Western Front was shattered as
German armies rolled into Denmark and Norway. On May 10, 1940, the world
was startled to hear of the German attack on France, Holland, Belgium and
Luxembourg. At 1:00 A.M., network headquarters in New York received a
United Press flash stating that German troops had invaded Holland. This
started a chain reaction of bulletins and special broadcasts, as Paul White's
"well-oiled news machine" immediately swung into action. At 2:00 A.M.,

Columbia's shortwave listening station picked up Goebbels's announcement of the invasion to the German people, and promptly relayed it to American listeners with simultaneous translation. NBC carried a special talk by the Dutch minister to the United States, Dr. Alexander Loudon. The high point of network coverage on the first day of the attack came when American listeners heard the resignation speech of Neville Chamberlain in the House of Commons.[171] Three days later, the voice of his indomitable successor, Winston Churchill, was heard offering his "blood, toil, tears and sweat," to Parliament and the British nation.[172]

As the Wehrmacht surged through France, the networks assembled a formidable team of military experts to discuss the strategic and technical aspects of the fighting. Maj.-Gen. Stephen Fuqua, USA (ret.), Maj. Leonard Nason, and Brig.-Gen. Henry Reilly, USA (ret.), covered land operations; Paul Schubert and Capt. Frederick Reinecke, USN (ret.), discussed naval matters; and Col. Charles Kerwood analyzed the situation in the air.[173] Maj. George Fielding Elliot, who had distinguished himself during the Polish crisis, was given his own 15-minute program for CBS.

On May 12, eyewitness accounts of conditions in war-torn Amsterdam were sent by Louise Wright (NBC), Piet Van T Veer (MBS), and Mary Marvin Breckinridge (CBS).[174] These were followed by Victor Luschini speaking "from a forward position" for Mutual and giving a vivid description of Luftwaffe attacks on nearby French border towns. While broadcasting from German lines along the River Scheldt that same day, William Shirer was almost hit by an errant British bomb.[175] Reports from the Western Front were so common in May that one MBS official noted, "Not a single musical number could be played without interruption."[176]

With French offensives failing all along the front, President Paul Reynaud appealed to the world for assistance in two shortwave broadcasts on June 2 and 6.[177] On June 3, Paul Archinard described a German air raid on Paris that leveled the buildings adjacent to NBC offices on the Rue Poessin. While the correspondent was not hurt, the studio in which he was broadcasting looked "as if a hurricane had struck."[178]

On June 9, Americans heard of the French capital's fall from a somber Eric Sevareid:

> The "City of Light" is now darkened by wartime blackouts. The people of Paris…are as calm as could be expected. They are a fatalistic people. It is this quality which makes Frenchmen stand half-naked in this withering heat, feeding their red-hot machine guns until literally crushed by German tanks.[179]

Sevareid's account of French heroism was the last voice Americans heard from Paris until the city was recaptured by Allied troops four bitter years later.

On June 10, the world was horrified to hear Italian dictator Benito Mussolini declare war on an already defeated France.[180] Il Duce's proclamation was immediately followed, as was now the custom, by the reactions of Premier Reynaud and British minister of information Alfred Duff Cooper.[181] On June 17, a stunned American nation learned of the collapse of French resistance through a shortwave address by the pro–German puppet Henri Petain.[182] The last broadcast to emanate from France came on June 19, when William Humphries described a German air raid on Bordeaux. With the silencing of the only remaining French shortwave unit by the approaching German army, all direct contact with that country ceased. As a result, Rome now replaced Paris as the third regular origination point in daily network round-ups.*

With the termination of radio communications, network correspondents in France endeavored to return to the United States by way of Madrid or Lisbon, but found it extremely difficult to arrange passage. For several jittery days, CBS and NBC headquarters in New York lost touch with their French-based reporters. Their whereabouts were unknown until on June 22 William L. Shirer of CBS and William C. Keirker of NBC were heard delivering an eyewitness account of the French surrender from the Compeigne Forest in Alsace.† In a powerfully moving broadcast, the two correspondents described the "ironic twist of fate" that saw the French forced to capitulate to Hitler in the same railroad car where Marshal Foch had accepted the German surrender in November 1918. Using radio's power to convey vivid narrative, Shirer recreated the scene that he had witnessed only moments before:

> Hitler steps up to the car followed by Göring and the others. We watch them entering the drawing room in Marshal Foch's car. We can see nicely now through the window. Hitler enters first and takes the place occupied by Marshal Foch the morning the first armistice was signed. The Germans salute, the French salute. The atmosphere is what Europeans call "correct," but you'll get the picture when I say we see no handshakes, not on occasions like these.[183]

Underscoring the humiliating nature of this spectacle, William C. Keirker reported:

> We are in the midst of a hurried turn of events which have been unleashed by Hitler with a kind of furious prodigality and unconcern for world opinion. Barely six weeks ago, he let loose with the biggest show of his career, and in this space of time, the clock of history has been set back almost a quarter of a century. And today we have witnessed the reversal of time![184]

The networks were so prompt in their reporting of the French surrender that American listeners received the news hours before the German and French

*London and Berlin were the other two. The advent of the Scandinavian Campaign in May and June 1940 saw the addition of Stockholm as another regular pickup point.

†Shirer and Keirker were the only correspondents present to report this momentous event. Most other reporters had taken up position in Berlin, thinking that the cease-fire would be signed in the German capital (Broadcasting, June 22, 1940, p. 44).

people became aware of it.[185] CBS and NBC had so streamlined their coverage that America was receiving no less than 20 foreign pickups a day in the summer of 1940.[186] A typical news day for an NBC station included the following schedule:

> Throughout the day, WJZ will continue its wide coverage of the world's news with the following broadcasts. At 7:55 this morning, there will be another complete news summary, followed at 8:00 a.m. by on-the-scene accounts by NBC war reporters in Berlin and London. Then a report from Washington. News summaries during the day are scheduled for 8:55 a.m., 12:55 p.m., 1:45, 4:55, 6:00, and 6:25. At 9:30 this evening you are invited to listen to the comments of John B. Kennedy. More news on WJZ will be heard at 11:00 p.m. and at 12:00 midnight. Late bulletins from the Associated Press go on the air at 12:57 and 1:57 tomorrow morning.[187]

Britain Under Siege

No one individual demonstrated radio's power to make the listener feel that he was a participant in distant events more effectively than Edward R. Murrow. Through his frequent broadcasts from London, Americans were able to follow the action firsthand as Germany endeavored to subdue England after the fall of France. As wave after wave of German bombers appeared in the skies over the city in the summer of 1940, Murrow "bridged the Atlantic" and brought the Battle of Britain home to the American public. Twice a day, listeners tuned to CBS's *News from Europe* program eagerly anticipated the correspondent's earnest "This is London…" air signature. On August 24, immediately after one of the heaviest bombing raids of the war, Murrow brought his microphone out of an air raid shelter in Trafalgar Square and allowed his American listeners to hear the sinister shriek of the sirens and the "sounds of frantic activity in the streets."[188] In his September 24 broadcast, he enabled the audience to actually "take part" in a Luftwaffe raid while it was still in progress. Standing on a rooftop, "looking out over London," Murrow used his remarkable descriptive faculties to "paint the scene" of devastation that unfolded before him. As he spoke, his microphone picked up the sound of sirens, anti-aircraft fire, and exploding bombs.

> In the course of the last twenty minutes there's been considerable action up here…. Just straight-away in front of me the searchlights are working. I can see one or two bursts of anti-aircraft fire far in the distance. Just on the roof across the way I can see a man wearing a tin hat, a pair of powerful night glasses to his eyes, scanning the sky…. There is a building with two windows gone….[189]

The most poignant part of this broadcast came when CBS correspondents interviewed British families that had sought haven in the crypt of St.

Edward R. Murrow, bridging the gap from war-torn London.

Martins-in-the-Field.* The *Christian Science Monitor*, commenting on this scene the next day, felt that it "conveyed a message which newspapers, even with the most brilliant reporting, photographing and editing, cannot deliver."[190]

Murrow was so close to the frontlines in Britain that his London studio

While Murrow enjoyed the largest audience of any foreign correspondent in 1940, he was by no means the only American broadcaster covering the English scene. His subsequent renown seems to have overshadowed the efforts of other talented network newscasters who also spent sleepless nights in Anderson shelters while endeavoring to illuminate conditions in wartime Britain for American listeners. These relative unknowns included Charles Collingwood, Larry LeSeur (CBS), John MacVane, and Fred Bate (NBC).

was thrice destroyed by enemy bombs.[191] Friends feared for his safety every time he ventured out into the street with his microphone. By the "time the last Dornier droned home" in mid–1941, Murrow had lost twenty pounds.[192] In a letter to his brother, Lacey Murrow, he acknowledged that he had "reached the point where my hands shake so much I can't even read my lines."[193]

Murrow was a "masterful speaker" and a "sensitive musician of the spoken word." He knew how to deliver his words in a way that made the "listener's imagination enlarge on the meaning of what he said."[194] When trying to convey the deathlike silence of the London streets between two successive air raids on the night of September 8, Murrow told them "how loudly the liquid from two pierced cans of peaches dripped inside a smashed shop."[195] According to his colleague, Bob Trout, he frequently employed "poetic images" to describe what he saw.[196] When viewing British defenses in action during one raid, he referred to the "faint red, angry snap of the anti-aircraft bursts against a steel-blue sky."[197] After returning from a bombing mission over Berlin, Murrow depicted the city as an "orchestrated hell—a terrible symphony of light and flame."[198] Always keeping the nature of his audience foremost in his mind, he organized his broadcasts in such a way to "describe things in terms that make sense to the truck driver without insulting the intelligence of the professor."[199] Eric Sevareid noted: "He could absorb and reflect the thoughts and emotions of day laborers, airplane pilots or cabinet ministers..."[200] Another contemporary observed that the strength of Murrow's broadcasts resided in their ability to "increase our knowledge of public facts, but sharpen it with feeling. They sensitize our intellect and educate our emotions about actual life."[201]

A typical example of Murrow's ability to convey the emotional tension of a situation can be found in his broadcast of September 13, 1940:

> This has been what might be called a 'routine night'—air raid alarm at about nine o'clock and intermittent bombing ever since. I had the opinion that more high explosives and less incendiaries had been used tonight. Only two small fires can be seen on the horizon. Again, the Germans have been sending their bombers singly or in pairs. The anti-aircraft barrage has been fierce but sometimes there are periods of twenty minutes when London has been silent.... one becomes accustomed to rattling conditions and the distant sound of bombs. In these comes the silence that can be felt. You know the sound will return—you wait, and then it starts again. That waiting is bad. It gives you a chance to imagine things.[202]

In another moving "word-picture," Murrow described how Britons spent their second wartime Christmas. On December 24, 1940, he told American listeners:

> Christmas began in London nearly an hour ago. The church-bells did not ring at midnight. When they ring again, it will be to announce invasion.... The rooftop watchers are peering across the fantastic forest of London's chimney pots. Anti-aircraft gunners stand ready.... The fire

fighters and ambulance drivers are waiting, too. The blackout stretches from Birmingham to Bethlehem.[203]

Murrow's effectiveness in bringing the London Blitz into the homes of America earned him the respect of the entire news community. Eric Sevareid remarked that his "physical, intellectual and moral performance in those deadly [months] is not likely to be equaled by any reportorial voice or pen in this generation."[204] At a dinner party given in his honor a year later, librarian of Congress Archibald MacLeish paid tribute to "our man in London" in this way:

> Sometimes you said you were speaking from a rooftop in London looking at the London sky. Sometimes you said you spoke from underground beneath that city. But it was not in London really that you spoke. It was in the back kitchens and the front living rooms and the moving automobiles and the hot-dog stands and the observation cars of another country that your voice was truly speaking.[205]

In October 1940, New York's Overseas Press Club singled Murrow out as the "foreign correspondent who most contributed toward the information of the American people and the formulation of American national policy in international issues."[206]

Through his vivid eyewitness accounts of Britain's plight, Murrow significantly increased the sympathy and compassion most Americans had for the British cause. No broadcaster more forcibly conveyed the pressing need to aid England. Many Americans who tuned in "personally felt the unpredictable terror of the German bombing raids."[207] By "undermining his listeners' sense of remoteness from the European struggle," Murrow helped to increase interventionist sentiment in America at a time when participation was an intensely disputed topic. Eric Sevareid commented:

> He made the British and their behavior human and thus compelling to his countrymen at home. He was a far greater influence than the American ambassador to London. *He* was the ambassador, in a double role, representing Britain in America as well as America in Britain. There is no doubt of his immense aid to the President in awakening the American people to the issue before them.[208]

Archibald MacLeish once told the correspondent: "You have destroyed ... the superstition that what is done beyond 3,000 miles of water is not done at all."[209] According to another observer: "The events he chose to describe and the manner in which he described them, implied, without need for explanation, a Nazi march of conquest which would not stop short of America's shores and therefore necessitated a militant administration response, possibly including war."[210] To the millions who heard Murrow's reports, it seemed as though the Battle of Britain and the Blitz were "merely preludes to the bombing of New York City." By "putting the listener into [the British] man's shoes," Murrow was even more successful than FDR in manipulating public opinion into accepting a "stronger American commitment to Germany's opponents."[211] Certainly, Lend-Lease was more palatable to an audience that tuned in to Murrow and had experienced the nightly ravages of the Blitz with him.*

A World at War

After failing to overcome British resistance, Hitler turned his attention elsewhere. On April 5, 1941, in order to secure his southern flank, Hitler ordered 33 Wehrmacht divisions and 1,500 aircraft into the Balkans. Because of the alertness of an NBC shortwave monitor, the network received the official German announcement of the invasion of Greece and Yugoslavia several minutes "before the other networks and well ahead of the press flash from Berlin." This was quickly followed by Hitler's order of the day to the German Balkan army. At 3:00 A.M., the nets presented a discussion by the Yugoslav and Greek ambassadors in Washington. To ensure an uninterrupted flow of news from southern Europe, CBS implemented a "new system of blind relays for emergency use," whereby its correspondents on the scene could broadcast four times a day over a special closed circuit. If they had anything vital to report, it was immediately put over the air.[212]

On June 22, 1941, the German army launched a massive invasion of the Soviet Union. In the greatest single offensive in military history, the Germans and their Axis satellites committed over 3 million men, 600,000 vehicles, 3,500 tanks and almost 2,000 planes along a front 1,800 miles long. First indications of Germany's move by Columbia's listening posts "brought its entire news staff to New York headquarters, some men still in their pajamas." At 11:30 P.M., a German announcer revealed that Goebbels was to make an important declaration. Eleven minutes later, NBC's Robert Waldrop went on the air with a full translation of the propaganda minister's war message. For the next 5½ hours, NBC presented no less than 20 periods of bulletins and commentaries on this momentous event.†

As in previous campaigns, enemy broadcasting centers were among the first German targets in Russia. *Broadcasting* noted:

> The task of the advance guards and bombers is to put radio stations out of commission, many of which have already been destroyed by their own

*On the evening of December 7, 1941, Murrow was a guest at the White House. Harry Hopkins and Felix Frankfurter were avid listeners of his London reports. During their discussion, FDR inquired about German air attacks and British resolve. According to David Culbert: "Roosevelt apparently believed that Murrow's broadcasts had helped greatly in making Americans accept the possibility of an [American] declaration of war" (p. 194).

†Federal officials also received advance warning of the German attack through its "newest intelligence adjunct," the Foreign Broadcast Monitoring Service, a shortwave agency established by Roosevelt's Defense Committee Board (Broadcasting, September 1, 1941, p. 54).

people so as not to fall into the hands of the enemy. When they capture transmitters before they can be destroyed, the Germans immediately begin distributing fake news and frightening the population into submission.... Almost every political, diplomatic and military move that has been launched by Germany occurred only after an intensive [radio] propaganda campaign.

By the fall of 1941, the Nazis succeeded in taking over nine of the twelve main long-wave transmitting centers of Europe. These included Hilversum (Holland), Karlundburg (Luxembourg), Oslo (Norway), Radio Paris (France), Lahti (Finland), Motala (Sweden) and Radio Rumania. The fact that the only two free facilities left were the BBC and Radio Switzerland caused one observer to lament: "There is no voice in Europe except that of Germany."[213]

For the radio networks, "Operation Barbarossa" meant expanding the scope of their coverage to global dimensions. The day after the attack had begun, CBS began carrying shortwave pickups from Moscow. For years, Joseph Stalin had forbidden western newsmen from covering events in the Soviet Union. Now, recognizing the importance of American opinion (and Lend-Lease assistance), the Soviet dictator sharply toned down his country's censorship. The nets, eager to exploit this new opportunity, hastened to send correspondents to the Russian capital. CBS dispatched the noted playwright Erskine Caldwell and his famous photographer wife, Margaret Bourke-White, while NBC sent Herman Mabicht and Robert Magidoff, and MBS sent Henry Shapiro.[214]

On June 24, NBC aired the first "International News" program in broadcast history.[215] On CBS, the new *World Today* program offered reports "direct from world centers."[216] Now Americans could not only hear regular reports from Continental Europe, but also from correspondents in Athens, Cairo, and Ankara. The nets also expanded their South American pickup system to include Panama, Buenos Aires, Rio de Janeiro and a host of other cities. At the same time, with Japan moving into Indochina, the Far East situation was now covered through frequent transmissions from Cecil Brown in Shanghai and Richard Tennelly in Tokyo.[217] No area of the world was inaccessible to the ubiquitous radio correspondent. CBS and NBC also gained access to the new AP subsidiary, Press Association, Inc., which presented data to stations in an improved "made for radio" format. By December 1941, radio newsrooms were able to draw upon the resources of four major news services: AP, Transradio, UP, and INS.[218]

Six months after the beginning of the Russo-German War, Americans learned of another devastating attack much closer to home. On December 7, 1941, radio became the first medium to report the shocking news of the Japanese raid on Pearl Harbor. The first bulletin was aired only one hour after the last wave of enemy planes returned to their aircraft carriers. At 2:24 P.M., White House press secretary Steve Early informed the three press associations of the attack. Two minutes later, Mutual's New York station WOR interrupted its broadcast of the Dodgers-Giants football game to read the UP flash to bewildered listeners. At 2:30, the news staffs of the other major networks, "seasoned by previous crises," came to life. At 2:35, NBC rang four chimes (instead of the usual three) over the air, to notify all network executives and news personnel to contact their offices. CBS sent out its own prearranged signals, and within the hour the "skeleton staffs began to receive reinforcements that soon swelled their numbers to unusual proportions."[219] At 2:45 Eastern Standard Time, an NBC announcer read the following bulletin that had just been received over shortwave from station KGU in Hawaii:

> We have witnessed this morning ... the severe bombing of Pearl Harbor by army planes that are undoubtedly Japanese. The city of Honolulu has been attacked and considerable damage done. This battle has been going on for nearly three hours.... It's no joke—it's a real war.... There has been severe fighting going on in the air and on the sea.[220]

At the same time, CBS, who happened to be in the middle of its *World Today* program, presented John Daly giving a report of a telephone conversation he had just had with an official at member station KGMB, Honolulu.

For the next two days, Americans remained by their sets, anxiously awaiting the official confirmation that their country was at war.[221] To satisfy the public demand for information, the networks remained on the air for 34 straight hours, presenting a continuous stream of coverage.* Bulletins and eyewitness accounts poured in from all over the Pacific. An NBC correspondent described the aftermath of the attack from atop the *Honolulu Advertiser* tower overlooking the harbor. As security measures began to reduce the number of on-the-spot reports from Hawaii, the airwaves were taken over by commentators, analysts, and military experts. In the first few hours alone, Americans heard interpretations of the situation by Upton Close, Morgan Beatty, H. V. Kaltenborn, John B. Hughes, Fulton Lewis, Jr., and Eric Sevareid.[222] Given the significance of the attack and the confusion that surrounded it, radio commentary had the effect of "allaying rumor and increasing public understanding."[223] Through radio's worldwide connections, listeners heard reactions to the attack from governments as distant as Lebanon. NBC, utilizing its newly assembled Far Eastern staff, brought in reports from Sidney Albright in Batavia, Harrison Forman in Singapore, Ed Mackay in Shanghai, and Mel Jacoby in Chungking.[224] From their domestic bureaus, the networks kept audiences informed of White House and congressional actions. In an unprecedented move, correspondents were allowed to broadcast the complete dialogue between government and cabinet officials, military advisors, and reporters during a White House press conference. On the evening of December 8, a record

After 1½ days of uninterrupted coverage, the networks returned to regular programming, but with intermittent reports every half hour. It was not until the middle of December that NBC and CBS returned to anything resembling a normal broadcast schedule.

81 percent of the American public tuned in to hear the president ask Congress for a declaration of war against Japan. Immediately afterward, microphones were placed within congressional chambers so that listeners could hear the actual deliberations that would determine the fate of millions of American men and women.

Late that night, NBC's Bert Silen informed listeners of Japanese incursions into American possessions in the Philippines. Speaking from an army dugout, he presented a graphic account of an enemy air raid as it occurred*:

> Manila has just been bombed! In fact, right now it is being bombed.... The first we knew of the bombing we heard terrible detonations and then saw huge flames from incendiary bombs coming out of Fort William McKinley and Nichols Air Field ... turning the sky absolutely crimson. We saw the real fireworks display of blood-red anti-aircraft tracer bullets going after those Japanese bombers ... and we thought we couldn't get this out because the bombers paid a visit to the transmitting stations through whose transmitter we are putting this broadcast.... It looks as though the Japanese are coming back again....[225]

By the time H. V. Kaltenborn returned to the air for the third time on December 8, it was obvious that "the world, entirely, [was] at war."[226]

Conclusion

As a result of radio's extraordinary power to inform, America would be one of the world's most "news conscious and internationally-aware" countries by the end of 1941.[227] By mobilizing all of their resources and refining their coverage techniques, the networks successfully kept Americans apprised of the world conflict that ultimately engulfed them. As a result, the Second World War was truly the first "living room war" in American history. Through its extensive coverage, on-the-spot reporting, eyewitness accounts, flash bulletins, discussion programs, current event dramatizations, and disaster relief efforts, radio surpassed the newspaper as the nation's dominant news medium. Time and again, radio demonstrated its unrivaled advantages of immediacy, directness, intimacy and dramatic appeal. By assuming the role of America's most efficient disseminator of news and information, radio radically redefined its role as a broadcast medium and stood as a potent example of the power of technology to serve in the public interest. In the process, radio during the 1930s fully developed its own dual nature. In its coverage of the war in Europe and the Far East, radio demonstrated its ability to mold public opinion by "creating a foreign policy consensus that would help to unify the country in time for

---

The Japanese advance on Manila was so swift, when Silen finished another air raid broadcast on December 25, he was immediately seized by enemy troops (Gordon, p. 122).

American involvement in the conflict." At the same time, the medium responded to popular interest in international affairs and satisfied the public's growing need for information.[228] Overall, radio's performance in the 1930s offers the clearest possible illustration of the medium's role as cultural mirror.

Part III
"Incredible As It May Seem..."

10. Orson Welles and the "War of the Worlds"

By 1938, radio had firmly established itself as a credible means of communication. Through the fireside chat and the news broadcast, Americans had come to rely on the medium as what they believed to be an "unimpeachable source of truth." For a majority of listeners, it was natural that anything coming through their loudspeakers that purported to be fact was believed. Radio playwright Archibald Macleish described this widespread phenomenon when he said, "The ear accepts; accepts and believes."[1] On Halloween Eve 1938, the true extent of the public's unquestioning faith in radio and its deference to the voices of its speakers would be illustrated with disastrous consequences. For when Orson Welles and his Mercury Theater took to the air in what was expected to be a routine dramatization of a classic H. G. Wells novel, over one million Americans would fail to separate fact from fiction. In a potent demonstration of radio's power to induce belief and to create a false reality in the minds of its listeners, the *War of the Worlds* broadcast sparked a nationwide panic. By the time the program ended, men, women and children in towns and cities all across the country were in desperate flight from creatures that "had no existence except in their own imaginations."[2]

Precedents

Before the Welles broadcast, there were a few notable incidents where individuals had used the aural power of the medium to hoodwink the public. For example, in 1935, the popular radio commentator Boake Carter simulated an on-the-spot report of the Oxford-Cambridge rowing competition from a small New York studio. To add an aura of authenticity to his broadcast, a phonograph recording provided the sounds of an excited British crowd as background.[3]

In September 1936 two other sports announcers enjoyed large audiences because of the vividness of their 'live' play-by-play descriptions of major league baseball games. When Red Barber (WLW-Chicago) and Ronald Reagan (WHO-Des Moines) spoke into the microphone each week, they were not even witnessing the on-field plays they reported. Their descriptions were so colorful that listeners would never have dreamed that each was actually in a small studio hundreds of miles from the scene of action. With "painterly imaginations" both would receive terse statements of the plays by telegraph, and would embroider them for listeners. Veteran radio actor Joseph Julian described how he had helped Red Barber "perpetrate [this] fraud on the fans":

> One afternoon I was ordered to report to a small studio with a turntable and two effects—a recording of a crowd cheering and a bat smacking a baseball. When I arrived, Barber was sitting in front of a ticker tape machine. It was ticking away, but no printouts were happening.... Barber explained that the Cincinnati Reds' baseball game was about to start and he would be broadcasting a play-by-play description....
>
> I tested the crowd cheers and batted-ball effect, so that the control room engineer could set his levels, then waited for the game to begin. The bat-clouting-a-ball effect was achieved without a ball. Only a bat and a leather-covered judge's gavel were used....
>
> Waiting for the game to start, I tried to fathom why these effects would be needed in reporting a game over a news ticker in a tiny studio. Only when we went on the air did I understand that I was a co-conspirator in a plot to make listeners believe they were hearing a game brought to them directly from the stadium by an eyewitness reporter. As the ticker started spewing tape, Barber began transposing cryptic facts of plays that had already happened into colorful descriptions of these plays as they were happening. He did it with such conviction he almost had me believing I was at the ball park. He would embellish the factual information from the tape with vivid accounts of a player's behavior—gestures and actions that were sheer invention. For instance, the tape might read: "The count was three and two. Thomas hit a single to center." Barber would turn that into: "Three and two on Thomas now. He seems a little nervous, walks away from the plate, rubs his hands in the dirt ... hefts his bat ... coming back now ... hunches over the plate ... the pitcher wipes the sweat from his face with his sleeve ... spits ... winds up and here's the pitch!" Then he'd cue me to thwack my baseball bat with the gavel and turn up the crowd cheers. His enthusiasm and excitement would rise above the noise. "It's a good one! It's a good one!" he would shout. "A straight drive to center field! There's the throw over to first ... and the man is safe!" If it were a double or a triple, he'd yell even louder, signaling me for more decibels from the crowd. After a few innings I caught on, and naturally put the thwacks and cheers in the right places without being told. On a home run, I'd goose up the crowd as loud as I could and Red would give it full throttle, screaming his description of the ball soaring over the left-field fence many moments after it had already been there. A great sleight-of-mouth artist, Red Barber.[4]

Reagan repeated this "elaborate creative process" in over 600 broadcasts of his own.[5] On one occasion, his aural deception almost met with disaster.

> I saw Curly start to type so I finished the windup and had Dean send the ball on its way to the plate, took the slip from Curly, and found myself

faced with a terse notice: "The wire has gone dead." I had a ball on the way to the plate and there was no way to call it back. At the same time, I was convinced that a ball-game tied in the ninth inning was no time to tell my audience we had lost contact with the game and they would have to listen to recorded music. I knew of only one thing that wouldn't get in the score column and betray me—a foul ball. So I had Augie foul this pitch down the left field foul line. I looked expectantly at Curly. He just shrugged helplessly, so I had Augie foul another one, and still another; then he fouled one back into the box seats. I described in detail the red-headed kid who had scrambled and gotten the souvenir ball. He fouled one into the upper deck that just missed being a home run. He fouled for 6 minutes and 45 seconds until I lost count. I began to be frightened that maybe I was establishing a new world record for a fellow staying at bat hitting foul balls, and this would betray me. Yet I was into it so far I didn't dare reveal that the wire had gone dead. My voice was rising in pitch and threatened to crack, and then, bless him, Curly started typing. I clutched at the slip. It read: "Galen popped out on first ball pitched." Not in my game he didn't—he popped out after practically making a career out of foul balls.[6]

Sports announcer Pat McSwain of Gastonia, N.C., also employed the Reaganesque technique. When he arrived in Forest City to cover a junior baseball game, he discovered that it had been relocated to another park. Witnessing the actual match five miles away was Vernon Upton, Jr. Using information relayed by automobile to his transmitter site, McSwain gave a detailed account of the game's proceedings "without a fan in the stands or a player on the field." Despite this discrepancy, many considered this to have been his "finest play-by-play ever."[7]

These anecdotes clearly demonstrate one of radio's most intriguing characteristics: One does not have to be physically present at an event in order to convey it to an audience. The announcer is merely the lense through which a listener "sees" an event. The listener projects the auditory images he receives onto the theater of his own mind and develops them into some kind of recognizable form, based on his own individual experience and preconceptions.

These mental pictures could be of a relatively innocuous nature, such as a sports event, or they could be more malevolent. The year 1926 saw unprecedented labor unrest and strike activity in Britain. On January 26, English listeners were shocked by a routine news broadcast that purported to relate the activities of an uncontrollable London mob. In an "eyewitness account," the BBC's Father Ronald Knox described how communist hordes attempted to raze the Houses of Parliament, detonate a bomb underneath Big Ben, and hang several prominent cabinet ministers. The broadcast terminated with the BBC station's own destruction.* As soon as the program concluded, law enforcement,

*In a 1970s recorded interview with noted film director Peter Bogdanovich, Welles specifically cited this broadcast as a direct inspiration for his Halloween program. "I thought it would be fun," he recalled, "to [simulate this kind of destruction] on a big scale ... from outer space."

newspaper, and radio stations were inundated with calls from unnerved listeners. Fortunately, the panic generated by this ruse was localized and the level of emotional trauma relatively slight.[8]

By 1937, this aural trickery was beginning to infiltrate network programming. When NBC's realistic cops and robbers drama *Gangbusters* took to the air, "police [were] sent on fruitless errands to many houses to prevent supposed crimes, only to discover that their informers had been hoaxed." Another crime-fighter, *The Shadow*, "caused many a swooning of listeners who took his macabre accounts too literally."[9]

On March 4, 1937, as Hitler consolidated his hold on the Rhineland, the French reinforced the Maginot Line, and civil war raged in Spain, the *Columbia Workshop* presented Archibald Macleish's true-to-life, militaristic drama, "Fall of the City."[10] In this program, clearly designed to mirror events in Europe, a radio announcer delivered a purportedly live, "eyewitness description" of a dictator's attempt to subjugate a peaceable (but unnamed) urban community. As the enemy force advanced upon the city, listeners heard the terrified and disoriented state of the citizens as they deliberated whether to resist. Director Irving Reis heightened the program's realism by presenting an appropriate "acoustical atmosphere." To simulate the vociferous masses of the mythical city square, Reis transmitted his program from the midst of an assembled crowd at New York City's Armory. The result was an ultra-real program in which the "texture of the sound gripped the attention and chilled the bone." Among those who participated in this production and noted its effect was a relatively unknown actor named Orson Welles, who played the role of the announcer.[11]

A few months later, Welles was again on hand to witness radio's power of deception, this time as a cast member in a *March of Time* reenactment of the Amelia Earhart tragedy. On July 8, 1937, less than a week after the actual disappearance, a radioman for Inter-Island Airways flying from Hawaii mistook the *March of Time* broadcast for an S.O.S. from Earhart's missing aircraft. The radioman immediately notified officials that he had heard a "conversation between the lost pilot and ships at sea." For the next few days, hopes revived of finding Earhart and her navigator, Fred Noonan. Eventually, it was discovered that the man had intercepted the "shortwave relay of the *March of Time* program from San Francisco to Hawaii." While there were some negative comments uttered, serious criticism of the dramatization was by no means widespread.[12]

The verisimilitude of *March of Time* broadcasts produced an abundance of similar, though less sensational, incidents. The actors who performed the impersonations on the program were so "versatile … and endowed with a variety of accents and characterizations," that Joseph Julian considered them the "aristocrats of the profession." Once, while playing the part of Japanese ambassador to the United States Hirosi Saito, Guy Repp was summoned to the studio telephone. It was the Japanese consulate wanting to know why the Ambassador hadn't notified them he was in town. Repp explained he was only an actor impersonating Saito, but the caller was not to be put off. He insisted he was very familiar with the ambassador's voice and invited Repp to a diplomatic dinner the next evening.[13]

Listeners were also frequently fooled by the talented array of FDR imitators on the program: Bill Adams, Gilbert Mack and Art Carney.

[One] time, Gilbert Mack's wife was at home listening to his voice coming over the radio as Franklin Roosevelt delivering his ringing Inaugural in which he said: "The only thing we have to fear is fear itself," when a man, who frequently stopped by to sell her fresh eggs, rang the doorbell. She hurriedly let him in, saying, "Shhh, I'm listening to my husband!" The man gave her a peculiar look and left—never to return.[14]*

For most Americans, the Earhart flight and the affairs of ambassadors and dictators were distant matters. But how would they respond if a crisis occurred that was much more immediate? As a young Orson Welles absorbed the lessons of his radio experience and moved on to bigger things, he would endeavor to find out.

Orson Welles and the Mercury Theater

In the mid–1930s, Orson Welles was an active radio personality. His broadcast commitments were so considerable, he often found it necessary to hire an ambulance to get him from studio to studio on time.[15] Despite the number of his appearances, however, he was not well known, for he performed "almost anonymously."[16] The only work for which he was truly recognized was as the great "man of mystery and student of science," *The Shadow*.

In the summer of 1938, Welles graduated out of his small supporting roles on network shows and was given a program of his own. In August, he brought his highly acclaimed Mercury Theater stage producing unit to radio in a series of dramatizations of classic novels. Though formally affiliated with the New Deal's Federal Theater Project, the Mercury Theater was given considerable autonomy in determining the nature of the material it chose to perform. As producer, director, and leading player of this gifted theatrical company, Welles developed a reputation for dabbling in the unorthodox.[17] Among his many unique creations were a black *Macbeth* set in Haiti and a modernized *Julius Caesar* in which actors in fascist-style garb performed in front of an austere stone wall.[18]

*Will Rogers was another convincing impersonator. On a 1927 Gulf Show, his imitation of Calvin Coolidge "was mistaken by thousands for an actual Presidential address" (Washington Post, November 1, 1938, p. 4).

The "boy genius" and his toy: Orson Welles at the microphone, 1937.

Welles applied this same innovative spirit to his radio productions. He frequently praised radio as a "popular, democratic machine for disseminating information and entertainment," but he felt the medium's dramatic potential had never been fully realized. Like Roosevelt and many network newscasters, Welles recognized that the radio was an "intimate piece of living room furniture" whose unseen audience should "never be considered collectively, but individually."[19] While he maintained that "radio was the best story-teller there is," he wanted to overcome the popular belief that radio was "just an extension of play-wrighting."[20] According to Welles:

> There is nothing that seems more unsuited to the techniques of the microphone than to tune in to a play and hear the announcer say: "The curtain is rising on another production of..." This method of introducing the characters and setting the locale seems hopelessly inadequate and clumsy.[21]

Such techniques, he maintained, "treated the listener as little more than an eavesdropper." To increase the personal quality of the medium, Welles endeavored to present the classic works of fiction in the first personal singular (*First Person Singular* was in fact the original title of the Mercury Theater series), together with such other literary devices as "streams of consciousness" and "dramatized diaries and letters." Through these techniques, the listener would develop a sense that the "narrator was taking him into his confidence, and thus acquire a personal interest in the resolution of the plot." Welles demonstrated the effectiveness of this method when, during an early broadcast version of *Julius Caesar*, he used the familiar voice of H. V. Kaltenborn to "guide listeners through another crisis in power politics."[22] Welles was also interested "in using his productions to explore the relationship between fictional versions of an event, and the shifting, evasive reality that underlies [it]."[23]

One of the reasons Welles so enjoyed working on radio was his fascination with sound and its ability to enhance the realism of a dramatic situation. According to Mercury member William Alland, Orson understood that "sound in radio was like lights in theater. It was more than just a background, it was a [vital] creative element." In addition to his manifold duties as writer, producer, director and actor, Welles also "took a personal role in maintaining the quality and accuracy of the sound effects used on his broadcasts." John Houseman relates how he and Welles spent three hours experimenting with various ways to represent a "severed head" during rehearsal for the July 25, 1938, production of *A Tale of Two Cities*.[24] While doing *Les Misérables* for Mutual in the summer of 1937, Welles conceived the idea of using the echoes produced in the studio urinals to replicate the sewers of Paris.[25] Welles greatly appreciated radio's illusion-creating power. As a lifelong student of magic, Welles felt that if his audience was forced to rely solely on their sense of hearing, his ability to deceive them would be greatly enhanced.

The small circle of writers, educators and intellectuals that regularly followed Welles's broadcasts marveled at his "imaginative grasp of the possibilities of radio."[26] In October 1938, the whole world would share this same sense of wonder, and Welles would become a household name.

Preparation for War of the Worlds

On October 24, 1938, Welles and his co-writers, Howard Koch and John Houseman, commenced work on the script for the upcoming Mercury Theater offering, *War of the Worlds*. Soon after they began, it became apparent that considerable obstacles had to be overcome in order to translate the Victorian novel into a viable radio play. While the H. G. Wells story of a Martian invasion of England seemed "futuristic" to audiences in 1898, the radio writers felt that forty intervening years had diminished much of its plausibility. After fretting over the script for twenty-four hours, Koch telephoned Houseman and stated his reservations about writing the play. He complained that there was no possible way "such an antiquated epic could be effectively adapted for modern radio." Koch suggested scrapping the Wells enterprise in favor of a rendition of *Lorna Doone*, but because of clearance problems, this plan was soon jettisoned.[27] It was well-known within the Mercury Company that Orson had wanted to try something "new" this time. After a successful opening season of historical dramas (*A Tale of Two Cities*, *The Count of Monte Cristo*) and biographical sketches (Abraham Lincoln, Julius Caesar), Welles felt that "a bit of science-fiction" would be a welcome departure.[28] Houseman and Koch preferred doing Matthew P. Shiel's *Purple Cloud*, but the young director could not be swayed from his "favorite project."[29] Welles instructed Koch to "revise the [Wells] story somewhat," by "modernizing the language, updating the dialogue," and presenting the story through a series of fake news bulletins.[30]

With these new guidelines to follow, Koch and Houseman pored over the script for the next 36 hours. Every twenty pages that were produced were immediately submitted to Welles for scrutiny. Because of his "exacting standards," the authors found themselves constantly rewriting scenes and "speeding back and forth to the studio."[31] By Thursday's rehearsal a complete draft was ready for his consideration. As was his custom, Welles had the script performed and recorded, then listened to the playback. (By this practice he felt he could fully "grasp its merits and defects better than if it was read.")[32] After hearing the recording, Welles decided the story still lacked a crucial ingredient to make it relevant to a 1930s audience. He directed his writers to "heighten the impact of the news simulations" and substitute actual American names and places for Wells's English locales. By changing the scene of action from London to Grover's Mill, New Jersey, and by "intensifying the pace of the bulletins," Welles hoped to give the "illusion of up-to-the-minute reality."[33] He also changed the time frame from the nineteenth century to "the thirty-ninth year of the twentieth century."

On Friday afternoon, the new script was submitted to the CBS censors. Network official Davidson Taylor and CBS attorneys felt that the script was too believable in its present form, and that its realism would have to be toned down before it could be aired. The network insisted on 28 script changes, including the elimination of official designations that might prove legally problematic. Welles was forced to change the Museum of Natural History to the "National History Museum," the National Guard to the "militia," and the U.S. Weather Bureau to the "Government Weather Bureau."[34] CBS argued that these alterations were necessary in order to underscore the fictional character of the broadcast.

While the network was concerned that the program might appear too authentic to many listeners, some on Welles's staff did not share this view. Houseman persistently hesitated about presenting *War of the Worlds*, because he suspected that "people might be bored or annoyed at hearing a tale so improbable."[35] Several others who were involved in the production spurned the script, which was held to be too "silly," "very dull," and "lacking in human interest."[36] One cast member confided to Houseman: "We're going to make fools of ourselves. Absolute idiots!"[37] This was also the prevailing view among the radio community at large. Radio critic Ben Gross remarked to a friend a few hours before airtime, "Yeah, good old Sunday-supplement fantasy, but he's dressed it up. Anyway, don't bother to listen. Probably bore you to death."[38] In an effort to reassure the pessimists and skeptics in his company that the production would not flop, Welles added several more personal touches to the script during the two hours prior to airtime.*

At 7:58 P.M., the Mercury Theater players assumed their positions before the microphones. Welles mounted a small podium at the far left of the soundstage and donned his headset. As the studio clock indicated 8:00 P.M., he gave the signal to announcer Dan Seymour to commence the program.

Much of the American public was not adequately prepared for what followed on that quiet Sunday evening. In the next hour, Welles would so brilliantly manipulate the properties and conventions of broadcasting that over a million listeners would believe the United States was actually under attack from marauding armies of Martians. By exploiting the public's deference to voices of authority, and by playing on their endemic fears of war and disaster, their faith in the familiar, and their views of science, Welles gave the country the greatest Halloween scare it had ever experienced. By pulling off the most monumental hoax in broadcast history, Welles provided Americans with the most potent demonstration yet of the enormous power radio wielded in their lives.

---

*H. G. Wells later claimed that Orson Welles's revisions were made "with a liberty that amounted to a complete rewriting" of his novel into "an entirely different story" (New York Times, October 2, 1938, p. 26).

11. The Broadcast

Those who routinely tuned in to the *Mercury Theater on the Air* on Sunday nights heard the greeting of a familiar voice on October 30, 1938. Regular listeners prepared themselves for another evening of classical entertainment when they heard:

> ANNOUNCER: The Columbia Broadcasting System and its affiliated stations present Orson Welles and the Mercury Theater on the Air in the "War of the Worlds," by H. G. Wells.[1]

Next, as was the custom, Welles was introduced as director, and the fictional setting was conveyed.

> WELLES: We know now that in the early years of the Twentieth Century, this world was being watched closely by intelligences greater than man.... Across an immense ethereal gulf ... intellects vast, cool and unsympathetic regarded this earth with envious eyes, and slowly, but surely, drew their plans against us.

As soon as Welles finished his opening monologue, an announcer gave a routine weather forecast. Immediately after, listeners heard another voice introduce a third-rate musical program featuring the Ramon Raquello Orchestra from New York's Hotel Park Plaza.

Those who had been listening to the program from the beginning surely understood that this was no more than a rather unusual start of another Mercury Theater play. But many listeners had just tuned in, after having scanned through the various stations at the top of the hour, looking for a good program. As a result, these late-tuners would have missed the opening announcement, which plainly designated the show as fantasy. It seemed that their dial had alighted upon one of the many jazz band programs that dominated the airwaves during this time slot.

Suddenly, the music ceased and another familiar sound was heard: "Ladies and gentlemen, we interrupt this program of dance music to bring you a special bulletin from the Intercontinental Radio News." Only a month had since the Munich Crisis, and listeners were well accustome announcers (often from the International News Service) break into programs with the latest flashes and news bulletins. On September 24, the *Mercury Theater* itself had been interrupted for a crisis report while the cast was performing "The Immortal Sherlock Holmes."[2]*

The *Mercury Theater* "announcer" reported that astronomers across the country had been observing several gas explosions on the planet Mars. Immediately after this terse communiqué, "regular programming" resumed. But after a few more minutes of dance music, another news flash was heard:

> ANNOUNCER: Ladies and Gentlemen, following on the news given in our bulletin a moment ago, the Government Meteorological Bureau has requested the large observatories of the country to keep an astronomical watch on any further disturbances occurring on the planet Mars.

This rapid-fire reporting was again what the Munich Crisis had conditioned listeners to expect: a series of reports, each following hot on the heels of the other.

To clarify the issue for the listening audience, Welles presented an interview with "a noted astronomer." In another recognizable expression that indicated radio's power to transport the listener to the site of an important event by remote hook-up, the announcer promised to "take you now to" the Princeton Observatory at Princeton, New Jersey. As usual, CBS had its man on the spot: "This is Carl Philips, speaking to you from the observatory at Princeton." In a familiar type of on-the-scene interview, Philips asked Professor Richard Pierson (probably a veiled reference to Newton L. Pierce, a noted Princeton University astronomer), "Would you please tell our radio audience exactly what you see as you observe the planet Mars through your telescope?" By means of realistic sound effects, listeners heard the clanking of the gears as Pierson maneuvered his telescope into position.

Those at home heard nothing to indicate that this "astronomer" was an actor. He spoke in an authoritative tone and employed the scientific jargon of "orbits," "atmospheric conditions, " and "celestial opposition." Since the late nineteenth century, Americans had increasingly become accustomed to accepting the word of science as fact. Listeners therefore became unsettled when Pierson stated that he could not account for the gas explosions he was witnessing.

Philips reminded the audience that they were listening to a remote broadcast from Princeton, then broke off to read a note he had just received. The note stated that the "National History Museum" had registered seismic shocks of "earthquake intensity" occurring within a twenty-mile radius of Princeton. After a brief piano interlude, another news flash informed listeners of

...ding to Welles biographer Frank Brady, this was the moment when Welles first thought ...his technique "as a dramatic device to add tension" in one of his later plays (p. 167).

more explosions on Mars, and reported that a "huge, flaming object, believed to be a meteorite," had fallen near Grover's Mill, New Jersey. Again, CBS quickly mobilized its news crew to cover the event: "We have dispatched a special mobile unit to the scene and will have our commentator, Mr. Philips, give you a description as soon as he can reach there from Princeton."

Another musical number was played, and then Philips was heard against a background of crowd noises and police sirens, reporting from the site where the meteorite had fallen. The correspondent stated that he traveled the eleven miles from Princeton in ten minutes, but in reality only ninety seconds had elapsed since listeners last heard his voice. This anomaly seemed credible because of a familiar aural device. In normal radio programming, it had been customary to provide a brief "musical bridge," signifying a change in the time or setting of a story. This technique had been applied so often in programs of all genres that many listeners apparently failed to notice the inconsistency of actual time.

Philips then used radio's extraordinary descriptive power to convey the spectacle before him. It was "something out of a modern *Arabian Nights* ... the thing, half-buried in a vast pit, struck with terrible force and knocked down trees." Listeners were intrigued to discover that it was not a meteorite, but a huge extraterrestrial cylinder. Adding an air of authenticity to this scene, Philips chided a curious spectator who ventured into his line of sight while he was on the air: "Would you mind standing to one side, please!" Eventually Philips found his way through the crowd and interviewed Mr. Wilmuth, the owner of the farm where the object had landed. The dialogue had all the earmarks of a real man-in-the-street interview:

PHILIPS: Mr. Wilmuth, would you please tell the radio audience as much as you remember of this unusual visitor that dropped in your backyard? Step closer, please.

WILMUTH: I was listenin' to the radio...

PHILIPS: Closer and louder, please.

WILMUTH: (*To pushy bystander*) Pardon me!

PHILIPS: Louder, please, and closer.

WILMUTH: Yes sir—While I was listenin' to the radio and kinda drowsin', that professor fellow was talkin' about Mars, so I was half dozin' and half...

This interview appeared completely authentic to listeners, especially in Wilmuth's colloquial speech and microphone-shy attitude. For many, the genuineness of the earlier news reports was confirmed by Wilmuth's acknowledgment that he had also heard them. Eventually, the farmer overcame his reticence and continued to talk until Philips cut him off.

Philips then described for his listeners the public awe over the object before him, and discerned a peculiar noise emanating from within.

PHILIPS: Listen (*long pause*) ... Do you hear it? It's a curious humming sound that seems to be coming from inside the object. I'll move the microphone nearer. Here (*pause*). Now we're not more than 25 feet away. Can you hear it now?

All of a sudden, the calmness around the cylinder was broken. As listeners drew closer to their sets in amazement, Philips exclaimed:

Just a minute! Something's happening! Ladies and gentlemen, this is terrific! The end of the thing is beginning to flake off! The top is beginning to rotate like a screw! ... Ladies and gentlemen, this is the most terrifying thing I have ever witnessed ... Wait a minute! Someone's crawling out of the hollow top. Someone or something. Good heavens, something's wriggling out of the shadow like a gray snake. They look like tentacles to me. There, I can see the thing's body. It's large as a bear and it glistens like wet leather. But that face. It ... it's indescribable. I can hardly force myself to keep looking at it. The eyes are black and gleam like a serpent. The mouth is V-shaped with saliva dripping from its rimless lips that seem to quiver and pulsate ... This is the most extraordinary experience. I can't find words ... I'm pulling this microphone with me as I talk. I'll have to stop the description until I've taken a new position. Hold on, will you please, I'll be back in a minute.

There was a brief pause while the announcer reminded the audience that they were hearing an eyewitness account of what was transpiring on the Wilmuth farm. Philips returned in a seemingly spontaneous moment asking his engineer, "Am I on?" The police cordoned off the pit, and a flag of truce was offered to those inside. Again things began to happen.

PHILIPS: Wait! Something's happening! A huge shape is rising out of the pit. I can make out a small beam of light against a mirror. What's that? There's a jet of flame springing from that mirror and it leaps right out at the advancing men! It strikes them head on! Good Lord, they're turning into flame!

(*Screams and shrieks*)

Now the whole field's caught fire (*explosion*) ... the woods ... the barns ... the gas tanks of the automobiles ... It's spreading everywhere. Its coming this way ... about twenty yards to my right.

Philips was cut off abruptly, and listeners heard the thud of the falling microphone and then a hair-raising silence. Then an announcer came on to explain, in terms that had been commonplace during the transatlantic reports of the previous month: "Ladies and gentlemen, due to circumstances beyond our control, we are unable to continue the broadcast from Grover's Mill. Evidently, there is some difficulty with our field transmission."

At this point, many listeners were bewildered and alarmed. They had just heard a major disaster unfold before their very ears. The intense drama of this part of the broadcast in no way betrayed it as fiction. Millions of Americans remembered hearing another live report of disaster only a year earlier from another location in New Jersey. As in the case of Herbert Morrison's *Hindenberg* broadcast, apparently radio had again proved its unique ability to convey the emotional impact of a destructive event direct from the scene. In its spontaneity and dramatic realism, the scene at Grover's Mill was almost identical to the *Hindenburg* broadcast. Indeed, the actor who portrayed Philips, Frank Readick, had listened repeatedly to a recording of Morrison's account just before going on the air and had decided to "recreate the reporter's emotional trauma in his own terms" when describing the carnage caused by the Martian death ray.[3]

The shock experienced by many listeners was suddenly replaced by feelings of confusion. A new bulletin announced that the "California Astronomical Society" was of the opinion that the explosions on Mars were nothing more than severe volcanic disturbances on the planet's surface. While the experts were telling listeners that nothing was wrong, their own ears had indicated otherwise. Which source was to be believed? Hadn't the California astronomers heard the report from the Wilmuth farm? The scientific community had evidently misdiagnosed the problem, and as a result, many Americans begin to succumb to sensations of helplessness.

Before listeners had time to compose themselves, they were confronted with another disturbing bulletin:

> ANNOUNCER: Ladies and gentlemen, I have just been handed a message that came in from Grover's Mill by telephone. Just a moment. At least forty people, including six state troopers, lie dead in a field east of the village of Grover's Mill, their bodies burned and distorted beyond all possible recognition.

The worst fears of many listeners had just been confirmed.

After this, events began to move fast. The radio audience heard the voice of Brigadier General Montgomery Smith, commander of the state militia, declaring a state of emergency in New Jersey and placing certain counties under martial law. Four companies of state militia were ordered to proceed from Trenton to Grover's Mill to aid in the evacuation of homes. The Red Cross had been mobilized. Contact was established with Professor Pierson, who had witnessed the tragedy, and he expressed his inability to identify the precise nature of the Martian heat weapon. By telling listeners that the beings possessed "scientific knowledge far in advance of our own," he underscored their feelings of vulnerability. Immediately following this assessment, listeners were informed that the incinerated body of Carl Philips had been identified among the dead at Grover's Mill.

Next, a special statement by Mr. Harry MacDonald, vice-president in charge of radio operations, was aired. MacDonald stated his intention to place all of his broadcasting resources at the disposal of the state militia. He proclaimed: "In view of the gravity of the situation, and believing that radio has a definite responsibility to serve in the public interest at all times, we are turning over our facilities..." By having his imaginary radio executive profess a desire to serve the public while the real McCoys were going to such lengths to unnerve it, Welles was again at his deceptive best. The radio industry's reaffirmation of its role in promoting the public welfare reassured many listeners that the medium would not be used to dupe them. Again, many reservations about the authenticity of the program were dismissed.

The next voice provided listeners some relief from their anxiety. It was Captain Lansing of the Signal Corps, telling the public that the army had arrived and the situation was under control. The pit at Grover's Mill was surrounded by eight battalions of heavily armed infantry. As a result, "All cause for alarm is now entirely unjustified.... With all their reported resources, these creatures can scarcely stand up against heavy machine gun fire." Surveying the scene before him, Lansing remarked, "It looks almost like a real war." But just as many Americans were breathing a sigh of relief, disaster again struck:

> LANSING: Wait, that wasn't a shadow! It's something moving ... solid
>   metal ... kind of a shield-like affair rising out of the cylinder
>   ... It's going higher and higher. Why, it's standing on legs ...
>   actually rearing up on a sort of metal framework. Now it's
>   reaching above the trees and searchlights are on it! Hold on!
>   (*break off*)

By now, many listeners were thoroughly terrified. A whole force of American soldiers had been overwhelmed in a matter of seconds. Nothing could stop the machines. The nation's best military equipment seemed but toys against this awesome extraterrestrial power. Now the feeling of defenselessness became most acute. This mood was exacerbated when the next voice clearly confirmed the nature of this pressing danger:

> ANNOUNCER: Ladies and gentlemen, I have a grave announcement to make.
>   Incredible as it may seem, both the observations of science and
>   the evidence of our own eyes lead to the inescapable assump-
>   tion that these strange beings who landed in the Jersey farm-
>   lands tonight are the vanguard of an invading army from the
>   planet Mars.

The voice of the radio announcer, who had so recently informed the American public of the movements of foreign armies in Europe, now heralded an even more startling invasion. The announcer went on to describe the extent of the damage suffered by American forces in this terrible confrontation.

ANNOUNCER: The battle which took place tonight at Grover's Mill has ended in one of the most startling defeats ever suffered by an army in modern times: 7,000 men armed with rifles and machine guns pitted against a single fighting machine of the invaders from Mars. One hundred and twenty known survivors. The rest strewn over the battle area from Grover's Mill to Plainsboro, crushed and trampled to death under the metal feet of the monster, or burned to cinders by its heat ray. The monster is now in control of the middle section of New Jersey, and has effectively cut the state through its center. Communication lines are down from Pennsylvania to the Atlantic Ocean. Railroad tracks are torn and service from New York to Philadelphia discontinued except routing some trains.... highways clogged with frantic human traffic, police and army reserves are unable to control the mad flight. By morning the fugitives will have swelled Philadelphia, Camden, and Trenton, it is estimated, to twice their normal populations. At this time martial law prevails throughout New Jersey and eastern Pennsylvania.

To many Americans, it seemed their world was disintegrating as they listened. The Northeast had been overrun; it was only a matter of time before the rest of the country met a similar fate. Anyone who was still skeptical was sure to be convinced by the next voice he heard: "We take you now to Washington for a special broadcast on the national emergency ... the secretary of the interior." With this introduction, a man sounding distinctly like President Roosevelt went on the air to address the nation.

SEC. OF INT.: Citizens of the nation, I shall not try to conceal the gravity of the situation that confronts the country, nor the concern of your government in protecting the lives and prosperity of its people. However, I wish to impress upon you—private citizens and public officials, all of you—the urgent need of calm and resourceful action. Fortunately, this formidable enemy is still confined to a comparatively small area, and we may place our faith in the military forces to keep them there. In the meantime, placing our faith in God, we must continue the performance of our duties each and everyone of us, so that we may confront this destructive adversary with a nation united, courageous, and consecrated to the preservation of human supremacy on this earth. I thank you.

Although introduced as the "secretary of the interior," there was little doubt in many minds that this was the president of the United States, once again using the airwaves to address the American public during a time of crisis. As he had done so often in the worrisome days of the Depression, Roosevelt had apparently come on the radio to calm the nation and forestall panic. The voice employed the same inspiring language that listeners had heard so often in numerous fireside chats. But this time the voice did not uplift. It was evident that the president, in typically bureaucratic fashion, was trying to underestimate American losses. His admission that the federal government was gravely concerned by the Martian menace, and his invoking the name of God to stave off disaster, struck listeners as particularly troubling. Here Welles was again turning the tables on the American public, for another common radio vehicle that had previously been used to quell fear was now employed to enhance it. After the speech of the "secretary," Americans had every reason to believe that the end of the world was at hand.

A flood of bulletins reinforced this conclusion. In quick succession, it was reported that central New Jersey was blacked out from radio communication; that astronomers were warning of Martian reinforcements arriving at regular intervals; and that scouting planes had observed three Martian machines, visible above the treetops, moving north of Somerville, with the population fleeing before them. Americans were also made aware that the Martians were "picking their way carefully," trying to "avoid unneeded destruction of cities and countryside." For many people, this explained why they hadn't seen the invaders yet. Another flash told how the machines halted to uproot power lines, bridges, and railroad tracks. "Their apparent objective is to crush resistance, paralyze communications, and disorganize human society." Americans were now confronted with a calculating enemy, well-versed in the art of modern warfare. The war strategies that had been played out in Europe were now being waged in America.

As the Martian machines attempted to link up, the United States military endeavored to make one final stand. By means of special wires to the battle zone, Americans heard a two-way conversation between an officer of the 22nd Field Artillery and one of his gunners. Listeners remembered hearing this technical device only months ago, during Munich, where it was employed on a large scale. The battery found its range and opened fire, debilitating the legs of one machine.

All of a sudden, something new entered the picture. An observer reported: "A black smoke, moving this way. Lying close to the ground. It's moving fast." All of the soldiers donned their gas masks, but strangely, the vapor penetrated and they began to cough. Radio contact was established between the ground and a bombing plane overhead. The plane observed the "heavy, black smoke hanging close to the earth, of extreme density, nature unknown." The pilot of the aircraft gave the radio audience a blow-by-blow description of what happened next:

> The enemy is crossing the Passaic River, another straddles the Pulaski Skyway. The giant arm raised—Green flash! They're spraying us with

flame! Two thousand feet. Engines are giving out. No chance to release bombs. Only one thing left ... drop on them, plane and all. We're diving on the first one. Now engines gone! Eight..."

The next voice informed the audience of the lethal nature of the "black smoke":

ANNOUNCER: Warning! Poisonous black smoke pouring in from Jersey marshes. Gas masks useless. Urge population to move into open spaces ... automobiles use routes 7, 23, 24 ... avoid congested areas.

Listeners were horrified to learn the enemy was using poisonous vapor to destroy the civilian population. It was a common belief in the 1930s that after heavy use of gas in World War I and then the development of the modern bomber, the next world conflict would be characterized by large-scale gas attacks on civilian targets from the air. Here, Welles cleverly exploited this popular fear, as well as Americans' perceptions and expectations of modern total war, with terrifying effect.

Next came a radio correspondent speaking by remote broadcast from the rooftop of "Broadcasting Building, New York City" (a fictionalized Radio City). Against a background of church bells warning the inhabitants to flee the approaching Martians, the reporter described the scene of pandemonium before him. His frequent use of familiar place names augmented the realistic character of his vivid and dramatic narrative.*

The Hutchinson Parkway is still kept open for motor traffic. Avoid bridges to Long Island ... hopelessly jammed. All communication with Jersey closed, no more defenses. Our army wiped out ... artillery, air force, everything wiped out ... This may be the last broadcast. We'll stay on the air to the end. Streets jammed, boats fleeing harbor overloaded ... Five machines above the Palisades in sight, wading the Hudson like a man wades a brook. Martian cylinders falling all over the country ... Buffalo, Chicago, St. Louis ... Now the first machine reaches the shore. He stands watching, looking over the city. His steel, cowlish head is even with the skyscrapers. Now they're lifting their metal hands. This is the end now. They're running towards the East River ... thousands of them, dropping like rats. Now the smoke's spreading faster. It's reached Times Square. People trying to run away from it, but it's no use. They're falling like flies.

*Here Welles was utilizing a device employed only four days earlier in the Columbia Workshop production of the Archibald MacLeish play, Air Raid. The drama opened with an announcer (the Mercury's own Ray Collins) observing children playing from a tenement rooftop. All of a sudden, his commentary was interrupted by the wail of an air raid siren. As bombs began to drop and machine guns chattered, horrifying screams were heard from below. Although the script was written in verse, the realistic way it was presented endowed it with a chilling, on-the-spot quality. William Robson directed the play, and Welles played one of the leads.

> Now the smoke's crossing Sixth Avenue … Fifth Avenue … 200 yards
> away … its 50 feet… (*long pause*)

At this point, as was the custom, the story temporarily ceased and the half-hour break was aired. During this time the Mercury Theater announcer reaffirmed the fictional nature of the broadcast:

> You are listening to a CBS presentation of Orson Welles and the Mercury Theater on the Air in an original dramatization of the *War of the Worlds*, by H. G. Wells. The performance will continue after a brief intermission. This is the Columbia Broadcasting System.

After a thirty-second pause for station identification, the announcer reintroduced the drama: "The *War of the Worlds* by H. G. Wells, starring Orson Welles and the Mercury Theater on the Air." With these two announcements, it was clear that what occurred had been only a play. But many people, thinking the Martians were spreading destruction all over the United States with heat rays and poisonous gas, had already made the decision not to wait around to hear more bad news.

Those who continued to listen heard no more bulletins, flashes, or disturbing on-the-spot reports. Instead, the broadcast resumed the character of a dramatic performance, featuring a monologue by Welles as Professor Pierson, committing his thoughts to his journal and tortured by the prospect that he was "the last living man on earth." The story continued with Pierson's struggle to stay alive until the Martians succumbed to the ordinary bacterial strains against which their systems could not cope; "slain after all man's defense had failed, by the humblest thing that God in His infinite wisdom put on the earth." Unfortunately, many Americans did not remain to hear the ending of this fine play.

By the end of the drama, Welles was perfectly aware that some listeners might not have taken his presentation as fantasy. Recognizing this, he went on the air in the closing minutes of the broadcast to reassure them:

> This is Orson Welles, ladies and gentlemen, out of character to reassure you that the *War of the Worlds* has no further significance than as the holiday offering it was intended to be: the Mercury Theater's own radio version of dressing up in a sheet and jumping out of a bush and saying "Boo!" Starting now, we couldn't soap all of your windows and steal all of your garden gates by tomorrow night. So we did the next best thing. We annihilated the world before your ears, and utterly destroyed the CBS. You will be relieved, I hope, to learn that we didn't mean it, and that both institutions are still open for business. So good-bye everyone, and remember please, for the next day or so, the terrible lesson you learned tonight. That grinning, glowing, globular invader of your living room is an inhabitant of the pumpkin patch, and if your doorbell rings and nobody's there, that was no Martian—it's Halloween.

Altogether, four announcements stating the program's fictional character were made to the full network during the course of the broadcast. Furthermore, when Walter Winchell went on the air at 9:00 P.M. for Jergens, he declared: "Mr. and Mrs. North America, there is no cause for alarm. America has not fallen. I repeat: America has not fallen."[4] At 10:30, 11:30, and midnight, the following announcement was issued:

> For those who tuned in to Orson Welles and the *Mercury Theater on the Air* broadcast from 8–9 EST tonight and did not realize that the program was merely a modernized adaptation of H. G. Wells' famous novel, *War of the Worlds*, we are repeating the fact which was made clear four times in the program, that, while the names of some American cities were used, as in all novels and dramatizations, the entire story and all its incidents were fictitious.[5]

In all, 60 percent of those stations that aired the program interrupted it to make local announcements when it became apparent that a misunderstanding had been perpetrated.[6] Unfortunately, the damage had already been done. These reassurances came over the radios of empty homes. More than a million Americans, convinced of the authenticity of Welles's Martian invasion and victimized by their own imaginations, were already in headlong flight.

12. The Public Reaction

Panic in the Streets

The public response to the Welles broadcast was nothing short of electrifying. Newspapers spoke of a "tidal wave of terror that swept the nation."[1] A contemporary psychologist observed: "Probably never before have so many people in all walks of life and in all parts of the country become so suddenly and so intensely disturbed as they did this night."[2] It was estimated that of the 6 million people who heard the program, over 1.7 million had believed it to be an authentic news broadcast, and 1.2 million had become severely frightened.[3] While only 12 percent of the total radio audience had tuned in, "more than half this number had taken the broadcast seriously."[4] Network surveys placed the national figures even higher (72 percent) and revealed that in the southern states 80 percent of those who had tuned in believed in the Martian invasion.[5]

The area of the greatest panic was in the Northeast, where the bulk of the program's action had taken place. In Trenton, N.J., the first urban center encountered by the imaginary invaders, every highway out of the city was clogged with fleeing traffic. One state trooper reported:

> Hundreds of automobiles began to flash along at speeds which normally indicate gangsters leaving scenes of assassination. But there were family parties in most of the cars.... When a motorcycle [officer] tried to overhaul one speeding auto, he was passed by two or three others. The stampede was in all directions.[6]

Those intrepid souls who decided to remain behind pulled out their World War I–era gas masks. Scores of frantic residents implored the electric company to turn out the city's lights as a defensive measure against the approaching aliens.[7] Newark police received 2,000 calls from terrified listeners. In one city block, twenty families rushed out of their homes with handkerchiefs and washcloths over their faces to flee the enemy's poisonous gas.[8] Others remained behind only long enough to pack their vehicles with "furniture, children, dogs, and whatever else" they could quickly jam into them.[9] St. Mary's and St. Michael's hospitals each treated more than fifteen people for shock.[10] In response to the report of the mobilization of 7,000 National

Guardsmen on the program, New Jersey armories in Sussex and Essex counties were overwhelmed by officers and men seeking to check in.[11] In the region around Grover's Mill, bewildered farmers armed with guns roamed the countryside, looking for the invaders. Many courageous citizens sought to link up with the militia that was supposedly deploying nearby. More than 100 New Jersey state troopers were ordered to the area to "calm the populace" and to disarm the trigger-happy volunteers.[12] Dozens of vehicles containing the curious descended upon the supposed crash site to take pictures and gather souvenirs.[13] In nearby Cranbury, local fire chiefs spent the night following up reports that the forest had been set ablaze by the enemy's heat rays. One couple, in their haste to escape, drove through their unopened garage door.[14]

In New York City, "communications were virtually immobilized" as frightened callers swamped switchboard operators seeking advice and help. One surprised agent reported: "The first few callers we thought were intoxicated. But when the calls persisted, with some people very excited and others crying, we knew it was serious."[15] The *New York Times* alone received more than 875 telephone calls, and the *Daily News* reported more than 1,100.[16] At the latter, lines were jammed for hours, and the staff stopped saying "Hello." They "merely plugged in" and assured, "No, madam/sir, there are no men from Mars. It is just a radio show."[17] One overwrought woman asked if they were abandoning New York, and scores of Red Cross volunteers requested directions to the nearest emergency relief shelter.[18] Police stations and army barracks received calls from men anxious to enlist against the invaders.[19] Many churches delivered end-of-the-world prayer meetings to record congregations, and priests were "flooded with calls from parishioners seeking confession."[20] While his wife remained at home clutching her rosary, one man overturned his car while speeding to find a cleric.[21] In Harlem:

> Folks tripped over each other getting in and out of houses. Strong men who had forgotten all about the meaning of prayer dropped to their knees to spend their last few moments with God. Children half frightened out of their wits screamed in terror and women fainted.[22]

Hospitals had their hands full, restraining frantic patients and attempting to retrieve the few cases, some seriously incapacitated, who had gotten out of bed and taken off into the night. Thousands of off-duty doctors and nurses offered their services to the victims of Martian aggression. All over the city, the call went out for sailors on home leave to return to ship. One woman started a "minor stampede" when she ran into a theater screaming that the city was on fire.[23] As people madly rushed about, many said they had actually seen the ghastly aliens. A Manhattan man in a tree claimed he could see the flames of battle through his binoculars.[24] The pandemonium on New York's streets surpassed even the "hysterical rejoicing that followed immediately upon the report of the armistice in November 1918."[25] The wardens of several county penitentiaries were compelled to commandeer radio sets when it seemed inmates were becoming restless.[26]

In cities and towns across the nation, the reaction was similar. In Boston, people gathered on rooftops to marvel at the colorful patterns in the night sky produced by the alleged "burning of New York"[27]—actually the hue of distant neon signs. Rumors that the city had been destroyed, with millions of casualties, compelled masses of southerners from Richmond to Atlanta to gather in churches. Many families fled into the Appalachian Mountains, where they were found by sheriffs' posses days later.[28] In a college sorority house in Birmingham, women lined up behind the telephone, tearfully waiting to speak to their parents for the last time. The campus at Brevard College, N.C., was completely paralyzed for a half-hour, and five male students fainted.[29] A man from Selma, Louisiana, catching his chin under a clothesline while running in the dark, "thought he had been hit with a death ray."[30] In Salt Lake City, a distraught suitor called his sweetheart and insisted: "Marry me before we're killed!"[31] In Pittsburgh, a man rushed home to find his wife in the bathroom, holding a bottle of poison and shrieking, "I'd rather die this way than that!" Elsewhere in Pennsylvania, citizens scanned the skies for falling meteors, and one woman sealed up her house with cement to keep the invaders out. In Montgomery, Alabama, citizens mistook the sound of a low-flying aircraft for a Martian cylinder. Perhaps the most frightening experience occurred in Concrete, Washington, where a sudden power failure "convinced its inhabitants that the end was near."[32] KMOX (St. Louis) and KIRO (Seattle) each received over 700 calls, and WJSV (Washington, D.C.) attracted 470—two from managers of local grocery chains "asking if extra food supplies were needed in New York and New Jersey."[33] The Chesapeake and Potomac Telephone Company topped all others, with a record 9,000 calls.[34] One midwestern mayor phoned CBS and bellowed: "There are mobs in my streets! Women and children crowding my churches! Violence! Looting! Rioting!"[35] A Flint, Michigan, chamber of commerce official stated that the population of his city had been "scattered far and wide, and that it would take days to reassemble it."[36] Yet another caller demanded: "CBS, what are you going to do about me? I'm 300 miles from home without a penny in my pocket."[37] After driving all night, a New Jersey man pulled into a fueling station in the nation's capital and demanded: "Give me some gas. I'm headed for Florida and in a hurry. All hell has broken loose in New Jersey."[38] Since public excitement still had not subsided by the late afternoon of October 31, the Rochester *Democrat and Chronicle* felt it necessary to remind citizens: "No! No! No! The U.S. is NOT attacked!"[39]

The panic was not confined exclusively to the United States. When families in Watertown and other northern New York State communities sought refuge across the border in Canada, they discovered the broadcast had caused "widespread alarm" there as well.[40] Ontario attorney general Gordon Conant was so dismayed by the reaction of his countrymen, he instructed his office to investigate methods for the rigid censorship of all future programs emanating from American sources.[41]

There were numerous injuries, but surprisingly, no one committed suicide or died of heart failure—despite widespread rumors to the contrary. A handful of people who had suffered severe shock or mental trauma as a result of the program attempted to sue CBS.[42] According to John Houseman, the network was even accused of causing several miscarriages.[43]

A poll conducted by the American Institute of Public Opinion six weeks after the broadcast revealed the true extent of the panic. In the course of their research, it was found that only 12 percent of the total listening audience had heard the program. The *Mercury Theater on the Air* was an unsponsored program that appealed primarily to educated listeners. It was scheduled in a time slot that CBS felt was "unsalable" because it had to compete with the *Charlie McCarthy Show*, the most popular program on network radio. In addition to this, many of the largest New England stations, including WEEI (Boston), had exercised their prerogative as CBS affiliates and decided not to carry the program.[44] The American Institute of Public Opinion came to the conclusion that had more people been listening in, the extent of the "panic would have been even more widespread" and less controllable.[45]

When considering survey data, it is important to realize that many people, fearing embarrassment, probably did not admit that they had been frightened. Conducting his survey less than two months after the event, Cantril received many evasive replies like the following:

> "Me scared? Course not. I knew it was a play all the time. Me and the old woman ran down the streets and mingled with the crowd, but we wasn't scared ourselves. Just for kicks, we wanted to see how the others were taking it. You know what I mean."[46]

Overall, the "large-scale, irrational behavior" of the few who did listen to the broadcast was sufficient for a *New York Herald-Tribune* writer to remark: "Not since the Spanish Fleet sailed to bombard the New England coast in 1898 has so much hysteria, panic, and sudden conversion to religion been reported to the press of the U.S., as when radio listeners heard about an invasion from Mars."[47]

Popular Gullibility?

For many prominent observers, the mass hysteria was clearly the result of a "deep-seated public gullibility." One of the most vociferous purveyors of this view was radio commentator and newspaper columnist Dorothy Thompson. In a November 2, 1938, "On the Record" article, she praised the Welles broadcast as "forcible testimony" of the power of American broadcasting:

> Welles and the Mercury Theater have made one of the most fascinating demonstrations of all time. They have proved that a few effective voices,

accompanied by sound effects, can so convince masses of people of a totally unreasonable and completely fantastic proposition as to create a nation-wide panic.[48]

The reason for the broadcast's success, she argued, was that listeners lacked the critical sense and "spark of skepticism" needed to identify the program as a play. Welles's deception, she wrote, "has cast a brilliant and cruel light upon the failure of popular education. It has shown up the incredible stupidity, lack of nerve and ignorance of thousands."[49] Dr. Alice Keliher, of the Religious Programs Education Association, conceded that "American education has a few embarrassing questions to answer."[50] University studies conducted shortly after the broadcast seemed to reinforce this view. One study revealed that the more educated segment of the listening audience had been far less inclined to believe the program than their unschooled counterparts.[51] Such evidence induced literary critic Alexander Woolcott to write Welles: "This only goes to prove that the intelligent people were listening to a dummy [Charlie McCarthy], and all the dummies were listening to you."[52]

The press had been waiting for an opportunity to pounce upon its electronic competitor. After having had to "bow to radio as a news source during the Munich Crisis, the press was only too willing to expose the perilous irresponsibility of the new medium."[53] In the days following the broadcast, it made the most of the opportunity. A scathing cartoon in the *New York World Telegram* on November 1 showed panicked masses fleeing as a radio loudspeaker blared words like, "The Martians are smashing New York!" "Cylinders from Mars are Falling all over the Country!" "Death Rays!" "Monsters as Tall as Skyscrapers!" The accompanying caption read, "What Has Happened to the American Mind?"[54]

Critics pointed out that "nothing in the dramatization was in the least bit credible," and that a twist of the tuning dial would "have established for anybody that the national catastrophe was not being noted on any other station." The fact that the broadcast was conspicuously advertised as a fictional program for days in the newspapers seemed to prove that "a second of logic would have dispelled any terror."[55] Indeed, the entertainment section of the Sunday *New York Times* displayed a large photograph of Welles and the Mercury cast above the heading: "Tonight's show is H. G. Wells's 'War of the Worlds'."[56]

Critics were astounded that listeners would believe that, in the course of forty-five minutes' actual time, "the invading Martians were presumably able to blast off from their planet, land on earth, set up their destructive machines, defeat our army, disrupt communications, demoralize the populace, and occupy whole sections of the country."[57] This seemed to confirm the suspicions of many radio advertisers that the audience "often listened to programs absent-mindedly, without being attentive to the subtle points of a broadcast."[58] H. V.

Kaltenborn's wife added, "How ridiculous. Anybody should have known it was not a real war. If it had been, the broadcaster would have been Hans."[59]

Even the radio industry itself took an opportunity to poke fun at the impressionable American public. In the script for a popular *Town Hall Tonight* program scheduled a week after the Welles ruse, comedian Fred Allen planned to open with the following warning:

> This is a comedy program. Any sound effects or dialogue you hear during the hour will be purely imaginary. If you hear a phone ringing [and he demonstrated] don't answer it. If you hear a knock on the door [another demo] don't rush to open it. Just sit back and relax. Nothing is going to happen.[60]

The reaction of foreign observers was not favorable. Britons seemed reluctant to believe the American public had swallowed such a well-known tale of fantasy. In an interview with H. G. Wells a year-and-a-half later, the British author explained the hysteria as "normal American Halloween fun-making." Soft-pedaling the dangerous nature of the panic, Wells said, "Have you never heard of Halloween in America when everyone pretends to see ghosts?"[61] European dictatorships found that the Welles broadcast provided "rich grist for their propaganda mills." The Italian fascist daily *Resto de Carlino* proclaimed that the "mythical Martians put a third-grade democracy into tragic confusion." Both Hitler and Mussolini "hailed the hysterical exhibition as a sign of the decadence and cowardice of American democracy."[62] One of Germany's main newspapers, *Der Angriff*, caustically stated:

> If Americans fall so easily for a fantastic radio broadcast of an invasion from Mars, that explains why they so readily believe Nazi atrocity tales.... Naivete is a gift of God, but it should not be abused.... This explains a lot for the Old World.[63]

The Welles Plan

While the public gullibility argument has its merits, it is a far too simplistic and convenient explanation that tends to obscure the true origins of the panic. It must be remembered that many intelligent and capable individuals proved susceptible to the feelings of helplessness and fear. In Elizabeth, N.J., one woman remarked: "The reason why the thing was so real to us was because, that evening, there were several people at our home, engineers and others who were very well-informed. They were convinced the thing was real too, and they were as frightened as we were."[64] When one family in Maplewood, N.J., called the local police asking for advice, the officer on duty responded: "We know as much as you do. Keep your radio tuned and follow the announcer's advice."[65] Countless officers on patrol became startled while listening to the program on their car sets; New York City and New Jersey state police had to dispatch a message assuring them that there was "no cause for alarm."[66] Atlanta police found "responsible people" to have been "among the most anxious information seekers." At the *New York Herald-Tribune*, photographers "put on gas masks in preparation to go into the streets and get pictures of the Martians."[67] The *Memphis Press-Scimitar* recalled its entire staff in order to get out an exclusive on the "bombing of Chicago."[68] The radio editor of a Syracuse newspaper fled with his family, and so many journalists sought validation of the reports that the Associated Press was compelled to issue the following notice: "Note to Editors: Queries to newspapers from radio listeners throughout the U.S. tonight, regarding a reported meteor fall which killed a number of New Jerseyites, are result of a studio dramatization."[69] A Howard University professor phoned the *Washington Post* to "verify reports of the alien invasion."[70] The New York City Public Health Department and the president of Washington's Red Cross tried to organize national disaster relief efforts.[71] In their barracks at Quantico, Va., a company of "hard-boiled Marines wept and prayed."[72] The "reports of falling meteors" even prompted two Princeton geologists, Dr. Arthur Buddington and Dr. Harry Hess, to grab flashlights and shovels and "set out in search for them."[73] An NBC executive who happened to be listening to the program was outraged that his network had failed to cover "a story so colossal that no one would survive long enough to report it."[74]

It is clear by these examples that "possession of critical faculties was not in itself enough to prevent a misreading of the situation." The *Washington Post* observed: "There are certain forms of fear against which common sense is apparently powerless."[75] According to Cantril, "while public naivete certainly played a role in the hysteria, it merely provided a more receptive setting for the broadcast."[76]

More than any other single factor, the clever manipulation of the various conventions of radio was responsible for inciting a nationwide panic. Only with this observation can one account for the fact that "people of widely different social classes and educational backgrounds behaved irrationally."[77] Despite the remark by Dorothy Thompson that "nothing whatever about the dramatization was in the least bit credible, no matter at what point the listener might have tuned in," no one examining the script today "can deny that the broadcast was so realistic" (especially its first half) that it was believable to "even the relatively sophisticated and well-informed listener."[78]

When Welles was confronted by an army of inquisitive reporters the morning after the broadcast, he was all innocence. To a question during a press conference inquiring whether he had been aware of the terror he was encouraging, Welles replied, "Definitely not. I had anticipated nothing unusual." In his "most sincere tone," he added:

I'm of course surprised that the H. G. Wells classic, which is the original for many fantasies about invasions by mythical monsters from the planet

Mars … and has become familiar to children through the medium of comic strips and many succeeding novels and adventure stories, should have had such a profound effect on radio listeners.[79]

To the Associated Press, he stated:

We've been putting on all sorts of things from the most realistic situations to the wildest fantasy and nobody ever bothered to get serious about them before. We just can't understand why this should have had such an amazing reaction….[80]

In an interview the next day, Welles assured the public, "I don't think we will choose anything like this again."[81] It was during the first morning-after interview that the myth of deaths caused by the panic probably began. Several press representatives, in their eagerness to discredit radio, confronted the Mercury cast with false reports of ever-increasing mortality figures. According to John Houseman, for many hours "we believed ourselves to be mass murderers."[82] Despite public statements to the contrary, this rumor persists to this day.

Much of the public accepted Welles's apology and absolved him from culpability. A *Daily News* writer spoke for many pardoning Americans when he remarked: "We're sure the 23-year-old actor, Orson Welles, didn't realize the panic he was spreading from coast to coast."[83]

Much of what Welles had told the press, however, was untrue. The young director had begun to get an inkling of the public response soon after the first few "bulletins" were aired. Fifteen minutes into the program, after the "Secretary of the Interior" finished speaking, CBS supervisor Davidson Taylor was called to the studio phone to respond to confused and frightened inquiries from hundreds of affiliate stations all around the country.[84] Taylor informed Welles of these communications and directed him to use the intermission to reassure listeners that the program was only a play. But this was more than ten minutes away, and "there were still many more terrifying moments in the script." A New York police station phoned the studio and demanded, "What's going on up there?" Welles himself, on the sound-room floor, could see police beginning to swarm around the halls. One officer tried to enter the area where the broadcast was in progress, but an actor pushed him away.[85]

Welles, then, had an indication of the popular reaction and "had ample opportunity to clarify the situation," but he deliberately chose not to. In fact, he had anticipated the public's reaction as part of a carefully calculated plan to "excite the passions" of the listening audience. As far as he was concerned, everything was proceeding satisfactorily. According to William Alland, when Davidson Taylor confronted Welles and said: "For God's sake, you're scaring people to death, please interrupt and tell them its only a show," the Mercury director replied: "What do you mean interrupt? They're scared? Good, they're supposed to be scared. Now let me finish!" At one point, Alland recalls looking down a hall and seeing William Paley "in a bathrobe and slippers ... trying to find out what the hell was going on."[86]

Welles first revealed his plot during an interview for BBC television in 1955, after time had mitigated public anger and had "taken the sting out" of the $12 million in lawsuits against CBS.* On this occasion, Welles disclosed for the first time that "in fact, we weren't as innocent as we meant to be when we did the Martian broadcast."[87] In a later interview with American film director Peter Bogdanovich, Welles admitted that the kind of response the program would elicit "was merrily anticipated by all of us." When the actual scale of the panic exceeded even his own expectations, Welles was delighted. In a 1978 appearance on the *Today Show* he confessed that the reaction to his trick had been "laughable." He told his host: "I never thought it was anything but funny."[88]

In his BBC interview, Welles explained the motivations behind his conscious attempt to deceive the American public:

> We were fed up with the way in which everything that came over this magic box, the radio, was being swallowed. People suspect what they read in the newspaper and what people tell them, but when radio came ... anything that came through that new machine was believed.
> Radio in those days, before the tube and the transistor, wasn't just a noise in somebody's pocket—it was a voice of authority. Too much so. At least I thought so. It was time for someone to take the starch ... out of some of that authority: hence my broadcast.[89]

Thus, Welles exploited the confidence listeners had developed towards the medium that had seen them through the Depression and had kept them informed of the latest foreign and domestic occurrences during the 1930s. Welles thought that "Halloween Eve was the perfect time to spoof not just the American people, but radio itself." In attempting to "diminish the authority and power of radio," and undermine the strong hold it had on the public, Welles manipulated virtually all of the medium's "inherent properties" and accepted usages.[90]

The precise total of damages varies from source to source—from Houseman's low of $750,000 to Welles's own high of $12 million. Fortunately for Welles, his attorney, L. Arnold Weissberger, had removed an indemnification clause from his CBS contract, which would have made him responsible for the network's legal costs in this case. While none of the claims ever went before a judge, several thousand dollars were dispensed in out-of-court settlements.

13. "It Was All So Real"

Manipulation

One week after the broadcast, Princeton University launched the Princeton Radio Project, a research study to determine exactly why so many people had been duped into believing the invasion from Mars. Under the direction of psychologist Hadley Cantril, the research group (which also included Dr. Paul Lazarsfeld, Hazel Gaudet, and Dr. Frank Stanton) interviewed 135 people who had heard the program and had been upset by it. Cantril endeavored to discover the psychology behind the mass hysteria by employing the most sophisticated research tools then available to social science.[1] CBS embarked upon its own study, with sociologist Herta Herzog leading a team of able investigators.

Referring to the unique characteristics of radio which made it conducive to inciting panic, Cantril remarked:

> By its very nature radio is the medium par excellence for informing all segments of the population of current happenings, for arousing in them a common sense of fear or joy and for inciting them to similar reactions directed towards a single objective.... The radio audience consists essentially of thousands of small, congregate groups united in time and experiencing a common stimulus—altogether making possible the largest grouping of people ever known.[2]

It was found that the program was accepted because Welles had so "capably handled the old familiar earmarks of credibility" that both the form and content of the broadcast seemed authentic.[3] The broadcast appeared so real because much of it "fell within the existing 'standards of judgment' of the listener." Cantril defined this phenomenon as the "organized mental context which provides an individual with a basis for interpretation." As such, "if a stimulus fits into the area of interpretation covered by the standard of judgment and does not contradict it, then it is likely to be believed." Welles was able to frighten American listeners because he used his program to create a mirror that reflected all of their apprehensions. By using various radio devices to play on the latent anxieties of listeners, he was successful in "arousing in them false standards of judgment that made them susceptible to feelings of panic."[4] John Houseman remarked: "If, that night, the American public proved gullible, it was because enormous pains and a great deal of thought had been spent to make it so."[5] With this in mind, a more thorough examination of Welles's methods is necessary for a complete understanding of this significant event.

Among the most prominent standards of judgment that Welles manipulated to induce "immediate acceptance of his broadcast" was radio's "role as an acknowledged vehicle for important announcements." As previously mentioned, only 35 days before the broadcast, millions of listeners had remained by their radios in order to receive the fast-breaking news from a continent on the brink of war. It had become natural to expect that musical programs, quiz shows, serials, dramas, and any other kind of programming would be preempted in an emergency, in order that an "anxious public could be informed."[6] A significant proportion of listeners had come to rely on radio as their main source of news. Indeed, most of those Cantril and Herzog interviewed mentioned the "confidence they had in radio and their expectation that it would be used for important announcements." Some of their comments:

> When I hear something on the radio like that I take it for granted it is true.[7]
> We have so much faith in broadcasting. In a crisis it has to reach all people. That's what radio is here for.
> The announcer would not say it if it was not true. They always quit if something is a play.
> I put credence in news bulletins. I feel that the radio is the official organ to let people know of tragedies. This sort of broke my faith in radio.[8]

Welles also exploited the public's respect for prestigious speakers and experts. According to Cantril: "It is a well known fact to psychologists, advertisers and propagandists that an idea has a better chance of gaining public acceptance if it is endorsed by some well known personality whose character, ability, or status is highly valued." The unusual events described by the announcer in the Mercury Theater broadcast "were so far removed from ordinary experience, and yet of such personal significance to the listener," that he was in need of expert interpretation.[9] Many listeners felt that in such extraordinary circumstances, only an informed observer could understand the situation and communicate it to the layman. To fulfill the public's need for expert opinion about the extraterrestrials, Welles provided an array of "scientists," including Professor Farrel of Mt. Jennings Observatory, Professor Morse from Macmillan University, and the chief character in the play, Professor Pierson of Princeton. When the situation required an armed response, listeners were given the military expertise of such figures as Brigadier General Montgomery Smith, commander of state militia, and Captain Lansing of the Signal Corps. The most effective prestigious speaker was undoubtedly the Rooseveltian "Secretary of the Interior." For this role, Welles had recruited the gifted impersonator Kenny Delmar. Sounding very much like a commander-in-chief, he apprised Americans of the grave situation facing them and issued evacuation instructions. While the speaker was not specifically referred to as the "president," many listeners automatically made the vocal connection. Instead of hearing and processing what was actually said, the listener "heard what accorded with his preconceptions."[10] While many of the official and professional appellations given on the program had been fabricated, they were nonetheless titles that "suggested authority."[11]

In Harlem, one man rushed into a police station insisting that he be evacuated because he had just heard "the President's voice" on the radio, advising all citizens to leave the cities. Another listener remarked, "I didn't tune in until the program was half over, but when I heard the names and titles of Federal, State, and municipal officials, and when the 'Secretary of the Interior' was introduced, I was convinced that it was the real McCoy."[12] At this point, a Syracuse woman stated: "Things went blackest and ... we sat back and waited for the end to come."[13]

To the list of conspicuous voices must be added those of Welles and his talented cast. The consummate "dramatic excellence of their vocal performances" greatly enhanced the lifelike quality of the broadcast.[14] Welles's "resonant, throbbing voice" had the effect of "investing a simple, declarative sentence with a sense of excitement and importance."[15] The magnificent acting demonstrated by the "horrified Philips and the choking announcer" also conveyed a strong sense of authenticity.

As the play unfolded, Houseman observed, a "strange fever seemed to invade the studio—part childish mischief and part professional zeal. First to feel it were the actors, who, suddenly realizing the chance to do a wonderful show, began to stretch the familiar elements of theatrical effect far beyond the normal point of tension." So convincing were their performances, Houseman continued, that "to this day, it is impossible to sit in a room and hear them without feeling ... in the back of your neck, some slight draft left over from that great wind of terror that swept the nation."[16]

The realistic nature of the broadcast was further magnified by the frequent use of vivid descriptions and idiomatic, colloquial, and folksy expressions. Examples of this would include the description of the gas as "a sort of yellowish-green," the policeman's warning, "One side there. Keep back, I tell you!" and the spectator's exclamation, "The darn thing's unscrewing!"[17]

Continual use of specific details added to the effect. Brigadier General Smith's edict is one of the best examples:

> I have been required by the governor of New Jersey to place the counties of Mercer and Middlesex as far west as Princeton, and east to Janesbury, under martial law. No one will be permitted to enter this area except by special pass issued by state or military authority. Four companies of state

militia are proceeding from Trenton to Grover's Mill and will aid in the evacuation of homes within the range of military operations.

The mention of familiar places proved particularly frightening to the inhabitants of New Jersey and New York, the areas in which the Martian machines were the most active. Princeton, Newark, Trenton, the Holland Tunnel, Allentown, Morristown, the Watchung Mountains, Bayonne, the Hutchinson River, Trenton, Times Square, Fifth Avenue, Plainsboro, and the Pulaski Skyway were all mentioned in the course of the broadcast. All are well known to Jerseyites and New Yorkers, as well as much of the nation at large.[18] The effectiveness of this device can again be proved by the remarks of listeners. One stated: "It must be real ... there is no other Grover's Mill. They said Grover's Mill, New Jersey."[19]

Particularly effective, too, was Welles's skillful manipulation of the audience's sense of time. Welles abided by the "real duration of time in the beginning of the program and then dramatically collapsed the action once the basic illusion had been established."[20] Houseman explained: "The first few minutes were intended to lull the audience into a false security and to furnish a solid base of realistic time from which to accelerate later."[21] At several points in the broadcast, Welles "allowed dead silence on the air," and he "dragged out" Ramon Raquello's musical numbers for an unusually long period, so as to make the "later, speeded-up and implausible occurrences seem real."[22] These artful devices "undermined the listener's critical faculties" and made such inconsistencies of time as a ninety-second journey of eleven miles (from Princeton to Grover's Mill seem believable.[23] Houseman has argued that only by "telescoping the reality of dramatic time" could listeners logically accept that within the span of three quarters of an hour, "large bodies of troops were mobilized, cabinet meetings were held, and savage battles were fought on land, air and sea."[24] The "sheer onrush of events in a rapid-fire manner" severely hindered the listener's ability to apply logical standards "to the incredible things he was hearing."[25] By alternating bulletins and music, Welles created a format in which tension was repeatedly introduced, released, and renewed, paralyzing his audience.[26]

At the same time, events reported in the broadcast began as fairly believable occurrences and gradually progressed to the incredible. The first announcement of the "atmospheric disturbances and explosions of incandescent gas" was quite credible and succeeded in gaining the confidence of the listener. As the story events grew more fantastic, Welles's characters maintained this trust by revealing that they also had trouble accepting what they saw and heard.* When he perceived that the object before him was not a meteor but a metal container, the reporter Carl Philips registered his astonishment at the "fantastic scene" that resembled "something out of a modern Arabian Nights." When the cylinder

---

*According to Professor Herzog, "It is quite understandable that people are more likely to believe a strange tale when the narrator himself expresses incredulity" (Herzog, p. 3).

began to open, he exclaimed: "Ladies and Gentlemen, this is terrific!... This is the most terrifying thing I have ever witnessed.... This is the most extraordinary experience. I can't find words..." After the massacre at Grover's Mill, the announcer says, "Incredible as it may seem..." Thus the listener knew that his own puzzlement was also experienced by those observing the situation.[27] Houseman believed the "credible to incredible" progression to have been "the great tensile strength of the show, the structural device that made the whole illusion possible." He added: "It could have been carried off in no other medium than radio."[28]

Another Welles technique that added an authentic aura to the program was his convincing use of sound effects. Acting director Paul Stewart worked for many days "trying to perfect the crowd scenes, the roar of the cannon in the Watchung Hills, and the sound of New York harbor as the ships, with the last remaining survivors, put out to sea."[29] Through the use of recently improved microphone filters, Stewart and Welles were able to maintain the illusion of genuine radio communication in the two-way field conversation between the artillery commander and his gunner, and the closed-circuit transmissions of the bomber pilot. The film *The Night That Panicked America* demonstrates how many of these effects were achieved. The eerie sound of the Martian machines was made by a makeshift, flute-like instrument. To simulate the sound of the opening spacecraft, Welles situated a microphone in the studio bathroom and had an engineer slowly unscrew the lid of a coffee jar inside a toilet.[30] The effectiveness of his sound effect innovations can be ascertained by the comments of numerous listeners. One remarked:

> I tuned in and heard buildings tumbling down in the Palisades and people fleeing Times Square. I could hear the noise in the radio and the announcer said so. It was not static, but things actually falling, so I did get up and looked out.[31]

Perhaps no single sound was employed with greater effect than the "lone piano" which "shattered the dead air with its ominous tinkle" after each report of catastrophe: the massacre at Grover's Mill, the ill-fated battle in the Watchung Mountains, and so on. As the piano played on, giving listeners' imaginations time to dwell upon the terrible implications of each bulletin, "its effect became increasingly sinister—a thin band of suspense stretched almost beyond endurance."[32] The absence of sound—"the technical use of silence"— was also extremely effective.[33] One listener remarked: "At one point we heard nothing and it seemed like they cut away. Then there was only silence—and that intensified our interest even more."[34]

Historical Environment

One cannot begin to understand the plausibility of the Welles program without first taking into account the historical context in which it was aired.

Since the crash of 1929, the United States had been experiencing severe economic and social turbulence. After nearly a decade of chronic unemployment, labor unrest, declining wages, bank failures, agricultural crisis, and the "inability to plan for a protected future," many Americans experienced intense feelings of insecurity. The year 1938 had been one of deteriorating circumstances, with over 20 percent (10 million) of the population jobless and capital investment falling to a new low of $121 million (from the previous year's $314 million).[35] The growing complexities of modern society, especially with the advent of an increasingly technocratic and interventionist government during the New Deal, and the contraction of educational, occupational, and professional opportunities made many citizens feel that they had been disenfranchised and no longer maintained control over their lives.[36] The activities of the Brownlow Commission (and the soon-to-be established Executive Reorganization Act) certainly heightened the fears of those who resented increasing federal encroachment. After the president's ill-conceived efforts to pack the Supreme Court and purge his own party, many were convinced that FDR was endeavoring to replace representative democracy with dictatorship. While the New Deal had certainly made great strides by 1938, many Republicans and many of those who remained in the breadlines worried that the Administration was incapable of mastering the Depression.

The increasing frequency of natural catastrophes such as floods, hurricanes, and dust storms exacerbated the pervasive sense of helplessness. Manmade disasters also affected the national mood. On June 19, 1938, one of the worst rail accidents in history claimed over 40 lives in Montana. That same year, 22 schoolchildren were killed in Utah when their bus was hit by a freight train; and in Linden, N.J., a gas and oil fire at the city service plant burned uncontrollably for three days. Religious notions had "long conditioned people to a general expectation of disaster, as a form of divine punishment." To many Americans, "all was not right with the world, and reports of rampaging Martians seemed to fit perfectly into the confusing picture with which they were already familiar." According to one listener: "I hated to think that the end of the world had come, but there are such unusual things happening in the world ... that I thought it was possible."[37]

Perhaps the most important contextual factor in making listeners accept the notion of a hostile invasion was the recent European war scare. Because of the constant and very real threat of another world conflict, the "mood of the American people was already one of insecurity and apprehension streaked with hysterical fear," even before the Welles broadcast.[38] Thanks to the accomplishments of network news correspondents in bringing the events of Europe home in September 1938, Americans were well aware that Nazi Germany was priming itself for war. Every day during the Munich Crisis, programs were constantly interrupted by flash announcements which "threatened disaster or uncertain peace." As a result, "nerves made jittery by actual, though almost incredible threats of war, had prepared a good many American radio listeners to believe the completely incredible 'news' that Martian hordes were here."[39] Thus, according to Cantril, "both the techniques and the content of the broadcast tended to fit into the existing mental context which had resulted from world events of the previous weeks."[40] Said listeners:

> The war news has everybody so tense, we more or less believe everything we hear.
> It was made up like a news flash exactly the way it was made during the Crisis. I thought it was some sort of disaster. One never knows what is going to happen these days."[41]

In the "general atmosphere of uncertainty," many listeners "translated the creatures" into a more familiar aggressor. Over one quarter of all those interviewed by Cantril believed it to be some sort of earthly foreign attack, and many of his subjects referred to the extraterrestrial onslaught in terms associated with First World War, such as "gas attacks" and "aerial bombings."[42] Many Americans who had marveled at Germany's employment of technological curiosities like the Stuka dive-bomber and Panzer II tank in Spain, Austria, and Czechoslovakia assumed that Hitler's engineers had developed some sort of super-weapon with which to conquer the world.[43] The suddenness of the Martian attack, and the speed of their advance, did not come as a surprise to a world that had witnessed the swift operations of the "Condor Legion" and mechanized armor, and would soon be introduced to blitzkrieg warfare.

A Newark housewife ran into the street and tried to flag down a car, screaming, "Don't you know New Jersey is being destroyed by the Germans?— it's on the radio."[44] Another frightened citizen commented: "While the U.S. thought everything was settled, they came down unexpected. The Germans are so wise, they were in something like a balloon." Other people believed the attack originated with another of America's potential enemies: "I felt it might be the Japanese—they are so crafty."[45] Still others ventured that it was another phase in Hitler's campaign against the Jews.* Reactions of this type reflected the deep xenophobia in the American psyche. Americans harbored a latent antipathy towards anything alien, whether Martian or German. Howard Koch remarked, "If the play had portrayed Martians as arrivals on a friendly mission, I suspect our audience would have been less ready to accept the drama as something actually happening."[46]

Many critics condemned Welles for his "untimely presentation." Heywood Broun of the *New York World Telegram* observed:

> I doubt if anything of the sort would have happened four or five months ago. The course of world history has affected national psychology. Jitters

---

The broadcast occurred only 10 days before Kristallnacht, Hitler's great campaign of terror and pillage against the Jews of Germany.

have come to roost. We have just gone through a laboratory demonstration of the fact that the peace of Munich hangs heavy over our heads, like a thundercloud.[47]

A writer for the *Daily News* sourly remarked: "Mr. Welles, student of Shakespeare, might have remembered Hamlet, and, remembering, might have foreseen the effects of too much dramatic realism on an audience already strung to a high nervous tension."[48] This view was shared by one of the editors of the *New York Times*: "Common sense might have warned the producer of the broadcast that our own people are just recovering from a psychosis brought on by the fear of war."[49]

Wonders of Science

In view of the popular conception of science in 1938, it is no surprise that even the most fantastic elements of the broadcast seemed credible. The first several decades of the twentieth century had been a period of rapid technological change. The early 1900s had seen the development of the telephone, automobile, light bulb, phonograph, typewriter, and camera. The First World War had demonstrated the ways in which science could be mobilized to produce weapons of mass destruction: fighter aircraft and zeppelin bombers, poison gas, tanks, submarines, machine guns, and flamethrowers. In the 1920s, Americans were introduced to a host of labor-saving electrical appliances: the vacuum cleaner, washing machine, electric sewing machine, and toaster. According to Cantril, many people without a scientific background saw these modern devices as "manifestations of a baffling power, in which the principles by which they operate are completely unknown." Even radio itself appeared to originate from a "world outside and lie within a universe of discourse completely foreign to the perplexed layman." It was a common belief among average Americans that if science could create the technical contraptions already in existence, could it not also "create rocket ships and death rays?"[50] After all, popular, pseudo-scientific magazines like *Amazing Science* advertised: "Today's extraordinary fiction [is] tomorrow's cold fact." The popular radio character *The Shadow* spoke for many of his countrymen when he said:

> Is anything really fantastic as the modern world of science? Thirty years ago, the notion that a human voice could circle the earth without the aid of wires could have been called, not only fantastic, but impossible. Radio, electric lights, the airplane, all were called fantastic in their time, but today they are accepted facts.[51]

Many of those Herzog questioned reinforced this view:

> So many odd things are happening in the world.... science has progressed so far that we don't know how far it might have gone on Mars. The way the world moves ahead, anything is possible.[52]

This last observation points to another popular myth, that Mars was inhabited. The prevailing opinion on this topic stemmed from the writings of Percival Lowell, who published a book entitled *Mars: As the Abode of Life* in 1901. In this work, readers were introduced to a superhuman race of intelligent creatures who had constructed canals on the planet's surface to channel water to their burgeoning cities. Lowell's successors revealed some of the planet's other life-sustaining features, including an atmosphere and cloud formations. Three days before the broadcast, newspapers published a statement by Dr. Knut Lundmark, director of the Lund Observatory in Sweden, confirming the existence of "living things on Mars."[53]

On some level, popular belief was also likely affected by the planet's name—Mars, the name of the Roman god of war—and by frequent descriptions of the "blood-red planet." Such descriptors suggested the inhabitants must be hostile. The threat from Mars was considered all the more immediate since the planet was earth's closest neighbor at 260 million miles—a distance Welles shortened, in his broadcast, to 40 million.

Many Americans who did not acquire their scientific knowledge from textbooks were familiar with Martians through various other media. In mid-1938, Mutual's Dave Driscoll and Charles Singer stood by with broadcasting equipment as Hayden Planetarium curator Dr. Clyde Fisher attempted to bounce radio signals off the red planet's surface.[54] In the Buck Rogers comic strip and the Flash Gordon movie serials, Americans could see the conflict with Mars regularly enacted.[55] (Herta Herzog found that these two interplanetary heroes were mentioned by many interviewees.) In the late thirties, the Buck Rogers character moved to a five-day-a-week spot on radio, and countless listeners soon became acquainted with ray guns, rocket ships, and "gyro-cosmic reletavators."[56] In 1938, *Flash Gordon's Trip to Mars* opened in theaters across the country.* While these sources were clearly fictional, many Americans nevertheless could honestly state, "All I know about Mars is what I read in the comic strips."[57] One has to agree with Dorothy Thompson that, in many ways, the popularization of science had produced "gullibility and new suspicions, rather than ... skepticism and the really scientific attitude of mind."[58]

Tuning in Late

Cantril notes that regardless of the broadcast's realistic flavor, "it would seem highly unlikely that any listener would take it seriously had he heard the announcements that were clearly made at the beginning of the hour" stressing the program's fictionality. The listener may still have become startled, but

Hollywood likewise capitalized on the increased interest in Mars after the Mercury broadcast. In the middle of November, Universal released a major new serial, Mars Attacks the Earth! *(Variety, November 9, 1938, p. 22).*

only on the basis of the intense drama of the play and without the strong "feeling of personal involvement." The listener "would know the events were happening 'out there' in the studio, and not 'right here' in his own state or county."[59]

Cantril and Herzog found that "the time a listener tuned in to the broadcast was a major determinant in shaping his later reactions." The following remarks were typical:

> We were listening to another favorite station at the time and did not get in the very beginning.
> We turned our radio on after the program started, so we didn't have any way of knowing it was a play or make-believe story.[60]

The CBS survey discovered that 42 percent of those who had accepted the program as actual news had tuned in late. A poll by the American Institute of Public Opinion put this figure at 61 percent.[61] In both cases, it was clear that tuning in late was a strong conditioning factor. Most latecomers had been scanning the dial at the top of the hour in an attempt to find something of interest. Some had been tuned into the *Classical Album*, the *Bach Cantata Series*, or Walter E. Ernst's "Symposium on the Judiciary Amendment." But the majority had been listening to the eminently more popular *Chase and Sanborn Hour* with Edgar Bergen and Charlie McCarthy,* and had switched over to the Welles program after the opening ventriloquist routine ended and Nelson Eddy's first song was about to begin. To this day, no historian has been able to locate a recording of the *Chase and Sanborn Hour* of October 30, 1938, so it is not possible to know precisely when the opening act ended. However, an examination of the show's other broadcasts from the same year suggests that the routine usually ended seven to eleven minutes into the program. Thus anyone tuning into *War of the Worlds* after this segment would have arrived either in the middle of the Philips-Pierson interview or directly before the announcement that the first meteorite had landed. Many other listeners, using older receivers, had switched them on exactly at 8:00 P.M. but had to wait for the tubes to warm up before they received any sound. Since this process could take up to two minutes, many missed the Mercury Theater's 36-second weekly opening sequence and Welles's 1½-minute introduction. (Even those who heard Welles's opening narration may have been confused, since Welles was also a character in the play—Professor Pierson—and listeners may have been unable to separate his factual and fictional roles.).

Still others tuned in to the middle of the program after excited family members or neighbors rushed in and made them listen, or nervous friends had

---

According to Broadcasting, *"By his [Charlie McCarthy's] near monopoly of the air at this time, he saved tens of millions" of those who did not tune out "from the Welles frightfulness." A Hooper survey estimated that the ratio of listeners to Welles and McCarthy was 3.6 to 34.7 (*Broadcasting, *February 1, 1940, p. 36, and March 1, 1940, p. 70).*

called. An American Institute of Public Opinion survey revealed that 21 percent of those who tuned in late did so at the prompting of someone else.[62] One listener who helped to perpetuate this "contagion of excitement" remarked: "I was listening to the program with a friend. When we heard the news, I thought I better go around and tell his mother. Then we went to his friend's parents house to tell them."[63] Some of the late tuners were "so overwhelmed by the sudden impression of flashes, that they overlooked the fact that everything was being carried on in an orderly fashion on the other stations."[64] Many believed that CBS had obtained a "scoop" on the story, as WOR (soon to be MBS) had in the 1932 Lindbergh kidnapping, when logistical constraints prevented the other networks from setting up in Hopewell in time to cover the initial stages of the case. One listener reported: "My mother said to turn it to another station. We did and they were having their regularly-scheduled program. My mother said they were not as sharp as CBS."[65]

On the other hand, Cantril discovered that over 20 percent of those who had been frightened by the broadcast had been listening from the very beginning. Many of these people believed that the Mercury Theater's play itself "had been interrupted in order to give space to the news bulletins."[66] Many had been so upset by the news flashes that they forgot what they had heard only minutes before. Some simply fell victim to the pervasive habit of ignoring a program's opening message. Cantril found that some people listen inattentively until "they are aware that something of particular interest is on." Since the top of each hour was generally dominated by station identifications, advertisements, and theme music, it was routinely ignored.* Half of those who misinterpreted the broadcast, despite having heard it from the beginning, said they disregarded the opening announcements. These people merely had their sets tuned to the local CBS affiliate and were unaware of that evening's program schedule.[67]

Cantril concluded that late-tuning and disinterested listening were "decisive in determining whether ... an individual would follow the program as a play or as a news report." The Martian story was presented so realistically that "misinterpretation was apt to arise without the proper warning signals."[68]

---

*The Washington Post *and other newspapers, keenly affected by the "flight of advertising dollars to radio," went to great lengths to point this out. One editorial queried potential sponsors: "Who listens to what your announcer tells them about your product? Who listened to him [Welles]?" (Brady, p. 176).*

14. Aftermath

Censorship

On the heels of the tumult generated by the broadcast, the radio industry braced itself for the inevitably harsh government reaction. On October 31, Federal Communications Commission officials indicated that they intended to review the script and conduct an inquiry to determine whether "public interest warranted official action." FCC chairman Frank McNinch ordered an immediate investigation into CBS's conduct. In the process, he set off a heated debate between those who had been continually advocating censorship of radio and those who staunchly opposed it.[1]

Because of radio's enormous influence and expansive reach, the United States government had always been "vitally concerned with the proper control and direction of this mighty medium of communication."[2] While the 1934 Federal Communications Act denied the FCC the power of direct censorship, it called upon that body to ensure that the public interest was in no manner threatened by radio programming. In the minds of many government officials, "this included programs that were meant to terrorize the population."[3]

During the New Deal, "there had been a movement, coincident with the increasing centralization of authority in Washington, for stronger control and firmer regulation of radio." Proponents of this scheme sought "to make the medium more an organ of government, if not a direct arm," as in many states of Europe.[4] Radio in the United States was government-licensed but not government-owned. In contrast to the continental system, "censorship was infrequent and federal agencies like the FCC had laid down few rules with which to govern the medium." As a result, "broadcast officials were expected to maintain this traditional liberty by acting responsibly."[5] Individual stations and networks were given the freedom to choose their own programs and fashion their own codes of conduct, but they were expected to be self-regulating. If the FCC determined that a station or network's policies were not in harmony with the public interest, "its broadcasting license could fail to achieve renewal, or could be revoked."[6]

In the late 1930s, the government appeared determined that no infraction should escape its vigilant eye. In 1935, the FCC initiated hearings against a Missouri station that had aired an astrology program. The station was charged with "taking advantage of listeners' credulity."[7] In October 1936, Senator Vandenburg had been banned from the air for unfair use of recorded material in a broadcast "debate" with FDR. In December 1937, an even more notable violation occurred on the popular *Chase and Sanborn Hour* when Mae West's overt sexual references during an "Adam and Eve skit" offended many listeners. The FCC was deluged with complaints, but it took no action other than scolding NBC's censors for not having excised the offensive passages beforehand. The commission's "raised eyebrow of displeasure" was sufficient encouragement for NBC to modify its operating policy.

In the months before the Welles broadcast in 1938, it seemed as though the FCC was preparing for a major crackdown. In September, Chairman McNinch severely reprimanded WCTN (Minneapolis) and several NBC affiliates for a scandalous adaptation of Eugene O'Neill's story "Beyond the Horizon."[8] Congress was intensely scrutinizing network anti-monopoly abuses, and had set aside the third week in October for an in-depth FCC "probe of all phases of broadcasting."[9]

When the Welles program sparked a nationwide panic, industry observers "felt that radio had gone too far, and that nothing could prevent immediate government retaliation." Upon initiating hearings, Frank McNinch declared the broadcast "regrettable" and remarked, "The widespread public reaction … is another demonstration of the power and force of radio, and points out again the serious public responsibility of those who are licensed to operate stations."[10] Radio commentator Hugh Johnson observed that "the witchburning Mr. McNinch" now had "a new excuse to extend the creeping hand of government restrictions of free speech by way of radio censorship."[11] George Henry Payne, who had spearheaded a campaign against the use of horror in children's programming, "rebuked the industry for its bad taste." Commissioner Paul A. Walker "resolved himself to be stern in this case," and Senator Clyde Herring of Iowa stated his intention to introduce a bill for "controlling such abuses as were heard over the radio" that night. Herring's legislation proposed the establishment of a censorship board "to which all radio scripts would have to be submitted prior to broadcast."[12]

There were also many voices that denounced any kind of government action. Commissioner T.A.M. Craven remarked:

> I feel that the Commission should proceed with the utmost caution to avoid the danger of censoring what shall or shall not be broadcast over the radio. I also feel that in this case caution should be exercised so that any FCC action will not tend to handicap the development of the dramatic arts in broadcasting.[13]

Many opponents of censorship believed that the broadcast had been nothing more than a "first-class bedtime story" and that the newspapers were responsible for making "nationwide turmoil out of a tempest in a teapot."[14] Surprisingly, some newspapers came out in support of their electronic rival. The editor of the New York *World Telegram* stated:

> Of course it should never happen again. But we don't agree with those who are arguing that the Sunday night broadcast showed a need for strict government censorship of radio programs.... Better to have American radio remain free to make occasional blunders than start on a course that might, in time, deprive it of the freedom to broadcast the uncensored truth.[15]

Columnist Heywood Broun warned: "We have much more reason to fear censors than octopi from the distant skies. The weapons they can use can be much more far-reaching and devastating than anything conjured up in a fantastic horror story."[16]

In another "gesture of media solidarity," a reporter for the *Seattle Star* declared: "Freedom of the spoken word is as important a part of our national policy as freedom of the printed word." Radio's own H. V. Kaltenborn added his distinguished voice to this debate when he said, "Keep [radio] completely free to all of those who have ideas to express. It is one of the bases of a democratic government."[17]

In numerous surveys, it was clear that those opposing censorship represented the majority. When asked, "Which do you think would be better for people in this country—if radio were run by the government or by private business?" over 73 percent opted for private ownership.[18] A 1939 *Fortune* poll found that only 26 percent of those interviewed favored some measure of government supervision of radio productions, while 32 percent advocated federal supervision of the film industry.[19]

CBS Responds

The full force of any government retaliation was sure to descend on CBS. As a result, the network, which had previously given Welles free rein, was incensed, and Paley was under considerable pressure to discipline the young prodigy. When reporters and policemen darted into the studio after the broadcast, network officials drove the entire Mercury cast into a back office. While this was going on, CBS staff commandeered every script and recording of the program and "locked them up or had them destroyed." To keep them away from public view, the Mercury Players were detained until the early morning hours.[20] Rumors that Welles and his company would be "expelled from the network" abounded.[21] The next day, the only souls to be seen at network headquarters were "sound mixers and elevator men."[22]

The public reaction to the program was so distressing to CBS executives that they refused any references to it over the air. This was the tacit policy of the industry as a whole. When Fred Allen intended to "lampoon the gullible public" in a comedic skit, NBC officials adamantly refused.[23] On October 31, CBS released an official statement of apology to its full network:

> The Columbia Broadcasting System regrets that some listeners to the Orson Welles *Mercury Theater on the Air* program last night mistook fantasy for fact.... Naturally it was neither Columbia's nor the Mercury Theater's intention to mislead anyone ... and when it became evident that a part of the audience had been disturbed by the performance, five announcements were read over the network later in the evening to reassure those listeners.[24]

Self-Regulation

The Welles broadcast and its aftershocks inspired in all four networks a profound "sense of responsibility in seeing to it that such a situation [did] not occur again."[25] Many industry executives came to agree with the *New York Times* when it opined:

> The trouble is inherent in the method of radio broadcasting as manifested at present in this country. It can only be cured by a deeply searching self-regulation in which every element of the radio industry should join. Radio is new but it has adult responsibilities. It has not mastered the materials it uses. It does many things which the newspapers learned long ago not to do, such as mixing its news with advertising. Newspapers know the two must be rigidly separated and plainly marked. The "War of the Worlds's" bloodcurdling fiction was offered in exactly the manner that real news was given and interwoven with convincing actualities.[26]

After careful consideration of its policy, CBS decided to redefine its role as both purveyor of news and provider of entertainment. To ensure that the two functions would remain distinct (and would never be allowed to dangerously and imperceptibly blend), the network issued an official statement on November 1: "The Program Department hereafter will not use the technique of a simulated news broadcast within a dramatization when the circumstances of the broadcast could cause immediate alarm to numbers of listeners."[27] In order to keep "what is fiction from striking the listener's ear as news," NBC, CBS and MBS all agreed that such terms as "flash" and "bulletin" would be used only with the utmost discretion and only in situations of transcendent importance.[28] Recognizing that the "human voice was a powerful instrument," radio announcers would henceforth endeavor to "handle news without the slightest color or melodrama."[29] It was suggested that fictional treatments of real-life situations and all dramatizations of controversial subjects that featured impersonations of prominent personages be strictly banned.[30] As a result, the *March of Time* had to change its format from "re-enactments to on-the-spot reports by remote broadcast."[31]

Since the Welles program demonstrated that tuning in late could lead to misinterpretation, it became necessary for announcers to reiterate the nature of their programs: "For those of you who have tuned in late..."* Live broadcasts and recordings had to be clearly distinguished by labels such as "This is coming to you live," "The following is transcribed," "By transcription," or "Portions of the preceding have been transcribed." In addition, the networks were careful that all warlike sound effects, particularly bomb explosions and rifle fire, were clearly distinguishable from their real-life counterparts. Thus, the trademark opening of the popular crime drama *Gangbusters*, which "had featured a number of martial sounds, whistles, and machine gun chatter," had to be altered.[32]

Paul White of CBS summarized the network's new approach to news coverage in a memorandum:

> We have to be as energetic and resourceful as possible in keeping the radio audience informed; at the same time, we have to see to it that we do not cause unnecessary and useless anguish, suspense or confusion among our own people.[33]

These changes significantly increased in importance when the Second World War began. Echoing many of the principles laid down by White, the networks joined in September 1939 to issue a combined "Memorandum of European War Coverage":

> [The networks will make] every effort consistent with the news itself to keep out of their broadcasts horror, suspense, and undue excitement. Particular effort will be made to avoid suspense in cases where the information carrying the suspense is of no particular use to the listener. For example, we will not handle news of the air raid alarms until we actually learn whether or not there has been an air raid.... In all broadcasts about the flight of refugees, number killed, wounded, and the details of battle, and so on, we will use our best judgment and try to avoid undue shock to the radio audience without taking upon ourselves an unjustifiable responsibility for communicating how bad the war really is.... Broadcasters will at all times, try to distinguish between official news obtained from responsible official or unofficial sources...."[34]

By the time of United States entry into the war in 1941, the radio industry had expanded its commitment to help the public differentiate between fact and fiction in programming through the publication of "Suggestions for Listeners to Newscasts in Wartime." In this list, prepared by the Bureau of Research in Education, listeners were advised to "listen to every word so as

---

*Even today, this responsibility is implicitly acknowledged by virtually all broadcasters. When CBS presented its modernized version of War of the Worlds for television in October 1994, it was deemed essential, given Welles's success, to provide an abundance of disclaimers highlighting the fictional nature of the program. At the beginning of the telecast, under the image of the news anchor, a caption declared: "This is not an actual newscast. It is a fictional movie." In addition to this, after every commercial break, the announcer stated: "This is a realistic depiction of fictional events. None of what you are seeing is actually happening."

not to miss its meaning," "check radio news with newspaper accounts of the same item," and "note the source of the news." In addition, those repeating information they had heard on radio news programs should be careful not to report "opinion and conjecture ... as fact."[35]

The efforts of CBS and the other networks had the desired effect: They prevented government intervention. On November 7, 1938, National Association of Broadcasters president Neville Miller declared:

> The Columbia Broadcasting System has taken steps to insure that such program techniques will never be used again. This instance emphasizes the responsibility we assume in the use of radio and renews our determination to fulfill to the highest degree our obligation to the public.[36]

The next day, the FCC announced that no reprisals would be initiated against CBS because in the commission's judgment, "steps sufficient to protect the public interest have been taken by the network."* Thus by "reaffirming [radio's] capacity to self-regulate, the networks forestalled the undemocratic measure of government censorship."[37] By "enforcing its professed code of ethics," the broadcast industry ensured that its credibility as a news carrier would be preserved. As radio entered the war years and public demand for news programming increased sharply, CBS and the other networks would endeavor to recapture some of the prestige they had lost as a result of the Welles broadcast, through the "high standards of journalistic excellence and the commitment to fairness and accuracy" exemplified by Edward R. Murrow, Eric Sevareid, Charles Collingwood, Douglas Edwards, Robert St. John, Quincy Howe, Quentin Reynolds, and Robert McCormack.[38] Unfortunately, some would take inspiration in the example Welles had set, and would continue to merge fact and fancy for personal, political, or economic purposes. The problems arising when news looks like entertainment, and vice versa, would never go away. In an era of *Inside Edition* and *Hard Copy*, it is still difficult to avoid "blurring the distinctions and standards between news and entertainment."[39]

Lessons

For many observers, the Welles broadcast provided no dearth of valuable lessons for the future. To some, *War of the Worlds* was a prime example of how broadcasting could encourage "that intellectual passiveness that had already taken root among the masses which induces [them] to accept ready-made opinions as they would gospel truths." Because it "appealed only to the sense of hearing, radio could encourage listeners to relapse into a state of purely

---

*Fortunately for CBS, the FCC's attention was suddenly diverted from the Welles case. On November 2, Chairman McNinch ordered a full-scale investigation of a complaint that WHOM of New Jersey "had permitted a fascist anti–Semitic broadcast" (Washington Post, November 2, 1938, p. 10).

receptive activity" and could "instill dangerous ideas in the popular psyche through constant repetition."[40] Ever since the media blitz that helped propel Hitler into power, Europe's intelligentsia had been warning Americans of radio's ability to manipulate the "unstable, incredulous, and irrational masses."[41] The Welles broadcast was yet another clear demonstration of the "appalling dangers and enormous effectiveness of popular and theatrical demagoguery."[42]* In the hands of manipulative firebrands, radio constituted one of the "most dangerous weapons ever invented."[43] According to Howard Koch:

> The politician can bend the airwaves to create an image of himself and his world that suits his purposes.... He can thrust upon us a false picture of reality as distorting as the trick mirrors in a Coney Island funhouse.[44]

Dorothy Thompson agreed:

> The greatest organizers of mass hysterias and mass delusions today are states using the radio to excite terrors, incite hatreds, inflame masses, win mass support for policies, create idolatries, abolish reason and maintain themselves in power.[45]

The Martian program proved beyond doubt that "by clever manipulation, people can be made to swallow poison—if administered in small doses, carefully timed, and with the label of an accepted authority."[46] The "immediate moral," Thompson asserted, "is that no political body must ever, under any circumstances, obtain a monopoly of radio."[47]

She also observed:

> If people can be frightened out of their wits by mythical men from Mars, they can be frightened into fanaticism by the fear of the Reds, or aroused to revenge against any minority or terrorized into subservience to leadership because of any imaginable menace.... Welles has made a greater contribution to an understanding of Hitlerism, Mussolinism, Stalinism, anti-Semitism, and all the other terrorism of our times, more than will all the words about them that have been written.[48]

Evidently that understanding had an effect on network executives. The aftermath of the Welles broadcast caused NBC, CBS and MBS to radically reconsider their policy of selling airtime to Father Coughlin, the Communist Party, the German-American Bund, and other proponents of political views that seemed too far out of the mainstream.

Also paying attention to the effects of the Welles broadcast was Franklin Roosevelt. The president had observed the chaos that resulted when someone counterfeited his voice during the broadcast. He was not the only one to

---

As Welles's notoriety earned him a Hollywood contract and virtually unlimited freedom over the production of his films, he would continue to explore the themes of demagoguery and political opportunism in his landmark work Citizen Kane.

recognize the power of the impersonation, and the number of requests from advertisers and dramatists for permission to imitate the chief executive's voice on the air increased markedly.[49] Not wanting to relinquish his vocal authority, Roosevelt imposed a strict ban on presidential impersonation on the air. Larry Nixon of WMCA, New York, and many other industry officials consented to this policy because

> too many in the radio audience might think it was actually Mr. Roosevelt at the microphone, whether the mimic delivers a serious speech or mere nonsense. Furthermore, mimicry is not good broadcasting entertainment, and by eliminating it, we protect the listener from confusion.[50]

As a result of the broadcast, Roosevelt also recognized the political value of securing Welles's services for radio campaign work during his third- and fourth-term bids.[51] During the 1944 election, Welles traveled the eastern seaboard delivering endorsements at pro–FDR rallies, and he played a key role in the success of the election eve radio extravaganza, work for which he was gratefully commended by the president.[52] In return, Roosevelt encouraged Welles's own political aspirations when the latter considered running for a senate seat in Wisconsin.

FDR was not the only politician who tried to recruit Welles after the broadcast. As an indication of the broadcaster's newfound political appeal, the *Washington Post* printed a cartoon showing the Democratic mule and Republican elephant holding contracts and running toward Welles's office door. The caption read: "News Item–Radio listeners in panic at 'War of the Worlds' broadcast."[53]

Welles was also the object of considerable commercial attention after the broadcast. While the *Mercury Theater*'s sustaining status had been based upon its supposedly low audience appeal, the mammoth extent of the panic had demonstrated that the number of listeners who tuned in to the program, even on a casual basis, was far higher than originally assumed. The notoriety the program received after the "War of the Worlds" increased ratings even more (although never to the point of rivaling Charlie McCarthy). The week after the broadcast, the *Mercury Theater* attracted its first sponsor, Campbell Soup, and became the *Campbell Playhouse*.

The State of American Preparedness

Another significant lesson derived from the Welles broadcast was that the United States of 1938 was woefully unprepared for an actual war. The *Times* of London caustically remarked, "Here is a nation which, alone of big nations, has deemed it unnecessary to rehearse for protection against attack from the air by fellow beings on earth, and suddenly believes itself faced with a more fearful attack from another world."[54] Government officials, army chiefs, and national defense heads expressed the view that, besides "revealing the jittery state of nerves brought on by war clouds over Europe," the broadcast "drove home how little prepared the nation was to cope with an abrupt emergency."[55] According to the *New York Times*, on the "mere suggestion of a foreign attack" the United States erupted into a panic, causing "thousands from one end of the country to the other to be frightened out of their senses, starting an incipient flight of hysterical refugees, taxing the police and hospitals, confusing traffic and choking the usual means of communication."[56] What would the American people have done if this had been a genuine invasion? What would happen if the Luftwaffe developed a heavy bomber capable of reaching New York or Washington? H. G. Wells was astonished that Americans reacted as they did, despite not having "the war right under [their] chimneys" as Britain had.[57] Dorothy Thompson wrote:

> Even though Hitler had managed to scare Europe to its knees during the Munich Crisis, he at least had a powerful army and air force to back up his threatening words. By contrast, Mr. Welles scared thousands into demoralization with nothing at all.[58]

Welles's broadcast drew public attention to the dangers of international detachment. In fact, so many Americans now renounced isolationism and rallied behind the president's defense campaign that one observer remarked: "The *Mercury Theater* will probably be sponsored by the DuPonts [munitions] starting next week."[59] Some people went so far as to accuse FDR of having "allowed his voice to be imitated as a means of promoting his militaristic policies."[60]*

The broadcast also aided the American war effort in another way. According to Long Island University professor Raymond Paynter: "The War Department could not have devised a cheaper or broader experiment. The panic can't help but reveal to the Department the extent to which emotions can be lifted by false, terrifying reports."[61] Observations on the "ease with which radio could be [used] as an instrument of national demoralization" would add enormously to the effectiveness of the American psychological warfare campaign during World War II.[62] Defense officials now recognized that in the war of words being conducted over the world's shortwaves, it was vital that enemy propaganda be clearly designated as such.[63] According to *Broadcasting*: "Radio waves, unless they are harnessed for public service, can be as deadly to morale as bullets are to bodies.... Americans must learn to differentiate between news and propaganda."[64] As the U.S. began to assume a more active role in the Euro-

Ironically enough, the America Firsters tried to use the War of the Worlds *hysteria to prove Americans were too concerned about the threat from Hitler. In one broadcast they declared: "An invasion of America in the immediate future by any known aggressor would be the most insane, asinine and reckless military venture imaginable. It would be almost as fantastic as an expedition from Mars"* (America First Committee *broadcast, UMP #0566*).

pean conflict, shortwave broadcasts from belligerent sources were heavily curtailed by the Roosevelt Administration. As *Broadcasting* noted:

> While all warring governments would be glad to furnish speakers to address American radio audiences, the strict censorship and abundance of propaganda makes the acceptance of such broadcasts a risky business, which might result in an emotional reaction similar to that caused by the Martian drama.[65]

Because the government deemed it necessary to maintain strict control over the material beamed into the United States from abroad, the networks had to make sure their European pickups featured either accredited American correspondents or "statesmen of such high rank as to be respectable as official spokesmen for their countries." Newspaper editors could cut dubious material before it was published, but radio had "no such power, and once the mike is open, the audience gets whatever goes into it."[66]

Despite these precautions, the dictators continued to direct a steady stream of pro–Axis propaganda into United States airspace. The day after the Welles program, Mussolini commenced the operation of a new imperial radio center near Rome. With eight of the world's most powerful transmitters (of 100 kilowatts each) using 22 separate wavelengths, the center was specifically designed to beam "fascist thought to the Americas," and to "echo faithfully the pulsing life of the new Italy" across the globe.[67]

The Credibility Gap

Another result of the broadcast was a noticeable, if temporary, decrease of credulity among the American public with regard to what they heard on the radio. Howard Koch remarked that "if the non-existent Martians ... had anything to teach us, I believe it is the virtue of doubting and testing everything that comes to us over the airwaves and on the printed page."[68]

Because of this new tendency to suspend belief, many observers feared that "should a real catastrophe take place, people may take it as another hoax, in spite of urgent pleas by the authorities to the contrary."[69] Their fears were justified. A little more than three years after America was invaded by Martians, it was attacked—this time in reality—by another foreign foe, and the public reacted to the radio announcement with skepticism. Ironically, the morning of the attack on Pearl Harbor, Welles was on the air reading from the works of Walt Whitman, when his program was interrupted with a news flash.[70] Listeners were inclined to dismiss the news as another Welles trick.* One listener remembered:

*The extent to which this skepticism permeated the public consciousness is demonstrated in two period films. In Howard Hawks's Air Force (1943), an unbelieving John Garfield, hearing reports of destruction over the air from Pearl Harbor, remarks: "What is this, more Orson

The radio was on. It was a quiet, tranquil Sunday afternoon. And then the announcer broke in: "The Japanese have attacked Pearl Harbor." My first question was, "Is this another Orson Welles 'War of the Worlds' broadcast?"[71]

When NBC's rooftop correspondent broadcast an eyewitness account of the raid to American listeners, he felt obliged to add an earnest assurance: "It's a real war, it's no joke!"[72] According to *Broadcasting*:

Nowhere did the straight radio reports of the terrific bombing of Honolulu—of Japanese pilots diving over the beautiful mountains to fire U.S. ships and kill U.S. men—create anything resembling the panic created three years ago by Orson Welles' famed faking of a Martian invasion.[73]

Because of Welles's clever manipulation, Americans had "become so inured to tragedy" that even real war and likely invasion could not frighten them.[74]

The Legacy

Despite the renewed public awareness that resulted from the numerous inquiries, surveys, studies, and writings after the *War of the Worlds* broadcast, it was not beyond the realm of possibility that America could panic again. Indeed, the continued influence of radio, and then television, on the public consciousness made a repeat of October 30, 1938, even more likely.[75]

In 1939, a similar type of script was enacted over a local station in Charleston, S.C. Entitled "Palmetto's Fantasy," the program dealt with a deadly anti-aircraft ray that went haywire and dropped into a nearby reservoir, killing hundreds of people and polluting the city's water supply. Even before the broadcast terminated, station WCSC, police, and newspapers in Charleston were deluged with calls from terrified listeners.[76]

In 1940, a radio plug for a planetarium show, "How the World Will End," had scientists predicting that the life on earth would cease at 3:00 P.M. on April 1. Since it followed directly after a news program, this advertisement created a local panic in the small city where it originated, jamming switchboards and overburdening the police.[77]

On a larger and more violent scale was the panic that resulted in Quito, Ecuador, in 1949, when the Welles program was translated into Spanish and a few local details were added.* Listeners heard that the invaders were advancing upon the town from the south, destroying all opposition. An appeal by the "Minister of the Interior" for an organized defense on the program prompted one provincial governor to place his troops and police on full alert. The town's church bells were tolled, and local priests went into the streets seeking divine

Welles?" *In the 1945 film* Pride of the Marines, *news bulletins announcing the attack are met with this response: "Is this another 'men from Mars' program?"*

*For a fuller examination of the various Welles repeats, see Buglatz.

intervention. The South American program not only evoked the same hysterical response as its earlier American counterpart, but upon realizing they had been deceived, listeners burned down the radio station and killed or injured over twenty people, many of whom had acted in the drama. Rioting around the studio was so intense, order could be restored only through the intervention of tanks and tear-gas.*

In a 1964 revision of his *Invasion from Mars: A Study in the Psychology of Panic*, Hadley Cantril stated his belief that late twentieth century society was not too sophisticated to be taken in again. Indeed, he maintained that a similar hoax could cause panic on an even more extensive scale. Even today, it seems possible. Since 1938, the world has witnessed the development of weapons of mass destruction "against which there appears little protection." With the 1969 moon landing and the development of universe-ranging satellites and radio telescopes, the earth no longer seems remote and inaccessible in space. Nightly newscasts frequently present the latest close-up photos of previously unviewed planetary bodies taken by the Hubble telescope. A Northwestern University psychologist has remarked: "I think we still have a mindset to be afraid of some unknown enemy and we've been socialized by a whole variety of movies and television shows to be open to the notion of extraterrestrial life—probably more than ever before."[78] These factors could only "enhance the possibility of delusions that would be even more plausible than the invasion of Martians, and would not take the combined talents of H. G. Wells and Orson Welles to set it off."[79]

Cantril's thesis seemed to have been proven in 1965, when a power failure caused a blackout in a New England city, and millions of "blind" citizens succumbed to feelings of fear that a missile had fallen and total destruction was imminent. In 1977, WPRO, Providence, presented a localized version of *War of the Worlds* that sparked a storm of protest from area listeners. During the great old-time radio revival of the seventies, as the Welles program became a Halloween staple for AM stations across the country, mini-panics of this sort occurred in countless localities (Buffalo, N.Y., being perhaps the most prominent).[80] In 1982, a German television dramatization depicting an alien visitation propelled thousands of anxious people to their telephones to get emergency instructions. A few years later, a British news announcer interrupted a radio music program to announce that Russian missiles were over the Channel. Before he had an opportunity to explain that the bulletin was a promo for another program, listeners swamped the police with calls.[81]

Despite these repeat performances, Cantril in 1964 felt that the Welles broadcast was unique in its effect on the American public. Television "could not compete with the scenes painted by the imaginations of frightened listeners,

---

A similar violent response occurred in Portugal in 1988, when 200 people attempted to destroy the facilities at Radio Braga after learning they had been duped.

nor could it adequately picture all of the situations described in the broadcast."[82] This could only be accomplished through radio. When CBS presented *Without Warning*, a modern television version of *War of the Worlds*, on October 30, 1994 (using the same bulletin-like format), the level of popular fright in no way approached that elicited on Halloween Eve 1938, despite the realistic additions of "live" video feeds, NASA computer simulations, satellite relays, and the employment of a very convincing Charles Kuralt–type anchor. But the fact that, in numerous localities across the United States, police stations and broadcast studios received calls from fearful viewers serves as potent testimony of the enduring power of Welles's manipulative formula. The public reaction in 1994 is all the more striking in view of the fact that viewers were given even more warning than their counterparts had received fifty years earlier. The modern recreation was not only listed in the newspaper and *T.V. Guide* weeks in advance, it was prefaced by a twenty-minute documentary discussing the Victorian novel and describing exactly how Welles had perpetrated his hoax. (For those who, against all odds, managed to miss every warning, CBS provided seven written and spoken disclaimers during the telecast itself.) Certainly popular credulity played a key role in eliciting a hysterical response in 1938, but the 1994 CBS production seems to reinforce the timeworn adage that as a society grows older, it does not necessarily grow wiser.

15. Conclusion

To those who witnessed radio's maturation in the 1930s, it was clear that the medium was the most powerful instrument of mass communication in America. One could not fail to see that "radio's spellbinding voice was everywhere, and its influence was felt in every phase of life."[1]

A majority of Americans had reached this conclusion through the broadcasts of Franklin Roosevelt, the newscasters, and Orson Welles. At no other time in its history did broadcasting more clearly demonstrate its unique ability to condition mental and social habits, inspire emotion, stimulate the imaginative process, influence political dispositions, mold opinion, and inform the public than in the period from FDR's election in 1932 to the attack on Pearl Harbor in 1941.

By December 7, 1941, it was apparent that radio had undergone a striking transformation. As a result of the efforts of several talented broadcasters, the medium had been successfully exploited and manipulated to such an extent that its very function in society was irrevocably altered. As a consequence of Roosevelt's brilliant use of radio as a political tool in his speeches and fireside chats, it was clear by 1941 that America would meet its greatest military challenge internationally aware, confident, and united behind its "radio president" and the policies he chose to pursue. It was firmly expected that the president would be on the air to guide his nation through another crisis. As a result of the accomplishments of network newscasters, commentators, and correspondents, Americans on the home front would be continuously informed of the course of World War II in the most direct, personal, and rapid manner possible through live on-the-scene broadcasts, remotes, multiple-voice conversations, shortwave pickups, world roundups, discussion programs, and news dramatizations. Because of the *War of the Worlds* broadcast, the public receiving this information would be predominantly more skeptical of what was heard and critical of the way it was interpreted.

By redefining its role as political instrument and disseminator of information, and by defining the limits of its power to manipulate a listener's mental process and implant a false picture of reality in his mind, radio had achieved the modern form it would assume for much of the rest of the twentieth century. As a result, every president following FDR would endeavor to master broadcasting as an essential prerequisite for achieving and maintaining political power. As recently as June 1994, the *New York Times* could ascribe President Bill Clinton's election success largely to his effective handling of the electronic media.[2] Once established in office, Clinton, like his predecessors, would use the weekly radio address as a central instrument for publicizing executive policy. His political opponents, too, would endeavor to use the airwaves as a platform from which to criticize government initiatives.* As a result, just as Roosevelt had to compete with Huey Long and Father Coughlin for the political loyalties of the nation, Clinton would have to contend with a new school of radio demagogues, led by the likes of Rush Limbaugh and G. Gordon Liddy.

Today, any viewer watching ABC television's *World News Tonight* must acknowledge its debt to the pioneering newscasters of the Anschluss and Munich for developing the essential components of modern international news coverage.† Those who prefer the pseudo-informational visual tabloids *Hard Copy* and *Inside Edition* must look to the *March of Time* and Orson Welles's clever mixture of news and entertainment for precedents.

Thus, not only did radio broadcasting have a significant impact on the lives of Depression–era Americans; it continues to affect the nation to this day. While the voices and sounds of radio's golden age have all but faded away, the legacy of early American broadcasting lives on. A closer examination of the 1930s "communications revolution" not only brings the formative aspects of this period into relief and helps to illuminate the contemporary media scene; it allows an unprecedented glimpse into the ways in which technology both interacts with and shapes all politics, popular culture, information, and psychology.

Like the President's weekly Radio Address, the Republican response continues to be a weekend boradcast fixture.

†*The last ten years have witnessed an explosion of television news channels (CNN, Headline News, C-Span, MSNBC, CNBC). While most offer "comprehensive, 24-hour service," their abundance has led to a fiercely competitive struggle for ratings, in which hard news stories are often replaced by sensationalism and human interest features. In substance, analysis and quality, modern newscasters have never been able to rise to the level established by H. V. Kaltenborn, Raymond Swing, Dorothy Thompson, and Elmer Davis and their contemporaries.*

Notes

Full citations will be found in the Bibliography. The following abbreviations are used:

AA	Audio Archives
FDRL	Franklin D. Roosevelt Library
LOC	Library of Congress
MCI	Mass Communications, Inc.
MISC	Miscellaneous Audio Sources
MR	Milo Ryan Archive of the National Archives
MWC	Metro Washington OTR Library
NA	National Archives
NARA	North American Radio Archives - Cassette
NRC	National Recording Company
NRL	North American Radio Archives - Reel
OF	Official File (Franklin D. Roosevelt Library)
PPF	President's Personal File (Franklin D. Roosevelt Library)
PSF	President's Secretary's File (Franklin D. Roosevelt Library)
RHAC	Radio Historical Association of Colorado
RVC	Radio Vault Collection
RYC	Radio Yesteryear Tape Archives
SEP	Steve Early Papers (Franklin D. Roosevelt Library)
SPERDVAC	refers to General and Archive Libraries of SPERDVAC
SRT	refers to recorded broadcasts ("sound recorded tapes") of FDR in the Franklin D. Roosevelt Library
UMP	University of Memphis

Introduction

1. Czitrom, p. 79.
2. Douglas, p. xix.
3. *New York Times*, July 23, 1937.
4. Culbert, p. 15.
5. Sterling and Kitross, p. 182.
6. *Broadcasting*, January 1, 1940, p. 11, and December 15, 1940, p. 46.
7. "Radio Set Sales and Saturation," table in Lichty and Topping, p. 521.
8. *Broadcasting*, November 15, 1939, p. 22.
9. Charnley, p. 6.
10. "Broadcast Stations," table in Lichty and Topping, p. 148.
11. Lynd, *Middletown in Transition*, p. 263.

12. Barnouw, p. 6.
13. "Radio, Most Popular Family Servant," NBC survey reproduced in Dryer, p. 161.
14. Lynd, *Middletown: A Study* , p. 244.
15. Hoover, vol. 2, p. 146.
16. Czitrom, p. 85.
17. Herzog, quoted in Willey, p. 245.
18. Barnouw, p. 69.
19. Franklin Roosevelt, quoted in *Broadcasting*, May 15, 1939, p. 9.
20. *Broadcasting*, January 1, 1940, p. 9.
21. Sterling and Kitross, p. 161.
22. Franklin Roosevelt, quoted in *Broadcasting*, December 1, 1940, p. 15.
23. Grandin, p. 23.
24. MacDonald, p. 298.
25. Cantril, *Psychology*, p. 20.
26. *Variety*, March 1938, p. 13.
27. Franklin Roosevelt, quoted in *Broadcasting*, December 1, 1940, p. 15.
28. *Broadcasting*, April 1, 1939, p. 7.
29. Cantril, *Psychology of Radio*, p. 211.

1. Roosevelt and Radio

1. *Radioland*, September 1938, p. 11.
2. Yeilding and Carlson, p. xiii.
3. Letter, Franklin Roosevelt to Merlin Aylesworth, November 8, 1933, PPF 477, FDRL.
4. Franklin Roosevelt, quoted in *Broadcasting*, August 1, 1939, p. 30.
5. Letter, Roosevelt to Herbert L. Pettey, Secretary of Federal Radio Commission, November 4, 1933, PPF 477, FDRL.
6. Letter, Roosevelt to Aylesworth, November 8, 1933, PPF 477, FDRL.
7. Letter, Roosevelt to Pettey, November 4, 1933, PPF 477, FDRL.
8. Franklin Roosevelt, quoted in *Broadcasting*, May 15, 1939, p. 9.
9. Becker, p. 11.
10. Letter, Richard Roper to Roosevelt, May 3, 1934, PSF Box 72, FDRL.
11. *Broadcasting*, May 15, 1939, p. 9.
12. Halford Ryan, *American Orators*, p. 36.
13. Memorandum, Steve Early to Roosevelt, November 15, 1933, PPF 984, FDRL.
14. Pearson, p. 120.
15. *New York Times*, March 14, 1933, p. 12.
16. Letter from a listener in Rochester, N.Y., to FDR, March 28, 1938, OF 136, FDRL.
17. Grandin, p. 81.
18. Saerchinger, "Radio as a Political Instrument," p. 258.
19. *Ibid.*
20. *Broadcasting*, November 1, 1940, p. 32.
21. Rutherford, p. 82.
22. *Broadcasting*, May 1, 1933, p. 11.
23. *Ibid.*
24. Rutherford, p. 90.
25. *Broadcasting*, March 15, 1933, p. 5.

26. Yeilding, p. xiv.
27. *Broadcasting*, September 1, 1933, p. 33.
28. *Broadcasting*, August 15, 1940, p. 49.
29. Letter, William Paley to Franklin Roosevelt, January 24, 1936, PPF 984, FDRL.
30. *Broadcasting*, November 15, 1936, p. 42.
31. *Broadcasting*, February 15, 1940, p. 22.
32. Paley, p. 141.
33. *Broadcasting*, August 15, 1940, p. 49.
34. Fang, p. 3.
35. *Ibid*, p. 128.
36. *Broadcasting*, April 16, 1945, p. 11.
37. Fang, p. 56.
38. Winfield, p. 112.
39. *Broadcasting*, August 15, 1940, p. 48.
40. Halford Ryan, *Rhetorical Presidency*, p. xi.
41. Yeilding, p. xv.
42. Rosenman, p. 261.
43. *Ibid.*, p. 76.
44. *Broadcasting*, February 15, 1936, p. 9.
45. Winfield, p. 107.
46. Rosenman, p. 56.
47. *New York Times*, June 22, 1938, p. 4.
48. Halford Ryan, *Rhetorical Presidency*, p. 29.
49. Sharon, p. 12.
50. Halford Ryan, *Rhetorical Presidency*, p. 31.
51. Cantril, *Psychology of Radio*, p. 203.
52. Gross, p. 227.
53. Halford Ryan, *Rhetorical Presidency*, p. xii.
54. Rosenman, p. 173.
55. *Newsweek*, January 11, 1936, p. 9.
56. Buhite and Levy, p. xi.
57. Sterling and Kitross, p. 179.
58. *Broadcasting*, August 1, 1933, p. 8.
59. Reinsch, p. xii.
60. *New York Times*, May 7, 1933, p. 2.
61. *Broadcasting*, August 1, 1933, p. 8.
62. Perkins, *The Roosevelt I Knew*, p. 72.
63. Letter from a listener to Franklin Roosevelt, February 12, 1940, OF 101-A, FDRL.
64. Strout, p. 13.
65. *Broadcasting*, August 1, 1936, p. 8.
66. Sharon, p. 3.
67. Cantril, *Psychology of Radio*, p. 21.
68. Yeilding, p. xviii.
69. Ryan, *Rhetorical Presidency*, p. 19.
70. Wolfe, p. 309.
71. Radio broadcast: Fireside Chat, June 28, 1934.
72. Rosenman, p. 249.
73. Yeilding, p. xvii.
74. Troy, p. 163.

75. Halford Ryan *Rhetorical Presidency*, p. 19; and Rosenman, p. 249.
76. Yeilding, p. xv.
77. Rosenman, p. 249.
78. *Broadcasting*, August 15, 1940, p. 44.
79. Comments of Walter Damrosch, quoted in Yeilding, p. xvii.
80. Letter from a listener to Franklin Roosevelt, December 20, 1938, OF 101-A, FDRL.
81. *Broadcasting*, August 15, 1940, p. 48.
82. Wolfe, p. 308.
83. Yeilding, p. xv.
84. Wooten, p. 17.
85. Sterling and Kitross, p. 141.
86. *Broadcasting*, April 1, 1936, p. 22.
87. *Broadcasting*, September 22, 1941, p. 63.
88. Cantril, *Psychology of Radio*, p. 40.
89. *Broadcasting*, October 23, 1944, p. 53.
90. Crosby, p. 243.
91. Steele, p. 22.
92. *Broadcasting*, July 28, 1941, p. 49.
93. *Broadcasting*, February 1, 1937, p. 18.
94. *Broadcasting*, November 11, 1935, p. 51.
95. *Broadcasting*, August 15, 1940, p. 49.
96. Radio broadcast: *Perspective*, ABC, December 1, 1974.
97. Radio broadcasts: "Hollywood March of Dimes Salute to FDR's Birthday," January 30, 1938 (UMP #0267); January 30, 1940, January 24, 1942, and January 30, 1943 (author's collection).
98. Troy, p. 163.
99. *Ibid.*, p. 171.
100. Sherwood, p. 46.
101. *Variety*, March 15, 1940, p. 12.
102. Letters from listeners to Franklin Roosevelt, OF 136, FDRL.
103. *Broadcasting*, March 15, 1932, p. 13.
104. *San Francisco Examiner*, November 2, 1936, p. 120.
105. Mayer and McManus, p. 11.
106. Troy, p. 160.

2. Campaigning by Radio

1. *Broadcasting*, November 6, 1944, p. 16.
2. *New York Times*, March 13, 1933, p. 12.
3. *Broadcasting*, September 1, 1940, p. 99.
4. NAB President Neville Miller, quoted in *Broadcasting*, December 1, 1940, p. 25.
5. Cantril, *Psychology of Radio*, p. 31.
6. Reinsch, p. xii.
7. *Broadcasting*, September 15, 1932, p. 12.
8. Radio broadcast: Fireside Chat, May 7, 1933 (MCI Tape 1).
9. Radio broadcast: Fireside Chat, April 14, 1938 (MCI Tape 5).
10. *Broadcasting*, June 1, 1933, p. 12.
11. *Broadcasting*, September 22, 1941, p. 45.
12. Sterling and Kitross, p. 194.

13. Letter from a listener, September 27, 1944, PPF 200B, Box 122, FDRL.
14. Halford Ryan, *Rhetorical Presidency*, p. 25.
15. Gross, p. 225.
16. Steele, p. 4.
17. Sterling and Kitross, p. 69.
18. Hinshaw, p. 134.
19. Troy, p. 128.
20. Halford Ryan, *Rhetorical Presidency*, p. 112.
21. Yeilding, p. xi.
22. *Broadcasting*, January 1, 1933, p. 15.
23. Yeilding, p. xii.
24. Rosenman, p. 39.
25. Franklin Roosevelt, quoted in Slate and Cook, p. 198.
26. Rosenman, pp. 41–47.
27. Herbert Pettey, quoted in Steele, p. 21.
28. *Broadcasting*, September 1, 1932, p. 8.
29. Paley, p. 124.
30. Rosenman, p. 74.
31. FDR speech of June 28, 1932, quoted in Davis, New York Years, p. 315.
32. Slate and Cook, p. 202.
33. FDR speech of April 7, 1932, quoted in Halford Ryan, *Rhetorical Presidency*, p. 40.
34. *Broadcasting*, September 15, 1932, p. 12.
35. *Los Angeles Evening Herald*, quoted in *Broadcasting*, November 15, 1932, p. 38.
36. Davis, *New York Years*, p. 272.
37. *Ibid.*, p. 9.
38. *New York Times*, November 11, 1932, p. 3.
39. Hoover, vol. 2, p. 219.
40. *Broadcasting*, November 15, 1935, p. 51.
41. Gross, p. 225.
42. *Broadcasting*, May 15, 1934, p. 11.
43. Halford Ryan, *Rhetorical Presidency*, p. 86.
44. Davis, *New Deal Years*, p. 10.
45. Halford Ryan, *Rhetorical Presidency*, p. 46.
46. Yeilding, p. xii.
47. *Broadcasting*, March 7, 1936, p. 28.
48. *Broadcasting*, January 15, 1936, p. 10.
49. Barnouw, p. 53.
50. *Broadcasting*, October 24, 1936, p. 16.
51. Radio broadcast: "Sen. Vandenburg's CBS Censored Attack on FDR," October 17, 1936 (UMP #0353).
52. *Broadcasting*, November 1, 1936, p. 11.
53. *Broadcasting*, March 7, 1936, p. 29.
54. *Broadcasting*, November 15, 1936, p. 63.
55. *Newsweek*, February 16, 1936, p. 9.
56. *New York Times*, November 1, 1936, p. 2.
57. Troy, p. 171.
58. *Time*, October 3, 1936, p. 16.
59. *New York Times*, November 6, 1936, p. 12.
60. Letter from a listener, October 1, 1936, PPF 200-B, Box 70, FDRL.
61. Halford Ryan, *Rhetorical Presidency*, p. 47.

62. *Time*, October 10, 1936, p. 8.
63. Roosevelt speech of October 1, 1936, *Public Papers & Addresses*, vol. 5, p. 408.
64. FDR speech of October 31, 1936, *Public Papers and Addresses*, vol. 5, p. 568.
65. Rosenman, p. 134.
66. Halford Ryan, *Rhetorical Presidency*, p. 52.
67. *Broadcasting*, November 15, 1932, p. 8.
68. *Broadcasting*, November 1, 1936, p. 9.
69. Davis, *New Deal Years*, p. 646.
70. *New York Times*, October 21, 1936, p. 12.
71. Letter, Owen D. Young to Roosevelt, November 5, 1936, PPF 61, FDRL.
72. Letter, Harry Butcher to Steve Early, November 4, 1936, OF 256, FDRL.
73. Farley, p. 318.
74. Letter, Sam Rayburn to Roosevelt, July 3, 1940, PPF 315, FDRL.
75. *Broadcasting*, November 15, 1936, p. 10.
76. *Broadcasting*, September 29, 1941, p. 19.
77. *Broadcasting*, February 1, 1940, p. 57.
78. *Broadcasting*, June 1, 1940, p. 22.
79. *Broadcasting*, August 1, 1938, p. 18.
80. Caro, pp. 433–436.
81. *Broadcasting*, June 23, 1941, p. 49.
82. Woolf, p. 52.
83. Kessner, p. 514.
84. Radio broadcast: "Mayor La Guardia Reads the Funnies," July 1945 (UMP #0753).
85. Porter, p. 43.
86. Kessner, p. 515.
87. *Broadcasting*, April 16, 1945, p. 17.
88. *Broadcasting*, May 1, 1940, p. 54.
89. Rockwell, p. 84.
90. *Broadcasting*, July 28, 1941, p. 14.
91. *Broadcasting*, November 1, 1940, p. 44.
92. *Broadcasting*, July 15, 1940, p. 82.
93. *Broadcasting*, October 15, 1940, p. 106.
94. Sterling and Kitross, p. 180.
95. Troy, p. 161.
96. Lynd, *Middletown in Transition*, p. 377.
97. Sterling and Kitross, p. 183.
98. *Broadcasting*, August 15, 1940, p. 48.
99. Culbert, p. 45.
100. Barnouw, p. 143.
101. *Broadcasting*, July 1, 1940, p. 10.
102. *Broadcasting*, October 26, 1940, p. 66.
103. *Broadcasting*, October 2, 1940, p. 22.
104. *Broadcasting*, October 15, 1940, p. 106.
105. Radio broadcast: "Willkie for President Rally," November 4, 1940 (LOC Tape 7965-15A).
106. Halford Ryan, *Rhetorical Presidency*, p. 62.
107. Drummond, p. 444.
108. *Broadcasting*, August 15, 1940, p. 48.
109. *Broadcasting*, September 1, 1940, p. 99.
110. *Ibid.*, p. 56.

111. *Broadcasting*, August 15, 1940, p. 48.
112. Dillon, p. 202.
113. Perkins, *The Roosevelt I Knew*, p. 118.
114. *Broadcasting*, November 1, 1940, p. 99.
115. Gross, pp. 229–230.
116. *Broadcasting*, October 26, 1940, p. 75.
117. *Saturday Evening Post*, October 26, 1940, p. 29.
118. Davis, *Into the Storm*, p. 544.
119. *Broadcasting*, September 15, 1940, p. 26.
120. *Broadcasting*, October 15, 1940, p. 106.
121. Kessner, p. 469.
122. *Broadcasting*, September 15, 1940, p. 20.
123. *Broadcasting*, November 15, 1940, p. 20.
124. *Ibid.*, p. 76.
125. Willkie Speech at Madison Square Garden, November 2, 1940, Belfer Archives Collection, Syracuse University.
126. Sherwood, p. 246.
127. *Time*, October 30, 1944, p. 13.
128. Radio broadcast: "FDR's Madison Square Garden Speech," October 28, 1940, tape recording, FDRL).
129. Rosenman, p. 241.
130. FDR speech of October 30, 1940, quoted in Halford Ryan, *Rhetorical Presidency*, p. 55.
131. Memorandum, Roosevelt to Early, January 7, 1943, SEP, Subject File, Box 34, FDRL.
132. Radio broadcast: Democratic Committee Program, November 4, 1940, (LOC Tape 8283).
133. *Broadcasting*, November 15, 1940, p. 106.
134. Fang, p. 147.
135. Lazarsfeld, p. 259.
136. Radio broadcast: "Republican Rally," November 4, 1940 (UMP #0284).
137. Davis, *FDR: Into the Storm*, p. 299.
138. *Broadcasting*, November 15, 1940, p. 50.
139. Rosenman, p. 255.
140. *Variety*, November 28, 1940, p. 3.
141. *Broadcasting*, October 30, 1944, p. 16.
142. *Broadcasting*, May 15, 1944, p. 11.
143. *Broadcasting*, June 1, 1944, p. 10.
144. *Broadcasting*, May 15, 1944, p. 11.
145. Bender, p. 11.
146. *Weekly Digest of Radio Opinion*, p. 12.
147. *Newsweek*, Election Supplement, November 13, 1944, p. 3.
148. Gross, p. 229.
149. *Broadcasting*, May 15, 1944, p. 11.
150. *Ibid.*
151. *Time*, October 2, 1944, p. 21.
152. *Broadcasting*, October 16, 1944, p. 6.
153. *Broadcasting.*, October 2, 1944, p. 61.
154. *Ibid.* p. 61.
155. *Broadcasting*, October 16, 1944, p. 6, and October 30, 1944, p. 16.
156. *Broadcasting*, May 15, 1944, p. 11.

157. *Time*, October 2, 1944, pp. 23–24.

158. *Newsweek*, Election Supplement, November 13, 1944, p. 3.

159. Roosevelt's "Fala Speech," September 23, 1944, quoted in Kingdon, p. 123.

160. Rosenman, p. 478.

161. *Time*, October 2, 1944, p. 21.

162. *Time*, September 24, 1944, p. 12.

163. *Atlanta Constitution*, quoted in Halford Ryan, *Rhetorical Presidency*, p. 67.

164. *Time*, October 2, 1944, p. 21.

165. *Newsweek*, October 15, 1944, p. 22.

166. Troy, p. 182.

167. *Time*, October 2, 1944, p. 23.

168. *Broadcasting*, October 2, 1944, p. 16.

169. *Broadcasting*, November 6, 1944, p. 18.

170. Radio broadcast: "FDR's Foreign Policy Association Speech," October 21, 1944, (tape recording, FDRL).

171. Letter from a listener to Franklin Roosevelt, October 26, 1944, PPF 8601, FDRL.

172. *Time*, October 30, 1944, p. 11.

173. *Newsweek*, November 13, 1944, p. 30.

174. *Broadcasting*, October 16, 1944, p. 6.

175. Lichty and Topping, p. 307.

176. *Broadcasting*, October 2, 1944, p. 16.

177. *Broadcasting*, September 11, 1944, p. 12.

178. *Broadcasting*, October 9, 1944, p. 70.

179. Reinsch, p. 16.

180. *Broadcasting*, February 1, 1936, p. 8.

181. Bannerman, p. 141.

182. *Ibid.*, p. 142.

183. Radio broadcast: "Democratic Committee Program," November 6, 1944, (RVC Cassette 881).

184. Gross, p. 112.

185. Herbert Brownell, quoted in Reinsch, p. 22.

186. Barnouw, p. 209.

187. Letter, Franklin Roosevelt to Norman Corwin, November 20, 1944, PPF 315, FDRL.

188. *Broadcasting*, October 30, 1944, p. 16.

189. *New York Times*, November 8, 1944, p. 1.

190. Lazarsfeld, p. 127.

191. *Broadcasting*, October 30, 1944, p. 16.

192. *Broadcasting*, October 2, 1944, p. 16.

193. Letter, J. Leonard Reinsch to Steve Early, November 17, 1944, PPF 4026, FDRL.

194. *Broadcasting*, October 2, 1944, p. 16.

195. Reinsch, p. 19.

196. *Broadcasting*, October 15, 1944, p. 40.

197. *Newsweek*, Supplement, November 13, 1944, p. 5.

198. Rosenman, p. 475.

199. *Broadcasting*, October 9, 1944, p. 7.

200. *Time*, October 2, 1944, p. 11.

201. Charlotte Observer, November 2, 1944, p. 23.

202. *Broadcasting*, November 13, 1944, p. 40.

203. NBC president Lohr, quoted in *Broadcasting*, February 1, 1936, p. 8.
204. Troy, p. 185.
205. *Newsweek*, November 13, 1944, p. 5.
206. *Time*, October 30, 1944, p. 11.
207. *Broadcasting*, April 16, 1945, p. 16.
208. Farley, p. 320.
209. Troy, p. 188.
210. Farley, p. 319.

3. Selling the Domestic Agenda

1. Badger, p. 33.
2. Shannon, p. 109.
3. Freidel, p. 11.
4. Cantril, *Psychology of Radio*, p. 21.
5. Buhite and Levy, p. 8.
6. Delano, p. 122.
7. Buhite and Levy, p. 10.
8. Farley, p. 317.
9. *Roosevelt Album*, p. 12.
10. Letter from a listener to Franklin Roosevelt, October 21, 1933, PPF 479, FDRL.
11. Halford Ryan, *Rhetorical Presidency*, p. 12.
12. Buhite and Levy, p. 14.
13. *Broadcasting*, March 15, 1933, p. 7.
14. Radio broadcast: "FDR's First Inaugural," March 4, 1933 (LP recording, Spoken Word Inc.; text in PSF, FDRL).
15. Schlesinger, *Coming of New Deal*, p. 23.
16. Leuchtenburg, *Franklin D. Roosevelt and New Deal*, p. 104.
17. Halford Ryan, *Rhetorical Presidency*, p. 83.
18. Hopkins, p. viii.
19. Radio broadcast: *Edwin C. Hill News*, March 6, 1933 (author's collection).
20. *New York Times*, June 18, 1933, p. 2.
21. Contemporary observer, quoted in Halford Ryan, *Rhetorical Presidency*, p. 19.
22. Geselbracht, p. ii.
23. *New York Daily News*, May 5, 1933, p. 5.
24. Halford Ryan, *Rhetorical Presidency*, p. 85.
25. *Broadcasting*, March 15, 1933, p. 25.
26. Badger, p. 71.
27. *Broadcasting*, May 15, 1938, p. 7.
28. *Broadcasting*, March 15, 1933, p. 5.
29. Roosevelt, *Public Papers and Addresses*, vol. 2., p. 112.
30. Halford Ryan, *Rhetorical Presidency*, p. 31.
31. Radio broadcast: Fireside Chat, March 12, 1933 (MCI Tape 1).
32. Rosenman, p. 92.
33. Gordon and Falk, p. 76.
34. Radio broadcast: Fireside Chat, March 12, 1933 (MCI Tape 1).
35. *New York Times*, March 14, 1933, p. 12.
36. Hill, p. 7.
37. Cantril, *Psychology of Radio*, p. 32.
38. Letter from a listener, March 13, 1933, PPF 479, FDRL.

39. Badger, p. 71.
40. Freidel, p. 221.
41. Buhite and Levy, p. 18.
42. *New York Times*, May 8, 1933, p. 1.
43. Rosenman, p. 95.
44. Letter, Merlin Aylesworth to Franklin Roosevelt, May 10, 1933, PPF 477, FDRL.
45. *Broadcasting*, May 15, 1933, p. 7.
46. Badger, p. 156.
47. Rosenman, p. 45.
48. Davis, *New Deal Years*, p. 22.
49. *New York Times*, July 25, 1933, p. 1.
50. Buhite and Levy, p. 36.
51. Rosenman, pp. 95–96.
52. *New York Times*, June 5, 1934, p. 28.
53. Fireside chat of April 28, 1935; text printed in Roosevelt, *Public Papers*, vol. 4.
54. Badger, p. 96.
55. Rosenman, p. 170.
56. *Ibid.* p. 175.
57. Leuchtenburg, *Franklin D. Roosevelt and the New Deal*, p. 255.
58. Steele, p. 21.
59. *Broadcasting*, August 1, 1933, p. 5.
60. *Broadcasting*, April 15, 1939, p. 11.
61. *Broadcasting*, May 15, 1939, p. 9.
62. *Broadcasting*, April 15, 1939, p. 69.
63. Federal Radio Commission circular; quoted in Hoover, vol. 3, p. 422.

4. Domestic Challenges

1. Davis, *New Deal Years*, p. 507.
2. Rosenman, p. 46.
3. Radio broadcast: "Democratic Victory Dinner Address," March 4, 1937 (FDRL).
4. Halford Ryan, *Rhetorical Presidency*, p. 118.
5. Radio broadcast: Fireside Chat, March 9, 1937 (MCI Tape 10).
6. Davis, *New Deal Years*, p. 614.
7. *New York Times*, March 10, 1937, p. 1.
8. Halford Ryan, *Rhetorical Presidency*, p. 118.
9. Davis, *FDR: New Deal Years*, p. 71.
10. *Broadcasting*, February 1, 1939, p. 89.
11. Buhite and Levy, p. 84.
12. Radio broadcasts: "Congressional Opinions in the Proposed Changes in the Federal Judiciary," February 9, 1937 (LOC Tape 12634-1); "Why Pack the Supreme Court?" February 19, 1937 (LOC Tape 8404-35); "Mass Meeting of Opponents to the President's Supreme Court Plan," March 12, 1937 (LOC Tape 12634-9); "Man-in-the-Street Interviews Regarding the President's Proposed Change in Supreme Court," February 7, 1937 (LOC Tape 2634-1).
13. Radio broadcasts: February 9–21, 1937 (LOC Tape 12634-8).
14. Davis, *FDR: New Deal Years*, p. 615.
15. *New York Times*, March 13, 1937, p. 2.

16. Radio broadcasts: "The Farmer and the Supreme Court," and "The Supreme Court: Bulwark of Liberty," 1937 (SPERDVAC #256).

17. Letter from a listener to Roosevelt, April 5, 1937, OF 136, FDRL.

18. Halford Ryan, *Rhetorical Presidency*, p. 129.

19. Buhite and Levy, p. 84.

20. Radio broadcast: Fireside Chat, June 24, 1938 (MCI Tape 6).

21. Fireside Chat of June 24, 1938, text reproduced in *New York Times*, June 25, 1938, p. 1.

22. *Philadelphia Inquirer, Baltimore Sun, Hartford Courant*, June 25, 1938.

23. Davis, *FDR: Into the Storm*, p. 295.

24. Rosenman, p. 179.

25. Halford Ryan, *Rhetorical Presidency*, p. 10.

26. Davis, *FDR: Into the Storm*, p. 241.

27. *New Orleans Item*, January 12, 1928, p. 5.

28. Barnouw, p. 49.

29. *Chicago Daily News*, January 19, 1935, p. 3.

30. Williams, p. 630.

31. Gross, p. 236.

32. *New York Daily News*, March 8, 1935, p. 5.

33. Williams, p. 629.

34. Barnouw, p. 50.

35. *Time*, March 18, 1935, p. 11.

36. *Radio Guide*, July 23, 1939, p. 13.

37. Bendiner, p. 116.

38. Brinkley, p. 256.

39. *Broadcasting*, December 15, 1933, p. 11.

40. Radio broadcast: "Relief that Fails to Relieve," April 11, 1937 (Audio Archives).

41. Barnouw, p. 47.

42. Fang, p. 100.

43. *Broadcasting*, December 15, 1933, p. 11.

44. Radio broadcast: "Christianity versus Chaos," February 1937 (NARA Reel).

45. *Broadcasting*, December 15, 1935, p. 30.

46. *Radio Guide*, July 23, 1939, p. 23.

47. *Broadcasting*, January 1, 1939, p. 56.

48. *Fortune*, February 1934, p. 5.

49. Barnouw, p. 47.

50. *Broadcasting*, March 1, 1936, p. 32.

51. Brinkley, p. 266.

52. *Broadcasting*, January 1, 1939, p. 18.

53. Fang, p. 91.

54. Radio broadcast: "Twenty Years Ago," April 4, 1937 (Audio Archives).

55. *Broadcasting*, March 1, 1939, p. 72.

56. Fang, p. 100.

57. *Broadcasting*, February 15, 1939, p. 88.

58. *Broadcasting*, August 1, 1939, p. 28.

59. *Broadcasting*, January 1, 1939, p. 18.

60. *Broadcasting*, August 1, 1939, p. 28.

61. *Broadcasting*, January 1, 1939, p. 18.

62. *Broadcasting*, October 1, 1939, p. 13.

63. Fang, p. 104.

64. Sterling and Kitross, p. 188.

65. Bendiner, p. 116.
66. Hugh S. Johnson, quoted in Barnouw, p. 48.
67. Gross, p. 240.

5. Selling the Foreign Policy Agenda

1. Buhite and Levy, p. 134.
2. Radio broadcast: speech from Chautauqua, N.Y., August 14, 1937 (tape recording at FDRL); *Public Papers and Addresses*, vol. 5, p. 287.
3. Radio broadcast: "Quarantine Speech," October 5, 1937 (tape recording SRT 72-12, FDRL); *Public Papers and Addresses*, 1937 volume, p. 412.
4. Borg, p. 412.
5. Buhite and Levy, p. 144.
6. Halford Ryan, *Rhetorical Presidency*, p. 138.
7. Dallek, p. 199.
8. Davis, *FDR: Into the Storm*, p. 491.
9. Radio broadcast: Fireside Chat of September 3, 1939, (MCI Tape 8).
10. Davis, *FDR: Into the Storm*, p. 493.
11. Radio broadcast: "FDR's Speech before Congress," September 21, 1939 (UMP# 0885-6).
12. *Fortune* Poll, October 1939, PPF 479, FDRL.
13. *Time*, September 11, 1939, p. 14.
14. Keegan, p. 215.
15. *New York Times*, May 29, 1940, p. 1.
16. Rosenman, p. 197.
17. Buhite and Levy, p. 153.
18. *Broadcasting*, May 30, 1940, p. 17.
19. Radio broadcast: Fireside Chat of May 26, 1940 (SRT 72, FDRL).
20. Rosenman, p. 197.
21. Letter from a listener to Franklin Roosevelt, May 29, 1940, PPF 200-B, FDRL.
22. Rosenman, p. 194–98.
23. *Time*, June 3, 1940, p. 5.
24. Gallup Poll, May 26, 1940, and June 2, 1940; quoted in Gallup, vol. 1.
25. Davis, *FDR: Into the Storm*, p. 546.
26. Radio broadcast: "Roosevelt's University of Virginia Address," June 10, 1940 (MR 200, National Archives).
27. *Broadcasting*, July 1, 1940, p. 75.
28. Rosenman, p. 199.
29. Radio broadcast: "Roosevelt's Message to Congress on Selective Service," July 18, 1940 (UMP #1228).
30. *Broadcasting*, November 15, 1940, p. 10.
31. Radio broadcast: "Frank Knox and Robert Patterson Supporting Selective Service," July 1940 (UMP# 1196).
32. *Broadcasting*, August 15, 1940, p. 26.
33. *Broadcasting*, November 1, 1940, p. 16.
34. Rosenman, p. 242.
35. Radio broadcast: "Selective Service Program," October 29, 1940 (LOC Tape 9485-34A).
36. Rosenman, p. 243.
37. Letters from Winston Churchill to Frnaklin Roosevelt: July 31, 1940 (Doc.

19, 107); August 15, 1940 (Doc. 21, 109); October 27, 1940 (Doc. 30, 118); December 7, 1940 (Doc. 35, 125). Reproduced in Lowenheim.

38. Gross, p. 241.
39. Barnouw, p. 146.
40. Buhite and Levy, p. 164.
41. Radio broadcast: December 17, 1940 (tape recording, FDRL).
42. Rosenman, p. 258.
43. *Ibid.*
44. Halford Ryan, *Rhetorical Presidency*, p. 145.
45. Radio broadcast: Fireside Chat of December 29, 1940 (NARA Reel).
46. Halford Ryan, *Rhetorical Presidency*, p. 112.
47. *Broadcasting*, June 2, 1941, p. 47.
48. Rosenman, p. 256.
49. Gallup Poll, December 30, 1940.
50. Gallup Poll, January 11, 1941.
51. Rosenman, p. 265.
52. Letter from a listener to Franklin Roosevelt, December 30, 1940, PPF 200, Container 78, FDRL.
53. Dallek, p. 260.
54. Davis, *FDR: Into the Storm*, p. 45.
55. Van der Vat, p. 83.
56. Rosenman, p. 144.
57. Radio broadcast: Fireside Chat, May 27, 1941 (MCI Tapes 8–9).
58. "Adult Radio Audiences When the President Speaks," from "Audience Radio Measurement" table, reproduced in Lichty and Topping, p. 520.
59. Gallup Poll, May 8, 1941, and June 9, 1941.
60. Gallup Poll, May 22, 1941, and June 2, 1941.
61. Radio broadcast: *Wythe Williams*, May 28, 1941 (UMP #0266).
62. Letter from a listener to Franklin Roosevelt, May 27, 1941, PPF 200, Container 93, FDRL.
63. Buhite and Levy, p. 188.
64. Bailey and Ryan, p. 170.
65. Halford Ryan, *Rhetorical Presidency*, p. 150.
66. Radio broadcast: Fireside Chat of September 11, 1941 (SRT 72, FDRL).
67. Davis, *FDR: Into the Storm*, p. 102.
68. Steele, p. 119.
69. Letter from a listener to Franklin Roosevelt, September 11, 1941, PPF 200, Container 103, FDRL.
70. Gallup Polls, September 19, October 2, and October 5, 1941.
71. Rosenman, p. 293.
72. Radio broadcast: "FDR's Navy Day Speech" of October 27, 1941 (NA Tape 36-140).
73. Rosenman, p. 295.
74. *Ibid.*
75. Van der Vat, p. 91.
76. Radio broadcast: *American Legion Speaks*, November 11, 1941 (UMP #1196).
77. Steele, p. 127.
78. Radio broadcast: "America First Committee Program" (NRL #435).
79. Radio broadcast: "Martin Dies on American Neutrality" (LOC Tape 12731).
80. Barnouw, p. 133.
81. *Broadcasting*, October 15, 1940, p. 34.

82. Sen. Burton K. Wheeler, "America First Broadcast" (UMP #0566).

83. Burton K. Wheeler, quoted in Cole, p. 397.

84. Radio broadcast: Burton K. Wheeler, "America First Committee" (NARA #1209).

85. Radio broadcast: Burton K. Wheeler, "America First Committee" (UMP #0568).

86. Radio broadcast: "America First Speech by Charles Lindbergh," May 23, 1941 (UMP #1312).

87. Davis, *FDR: Into the Storm*, p. 497.

88. Radio broadcast: *America First Committee*, September 1939 (LOC Tape 11800).

89. Radio broadcasts by Charles Lindbergh: "Keeping America Out of War," September 1939 (LOC Tape 11800); October 12, 1939 (UMP# 0075); May 23, 1941 (UMP# 1312).

90. Davis, *FDR: Into the Storm*, p. 498.

91. Radio broadcast: "FDR's Speech Before Congress," September 21, 1939 (UMP #0885).

92. Radio broadcast: *American Radio Newsreel*, October 4, 1939 (NRL).

93. Radio broadcast: Fireside Chat, December 29, 1940 (MCI Tape 7).

94. Radio broadcast: "FDR's Third Inaugural Address," January 20, 1941 (LP recording, Spoken Word, Inc.).

95. Cole, p. 112.

96. Dryer, p. 205.

97. Steele, p. 139.

98. *Broadcasting*, August 15, 1940, p. 28.

99. *Ibid.*, p. 50.

100. Steele, p. 140.

101. *Broadcasting*, November 15, 1940, p. 19.

102. Memorandum, Lowell Mellett, Council for Democracy member, Mellett Papers, FDRL.

103. Radio broadcasts: *Fibber McGee and Molly*, December 9, 1941, and *Eddie Cantor*, April 23, 1941 (NARA cassettes # 3271 and 526).

104. Listener, quoted in Steele, p. 140.

105. Stenehjem, p. 155.

106. *Broadcasting*, January 1, 1941, p. 13.

107. *Broadcasting*, February 15, 1939, p. 44.

108. Radio broadcast: "We Hold These Truths," December 15, 1941 (UMP #0065).

109. Julian, p. 73.

110. Radio broadcasts: "Uncle Sam Makes and the World Takes," "Yankee Ships and Yankee Trade," and "U.S. Foreign Trade Comes of Age" (LOC Tapes 5441-19, 5441-18, 544-15).

111. Radio broadcasts: *The Other Americas*, November 22 and 29, 1942 (NCL Cassette #7780); December 6 and 13, 1942 (NCL Cassette #7781).

112. Radio broadcasts: LOC tapes 5320-16A and 16-B.

113. *Broadcasting*, July 7, 1941, p. 37.

114. Radio broadcast: *Young America Wants to Help* (NARA Cassettes).

115. *Broadcasting*, September 15, 1941, p. 38.

116. *Broadcasting*, November 10, 1941, p. 58.

117. *Broadcasting*, September 15, 1939, p. 79.

118. *Broadcasting*, July 15, 1940, p. 42.

119. *Broadcasting*, May 1, 1939, p. 26.

120. *Broadcasting*, June 15, 1940, p. 50.

121. Radio broadcasts: "Greek War Relief Program," February 8, 1941 (SPERD-VAC), and "China Relief Talk," June 25, 1941 (UMP# 1212).

122. Steele, p, 141.

123. Howe, p. 205.

124. *Broadcasting*, October 1, 1939, p. 32.

125. Sevareid, p. 195.

126. Culbert, p. 57.

127. Assistant Secretary of State Adolf Berle, quoted in Steele, p. 144.

128. *Broadcasting*, July 28, 1941, p. 51.

129. Radio broadcast: Edwin Johnson, "America First Committee Program," ca. 1940 (UMP # 0566).

130. Radio broadcast: *American Radio Newsreel*, October 4, 1939 (NRL).

131. Radio broadcasts *News and Views with John B. Hughes*, July 23, 1941 (UMP #1211); July 23, 24 and 25, 1941 (UMP #1300).

132. Radio broadcasts: *Fulton Lewis, Jr.*, June 10, 1941 (NRL); July 1, 1941 (UMP #1212); and August 1, 1941 (UMP #1204).

133. Radio broadcast: "FDR's Speech on the Launching of the Patrick Henry," September 27, 1941 (NRL).

134. Radio broadcast: "FDR's Address to the International Labor Conference," November 6, 1941 (UMP #0264).

135. Culbert, pp. 7–8.

136. Steele, p. 143.

137. Stenehjem, p. 143.

138. *Broadcasting*, September 1, 1940, p. 76.

139. Fang, p. 127.

140. Stenehjem, p. 153.

141. Culbert, p. 12.

142. *New York Times*, October 29, 1941, p. 11.

143. Buhite and Levy, p. 197.

144. Radio broadcast: "Roosevelt's December 8, 1941, Address to Congress" (NA, MR200).

145. Halford Ryan, *Rhetorical Presidency*, p. 153.

146. *Time*, December 15, 1941, p. 18.

147. Rosenman, p. 307.

148. Barnouw, p. 151.

149. Buhite and Levy, p. 197.

150. Radio broadcast: Fireside Chat, December 9, 1941 (MCI Tape 19).

151. Rosenman, p. 308.

152. *Ibid.*, p. 313.

153. Radio broadcast: "NBC Tribute to FDR," April 15, 1945 (NCL #765).

154. *Time*, December 15, 1941, p. 18.

155. Letter from a listener to Franklin Roosevelt, December 9, 1941, PPF 200-B, FDRL.

156. *Time*, December 15, 1941, p. 19.

157. Radio broadcast: "NBS Tribute to FDR," April 15, 1945 (NCL #764).

158. Sevareid, p. 193.

159. Towne, p. 144.

160. Cantril, *Public Opinion*, pp. 965–971.

161. Halford Ryan, *Rhetorical Presidency*, p. 146.

162. Buhite and Levy, p. 219.
163. "Adult Radio Audiences When the President Speaks," table in Lichty and Topping, p. 520.
164. Yeilding, p. xxi.
165. Rosenman, p. 8.

6. *The Death of FDR*

1. Radio broadcast: *American Album of Familiar Music*, April 15, 1945 (UMP #0987).
2. Radio broadcast: *Lest We Forget: These Great Americans*, "FDR," April 12, 1945 (UMP #0718).
3. *Broadcasting*, April 16, 1945, p. 17.
4. Asbell, p. 117.
5. *Broadcasting*, April 16, 1945, p. 66.
6. Radio broadcast: "NBC Tribute to FDR," April 15, 1945 (NCL # 764 and 765).
7. Radio broadcasts: "FDR Funeral Procession at Warm Springs," April 13, 1945 (NA #3946-51); "Hyde Park Service for FDR," April 16, 1945 (NARA Reel).
8. Radio broadcast: "FDR Funeral Procession in Washington, D.C.," April 14, 1945 (NA #208-134).
9. *Broadcasting*, April 15, 1945, p. 2.
10. Radio broadcast: "CBS Coverage of FDR's Death," April 13, 1945 (NA #208).
11. *Broadcasting*, April 15, 1945, p. 18.
12. Delano, p. 253.
13. Walter Johnson, p. 195.
14. Rosenman, p. 548.
15. *Broadcasting*, April 15, 1945, p. 12.
16. Czitrom, p. 159.
17. *Broadcasting*, April 15, 1945, p. 15.
18. Leuchtenburg, *In the Shadow of FDR*, p. x.
19. Radio broadcast: "Truman's Speech After the Death of Roosevelt," April 16, 1945 (UMP #0241).
20. *Broadcasting*, April 16, 1945, p. 15.
21. Leuchtenburg, *In the Shadow of FDR*, p. 23.
22. *Broadcasting*, April 16, 1945, p. 16.

7. *Early History of Broadcast News*

1. Fang, p. 3.
2. Desmond, p. 381.
3. Grandin, p. 7.
4. Culbert, p. 24.
5. Cantril, *Psychology of Radio*, p. 24.
6. *Broadcasting*, January 1, 1940, p. 66.
7. Culbert, p. 5.
8. Dryer, p. 143.
9. Bureau of Applied Social Research, p. 43.
10. Lichty and Topping, p. 662.

11. Mitchell, p. 65.
12. Danna, "*Press-Radio War*," p. 339.
13. Barnouw, p. 7.
14. *Broadcasting*, March 15, 1932, p. 6.
15. MacDonald, p. 298.
16. *Broadcasting*, January 15, 1935, p. 18.
17. *Broadcasting*, March 1, 1935, p. 5.
18. Contemporary observer, quoted in Fang, p. 289.
19. *Broadcasting*, March 15, 1932, p. 13.
20. Poteet, p. 106.
21. Paul White, p. 40.
22. Danna, "Rise," p. 5.
23. *Broadcasting*, May 1, 1933, p. 10.
24. *Broadcasting*, February 1, 1939, p. 13.
25. *Broadcasting*, January 1, 1935, p. 16.
26. Paul White, p. 44.
27. Charnley, p. 25.
28. *Broadcasting*, May 1, 1939, p. 12.
29. *Broadcasting*, May 15, 1939, p. 62.
30. *Broadcasting*, February 1, 1939, p. 42.
31. *Broadcasting*, January 15, 1941, p. 32.
32. Sterling and Kitross, p. 178.

8. Radio Covers Domestic Events and Crises

1. MacDonald, p. 299.
2. Radio broadcast: "Ohio and Mississippi Flood News," January 27, 1937, (LOC Tape 11796).
3. Sterling and Kitross, p. 178.
4. Radio broadcast: "Red Cross Program for the Relief of Flood Victims," February 11, 1937 (LOC Tape 15778-69B).
5. Radio broadcast: "WREC Flood Coverage," January 1, 1937 (UMP #0510).
6. *Broadcasting*, February 15, 1937, p. 31.
7. Sterling and Kitross, p. 177.
8. *Broadcasting*, February 1, 1937, p. 9.
9. *Bluefield News and Times*, quoted in *Broadcasting*, February 15, 1937, p. 71.
10. *Broadcasting*, October 1, 1938, p. 12.
11. Radio broadcast: "Herb Morrison Interview for WOR," May 7, 1937 (UMP #0545).
12. *Broadcasting*, May 15, 1937, pp. 14–15.
13. Radio broadcast: "The Hindenburg Disaster," May 6, 1937 (LOC Tape 16798-62A).
14. Schecter, pp. 257–58.
15. *Broadcasting*, May 15, 1937, p. 15.
16. Interview with Herbert Morrison, reproduced in Gordon and Falk, p. 98.
17. Sterling and Kitross, p. 181.
18. Schechter, p. 544.
19. *Broadcasting*, May 15, 1937, p. 12.
20. Schecter, p. 265.
21. *Broadcasting*, June 1, 1939, p. 13.
22. *Broadcasting*, June 30, 1941, p. 18.

23. *Radio Guide*, June 28, 1939, p. 18.
24. *Broadcasting*, November 1, 1940, p. 22.
25. *Broadcasting*, May 1, 1940, p. 86.
26. *Broadcasting*, August 1, 1940, p. 23.
27. *Broadcasting*, July 1, 1940, p. 12.
28. *Broadcasting*, November 15, 1940, p. 22.
29. Radio broadcast: *Fibber McGee and Molly*, November 5, 1940 (NARA Cassette #3257).
30. Rosenman, p. 137.
31. *Broadcasting*, December 1, 1940, p. 24.
32. *Broadcasting*, August 1, 1939, p. 30.
33. Barnouw, p. 143.
34. Gross, p. 240.
35. Dryer, p. 169.
36. MacDonald, p. 290.
37. Dunning, p. 624.
38. *Broadcasting*, February 1, 1936, p. 31.
39. Dryer, p. 186.
40. *Broadcasting*, February 1, 1936, p. 31.
41. MacDonald, p. 300.
42. *Radio Mirror*, October 1936, p. 21.
43. *Broadcasting*, May 1, 1939, p. 20, and April 7, 1941, p. 10.
44. *Broadcasting*, January 15, 1940, p. 87.
45. *Broadcasting*, June 15, 1940, p. 59, and April 7, 1940, p. 10.
46. *Broadcasting*, February 1, 1939, p. 76.
47. *Broadcasting*, August 1, 1940, p. 37.
48. Dunning, p. 28.
49. *Broadcasting*, November 1, 1939, p. 76.
50. *New York Times*, July 23, 1937, p. 11.
51. *Broadcasting*, March 15, 1932, p. 33.
52. Radio broadcast: *March of Time*, June 9, 1938 (NRL).
53. Radio broadcast: *March of Time*, March 6, 1931 (RVC #3670).
54. Radio broadcast: *March of Time*, "The Hauptmann Trial," October 5, 1934 (RVC #598).
55. *Broadcasting*, July 15, 1939, p. 27.
56. Czitrom, P. 88.
57. MacDonald, p. 311.

9. *Radio Covers the World*

1. MacDonald, p. 288.
2. Sterling and Kitross, p. 178.
3. MacDonald, p. 302.
4. Culbert, p. 208.
5. *Broadcasting*, June 15, 1934, p. 13.
6. Saerchinger, *Hello America*, p. 180.
7. *Broadcasting*, October 1, 1933, p. 10, and June 15, 1934, p. 13.
8. Schecter, p. 101.
9. William Paley, quoted in *New York Times*, August 3, 1931, p. 1.
10. *Broadcasting*, January 11, 1933, p. 23.
11. Charnley, p. 26.

12. Saerchinger, *Hello America*, p. 180.
13. Jordan, p. 13.
14. Paul White, p. 45.
15. Saerchinger, *Hello America*, p. 236.
16. Paul White, p. 44.
17. Saerchinger, *Hello America*, p. 237.
18. *Ibid.*, p. 238.
19. *Ibid.*, p. 244.
20. Radio broadcast: "Abdication of Edward VIII," December 12, 1936, CBS recording via shortwave (NRL).
21. Saerchinger, pp. 279–80.
22. *Broadcasting*, May 21, 1937, p. 3.
23. Radio broadcast: "Coronation of George VI," May 12, 1937 (NRL).
24. *Radio Guide*, May 29, 1937, p. 3.
25. Saerchinger, *Hello America*, p. 236.
26. Radio broadcasts: May 8, 1939, and May 17, 1939 (NRL).
27. Saerchinger, *Hello America*, p. 177.
28. Schecter, p. 111.
29. Charnley, p. 265.
30. Gordon and Falk, p. 87.
31. Stein, p. 54.
32. *The Home Front 1938–45* Tape #1.
33. Shirer, p. 110.
34. *Broadcasting*, June 1, 1940, p. 58.
35. Paley, p. 139.
36. "Austria's Annexation Illustrates Radio's Growth in Power to Inform," *Newsweek*, March 28, 1936, p. 12.
37. Fang, p. 309.
38. *Broadcasting*, September 1, 1940, p. 64.
39. Gordon and Falk, p. 90.
40. *Broadcasting*, September 11, 1944, p. 36.
41. Bliss, pp. 4–5.
42. "We Take You Back," March 13, 1958 (NA, MR 200).
43. Shirer, p. 105.
44. Bob Trout, quoted in *Washington State University*, p. 612.
45. Interview with Murrow, *This Is Edward R. Murrow*, April 30, 1965 (SPERD-VAC).
46. Murrow, quoted in *Washington State University*, p. 613.
47. Fang, p. 308.
48. *Broadcasting*, September 1, 1940, p. 64.
49. *Newsweek*, March 28, 1938, p. 11.
50. Kaltenborn, *I Broadcast*, p. 7.
51. Danna, "Rise," p. 3.
52. Kaltenborn, *I Broadcast*, pp. 56–208.
53. *Variety*, October 1, 1938, p. 11.
54. Rorty, p. 372.
55. *Broadcasting*, November 1, 1938, p. 7.
56. NBC advertisement, *Broadcasting*, November 1, 1938, p. 7.
57. Kaltenborn, *I Broadcast*, p. 7.
58. *Broadcasting*, June 1, 1940, p. 26.
59. William L. Shirer, quoted in *Broadcasting*, June 30, 1941, p. 16.

60. "Trials and Tribulations of a Radio Reporter: A New Type of Correspondent," *Newsweek*, October 17, 1938, p. 32.
61. CBS Pamphlet, "CBS Fan-Way Roundup Links Hemispheres," March 20, 1939; reproduced in Grandin, p. 19.
62. Maurice Hindus broadcast, reproduced in Gordon and Falk, p. 106.
63. Radio broadcast: "Chamberlain's Arrival at Croydon," September 28, 1938 (UMP #0035).
64. Rorty, p. 374.
65. Radio broadcast: "Shirer on the Munich Agreement," September 29, 1938 (LOC Tape 1267).
66. Kaltenborn, *I Broadcast*, p. 3.
67. Radio broadcasts: German News Shortwave," and "Italian Radio," September 16, 1938 (LOC Tape 11766).
68. Rorty, p. 372.
69. *Broadcasting*, November 1, 1938, p. 63.
70. *Radio Guide*, March 17, 1939, p. 4.
71. Radio broadcasts: Chamberlain, September 24, 1938 (LOC Tape 11786); Hitler, September 26, 1938 (LOC Tape 5742-1A) and October 9, 1938 (LOC Tape 2873-4).
72. *Broadcasting*, November 1, 1938, p. 11.
73. Rorty, p. 372.
74. "The New Diplomacy," *Broadcasting*, October 1, 1938, p. 34.
75. Kaltenborn, *I Broadcast*, p. 8.
76. *Ibid.*, p. 5.
77. *Broadcasting*, November 1, 1938, p. 63.
78. Sterling and Kitross, p. 176.
79. Kaltenborn, *I Broadcast*, p. 11.
80. *Broadcasting*, September 1, 1939, p. 80.
81. Rorty, p. 374.
82. Sterling and Kitross, p. 172.
83. Grandin, p. 68.
84. *Broadcasting*, October 15, 1938, p. 62.
85. Paley, p. 135.
86. "War Service a High Spot for Radio," *Broadcasting*, October 15, 1938, p. 15.
87. *Calvacade*, quoted in Rorty, p. 373.
88. *Radio Guide*, November 5, 1938, p. 2.
89. Roosevelt Presidential Press Conference, No. 487, September 30, 1938, in Roosevelt, *Complete Presidential Press Conference*, vol. 12, p. 167.
90. Rorty, p. 374.
91. Cantril, *Invasion*, p. 159.
92. Langer and Gleason, vol. 2, p. 35.
93. Lothian, p. 325.
94. Charnley, p. 28.
95. *Broadcasting*, July 15, 1939, p. 27.
96. Culbert, p. 73.
97. Fang, p. 31.
98. Paul White, p. 45.
99. Rorty, p. 372.
100. Grandin, p. 68.
101. William Shirer, quoted in *Broadcasting*, August 1, 1940, p. 76.
102. Kaltenborn, *I Broadcast*, p. 3.

103. Roosevelt Press Conference, No. 487, September 30, 1938, in *Roosevelt, Complete Presidential Press Conferences*, vol. 12, p. 117.

104. *Broadcasting*, October 15, 1938, p. 16.

105. Rorty, p. 373.

106. *Broadcasting*, July 1, 1939, p. 10.

107. *Broadcasting*, October 1, 1939, p. 70.

108. Culbert, p. 5.

109. Kaltenborn, *I Broadcast*, p. 5.

110. Paul White, p. 46.

111. Culbert, p. 206.

112. *Ibid.*, p. 4.

113. *Broadcasting*, August 15, 1939, p. 26.

114. Dryer, p. 154.

115. Fang, p. 290.

116. Swing, p. 194.

117. Street, p. 11.

118. Cantril, *Psychology of Radio*, p. 32.

119. *Broadcasting*, September 15, 1939, p. 80.

120. *Broadcasting*, November 1, 1938, p. 63.

121. Culbert, p. 4.

122. Letter from Bernard DeVoto sent to Elmer Davis; quoted in Culbert, p. 25.

123. MacDonald, p. 290.

124. Rorty, p. 374.

125. *Ibid.*, p. 373.

126. Lazarsfeld and Stanton, p. 259.

127. "The Press and the People," *Fortune*, August 1, 1939, p. 65.

128. Llewellyn White, p. 47.

129. Culbert, p. 13.

130. *Broadcasting*, September 1, 1939, p. 12.

131. *Broadcasting*, April 1, 1939, p. 82.

132. *Broadcasting*, May 1, 1939, p. 60.

133. Paley, p. 137.

134. Sterling and Kitross, p. 176.

135. Shirer, p. 135.

136. *Broadcasting*, August 1, 1939, p. 30.

137. *Broadcasting*, February 1, 1939, p. 20.

138. Radio broadcast: *University of Chicago Roundtable*, April 9 and April 21, 1939 (LOC Tape 1266-5); May 14, 1939 (LOC Tape 1266-5).

139. Radio broadcast: *March of Time*, "Conquest of Czechoslovakia," October 21, 1938 (RYC #456).

140. Paley, p. 138.

141. Radio broadcast: "Max Jordan Reporting from France," *We the People*, January 1940 (RVC #321).

142. *Broadcasting*, September 1, 1939, p. 12.

143. Kaltenborn, "Danzig," p. 3.

144. *Broadcasting*, September 1, 1939, p. 12.

145. Radio broadcasts: Lord Halifax, August 24, 1939 (LOC Tape 12662-2B); Daladier, August 25, 1939 (LOC Tape 3742-4); and Pope Pius XIII, August 24, 1939 (LOC Tape 12662-5).

146. Radio broadcasts: "Report on British Cabinet Reaction to War Crisis,"

August 26, 1939 (LOC Tape 16941-4A), and "Polish News in English," August 26, 1939 (LOC Tape 11776).

147. *Broadcasting*, September 15, 1939, p. 80.

148. Radio broadcast: "Hitler's Speech to the Reichstag on the Polish Crisis," September 1, 1939 (LOC Tape 5742-4B), and "The Polish Crisis" (RVC #602).

149. Jacquith, p. 9.

150. "War in the Living Room," p. 42.

151. Jacquith, p. 10.

152. *Broadcasting*, September 15, 1939, p. 18.

153. *Ibid.*, p. 80.

154. *Ibid.*, p. 19.

155. Radio broadcast: "Chamberlain's Declaration of War," September 3, 1939 (UMP #0070).

156. Edward R. Murrow broadcast, September 3, 1939; reproduced in Bliss, p. 16.

157. *Radio Guide*, October 1, 1939, p. 2.

158. *Broadcasting*, September 15, 1939, p. 80.

159. Swing, p. 205.

160. *Broadcasting*, September 1, 1939, p. 12.

161. *Broadcasting*, September 15, 1939, p. 19.

162. *Broadcasting*, January 1, 1940, p. 18.

163. *Broadcasting*, November 1, 1939, p. 86.

164. Jacquith, p. 30.

165. Fireside Chat, Sept. 3, 1939, Roosevelt, *Public Addresses and Papers*, vol. 1, p. 430.

166. Radio broadcast: *New York Herald-Tribune* Forum, October 26, 1939 (NRL).

167. Radio broadcast: "News Report from Montevideo on the Destruction of German Warship *Graf Spee*," December 17, 1939 (LOC Tape 5078-1A).

168. *Broadcasting*, January 1, 1940, p. 26.

169. Radio broadcast: "Twelve Crowded Months," December 30, 1939 (NA, MR 200).

170. *Broadcasting*, January 1, 1940, p. 11.

171. Radio broadcast: "Neville Chamberlain's Speech Before the House of Commons," BBC Shortwave, May 10, 1940, (LOC Tape 11795).

172. Radio broadcast: "Winston Churchill in the House of Commons," May 13, 1940 (LOC Tape 11795-1A).

173. Radio broadcast: "Analysis of German Invasion of France," MBS, May 22, 1940 (UMP #1189).

174. *Broadcasting*, May 15, 1940, p. 17.

175. *Broadcasting*, June 1, 1940, p. 26.

176. *Broadcasting*, May 15, 1940, p. 17.

177. Radio broadcasts by Paul Reynaud: June 2 and 6, 1940 (LOC Tape 4241-5).

178. *Broadcasting*, June 15, 1940, p. 30.

179. Radio broadcast: "Eric Sevareid on the Fall of Paris," June 9, 1940 (NRL).

180. Radio broadcast: "Benito Mussolini's Declaration of War on France," June 10, 1940 (LOC Tape 11798).

181. *Broadcasting*, June 15, 1940, p. 18.

182. Radio broadcast: "Henri Petain on the Defeat of France," French Shortwave, June 17, 1940 (LOC Tape 3822).

183. Radio broadcast: "William L. Shirer from Compeigne," June 22, 1940 (NRC #265).

184. Radio broadcast: "William C. Keirker on the French Surrender," June 22, 1940 (LOC Tape 11798).

185. Charnley, p. 29.

186. Barnouw, p. 140.

187. NBC-Blue Network Schedule, September 21, 1940, reproduced in Culbert, p. 20.

188. Radio broadcast: "Edward R. Murrow—London After Dark," August 24, 1940 (NRC #266).

189. Radio broadcast: Edward R. Murrow in London, September 22, 1940, *I Can Hear It Now* (MISC).

190. *Christian Science Monitor*, September 25, 1940, p. 11.

191. Fang, p. 312.

192. *Time*, December 15, 1941, p. 50.

193. Letter from Edward R. Murrow to Lacey Murrow; quoted in Kendrick, p. 126.

194. Culbert, p. 185.

195. Radio broadcast: Murrow in London, September 8, 1940, *A Reporter Remembers*.

196. *This Is Edward R. Murrow* interview.

197. Radio broadcast by Edward R. Murrow, *Edward R. Murrow: The War Years* (LP recording).

198. "Murrow's Orchestrated Hell Broadcast," December 3, 1943, Tape #30 (RVC).

199. Murrow, quoted in Gordon and Falk, p. 30.

200. Sevareid, p. 177.

201. Letter from a listener, quoted in Culbert, p. 207.

202. Murrow broadcast of September 13, 1940; reprinted in Bliss, pp. 35–36.

203. Murrow broadcast of December 24, 1940; reprinted in Bliss, pp. 42–44.

204. Sevareid, p. 176.

205. Archibald MacLeish, speech to dinner guests honoring Murrow; reproduced in Friendly, p. xvi.

206. *Broadcasting*, October 15, 1940, p. 28.

207. *This Is Edward R. Murrow* interview.

208. Sevareid, p. 178.

209. *Time*, December 15, 1940, p. 50.

210. Steele, p. 142.

211. Culbert, p. 203.

212. *Broadcasting*, April 14, 1941, p. 41.

213. *Broadcasting*, September 8, 1941, p. 17.

214. *Broadcasting*, June 30, 1941, p. 18.

215. Radio broadcast: "International News," June 24, 1941 (LOC Tape 12736-7B).

216. Radio broadcast: *The World Today*, November 29, 1941 (RVC #629).

217. Radio broadcast: *World News Round-up*, December 5, 1941 (NA, MR 200-59).

218. Lichty, p. 350.

219. Rose, p. 285.

220. Radio broadcast: "KGU (Honolulu) News," December 7, 1941 (NRL).

221. Letters from listeners, December 13, 1941, reprinted in Litoff and Smith, pp. 8–10.

222. Radio broadcasts: "Network Coverage of the Pearl Harbor Attack," CBS, December 7–8, 1941 (NA, MR 200).

223. Barnouw, p. 154.

224. *Broadcasting*, December 15, 1941, p. 5.

225. *Ibid.*, p. 60.

226. Radio broadcasts: "Network News Coverage of the Pearl Harbor Attack," NBC-Blue, December 7–8, 1941 (NA, MR 200-20).

227. Barnouw, p. 154.
228. Steele, p. 143.

10. Orson Welles and the "War of the Worlds"

1. Archibald MacLeish, quoted in Czitrom, p. 86.
2. Koch, *Panic Broadcast*, p. 11.
3. Gordon and Falk, p. 83.
4. Julian, pp. 22–23.
5. Reinsch, p. xi.
6. Ronald Reagan, quoted in Wills, p. 130.
7. *Broadcasting*, July 28, 1941, p. 51.
8. Cantril, *Invasion*, p. xi.
9. *Christian Science Monitor*, October 31, 1938, p. 18.
10. Radio broadcast: *Columbia Workshop*, "Fall of the City," April 11, 1937 (LOC Tape 5410-23).
11. Barnouw, p. 168.
12. Lichty and Bonn, p. 462.
13. Julian, p. 10.
14. *Ibid.*
15. John Houseman, interviewed for *Mercury Company Remembers*, (MISC).
16. Barnouw, p. 68.
17. John Houseman introduction to Koch, *As Time Goes By*, p. xii.
18. Brady, p. 84.
19. Naremore, p. 21.
20. *Saturday Evening Post*, January 27, 1940, p. 51.
21. Naremore, p. 21.
22. Barnouw, p. 84.
23. Naremore, p. 25.
24. William Alland and John Houseman, interviewed for *Mercury Company Remembers* (MISC).
25. Radio broadcast: *Les Misérables*, MBS (RHAC #055).
26. Gross, p. 197.
27. Dunning, p. 409.
28. John Houseman introduction in Koch, *As Time Goes By*, p. xiii.
29. Koch, *As Time Goes By*, p. 4.
30. "Interview with Orson Welles and H. G. Wells," KTSA, November 7, 1940 (RYC).
31. Koch, *As Time Goes By*, p. 4.
32. *Saturday Evening Post*, February 3, 1940, p. 6.
33. Dunning, p. 410.
34. Brady, p. 164.
35. *New York Times*, October 31, 1938, p. 4.
36. *Saturday Evening Post*, February 3, 1940, p. 38.
37. Houseman, p. 392.
38. Gross, p. 197.

11. The Broadcast

1. Radio broadcast: "War of the Worlds," *Mercury Theater on the Air*, October 30, 1938 (NRC #008).

2. Radio broadcast: "Immortal Sherlock Holmes," *Mercury Theater on the Air* (UMP #0832).

3. Houseman, p. 399.

4. Brady, p. 173.

5. *New York Times*, November 1, 1938, p. 4.

6. Cantril, *Invasion*, p. 44.

12. The Public Reaction

1. *New York Times*, October 31, 1938, p. 1.

2. Cantril, *Invasion*, p. ix.

3. "Anatomy of a Panic," *Time*, April 15, 1940, p. 11.

4. Higham, p. 127.

5. *Time*, April 15, 1940, p. 11.

6. *Saturday Evening Post*, February 3, 1940, p. 6.

7. Brady, p. 172.

8. Listener testimony, "Orson Welles and the Controversy Over Citizen Kane," *The American Experience*, PBS television broadcast, 1996.

9. Radio broadcast: "War of the Worlds Plus Thirty," October 1968 (UMP #0083).

10. "Boo!" *Newsweek*, November 7, 1938, p. 34.

11. *New York Times*, October 31, 1938, p. 2.

12. Koch, *Panic Broadcast*, p. 120.

13. *Washington Post*, October 31, 1938, p. 12.

14. Koch, *As Time Goes By*, p. 5.

15. Radio broadcast: "War of the Worlds Plus Thirty" October 1968 (UMP #0083).

16. *New York Times*, October 31, 1938, p. 2; and *New York Daily News*, October 31, 1938, p. 1.

17. Radio broadcast: "The Night America Trembled," CBS, ca. 1950 (UMP #0082).

18. Gross, p. 199.

19. "Interview with Orson Welles and H. G. Wells, KTSA, November 7, 1940 (RYC).

20. Oxford, p. 21.

21. Radio broadcast: "The Night America Trembled," CBS, ca. 1950 (UMP #0082).

22. *New York Amsterdam News*, November 5, 1938, p. 1.

23. *New York Times*, October 31, 1938, p. 2.

24. "Dialed Hysteria," *Newsweek*, November 7, 1938, p. 26.

25. *Christian Science Monitor*, October 31, 1938, p. 5.

26. *New York Times*, October 31, 1938, p. 10.

27. *Boston Globe*, October 31, 1938, p. 1.

28. Dunning, p. 412.

29. *Rochester Democrat and Chronicle*, October 31, 1938, p. 1.

30. Listener testimony, WBBM-Chicago Radio, "War of Worlds 50th Anniversary Show."

31. *New York Daily News*, October 31, 1938, p. 1.

32. Cantril, *Invasion*, P. 47.

33. *Variety*, November 2, 1938, p. 1.

34. *Washington Post*, October 31, 1938, p. 1.

35. John Houseman, interviewed for *Mercury Company Remembers* (MISC).

36. *Saturday Evening Post*, February 3, 1940, p. 38.

37. Radio broadcast: "The Night America Trembled," CBS, ca. 1950 (UMP #0082).

38. Bulgatz, p. 128.

39. *Rochester Democrat and Chronicle*, October 31, 1938, p. 13.

40. *Syracuse Herald*, October 31, 1938, p. 1.

41. *Toronto Star*, October 31, 1938, p. 1.

42. Paley, p. 112.

43. John Houseman introduction in Koch, *As Time Goes By*, p. xiv.

44. *Boston Globe*, October 31, 1938, p. 1.

45. Cantril, *Invasion*, p. 56.

46. Listener testimony, radio broadcast: "The Night America Trembled," CBS, ca. 1950 (UMP #0082).

47. *New York Herald-Tribune*, November 1, 1938, p. 3.

48. "On the Record," *New York Herald-Tribune*, November 2, 1938, p. 11.

49. *Ibid.*

50. *New York Times*, November 1, 1938, p. 12.

51. Cantril, *Invasion*, p. 112.

52. Alexander Woolcott, quoted in Welles and Bogdanovich, p. 18.

53. Houseman, p. 405.

54. *New York World Telegram*, November 1, 1938, p. 36.

55. Dorothy Thompson, "On the Record," *New York Herald-Tribune*, November 2, 1938, p. 13.

56. *New York Times*, October 30, 1938, p. 2.

57. Koch, *Panic Broadcast*, p. 11.

58. *Variety*, November 2, 1938, p. 2.

59. *Saturday Evening Post*, February 3, 1940, p. 37.

60. Proposed *Town Hall Tonight* script for November 5, 1938, quoted in Crosby, p. 277.

61. Interview with Orson Welles and H. G. Wells," KTSA, November 7, 1940 (RYC).

62. Gross, p. 202.

63. *Der Angriff*, November 2, 1938, p. 1.

64. Listener testimony, "War of Worlds Plus Thirty," October 1968 (UMP #0083).

65. *Time*, April 15, 1940, p. 60.

66. *New York Times*, October 31, 1938, p. 2.

67. *New York Herald Tribune*, October 31, 1938, p. 3.

68. Dunning, p. 412.

69. *Variety*, November 9, 1938, p. 3.

70. *Washington Post*, October 31, 1938, p. 1.

71. *Christian Science Monitor*, October 31, 1938, p. 13.

72. *Washington Post*, November 1, 1938, p. 4.

73. *New York Times*, October 31, 1938, p. 1.

74. Bulgatz, p. 129.

75. *Washington Post*, November 1, 1938, p. 10.

76. Cantril, *Invasion*, p. 58.

77. Naremore, p. 23.

78. Cantril, *Invasion*, p. 67.

79. *New York Times*, October 31, 1938, p. 2.

80. *Washington Post*, October 31, 1938, p. 12.
81. *New York Times*, November 1, 1938, p. 1.
82. Koch, *Panic Broadcast*, xiv.
83. *New York Daily News*, October 31, 1938, p. 1.
84. "Various Works by Orson Welles" (NARA).
85. Interview with Paul Stewart, assistant director of the Mercury Theater, quoted in Barnouw, p. 87.
86. William Alland, interviewed for *American Experience*.
87. Interview with Orson Welles, BBC television, 1955.
88. *Today Show* interview, 1978, quoted in Brady, p. 175.
89. Interview with Orson Welles, BBC television, 1955.
90. Naremore, p. 22.

13. *"It Was All So Real"*

1. Cantril, *Invasion*, p. ix.
2. *Ibid.*, p. xii.
3. *Saturday Evening Post*, February 3, 1940, p. 6.
4. Cantril, *Invasion*, p. 68.
5. Houseman, p. 40.
6. *Broadcasting*, March 1, 1940, p. 70.
7. Cantril, *Invasion*, p. 68.
8. (All three quotes.) Herzog, p. 492.
9. *Broadcasting*, March 1, 1940, p. 20.
10. Koch, *Panic Broadcast*, p. 110.
11. *Broadcasting*, March 1, 1940, p. 46.
12. *New York Times*, October 31, 1938, p. 2.
13. *Syracuse Herald*, October 31, 1938, p. 3.
14. Comments by Mercury cast members, radio broadcast: *Mercury Company Remembers*.
15. Koch, *Panic Broadcast*, p. 151.
16. Houseman, p. 398.
17. *Broadcasting*, March 1, 1940, p. 20; and Cantril, *Invasion*, P. 72.
18. Cantril, *Invasion*, p. 72.
19. Radio broadcast: "War of Worlds Plus Thirty," October 1968 (UMP #0083).
20. Naremore, p. 23.
21. Houseman, p. 398.
22. Naremore, p. 24.
23. Sterling and Kitross, p. 167.
24. Houseman, p. 401.
25. *Broadcasting*, March 1, 1940, p. 20.
26. Houseman, p. 398.
27. Cantril, *Invasion*, pp. 73–74.
28. Houseman, p. 400.
29. *Ibid.*, p. 394.
30. Film: *The Night That Panicked America*, 1975.
31. Listener testimony, quoted in Cantril, *Invasion*, p. 94.
32. Houseman, p. 400.
33. Welles and Bogdanovich, p. 32.
34. Listener testimony, quoted in Alland, *American Experience*.
35. Leuchtenburg, *Franklin D. Roosevelt and the New Deal*, p. 211.

36. Cantril, *Invasion*, p. 154.
37. Herzog, p. 495.
38. Davis, *FDR: Into the Storm*, p. 362.
39. *Daily News*, October 31, 1938, p. 2.
40. Cantril, *Invasion*, p. 160.
41. Herzog, p. 495.
42. Cantril, *Invasion*, p. 161.
43. Koch, *Panic Broadcast*, p. 104.
44. *New York Times*, October 31, 1938, p. 12.
45. Cantril, *Invasion*, p. 33.
46. Koch, *Panic Broadcast*, p. 28.
47. *New York World-Telegram*, November 2, 1938, p. 11.
48. *Daily News*, October 31, 1938, p. 5.
49. *New York Times*, October 31, 1938, p. 23.
50. Cantril, *Invasion*, p. 158.
51. Radio broadcast: *The Shadow*, January 1, 1939 (NCL #2389).
52. Herzog, p. 494.
53. *Christian Science Monitor*, October 27, 1938, p. 2.
54. *Broadcasting*, August 15, 1939, p. 20.
55. Film: *Invasion from Mars*, 1978.
56. Radio broadcast: *Buck Rogers in the 25th Century* (NCL #1230).
57. Herzog, p. 494.
58. "On the Record," *New York Herald-Tribune*, November 2, 1938.
59. Cantril, *Invasion*, p. 76.
60. Listener testimony, WBBM program.
61. Cantril, *Invasion*, p. 77.
62. *Broadcasting*, March 1, 1940, pp. 70–71.
63. Listener testimony, radio broadcast: "War of Worlds Plus Thirty," October 1968 (UMP #0083).
64. Herzog, p. 495.
65. Listener testimony, quoted in Alland, *American Experience*.
66. *Broadcasting*, March 1, 1940, p. 20.
67. Cantril, *Invasion*, p. 80.
68. *Broadcasting*, March 1, 1940, p. 70.

14. *Aftermath*

1. *New York Times*, October 31, 1938, p. 1.
2. Cantril, *Psychology of Radio*, p. 32.
3. *New York Times*, November 6, 1938, p. 6.
4. Charles Hurd, "Will the Radio be Censored?" *New York Times*, November 6, 1938, p. 19.
5. Cantril, *Psychology of Radio*, p. 36.
6. Dryer, p. 154.
7. Sterling and Kitross, p. 189.
8. *Washington Post*, November 1, 1938, p. 4.
9. *Broadcasting*, October 1, 1938, p. 3.
10. *Variety*, November 2, 1938, p. 11.
11. *Chicago Tribune*, November 3, 1938, p. 27.
12. *New York Daily News*, October 31, 1938, p. 4.
13. *Variety*, November 2, 1938, p. 3.

14. *Variety*, November 9, 1938, p. 5.
15. *New York World Telegram*, November 1, 1938, p. 2.
16. Heywood Broun, November 3, 1938, p. 5.
17. *Variety*, November 9, 1938, p. 4.
18. Lazarsfeld and Stanton, p. 86.
19. *Broadcasting*, June 1, 1939, p. 12.
20. Houseman, p. 399.
21. Houseman introduction in Koch, *As Time Goes By*, p. xiv.
22. Welles and Bogdanovich, p. 18.
23. Crosby, p. 277.
24. *New York Times*, October 31, 1938, p. 2.
25. Gross, p. 201.
26. *New York Times*, November 1, 1938, p. 13.
27. *Variety*, November 2, 1938, p. 1.
28. *New York Times*, November 8, 1938, p. 9.
29. *New York Times*, November 6, 1938, p. 3.
30. *Broadcasting*, February 1, 1940, p. 46.
31. Lichty and Bohn, p. 460.
32. Lichty and Bohn, p. 459.
33. Paul White, "Memorandum to CBS News Organization," quoted in Dryer, p. 144.
34. "Memorandum of European War Coverage," September 5, 1939, OF 136, FDRL.
35. Bureau of Research in Education, "Suggestion for Listeners in WarTime," reproduced in Dryer, p. 165.
36. *Variety*, November 9, 1938, p. 11.
37. *New York Times*, November 9, 1938, p. 2.
38. Paley, p. 127.
39. Dan Rather, "When News and Entertainment Look Alike," *New York Times*, March 8, 1994, p. 37.
40. Grandin, p. 75.
41. Troy, p. 170.
42. "On the Record," *New York Herald-Tribune*, November 2, 1938, p. 11.
43. Gross, p. 202.
44. Koch, *Panic Broadcast*, p. 162.
45. "On the Record."
46. Koch, *Panic Broadcast*, p. 164.
47. "On the Record," *New York Herald-Tribune*, November 2, 1938, p. 11.
48. *Ibid.*
49. PPF 101-A, FDRL.
50. Yeilding, p. xx.
51. Welles and Bogdanovich, p. 386.
52. Letter, Franklin Roosevelt to Orson Welles, November 25, 1944, PPF 8921, FDRL.
53. *Washington Post*, November 1, 1938, p. 10.
54. *Times* (London), November 1, 1938, p. 15.
55. "Preparedness vs. Panic Issue," *Variety*, November 2, 1938, p. 2.
56. *New York Times*, November 1, 1938, op. ed.
57. "Interview with Orson Welles and H. G. Wells," KTSA, November 7, 1940 (RYC).
58. "On the Record," *New York Herald-Tribune*, November 2, 1938, p. 11.

59. "Preparedness vs. Panic Issue," *Variety*, November 2, 1938, p. 1.
60. *Seattle Times*, November 8, 1938, quoted in Higham, p. 128.
61. *Chicago Tribune*, November 1, 1938, p. 3.
62. *Washington Post*, November 1, 1938, p. 10.
63. Jackson, p. 31.
64. *Broadcasting*, July 28, 1941, p. 14.
65. *Broadcasting*, December 15, 1941, p. 6.
66. *Broadcasting*, September 15, 1939, p. 79.
67. *Washington Post*, November 1, 1938, p. 12.
68. Koch, *Panic Broadcast*, p. 163.
69. Letter to the editor, *New York Times*, November 2, 1938.
70. Welles and Bogdanovich, p. 20.
71. Strock, p. 10.
72. Radio broadcast: "NBC Pearl Harbor Coverage," December 7, 1941 (NA, MR 200).
73. *Broadcasting*, December 15, 1941, p. 48.
74. Gross, p. 241.
75. Cantril, *Invasion*, p. xi.
76. Dunning, p. 423.
77. "Anatomy of a Panic," *Time*, April 15, 1940, p. 17.
78. Bulgatz, p. 140.
79. Cantril, *Invasion*, revised edition 1964, p. xi.
80. Koch, *As Time Goes By*, p. 9.
81. Brady, p. 186.
82. Cantril, *Invasion*, revised edition, p. xii.

15. Conclusion

1. Settel, p. 74.
2. *New York Times*, June 23, 1994, p. 37.

Bibliography

"Anatomy of a Panic." *Time*, April 15, 1940.

Asbell, Bernard. *When FDR Died*. New York: Holt, Rinehart and Winston, 1961.

"Austria's Annexation Illustrates Radio's Growth in Power to Inform." *Newsweek*, March 28, 1938.

Badger, Anthony. *The New Deal: The Depression Years, 1933–1940*. New York: Hill and Wang, 1989.

Bailey, Thomas A., and Paul Ryan. *Hitler vs. Roosevelt: The Undeclared Naval War*. New York: Free Press, 1979.

Bannerman, R. LeRoy. *On a Note of Triumph: Norman Corwin and the Golden Years of Radio*. New York: Carol, 1986.

Barnard, Elizabeth. *Wendell Willkie: Fighter for Freedom*. Marquette: Northern Michigan University Press, 1966.

Barnouw, Erik. *A History of Broadcasting in the United States*. Vol. 2: *The Golden Web, 1933–1953*. New York: Oxford University Press, 1968.

Becker, Samuel L. "Presidential Power: The Influence of Broadcasting," *Quarterly Journal of Speech* **47** (February 1961), pp. 11–14.

Behn, Noel. *Lindbergh: The Crime*. New York: Atlantic Monthly, 1994.

Bellush, Bernard. *Franklin D. Roosevelt as Governor of New York*. New York: Columbia University Press, 1955.

Bender, James. "The Two Men: A Radio Analysis." *New York Times Magazine*, September 17, 1944, pp. 11–36.

Bendiner, Robert. *Just Around the Corner: A Highly Selective History of the Thirties*. New York: Dutton, 1968.

Bishop, Jim. *FDR's Last Year: April 1944–April 1945*. New York: Morrow, 1974.

Bliss, Edward Jr., ed., *In Search of Light: The Broadcasts of Edward R. Murrow, 1938–1961*. New York: Knopf, 1967.

"Blitzkrieg on the Dial: NBC, CBS, and Mutual Prepare for New York War Games." *Newsweek*, August 17, 1940.

"Boo!" *Newsweek*, November 7, 1938.

Borg, Dorothy, "Notes on Roosevelt's 'Quarantine Speech.'" *Political Science Quarterly* **72** (1957), pp. 405–33.

Brady, Frank. *Citizen Welles: A Biography of Orson Welles*. New York: Anchor, 1989.

Brinkley, Alan. *Voices of Protest: Huey Long, Father Coughlin and the Great Depression*. New York: Vintage, 1982.

Broadcasting, 1933–1945.

Brown, Robert J. "Radio's First Courtroom Thriller." *Journal of Vintage Radio*, Fall 1994.

_____. "Radio's Time Machine." *Journal of Vintage Radio*, Fall 1995.

Buhite, Russel D., and David W. Levy, eds. *FDR's Fireside Chats*. Norman: University of Oklahoma Press, 1992.

Bulgatz, Joseph. *Ponzi Schemes, Invaders from Mars and Other Extraordinary Popular Delusions.* New York: Harmony, 1992.

Bureau of Applied Social Research. *The People Look at Radio: Report on a Survey Conducted by the National Opinion Research Center.* Chapel Hill: University of North Carolina Press, 1946.

Burlingame, Roger. *Don't Let Them Scare You: The Life and Times of Elmer Davis.* Philadelphia: Lippincott, 1961.

Buxton, Frank, and Bill Owen. *The Big Broadcast, 1920–1950.* New York: Viking, 1972.

Cantril, Hadley. *The Psychology of Radio.* New York: Harper, 1935.

_____. *The Invasion from Mars: A Study in the Psychology of Panic.* Princeton: Princeton University Press, 1940.

_____. *Public Opinion 1935–1946.* Princeton: Princeton University Press, 1951.

Caro, Robert. *The Path to Power: The Years of Lyndon Johnson.* New York: Vintage, 1983.

Charlotte Observer, 1933–45.

Charnley, Mitchell V. *News by Radio.* New York: Macmillan, 1948.

Chicago Daily News, 1924–40.

Chicago Tribune, 1933–45.

Cole, Wayne S. *Roosevelt and the Isolationists.* Lincoln: University of Nebraska Press, 1983.

Crosby, John. *Out of the Blue: A Book About Radio and Television.* New York: Simon and Schuster, 1946.

Crowell, Laura. "Building the 'Four Freedoms' Speech." *Speech Monographs* 22 (1955), pp. 266–283.

Culbert, David Holbrook. *News for Everyman: Radio and Foreign Affairs in Thirties America.* Westport CT: Greenwood, 1976.

Czitrom, Daniel J. *Media and the American Mind: From Morse to McLuhan.* Chapel Hill: University of North Carolina Press, 1982.

Dallek, Robert. *Franklin D. Roosevelt and American Foreign Policy, 1932–45.* New York: Oxford University Press, 1979.

Danna, Sammy R. "The Rise of Radio News," *Freedom of Information Center Report No. 211.* New York: Columbia School of Journalism, 1968. Pp. 1–7.

_____. "The Press-Radio War." *Freedom of Information Center Report No. 213.* New York: Columbia School of Journalism, 1968.

Davis, Kenneth S. *FDR: The Beckoning of Destiny, 1892–1928.* New York: Putnam, 1971.

_____. *FDR: The New York Years, 1928–1933.* New York: Random House, 1985.

_____. *FDR: The New Deal Years, 1933–1937.* New York: Random House, 1989.

_____. *FDR: Into the Storm, 1937–1940.* New York: Random House, 1993.

Delano, Daniel W. *Franklin Roosevelt and the Delano Influence.* Pittsburgh: Nudi, 1946.

Desmond, Robert W. *Crisis and Conflict: World News Reporting Between Two Wars, 1920–1940.* Iowa City: University of Iowa Press, 1982.

"Dialed Hysteria." *Newsweek,* November 7, 1938.

Dickinson, Terence. "Martians Invade Earth!" *Sky and Telescope,* September 1988.

Dillon, Mary Earhart. *Wendell Willkie.* Philadelphia: Lippincott, 1952.

Douglas, Susan. *Inventing American Broadcasting, 1899–1922.* Baltimore: Johns Hopkins University Press, 1987.

Drummond, Frank. "Wendell Willkie." In Isabel Leighton, ed., *The Aspirin Age, 1919–1941.* New York: Simon and Schuster, 1976.

Dryer, Sherman. *Radio in Wartime.* New York: Greenberg, 1942.

Dunning, John. *Tune in Yesterday: The Ultimate Encyclopedia of Old-Time Radio.* Englewood Cliffs NJ: Prentice-Hall, 1976.

Fang, Irving E. *Those Radio Commentators!* Ames: Iowa State University Press, 1977.

Farley, James. *Behind the Ballots: The Personal History of a Politician.* New York: Harcourt, Brace, 1938.

"Fast and Vivid War Sevice Given Nation by Broadcasts." *Broadcasting,* November 1, 1938.

Freidel, Frank. *Franklin D. Roosevelt: Launching the New Deal.* Boston: Little, Brown, 1973.

Friendly, Fred. *Due to Circumstances Beyond Our Control.* New York: Random House, 1967.

Furnas, J.C. "The War of Lies and Laughs: The Story of Radio's 24-Hour-a-Day Word Battle." *Saturday Evening Post,* February 3, 1940.

Gallagher, Hugh Gregory. *FDR's Splendid Deception.* New York: Dodd, Mead, 1985.

Gallup, George H. *The Gallup Poll: Public Opinion 1935–71.* Vol. 1: *1935–48.* New York: Random House, 1962.

Gannon, Michael. *Operation Drumbeat.* New York: Harper & Row, 1990.

Geselbracht, Raymond H. Introduction. In *Franklin D. Roosevelt's Inaugural Address of 1933.* Milestone Documents in the National Archives. Washington D.C: National Archives and Records Administration, 1988.

Gordon, George N., and Irving A. Falk. *On-the-Spot Reporting: Radio Records History.* New York: Messner, 1967.

Grandin, Thomas. *The Political Use of the Radio.* Newark: Arno, 1971.

Gross, Ben. *I Looked and I Listened: Informal Recollections of Radio and T.V.* New Rochelle: Arlington House, 1954.

Herzog, Herta. "Why Did People Believe in the Invasion from Mars?" Memorandum to Dr. Frank Stanton, Director of Research, Columbia Broadcasting System (1939). In Lichty, Lawrence W., and Malachi C. Topping, *American Broadcasting: A Sourcebook on the History of Radio and Television.* New York: Random House, 1975.

Higgins, C.S. *Sounds Real: Radio in Everyday Life.* St. Lucia: Univeristy of Queensland Press, 1982.

Higham, Charles. *Orson Welles: The Rise and Fall of an American Genius.* New York: St. Martin's, 1985.

Hill, Edwin C. "Radio's New Destiny." *Radio Stars,* June 1933.

Hinshaw, David. *Herbert Hoover: American Quaker.* New York: Farrar, Straus, 1950.

Hoover, Herbert. *The Memoirs of Herbert Hoover.* Vol. 2: *The Cabinet and the Presidency, 1920–33.* Vol. 3: *The Great Depression, 1934–41.* New York: Macmillan, 1952.

Hopkins, Harry. Foreword. In *Nothing to Fear* by B.D. Zevin. Boston: 1946.

Houseman, John. *Run Through: A Memoir.* New York: Simon and Schuster, 1972.

"How Radio Saved the *Squalus* Survivors." *Radio Guide,* June 28, 1939.

Howe, Quincy. *The News and How to Understand It.* New York: Simon and Schuster, 1940.

Huntemann, Jacque D. "War of the Worlds." *Good Old Days,* October 1993.

Hurd, Charles W. "Will the Radio be Censored?" *New York Times,* November 6, 1938.

Hutchens, John K. "His Honor, the Radio Showman." *New York Times Magazine,* July 16, 1944.

Jackson, Charles. "The Night the Martians Came" (1949), in Isabel Leighton.

Jansky, C.M. "The Contribution of Herbert Hoover to Broadcasting." *Journal of Broadcasting* 1 (Summer 1957).

Jaquith, Priscilla. "How We Give—and Take—the War News." *Rockefeller Center Magazine,* October 1939.

Johnson, Hugh S. "Mars Panic Useful." *Chicago Tribune,* November 3, 1938.

Johnson, Walter. *1600 Pennsylvania Avenue: Presidents and People, 1933–1959.* Boston: Little, Brown, 1960.

Johnston, Alva, and Fred Smith. "How to Raise a Child: The Education of Orson Welles." In 3 parts. *Saturday Evening Post*, January 20, January 27, February 3, 1940.

Jordan, Max. *Beyond the Microphone*. New York: Random House, 1943.

Julian, Joseph. *This Was Radio: A Personal Memoir*. New York: Viking, 1975.

Kaltenborn, Hans von. "Danzig the Dangerous," *Radio Guide*, August 28, 1939.

_____. *I Broadcast the Crisis*. New York: Random House, 1938.

Keegan, John. *The Second World War*. London: Penguin, 1989.

Kendrick, Robert. *Prime Time: The Life of Edward R. Murrow*. New York: Random House, 1955.

Kershaw, Ian. *Popular Opinion and Political Dissent in the Third Reich: Bavaria 1933–45*. Oxford: Clarendon, 1983.

Kessner, Thomas. *Fiorello La Guardia and the Making of Modern New York*. New York: McGraw-Hill, 1989.

Kingdon, Frank. *As FDR Said: A Treasury of His Speeches, Conversations, and Writings*. New York: Duell, Sloan and Pearce, 1950.

Klurfeld, Herman. *Winchell: His Life and Times*. New York: Praeger, 1976.

Koch, Howard. *As Time Goes By: Memoirs of a Writer*. New York: Harcourt, Brace, Jovanovich, 1979.

_____. *The Panic Broadcast: Portrait of an Event*. Boston: Little, Brown, 1970.

Langer, William L., and S. Everett Gleason. *The Challenge to Isolation*. Vol. 2: *The World Crisis of 1937–40 and American Foreign Policy*. New York: Harper and Row, 1952.

Lazarsfeld, Hazel Gaudet, and Bernard Berelson. *The People's Choice: How the Voter Makes Up His Mind in a Presidential Campaign*. New York: Columbia University Press, 1948.

Lazarsfeld, Paul F., and Frank Stanton, eds. *Radio Research 1942–43*. New York: Arno, 1979.

Leaming, Barbara. *Orson Welles: A Biography*. New York: Penguin, 1983.

Leuchtenberg, William E. *Franklin D. Roosevelt and the New Deal, 1932–1940*. New York: Harper and Row, 1963.

_____. *In the Shadow of FDR: From Harry Truman to Bill Clinton*. Ithaca NY: Cornell University Press, 1983.

Lichty, Lawrence, and Thomas W. Bohn. "Radio's *March of Time*: Dramatized News." *Journalism Quarterly* 51:3 (Autumn 1974), pp. 458–62.

Lichty, Lawrence W., and Malachi C. Topping. *American Broadcasting: A Sourcebook on the History of Radio and Television*. New York: Hastings House, 1975.

Litoff, Judy Barrett, and David C. Smith, eds. *Since You Went Away: World War II Letters from American Women on the Home Front*. New York: Oxford University Press, 1991.

Loewenheim, Francis L., ed. *Roosevelt and Churchill: Their Secret Wartime Correspondence*. New York: E.P. Dutton, 1975.

Lothian, Lord. "The U.S. and Europe." *International Affairs*, May–June 1939.

Lynd, Robert, and Lynd, Helen. *Middletown: A Study in Contemporary American Culture*. New York: Harcourt, Brace, Jovanovich, 1929.

MacDonald, J. Fred. *Don't Touch That Dial! Radio Programming in American Life, 1920–1960*. Chicago: Nelson-Hall, 1979.

MacNeil, Neil. "How to Rig a Convention." *Saturday Evening Post*, October 26, 1940.

MacVane, John. *On the Air in World War II*. New York: Morrow, 1979.

Mayer, Jane, and Doyle McManus. *Landslide: The Unmaking of the President, 1984–88*. Boston: Houghton-Mifflin, 1988.

Mitchell, Curtis. *Cavalcade of Broadcasting*. New York: Rutledge, 1970.

Naremore, James. *The Magic World of Orson Welles*. New York: Oxford University Press, 1978.

"Nation Pays Tribute to Radio's Flood Aid." *Broadcasting*, February 1, 1937.

"The New Diplomacy." *Broadcasting*, October 15, 1938.

New Orleans Item, 1923–40.

New York Daily News, 1933–45.

New York Herald-Tribune, 1933–45.

New York Times, 1933–45.

New York World-Telegram, 1933–45.

Oxford, Edward. "Night of the Martians." *American History Illustrated*, October 1988.

Paley, William S. *As It Happened: A Memoir*. New York: Doubleday, 1979.

Patterson, Thomas. *Out of Order*. New York: Vintage, 1994.

Pearson, Drew. *Diaries, 1949–59*. New York: Holt, Rinehart and Winston, 1974.

Perkins, Frances. "The Roosevelt I Know." *Common Sense*, February 1934.

_____. *The Roosevelt I Knew*. New York: Viking, 1946.

Poindexter, Ray. *Golden Throats and Silver Tongues: The Radio Announcers*. Conway: River Road Press, 1978.

Porter, Amy. "Butch Says Cut It Out." *Colliers*, April 28, 1945.

Poteet, G. Howard. *Radio!* Dayton OH: Pflaum, 1975.

"Preparedness vs. Panic Issue." *Variety*, November 2, 1938.

"The Press and the People." *Fortune*. August 1939.

"Radio Again Succors Stricken Area." *Broadcasting*, October 1, 1938.

"Radio Gives Fast Zeppelin Coverage." *Broadcasting*, May 15, 1937.

Radio Guide, 1933–45.

Radio Stars, 1933–45.

Radioland, 1935–41.

"Radio's Pow-Wow Man." *Radio Guide*, February 12, 1939.

Rather, Dan. "When News and Entertainment Look Alike." *New York Times*, March 8, 1994.

Reinsch, J. Leonard. *Getting Elected: From Radio and Roosevelt to Television and Reagan*. New York: Hippocrene, 1988.

Rockwell, Don, ed. *Radio Personalities: A Pictorial and Biographical Annual*. New York: 1935.

Rorty, James. "Radio Comes Through." *Nation*, October 10, 1938.

Roosevelt, Franklin Delano. *Public Papers and Addresses of Franklin D. Roosevelt*. Vol. 1: *A New Deal for America*. New York: Random House, 1938. Vol. 2: *Year of Crisis 1933*. New York: Random House, 1938. Vol. 4: *The Court Prevails 1937*. New York: Random House, 1938. Vol. 5: *The People Approve 1938*. New York: Random House, 1941.

_____. 1941 Volume: *The Call to Battle Stations*. New York: Random House, 1941

_____. 1944–45 Volume: *Victory and the Threshold of Peace*. New York: Random House, 1950.

_____. *Complete Presidential Press Conferences of Franklin D. Roosevelt*. Vols. 11–12: *1938*. New York: Da Capo, 1972.

Roosevelt, Franklin D., Library (FDRL). Hyde Park, New York: Official File (OF), President's Personal File (PPF), President's Secretary's File (PSF), President's Speech File, Recorded Speech Collection, Steve Early Papers (SEP).

Roosevelt Album. New York: Knickerbocker, 1945.

Rose, Ernest D. "How the U.S. Heard About Pearl Harbor." *Journal of Broadcasting* 11:4 (Fall 1961).

Rosen, Phillip. *The Modern Stentor: Radio Broadcasting and the Federal Government, 1920–34*. Westport CT: Greenwood, 1982.

Rosenman, Samuel I. *Working With Roosevelt*. New York: Harper, 1952.

Rutherford, Ward. *Hitler's Propaganda Machine*. New York: Grosset and Dunlap, 1978.

Ryan, Halford. "Franklin D. Roosevelt." In *American Orators of the Twentieth Century: Critical Studies and Sources*. Westport CT: Greenwood, 1987.

_____. *Franklin D. Roosevelt's Rhetorical Presidency*. Westport CT: Greenwood, 1988.

Ryan, J.H. "Radio Censorship Code." *The Radio Daily 1942 Radio Annual*, 1942, pp. 67–73.

Saerchinger, Caesar. "Radio as a Political Instrument." *Foreign Affairs* **56** (January 1938).

Saerchinger, Caesar. *Hello America! Radio Adventures in Europe*. Boston: Houghton-Mifflin, 1939.

San Francisco Examiner, 1933–45.

Schecter, A.A. *I Live on Air*. New York: Stokes, 1941.

Schlesinger, Arthur M., Jr. *The Coming of the New Deal*. Boston: Houghton-Mifflin, 1956.

_____. *The Politics of Upheaval*. Boston: Houghton-Mifflin, 1960.

Settel, Irving. *A Pictorial History of Radio*. New York: Grosset & Dunlap, 1971.

Sevareid, Eric. *Not So Wild a Dream*. New York: Knopf, 1946.

Shannon, David A. *Between the Wars: America, 1919–41*. Boston: Houghton-Mifflin, 1963.

Sharon, John T. "Psychology of the Fireside Chat." Senior Honors Thesis, Princeton University, 1949.

Sherwood, Robert. *Roosevelt and Hopkins: An Intimate History*. New York: Grosset & Dunlap, 1950.

Shirer, William L. *Berlin Diary*. New York: Knopf, 1941.

Slate, Sam J., and Joe Cook. *It Sounds Impossible*. New York: Macmillan, 1963.

Smead, Elmer E. *Freedom of Speech by Radio and Television*. Washington DC: Public Affairs, 1959.

Smith, Robert K. "The Origins of Radio Network News Commentary." *Journal of Broadcasting* **9** (Spring 1965).

Steele, Richard W. *Propaganda in an Open Society: The Roosevelt Adminstration and the Media, 1933–1941*. Westport CT: Greenwood, 1985.

Stein, M.L. *Under Fire: The Story of American War Correspondents*. New York: Messner, 1968.

Stenehjem, Michele Flynn. *An American First: John T. Flynn and the American First Committee*. New York: Arlington House, 1976.

Sterling, Christopher, and John M. Kitross. *Stay Tuned: A Concise History of American Broadcasting*. Belmont CA: Wadsworth, 1978.

Street, James. "Radio's Pow-Wow Man." *Radio Guide*, February 12, 1939.

Strock, Clancy, ed. *We Pulled Together ... and Won*. Greendale: Reminisce, 1993.

Strout, Richard Lee. "The President and the Press." In Katie Loucheim, ed. *The Making of the New Deal: The Insiders Speak*. Cambridge MA: Harvard University Press, 1983.

Summers, Harrsion B. *A Thirty-Year History of Programs Carried on National Radio Networks in the United States, 1926–1956*. New York: Arno, 1971.

Swing, Raymond. *"Good Evening!": A Professional Memoir*. New York: Harcourt, Brace, and World, 1964.

Taylor, Robert. *Fred Allen: His Life and Wit*. New York: Little, Brown, 1989.

Times (London), September-October 1938.

Towne, Ralph Louis, Jr. "Roosevelt and the Coming of World War II: An Analysis of
    War Issues Treated by Franklin D. Roosevelt in Selected Speeches, October 5, 1937
    to December 7, 1941." Ph.d. dissertation, Michigan State University, 1961.
"Trials and Tribulations of the Radio Reporter: A New Type of Correspondent." *News-
    week*, October 17, 1938.
Troy, Gil. *See How They Ran: The Changing Role of the Presidential Candidate.* New York:
    Free Press, 1991.
Van der Vat, Dan. *The Atlantic Campaign.* New York: Harper & Row, 1988.
Variety, 1932–45.
"War in the Living Room: Radio Gives the Public the News and the Jitters as Well."
    Newsweek. September 11, 1939.
"War Service a High Spot for Radio." *Broadcasting*, October 15, 1938.
Washburn, Philo C. *Broadcasting Propganda: International Radio Broadcasting and the
    Construction of Political Reality.* Westport CT: Praeger, 1992.
Washington Post, 1933–45.
Washington State University. *History in Sound: A Descriptive Listing of the KIRO-CBS
    Collection of Broadcasts of the World War II Years and After.* Seattle: 1964.
Weekly Digest of Radio Opinion. New York: Radio Reports, 1944.
Welles, Orson, and Peter Bogdanovich. *This Is Orson Welles.* New York: HarperCollins,
    1992.
"A Welles Fantasy in America." *Times* (London), November 1, 1938.
"What Is Father Coughlin Doing These Days?" *Radio Guide*, July 23, 1939.
White, Graham J. *FDR and the Press.* Chicago: University of Chicago Press, 1979.
White, Llewellyn. *The American Radio: A Report on the Broadcasting Industry in the U.S.
    from the Commission on Freedom of the Press.* Chicago: University of Chicago Press,
    1947.
White, Paul W. *News on the Air.* New York: Harcourt, Brace, 1947.
"Will FDR Be the Next Radio Czar?" *Variety*, March 15, 1940.
Willey, George A. "The Soap Operas and the War." *Journal of Broadcasting* 7:4 (Fall
    1963), pp. 339–352.
Williams, Harry T. *Huey Long: A Biography.* New York: Knopf, 1978.
Wills, Gary. *Reagan's America.* New York: Penguin, 1985.
Winfield, Betty Houchin. *FDR and the News Media.* Chicago: University of Illinois
    Press, 1990.
Wolfe, G. Joseph. "Some Reactions to the Advent of Campaigning by Radio." *Journal
    of Broadcasting* 13 (Summer 1969).
Woolf, S.J. "The Mayor Talks About Our Town." *New York Times Magazine*, Septem-
    ber 30, 1945.
Wooten, James. *Dasher: The Roots and Rising of Jimmy Carter.* New York: Summitt,
    1978.
Yeilding, Kenneth D., and Paul H. Carlson. *Ah That Voice: The Fireside Chats of Franklin
    Delano Roosevelt.* Odessa TX: Library of the President Museum, 1974.
Zevin, B.D., ed. *Nothing to Fear: Selected Addresses of Franklin D. Roosevelt, 1932–45.*
    Freeport ME: Houghton-Mifflin, 1946.

Selected Radio Broadcasts

The following is a highly selective list of some of the thousands of broadcasts used in the preparation of this volume. The reference number of each item, where available, is indicated.

Library of Congress Sound Collection (LOC)

"Benito Mussolini's Declaration of War on France," June 10, 1940, Tape 11798.
"British War Relief Program," 1940, Tape 5320-16A.
"Bundles for Britain," 1940, Tape 5320-16A.
"Burton K. Wheeler," February 12, 1937, Tape 12634-8.
"Chamberlain on Munich" September 24, 1938, Tape 11786.
"Chamberlain at Heston Airport," September 30, 1938, Tape 11786.
"Chamberlain's Speech Before House of Commons," BBC Shortwave, May 10, 1940, Tape 11795.
"Charles Lindbergh: Keep America Out of War," 1940, Tape 11800.
"Congressional Opposition to Proposed Changes in the Federal Judiciary," February 9-10, 1937, Tape 12634-1.
"Daladier on Polish Crisis," August 25, 1939, Tape 3742-4.
"Democratic Committee Program," November 4, 1940, Tape 8283.
"Fall of the City," *Columbia Workshop*, April 11, 1937, Tape 5410-23.
"FDR Speech at University of Virginia Commencment Exercises," June 10, 1940, Tape 3822-1.
"Frederick Van Nuys," February 9-21, 1937, Tape 12634-8.
"Gerald P. Nye on American Neutrality," 1940, February 9-21, 1937, Tape 12634-8.
"German News by Shortwave," September 16, 1938, Tape 11766.
"Henri Petain on the Defeat of France," June 17, 1940, Tape 3822.
"Hindenburg Disaster: Eyewitness Account by Herbert Morrison," May 6, 1937, Tape 16798-62A.
"Hitler's Speech to Reichstag on the Polish Crisis," September 1, 1939, Tape 5742.
"Hitler's Speeches during Munich," September 26, 1938, Tape 5742-1A, October 9, 1938, Tape 2873-4.
"Hospital on the Thames," 1940, Tape 5320-16B.
"International News," June 24, 1941, Tape 12736-7B.
"Italian Radio," September 10, 1938, Tape 11766.
"Lord Halifax," August 24, 1939, Tape 12662-2B.
"Man-in-the-Street Interviews Regarding the President's Proposed Changes in the Supreme Court," February 7, 1937, Tape 2634-1.
"Martin Dies on American Neutrality," 1940, Tape 12731.

"Mass Meeting of Opponents to the President's Supreme Court Plan," March 12, 1937, Tape 12634-9.
"News Report from Montevideo on the Destruction of the German Warship *Graf Spee*, December 17, 1939, Tape 5078-1A.
"Ohio and Mississippi Flood News," June 27, 1937, Tape 11796.
"Paul Reynaud," June 2, 1940 and June 6, 1940, Tape 4241-5.
"Polish News in English," August 26, 1939, Tape 11776.
"Pope Pius XIII," August 24, 1939, Tape 12662-5.
"Red Cross Program for Relief of Flood Victims," February 11, 1937, Tape 15778-69B.
"Report on British Cabinet Reaction to War Crisis," August 26, 1939, Tape 16941-4A.
"Selective Service Prgram: First Peacetime Draft Lottery," October 29, 1940, Tape 9485-34A.
"Uncle Sam Makes and the World Takes," October 22, 1939, Tape 5441-14.
University of Chicago Roundtable, April 9, 1939, Tape 1266-2; April 21, 1939, Tape 1266-2; May 14, 1939, Tape 1266-5; June 6, 1939, Tape 12666-4.
"U.S. Foreign Trade Comes of Age," November 5, 1939, Tape 5441-15.
"White Cliffs of Dover," 1940, Tape 5320-16A.
"Why Pack the Supreme Court?" February 19, 1937, Tape 8404-35.
"William C. Kierker on French Surrender," June 22, 1940, Tape 11791.
"William E. Borah on Neutrality and the Arms Embargo," October 22, 1939, Tape 5404-44.
"William L. Shirer on Munich Agreement," September 29, 1938, Tape 1267.
"Willkie for President Rally," November 4, 1940, Tape 7965-15A.
"Winston Churchill Before the House of Commons," BBC Shortwave, May 13, 1940, Tape 11795-1A.
"Yankee Ships and Yankee Trade," October 29, 1939, Tape 5441-18.

Franklin D. Roosevelt Library (FDRL)

Fireside Chats SRT-72 and Mass Communications Inc. (MCI) Tapes 1-20: March 12, 1933; July 24, 1933; October 22, 1933; April 28, 1935; February 5, 1937; March 9, 1937; October 12, 1937; April 14, 1938; June 24, 1938; September 3, 1939; May 26, 1940; December 29, 1940; May 27, 1941; September 11, 1941; December 9, 1941; "Quarantine Speech," October 5, 1937, SRT 72-12.

Audio Archives Inc., Latexo, TX (AA)

Father Coughlin, "Twenty Years Ago," April 4, 1937, #182
Father Coughlin, "Relief that Fails to Relieve," April 11, 1937.

Metro Washington OTR Library (MWC)

"Dick Cavett Interview with Orson Welles," two-hour television audio from 1978, #Z-0002 and Z-0003.

National Archives (NA)
(All programs are from the Milo Ryan Phonoarchive [MR 200] unless otherwise indicated)

"Behind the Scenes in CBS Newsroom," June 1, 1941.
"CBS Coverage of the Democratic National Convention," July 19, 1944.

European Situation, May 31, 1941.

"FDR Address to Congress," December 8, 1941, Tape 200-61.

"FDR-Churchill Meeting," August 14, 1941, with Albert Warner.

"FDR's Funeral Procession from Warm Springs," April 13, 1945.

"FDR's Funeral Procession in Washington DC," April 14, 1945, 208-134.

"Hitler Address to Nazi Congress at Nuremberg," September 12, 1938.

"Network News Coverage of Pearl Harbor Attack," NBC-Red and NBC-Blue, December 7–8, 1941, Tapes 200-1 to 200-21.

Report to the Nation, "Conscription," November 30, 1940.

"Second Anniversary of Start of War," September 1, 1941.

"Speech by Benito Mussolini Declaring War on France and Britain" (in Italian), June 10, 1940.

This Week in Washington, November 11, 1939.

Today in Europe, November 1939, Tape 200-802.

Twelve Crowded Months, December 30, 1939.

War This Week, October 15, 20, 1939; November 5, 19, 26, 1939; December 10, 17, 1939; January 7, 21, 1940.

"We Take You Back," CBS Commemorative Program with Bob Trout, March 13, 1958, MR 200.

World News Round-Up, December 5, 1941, Tape 200-59.

World Today, consecutive broadcasts, June to December 1941.

National Recording Company (NRC)

"Edward R. Murrow—London After Dark," 1940, Cassette 266.

"William L. Shirer from Compeigne Forest," June 22, 1940, Cassette 265.

North American Radio Archives—Cassettes (NARA)

"America First Committee," 1940, Cassette 1209.

Buck Rogers in the Twenty-Fifth Century, July 1938, Cassette 1230-31.

The Shadow, "The Man Who Murdered Time," January 1, 1939, Cassette 2389.

"Various Works by Orson Welles," series of oral interviews with Mercury Theater cast members.

We the People, January 1940.

You Are There, April 24, May 1, 8, 15, 22, 1949, #659-661.

North American Radio Archives—Reels (NRL)
(Reel access numbers are indicated, unless they originate
with a part of the collection that has not yet been catalogued)

"Adolf Hitler" (in German), October 6, 1939.

Ahead of the Headlines, ca. 1940.

Album of Manhattan, February 21, 1940, #696.

America First Committee, Various Broadcasts, ca. 1940, #655.

"America Today," December 7, 1941, with Gabriel Heatter, #333.

American Radio Newsreel, October 2, 4, 6, 1939.

Americans All, Immigrants All, ca. 1938, #072.

"Anthony Eden on Dunkirk," June 2, 1940.

"Arrival of King George VI and Queen Elizabeth," May 17, 1939, #696.

"Arthur Mann," July 4, 1940.
Associated Press News, December 25, 1939.
Bob Trout News, September 14–17, 1939.
CBS News, December 1 and 2, 1941, #295; December 3 and 4, 1941, #659.
"Chamberlain from Birmingham," February 24, 1940.
"Chamberlain Resigns," May 10, 1940.
"Chamberlain's Declaration of War," September 3, 1939, #656.
"Charles Lindbergh," September 15, 1939.
"Coronation of George VI," six hours of coverage, June 12, 1937.
Dorothy Thompson, September 2 and 3, 1939; June 22, 1940.
Dorothy Thompson Commentary, September 9, 1939, and June 22, 1941, #656.
"Duke of Windsor from Verdun Battlefield," May 8, 1939, #696.
"Edward VIII Abdicates," December 11, 1936.
Edward R. Murrow, August 31, 1939, and June 2, 1940, #517.
Edward R. Murrow, September 3, 4, 17, 1939; January 7, 10, 18, 1940; March 10, 31,
     April 9, 22, 1940; May 2, 8, 10, 1940.
Elmer Davis and the News, September 15 to December 30, 1939; August 27, 1940, to
     February 12, 1941; #697 and 698.
"English Summary of Hitler's Speech," October 16, 1938, #192.
European News Round-Up, August 28, 1939, and May 19, 1940.
European Situation, "Italy Declares War," June 10, 1940.
Father Coughlin, April 4, 1937, #496.
Father Coughlin, "Christianity versus Chaos," February 1937.
"FDR Speech at the Launching of USS *Patrick Henry* in Portland," September 27, 1941,
     #331.
"Fiorello La Guardia," May 28, 1941, #696.
Five Star Final, October 17, 1939.
Frank Singiser News, December 8, 1940, #334.
Fulton Lewis, Jr., November 4, 1941, and October 30, 1940, #448.
Gabriel Heatter, June 16, 1942, #669.
"General A.V. Alexander," July 4, 1940.
"George VI on German Invasion of Poland," September 3, 1939.
"German Advance in France," various reports by Eric Sevareid, May 1940.
"German-American Bund Rally," from Madison Square Garden, February 20, 1939.
"Hamilton Fish Speech," September 25, 1939, #867.
"Hitler Speech Summary," April 28, 1939.
"Hitler's Reply to FDR's Peace Appeal," April 29, 1939.
H.V. Kaltenborn, September 3 to October 27, 1939.
"Hyde Park Service for FDR," April 15, 1945, #092.
I Can Hear It Now, recordings of world events 1919–49, two hours, #289.
"Interview with Orson Welles," ca. 1970s.
"Irving S. Cobb Speech," November 1, 1940, #545.
Jergens Journal with Walter Winchell, May 18, 1941, #333.
Kaltenborn Edits the News, August 27, 1939, #699; October 20, 1939, #471.
"King George VI Speech," September 23, 1940, #656.
"League of Nations" Shortwave from Geneva, September 21, 1938, #656.
March of Time, December 31, 1936, #470; December 30, 1937, June 9, 1938, March 3,
     1939, and May 3, 1945, #229.
"Max Jordan," two reports from Munich, September 29, 1938.
"Munich Report," September 29, 1938, #192.
NBC News, September 29, 1939, #411.

NBC Tribute to FDR, two hours, April 15, 1945, #403.
NBC War News, September 23, 1939.
New York Herald-Tribune Forum, with Mayor La Guardia, October 4, 1937.
News of Europe, August 29 to September 21, 1939, #654.
News of the World, December 4, 1941, #653.
News Round-Up, May 19, 1940, #656; December 7, 1941, #696.
"1939 in Review," with Raymond Gram Swing, Janury 1940, #696.
"Premier Daladier from France," September 21, 1939.
"Premier Reynaud," May 18, 1940.
Press Association News, September 1, 9, 18, 1939.
"Queen Wilhelmina of the Netherlands," May 15, 1940.
Raymond Gram Swing, March 4, 1938; July 19, 1940.
Raymond Gram Swing, July 19, 1940, #656.
"Resignation of Chamberlain," May 10, 1940, #656.
"Summation of News," September 3, 1939, #867.
Town Meeting of the Air, "Which Way America?" May 30, 1935, #470.
United Press Reports, June 6, 13, 20, 1941.
"U.S. Declares War on Italy and Germany," December 11, 1941, #694.
Wake Up, America, "America's Stake in the War," and "The Future of Free Enterprise,"
    both programs ca. 1940.
"War Begins in Europe," September 1, 1939, with Elmer Davis.
"War That Did Not Come," October 20, 1938.
"Wendell Willkie Speech," November 1, 1940, #550.
"Winston Churchill on Dunkirk Evacuation," June 19, 1940, #191.
"Winston Churchill on Hitler," October 16, 1938, #192.
"Winston Churchill Speech," December 1940, #188.
"Winston Churchill's First Speech as Prime Minister," May 19, 1940.
World Today, November 5, 17, and 20, 1941, #696; and December 9, 1941, #699.

Radio Historical Association of Colorado (RHAC)

CBS News of Europe
June 29 to July 17, 1940, #272.
July 18 to August 5, 1940, #296.
August 6 to August 23, 1940, #297.
August 24 to September 16, 1940, #298.
September 17 to September 28, 1940, #311.
H.V. Kaltenborn, September 21, 25, 27, 29, 1939, and October 2, 1939, #311.
Les Misérables, Orson Welles and Company, July–September 1937, 7 parts, #055.
"Report on the Eclipse," June 7, 1937, #244.

Radio Vault Collection (RVC)

"Democratic National Committee Program," November 6, 1944, Cassette 881.
"The Polish Crisis," September 1, 1939, Cassette 602.
World Today, November 29, 1941, Cassette 629.

Radio Yesteryear Tape Archives (RYC)

Arrow News Reporter, September 21, 1939.
"Congressional Remote: Reaction to FDR's Embargo Repeal Speech," September 21, 1939.

"Edwin C. Hill News," March 6, 1933, Cassette 2439, September 21, 1939.
"Interview with Orson Welles and H.G. Wells," KTSA, San Antonio Radio, November 7, 1940, Radiola Records.
Midweek Review, September 21, 1939.
News with Charles Daly, September 21, 1939.
"Premier Daladier from France," September 21, 1939.
Fibber McGee and Molly, December 23, 1940, Cassette 304.

SPERDVAC (Society to Preserve and Encourage Radio Drama, Variety and Comedy)—General and Archives Libraries

"America's Salute to FDR on His Birthday," January 30, 1943, #169.
"Edward VIII Abdication Speech," CBC Shortwave, December 11, 1936, #463.
"Eugene Cerut Campaign Speech for FDR," November 1, 1944, #1405.
European War News, September 25, 1938, #347.
"Farmer and the Supreme Court," ca. 1937, #256.
"Greek War Relief Program," February 8, 1941.
H.V. Kaltenborn, December 19, 1940; April 24, 1941; May 6, 27, 1941; #31.
"I Am an American Panegyric," June 12, 1939, #227.
I Was There, "Duke of Windsor Married," June 8, 1941; and "Chancellor Dollfuss Murdered," October 27, 1941, #1069.
"London Broadcast," August 12, 1943, #24.
March of Time, January 1, 1942, #364.
Perspective, ABC News Program, December 1, 1974, #714.
Raymond Gram Swing, March 5, 1943, #325.
Robert Arden, Foreign Correspondent, April 15 and 20, 1940, #787.
"Salute to Labor," September 1, 1941, #234.
"The Supreme Court: Bulwark of Personal Liberty," ca. 1937, #256.
This Is Edward R. Murrow. Broadcast interview with Bob Trout for CBS News, April 30, 1965, #1355.
"Tribute to Orson Welles," recorded for KBIG, Los Angeles, December 15, 1985, #1084.
"We Hold These Truths," December 14, 1941, #42.

University of Memphis (UMP)

"Adolph Hitler Speech," April 28, 1939, #1310.
Ahead of the Headlines, ca. 1940, #0266.
Albert Warner Commentary, September 21, 1939, #0894.
Along the Newsfront, January 7, 1940, with Graham McNamee, #1188.
America Calling, "Bill of Rights," December 14, 1938, #0930.
America First Committee, speech by Charles Lindbergh, May 23, 1941, #1312.
America First Committe, speeches by Boake Carter, Col. Macinider, James Van Zandt, Alf Landon, A. Capper, Burton K. Wheeler, David I. Walsh, E.C. Johnson, Robert Taft, and William Castle, #0567-0568.
America Salutes FDR's Birthday, January 29, 1944, #1090.
American Album of Familiar Music, "On Roosevelt's Death," April 15, 1945, #0987.
American Challenge, "Bombers to Britain" and "Lafayette Escadrille," ca. 1940, #0219.
American School of the Air, "Romeo and Juliet," November 24, 1936, #1112.
"Analysis of German Invasion of Holland," MBS, May 22, 1940, #1189.
"Arthur Mann from London," July 4, 1940, #0548.

BBC Shortwave from London, June 11, 1940, #1192; July 7, 1940, #1193; August 3, 1941,
    #1204; July 27, 1941, #1213.
Bundles for Britain, February 2, 1941, #0773.
"Carl Midan on the Soviet Invasion of Finland," March 2, 1940, #1187.
"CBS All-Star Salute to FDR on his Birthday," January 22, 1938, #0989.
"Charles Lindbergh on Neutrality," October 12, 1939, #0075.
"China Relief Program," June 25, 1941, #1212.
"Congressional Declaration of War—Voting," December 8, 1941, #0579.
"Dr. John J. Brinkley," #1099.
European News Round-Up, May 19, 1940, #0235.
"European Situation from London," September 24, 1938, #0035.
Federal Theater—W.P.A, "Drums," #1111.
"First Selective Service Lottery," October 29, 1940, #0544.
"Frank Knox on Selective Service," #1196.
Fulton Lewis, Jr., misc. broadcasts from July through September 1941, #1221-1306.
"Henry Wallace, VP Candidate," October 28, 1940, #0283.
"Hindenburg Disaster," May 7, 1937, #0545.
"Hitler Speech," March 18, 1938, #0548; and April 28, 1939, #0234.
"Invasion of France," NBC, June 7, 1940, #1192.
"Italy Declares War on France," NBC, June 10, 1940, #1192.
John B. Hughes News, July 18, 22–25, 28, 31, 1941, #1228-1300.
John Gunther Commentary, May 11, 1940, #1191.
"John J. Pershing on the Security of the Americas," August 4, 1940, #0738.
"Max Jordan from Munich," September 29, 1938, #0235.
"Mayor La Guardia Reads the Funnies," July 1945, #0753.
Mercury Theater on the Air, "Immortal Sherlock Holmes," September 25, 1938, #0832.
"Military Analysis," MBS, June 9, 1940, #1192.
"Munich Report," September 24, 1938, #0234.
"Munich Report," September 27, 1938, #0292.
"Munich Report," September 29, 1938, #0035.
NBC Round-Up, May 12, 1940, #1191.
NBC Round-Up, July 7, 1940, #1193.
"News from Prague via Shortwave," September 28, 1938, #0035.
"Night America Trembled," ca. 1950, #0082.
Press-Radio News, September 29, 1938, #0233.
"Republican Election Rally," November 4, 1940, #0274.
"Report on Churchill-Roosevelt Meeting," August 14, 1941, #1302.
"Robert Patterson on Selective Service," #1196.
"Roosevelt Flag-Day Speech," June 14, 1942, #0240.
"Roosevelt Message to Congress on Selective Service," July 18, 1941, #1228.
"Roosevelt Speech on Labor," November 6, 1941, #0264.
"Roosevelt Speech on Neutrality," September 21, 1938, #0885.
"Senator Arthur Vandenburg's Censored Attack on FDR," October 17, 1936, #0353.
"Shortwave from Paris," April 9, 1940, #1194.
"Sigrid Schultz from Berlin," March 2, 1940, #1189.
These Great Americans, "FDR's Death," April 15, 1945, # 0778.
Town Meeting of the Air, March 12, 1942, #0291; May 21, 1942, #1210.
"Tribute to Late George V," January 26, 1936, #0353.
"Truman Speech after FDR's Death," April 16, 1945, # 0241.
"War of the Worlds Plus Thirty," October 1968, #0083.
We the People, February 6, 1940, #0732.

"William L. Shirer from Munich," September 29, 1938, #0510.
"WREC Flood Coverage," January 21, 1938, #0510.
Wythe Williams, July 27, 1941, #1213; September 2, 1941, #1209.

Miscellaneous Sources—Audio

Edward R. Murrow: The War Years. LP Recording, Columbia Masterworks, 1966.
Franklin D. Roosevelt's Inaugural Address, March 4, 1933; January 20, 1937; January 20, 1941; January 20, 1945. LP recordings, The Spoken Word, Inc.
The Home Front: 1938–45. Audio cassettes, Metacom Enterprises.
"Howard Koch Interview." *Morning Edition*, National Public Radio, February 1995.
Mercury Company Remembers. "Theater of the Imagination" Collection. New York: Voyager.
Murrow, Edward R. *I Can Hear It Now, 1933–45*. LP recordings, Columbia Records, 1948.
A Reporter Remembers. LP Recording, Columbia Masterworks, 1966.
This Is Orson Welles. Four hours of recorded interviews with Orson Welles. New York: HarperCollins Audio, 1992.
WBBM-Chicago Radio, "War of the Worlds 50th Anniversary Show," October 30, 1988.

Miscellaneous Sources—Film Sources

Invasion From Mars, BBC Television Documentary, 1978.
The Night That Panicked America. Made-for-Television film. Director: Joseph Sargent. 1975.
"Orson Welles Interview." BBC Television. Museum of Broadcasting.
"Without Warning," CBS Made-for-Television film. October 30, 1994.

Index